D0206210

Contents

viii

Figures and Maps

Acknowledgments

The papers published here were first presented in two lecture series at the University of Montana as part of a curriculum development program in international environmental studies. The program and the preparation of the book were funded by a grant from the United States Department of Education and the University of Montana. The support of both is gratefully acknowledged.

Ronald Erickson, in addition to contributing a paper, was co-director of the international environmental studies program. In large part, his efforts made the preparation of these essays possible.

Michael Kupilik, also a contributor, has been extraordinarily generous with his time, effort, and technical advice on the use of the University of Montana computer word processing and editing facilities.

Edie Cox has typed, edited, and proofread with great skill, perseverance, and good humor.

To these friends for their excellent assistance and to my family for its exemplary patience I extend my sincere thanks.

Richard N. Barrett

Preface

In 1978 a group of faculty members at the University of Montana initiated a program of international environmental studies. Consisting of economists, political scientists, geographers, a linguist, a sociologist, a historian, a chemist, and a forester, the group was drawn together by several important convictions. One of these was that environmental degradation is a worldwide phenomenon with extremely serious implications not just for Americans or the citizens of the other industrial nations, but for all the world's people. Another was that an adequate understanding of this issue could not be provided by a single discipline but rather must come from a variety of viewpoints. Finally, all were convinced that an understanding of the international dimensions of the environmental crisis was an obvious first step in learning to cope with one of our most serious problems.

One part of the international environmental studies program consisted of the presentation of two lecture series by participating faculty. The papers published in this book are the written versions of those lectures.

These papers reflect not only the variety of disciplines from which their contributors come. They also concern many aspects of the environmental problem and its manifestation in several areas of the world. But despite this variety of topics, areas, and approaches, several common themes emerge.

One of the most important and pervasive of these themes is that throughout the Third World efforts at agricultural development are accelerating the destruction of land, water, and forest resources at a fearful rate. The most sobering implication of this finding is that in trying to raise agricultural production in the short term, mankind appears to be destroying the basis for a sustainable agriculture and food supply in the future. The papers published here elaborate these themes in a number of ways.

Darshan Kang and Peter Koehn emphasize in particular the role of large scale and "green revolution" technologies of agricultural development. Drawing on the experiences of India, Ethiopia, and Nigeria, they trace the relationship between these technologies and degraded land use, water pollution, increased reliance on inorganic fertilizers and pesticides, and disruption of rural social structures.

Chris Field and Ronald Erickson analyze the problem of expanding cattle production in Costa Rica and Brazil respectively. Field examines its impact on land use and erosion, food supply, and ultimately social continuity. Erickson traces the impact of Amazonian development on local and world climate and on the indigenous people of the Amazon basin. He finds the roots of Amazonian development in part in the desire of the Brazilian government to extend its control over the region, a theme developed further by Fred Reed in his paper on the Sahel of Africa.

Two papers emphasize the link between environmental degradation and excessive levels of consumption. Thomas Power argues that such excessive consumption results from a basic misconception, namely that material welfare depends on the amount consumed rather than the social context in which the consumption occurs. Albert Borgmann contends that under the impact of technology much of what we consume can provide us with little but novelty. This sense of novelty, he suggests, can only be maintained by an ever growing flow of new products.

Several contributors analyze the relationship between environmental problems and systems of social decision making.

Michael Kupilik provides several interesting examples of environmental destruction in the Soviet Union and argues that their roots lie in the Soviet planning and resource pricing process. John Duffield also emphasizes the role of prices in his analysis of energy conservation. He finds that relatively low levels of energy use in Scandanavia are attributable to a policy of keeping energy prices high and discouraging consumption through a variety of regulations. Dennis O'Donnell argues that many environmental problems stem from the absence of supranational decision making authority, and Forest Grieves reviews the efforts that have been made in Europe to establish such authorities. Finally, Robert Eagle analyzes the Chinese and Tanzanian models of development and their relation to the environment. He reports that both countries have to some extent abandoned the principles of small scale, decentralized, and egalitarian development which many observers believe are essential to environmentally acceptable social progress.

Two papers deal with the theme of resource exhaustion. Daniel Kemmis and Richard Barrett argue that the pace and character of resource use must be controlled to protect the economic and social continuity of the resource producing communities. Herman Daly outlines the design of a steady state economy in which the principle of sustainability in resource use would play an important role absent from current forms of economic organization.

Several contributors discuss the relationship between environmental destruction and human values and ethics. Philip Maloney examines reverence for nature as a recurrent theme in Western culture and depicts the conflict between this theme and official ideology in the Soviet union. Albert Borgmann argues that humanity has entered into a relationship with nature of technological domination which threatens not only the natural world but the quality of human existence. Thomas Birch maintains that by valuing nature only for its ability to promote human welfare, we reject what many sense is a fundamental ethical imperative to protect and maintain the world in a wild state.

Finally, one contributor, Paul Lauren, describes the consequences, both for humanity and the natural environment, of modern warfare. As Lauren points out, this theme is fundamentally different from all others in this book. Environmental destruction is the intended consequence when weapons are used, not the accidental by-product. The solution to this gravest of threats can only lie in peace.

Richard N. Barrett

Contributors

Richard N. Barrett   Department of Economics, University of Montana, Missoula, Montana

Thomas H. Birch   Department of Philosophy, University of Montana, Missoula, Montana

Albert Borgmann   Department of Philosophy, University of Montana, Missoula, Montana

Herman E. Daly   Department of Economics, Louisiana State University, Baton Rouge, Louisiana

John Duffield   Department of Economics, University of Montana, Missoula, Montana

Robert E. Eagle   Department of Political Science, University of Montana, Missoula, Montana

Ronald E. Erickson   Department of Chemistry and Director, Environmental Studies Program, University of Montana, Missoula, Montana

Chris Field   Department of Geography, University of Montana, Missoula, Montana

Forest L. Grieves   Department of Political Science, University of Montana, Missoula, Montana

Darshan S. Kang   Department of Geography, University of Montana, Missoula, Montana

Daniel Kemmis   Montana House of Representatives

Peter Koehn   Department of Political Science, University of Montana, Missoula, Montana

Michael Kupilik — Department of Economics, University of Montana, Missoula, Montana

Paul Gordon Lauren — Department of History, University of Montana, Missoula, Montana

Philip Maloney — Department of Foreign Languages and Literature, University of Montana, Missoula, Montana

Dennis J. O'Donnell — Department of Economics, University of Montana, Missoula, Montana

Thomas Michael Power — Department of Economics, University of Montana, Missoula, Montana

Fred W. Reed — Department of Sociology, University of Montana, Missoula, Montana and United Nations Fund for Population Activities, Jakarta, Indonesia

Part I

Practical and Philosophical Problems

1
Technology and Nature
In Europe and America

Albert Borgmann

When we distinguish nature from other realms of the world, we think of it as the totality and unity of those things that exist and grow in their own right, without the intervention of man. Nature in this sense contrasts with culture, which in the modern world typically has the shape of technology. Nature is older than culture, and culture rests on nature. Today it is becoming doubtful if nature can continue to support culture. Modern technology sometimes seems like a parasite that is about to devour its host. This danger calls for reflection on the relation of nature and technology. The relation will turn out to be deeply ambivalent. To resolve the ambivalence, it is helpful to consider some of the aspects of the last pretechnological positions in Europe and America from which the relation developed into its contemporary form.

This approach may seem to be unable to contain the complexity of the issues in question. The problems of energy, the environment, and the economy seem to confound the best efforts of government; the flood of analyses and prescriptions seems only to aggravate the confusion. Where can one begin to sort out the problems? We must remember, however, that amidst the turmoil over policies, everyday life in the advanced industrial countries proceeds at a steady and disciplined pace . Just consider how many schedules and devices have to interact smoothly so that a seed can grow into a head of lettuce in California and the lettuce can reach a supermarket shelf in Montana. If we consider all the other lines of procurement that converge in the supermarket or on the television screen we get an impression of how strong and tight the network is of the technological universe in which we move with such ease and familiarity.

TECHNOLOGY AS AN APPROACH TO REALITY

This suggests that underneath the controversies and perplexities there is a firm common understanding of the structure of our world and a tacit agreement on how to sustain, advance, and utilize that world. Since the modern technological reality is unlike any other in history, it must be correlated with a distinctive approach to reality, and it is this approach that I want to call technology. Technology for present purposes is the characteristic way in which

3

modern man has agreed to take up with reality. When such an
agreement becomes firmly entrenched, it also becomes unspoken and
invisible. It is understood in the sense of being taken for granted;
it surfaces only in occasional reminders of the obvious. However, we
can catch a glimpse of its distinctive features when we return to
those statements at the beginning of the modern period where this
approach was first articulated.

Both Bacon and Descartes, writing in the first half of the 17th
century, saw themselves at the beginning and as initiators of a new
era (Bacon, 1960:3-4; Descartes, 1956:4,39). It was to be
distinguished by a radical scientific illumination of reality and by
an equally fundamental improvement of the human lot on the basis of
scientific insight. "...I am laboring," Bacon emphasized, "to lay
the foundation, not of any sect or doctrine, but of human utility and
power" (Bacon, 1960:16). And Descartes, speaking of his insights in
physics, said: "...they have satisfied me that it is possible to
reach knowledge that will be of much utility in this life; and
instead of the speculative philosophy now taught in the schools we
can find a practical one, by which, knowing the nature and behavior
of fire, water, air, stars, the heavens, and all the other bodies
which surround us, as well as we now understand the different skills
of our workers, we can employ these entities for all the purposes for
which they are suited, and so make ourselves masters and possessors
of nature" (Descartes, 1956:40). The main goal of these efforts
seems to be the domination of nature, but we must be more precise.
The desire to dominate does not just spring from a lust for power or
from sheer human imperialism. It is from the start connected with
the aim of liberating man from disease, hunger, and toil, and to
enrich his life with learning, art, and athletics. Descartes says
further of his studies that they "would not only be desirable in
bringing out about the invention of an infinity of devices to enable
us to enjoy the fruits of agriculture and all the wealth of the earth
without labor, but even more so in conserving health, the principle
good and the basis of all other goods in this life" (Descartes,
1956:40). And in Tommaso Campanella's City of the Sun of 1623, new
machines and more efficient labor lead to a greatly enriched life
where leisure is spent in "learning joyously, in debating, in
reading, in reciting, in writing, in walking, in exercising the mind
and body and with play" (Sibley, 1971:40). Bacon's New Atlantis
represents the most influential picture of the liberated and enriched
life in a society based on science and technology.

These visions preceded reality by more than a century. When in
the second half of the 18th century the industrial revolution began
to employ new machines and more efficient methods of production, it
at first increased the common toil and misery. But even such a
penetrating critic of these developments as Karl Marx held on to the
promise of modern technology and looked forward to an advanced
industrial and communist society where people "do this today and that
tomorrow, who hunt in the morning, go fishing in the afternoon, raise
cattle in the evening, are critics after dinner as they see fit,
without for that matter ever becoming hunters, fishermen, sheperds,
or critics" (Marx and Engels, 1959:33).

The splendor of the promise of technology appears bright even today when we remember how recently misery and deprivation shaped human life, especially in the newly settled areas of this country. In the older cemeteries of the American West, one can find tombstones from the early part of this century which record the deaths of siblings two, three, or four years old who died within a few winter weeks, weakened from poor food and shelter and taken away by contagious diseases. Granville Stuart speaks eloquently of how he and his brother "were famished for something to read" in the camp on Gold Creek, Montana, in the winter of 1860 (Stuart, 1925,I:159). They heard of a trunk of books in the Bitterroot Valley. "...we started for those books," Stuart wrote, "a hundred and fifty miles away, without a house, or anybody on the route, and with three big rivers to cross..." (Stuart, 1925,I:160). They spent half of all the money they had on five books. "...but then we had the blessed books," Stuart says, "which we packed carefully in our blankets, and joyfully started on our return ride of a hundred and fifty miles. Many were the happy hours we spent reading those books..." (Stuart, 1925, I:161).

The argument that the conquest of nature has liberated us from toil and misery is strong and it covers, of course, many more aspects of life than have become apparent so far. Eugene Ferguson gives a more detailed view of the matter.

> Relief became possible from the drudgery of threshing wheat, digging dirt, carrying water, breaking rocks, sawing wood, washing clothes, and indoors spinning and weaving and sewing; many of the laborious tasks of living were being made easier by the middle of the 19th century. Relief from toil does not necessarily mean a better, higher life; nevertheless, any attempt to get at the meaning of American technology must give a prominent place to machines that have lifted burdens from the shoulders of millions of individual human beings (Ferguson, 1979:16).

The liberating and disburdening character of certain phases and forms of technology is obvious and significant. Ferguson is a little more guarded but still confident as regards the enrichment that comes from technology. He says:

> The democratic ideal of American technology shone brightly, too, as countless low-priced pictures, books, lamps, rugs, chairs, cookstoves, and musical instruments served to lift hearts and reduce boredom and despair. The mail-order catalogs that appeared at the end of the 19th century epitomize the democratization of the amenities that has marked the rise of American technology. Rail, if you will, at the decline of taste; but look first at the real alternatives of bare walls, dirt floors, and minds untouched by the imaginative works of writers, poets, painters, and sculptors (Ferguson, 1979:16).

THE FAILED PROMISE OF TECHNOLOGY

Today, however, the confidence in the promise of technology that speaks from these passages is no longer commonly shared.[1] The doubts about that promise are complex, however, and spring from two very different concerns. One is the question whether the promise of disburdenment and enrichment can be made good for all people and times. The other concern is more concealed and difficult and asks whether the promise is not altogether misconceived, too vaguely given at first and no longer sensible where technology is most advanced.

To clarify these doubts and the implications they have for our relation to nature, we must be more precise about the pattern which evolves as modern man proceeds to conquer nature in order to gain a free and rich life. Let us proceed concretely and look at a woodburning cookstove. It provides more constant fire and heat than an open fire; it rids us of smoke and soot and allows us to cook with many pots at once. Still, the intensity of the fire is not easily regulated, and there remains the daily chore of carrying wood and building a fire. An electric range frees us of those labors, but someone will still be slaving over the stove, perhaps for hours, stirring, turning, and watching the food. Finally, the microwave oven lifts those burdens from the cook's shoulder and meals are ready within minutes and at the touch of a button. But it is apparent now that liberation by way of disburdenment has given way to disengagement. With microwave cooking, all direct and bodily engagement with fire and flame, with the texture of food, with the processes of simmering, boiling, and frying has disappeared.

What happens to the promise of enrichment through technology? In time bridges were built across Montana's rivers, all-weather highways were constructed, and cars and libraries were built. Within hours and without danger to life and limb, anyone could borrow however many books at no cost. But did our reading become more substantial and happier than that of the Stuarts? They had chosen Shakespeare, Byron, Adam Smith, the Bible, and a history of Napoleon's army. How does this compare with our best seller lists? And how do our typical leisure activities stack up against Campanella's vision of artistic, intellectual, and athletic pursuits? Ironically, we become less confident of positive answers to such questions as we consider the progress of the technologies of enrichment and weigh the excessive contributions that radio, films, and television have in fact made to the richness of our lives. Enrichment, we must admit, has yielded to diversion and distraction.

Why this change from liberation to disengagement and from enrichment to distraction? There is no necessity in this development as though a law of history had decreed it. It is a fact, and to understand it is to see its salient features in light of our deepest concerns. We must remember that the conquest of nature was to proceed from fundamental, i.e., scientific, insights into the workings of nature. Such insights were to allow us to procure and secure "all the wealth of the earth" in a correspondingly fundamental way, i.e., once and for all, without an ever renewed struggle. Thus diptheria is not to be battled time and again at the child's bedside, but to be conquered once and for all through a vaccination. Water is not to be had through a daily walk to the fountain or spring, in heat or cold, and by carrying buckets. Rather a water supply system is installed once and water is then on tap at all times. Everything is made available so that it is present at once, wherever it may be wanted, without risk and need of skill or attention. But things are so commodiously present only if there is a technological device that procures them and so disburdens us. In disburdening us, these devices intervene between us and nature. Between us and the springs and wells, there is the utility and plumbing system. Between us and the wheat fields are agribusiness and supermarkets. Moreover the devices of technology also come between us and culture. For we are separated from the musicians by the recording studio and the high fidelity system and from the distant poet's voice by a translation and by print.

In a pretechnological setting we are engaged with the things of nature and culture through a tightly woven context of means and ends. Such a context takes account of local and historical conditions and puts us in touch with them. Technology however conquers and subdues the local context and reduces nature and culture to resources. On that resource base it provides us with whatever commodities wherever we live. It procures oranges for Montanans and skiing for Texans. It makes Lowenbrau available to Americans and hamburgers to Bavarians.

We can now see why technology is an international phenomenon. It gains entry into all cultures and nations through its promise of liberation and enrichment. But it fulfills its promise by dividing the fabric of a culture into resources and commodities. It is a global phenomenon because it levels down all local and historical idiosyncrasies. Rice is as much a resource as wheat, tacos as much as pizzas, baroque music as much as jazz.

Technology is obviously a global phenomenon in very unequal ways. Some countries have their resources ravaged without a corresponding benefit of commodities. Others have a surfeit of consumer goods. Some countries rightly and urgently seek liberation from hunger, disease, and illiteracy through technology while in others the progress of technology mainly promotes distraction and dissolution. Still, technology is the decisive if not the sole force that is transforming the face of the earth. It has become the dominant culture. The question with which we began was whether nature could continue to support this sort of culture. Let us turn to some possible answers.

NATURE AND THE SUSTAINABILITY OF TECHNOLOGY

It seems at first that the procurement of commodities through technological devices is an endlessly voracious and inherently unstable process that will eventually devour its natural base. This is most apparent where technology has been most successful, i.e., in the advanced industrial countries. Here the liberation from toil and misery has been successful, but it has also disengaged us from the forces of nature and the intense experiences such engagement brings. The resulting boredom has been met with entertainment, but entertainment provided technologically, as a commodity that has no roots and fails to engage. Thus the consumption of commodities is also threatened by boredom and malaise unless it is spiced with novelty.

A stable technology would be boring and unbearable. Hence technology must forever progress and in so doing use up more and more resources. But since the latter are finite, a crash landing of technology seems inevitable.

Yet this analysis is incomplete since there is in fact a stabilizing tendency in technology. To make a commodity available is to secure it so that one can be assured of it. Technology would not truly liberate and disburden us if its blessings were accompanied by risks, if it were truly dangerous to cross a bridge or receive a vaccination, and if the water supply from a tap were unreliable.

From this point of view, environmental pollution and the energy shortage are merely embarrassing legacies of technology. They are embarrassing because we should have known and could have done better. We simply have been remiss in carrying the paradigm of the technological _device_ to its conclusion. We have employed devices here and there, in medicine, in agriculture, in transportation, and elsewhere. But we have neglected to take the earth itself as a device and to transform it accordingly. Buckminster Fuller admonishes us to recognize the earth as a spaceship, and in his _Manual_ for its operation he clearly urges the final extension of the device paradigm.

> One of the interesting things to me about our spaceship is that it is a mechanical vehicle, just as is an automobile. If you own an automobile, you realize that you must put oil and gas into it, and you must put water in the radiator and take care of the car as a whole. You begin to develop quite a little thermodynamic sense. You know that you're either going to have to keep the machine in good order or it's going to be in trouble and fail to function. We have not been seeing our spaceship Earth as an integrally-designed machine which to be persistently successful must be comprehended and serviced in total (Fuller, 1969:52).

Can we trust the self-righting tendency of technology? There are many environmentalists who would despair of it. They see no constraints on the voraciousness of technology and foresee a massive catastrophe before, on the ruins of technology, an ecologically sane world can be established. In light of what we know about pollution and resource depletion, this is not an unreasonable view.

But we must also bear in mind what we know about the evolution of common attitudes toward resources. That the latter are limited is a totally new experience for technology. Shortages were always understood to be local and temporary. Science fiction writers and futurologists have spared no effort to unfold all possible scenarios of the future. But the limitations of the resource base have had no place in them. Anthologies about problems of technology that are more than ten years old pay no attention to the environmental crisis (Baier, 1969; Burke, 1966; Walker, 1968).[2] In this light, the common consciousness of an environmental crisis has risen quickly. The crisis is now at the center of public attention. And as the quotation from Fuller has shown, the paradigm of technology has the conceptual resources to deal with the crisis.

But is it a satisfactory solution? It is obviously homocentric, i.e., man-centered. That man is at the center of all there is can be taken in many ways. Man is central in a distinctive manner in the technological approach to reality. He is the radical conqueror of nature and culture and the disengaged and distracted consumer of the fruits of his conquests. One may be disturbed about such conquest and consumption because of their possible self-destructive tendencies. But let us assume that this danger is met in accordance with Fuller's suggestion. It is precisely then that the more profound and consequential doubt about technology comes to the surface. Many environmentalists would oppose the total domination of nature even if man's reign can be sustained indefinitely. They do not want to see all of nature used no matter how shrewdly or prudently. They feel a deep respect for nature and for all forms of life. But they have difficulty in articulating this attitude, in justifying it, and in making it heard in public policy discussions. These problems often lead them to lapse into the discourse of technology: their predicament has been repeatedly noted. Christopher Stone, considering the case where environmentalists argue for the preservation of a useless species by reminding us that it may yet turn out to be useful, says:

> . . . when conservationists argue this way to the exclusion of other arguments, or find themselves speaking in terms of "recreational interests" so continuously as to play up to, and reinforce, homocentric perspectives, there is something sad about the spectacle. One feels that the arguments lack even their proponents' convictions. I expect they want to say something less egotistic and more emphatic but the prevailing and sanctioned modes of explanation in our society are not quite ready for it (Stone, 1974:43).

Robert Socolow says similarly:

> The conservationists have separate languages for talking to one another, to politicians, and to their avowed opponents. Except when they talk to one another (and perhaps even then) they refrain all too often from articulating what really matters to them (Socolow, 1976:20-21).

Tribe (1974) makes a similar point.

ALTERNATIVES TO THE TECHNOLOGICAL VIEW OF NATURE

Perhaps it is possible to break through the technological framework for dealing with nature by considering the different circumstances that prevailed in Europe and America when this framework began to take shape, i.e., when the modern technological conquest of nature got under way. The European and the American experiences differ in what they reveal and obscure, and, when seen together, cancel some of their concealments. The American experience obscures the fact that the conquest of nature entails of necessity

the destruction or loss of genuine culture. And this also is just
what an analysis of the European experience shows. But that analysis
alone may leave us defeated because the simultaneous erosion of
nature and culture reveals no ready basis for the rebuilding of a
sustaining culture and a new relationship to nature. On the American
side, however, the experience of the grandeur of nature is never
wholly suppressed by the advancing conquests of nature, and that
experience provides a point of salutary discontent with technology.

The American setting is, to begin with, particularly instructive
because the lines between technology and nature appear to have been
so clearly drawn: Western man was poised at the edge of a pristine
and gigantic continent to conquer the virgin land. In fact, the
relation was much more complex and difficult. The continent was not
untouched at all; it was well settled and populated by a culture
that Western man for the most part did not understand. And so the
conquest of the American continent was at the same time the
destruction of great cultures and peoples.

How was this conquest of nature to be regarded? There were, it
seemed, two traditional frameworks already in place for meeting the
challenge of the continent. In the one framework America appeared as
a garden, a pastoral setting of fertility and beauty for the life of
simplicity and joy that had long been a dream of European man (Marx,
1964:36-40).[3] Though Virginia may have answered to the physical
characteristics of that dreamscape, other parts of America did not.
What decisively damaged the pastoral view of America, however, was
the early realization that even where nature contributed its share of
peace, order, and beauty, man failed to provide his (Marx, 1964:
75-86). As Leo Marx has shown, the ideal remains crucial for the way
in which Americans try to understand their world and themselves. But
the early damage to this ideal made prominent the other traditional
framework in which European man saw the new continent, a framework
which was far more robust, better suited to the task of settling
America, and able to coopt, if not absorb, the other framework. It
was the view of America as a wilderness. Roderick Nash (1978), who
has chronicled the development of the American attitude toward
wilderness, points out that this attitude has strong and deep roots
in the Old World. From this mooring nature in its wild state
appeared hostile and terrifying, an enemy from whom one had to wrest
enclaves of culture. Nature was beautiful only when it had been
cultivated and turned into a garden. The premodern attitude toward
wilderness is not as relentlessly negative as Nash makes it out to
be, but in any case it obtained a cutting edge in the New World which
it had long lost in the Old. To be sure, there were large wilderness
areas in Medieval Europe and the notion of colonization or
cultivation was still alive within England at the beginning of this
century. But throughout this period this view gave way to one in
which man had come to terms with nature. Wilderness was seen from
within a long and finely developed tradition of commerce and
familiarity with the natural world. There were catastrophies and
changes in man's dealings with cultivated nature, but they never
entirely erased the experience of its intimacy and bounty. All this
was left behind in the New World where Western man found himself on a
continent that he thought of as wild simply and entirely.

The conquest of the American continent by the white man is a

long and complex story. Our concern is with one feature of this
process. It emerged after the first phase of colonization. The
first settlements were erected in a struggle with nature that was
still fought on pretechnological terms. But gradually, the forces of
colonization gathered momentum, and the assault on the entire
continent was launched.[4] It coincided roughly with the industrial
revolution in America, and it mirrored the ambivalence of the
domination of nature that we have noticed before. There were
certainly romantic and heroic components in the struggle with the
wilderness (Ferguson, 1979:4-6; Turner, 1958:1-38). And there were
attempts at settling down in the true sense, making a place one's own
and doing justice to the land. But there was also and increasingly
the tendency to look at nature merely as raw material that was to be
used and to be abandoned after it was used up (Berry, 1978:3-48).
What made the tendency a gigantic transformative force was the
systematic development and refinement of technology. Driving nature
to submission was finally not the work of individual adventurous
pioneers, but the extension and application of an approach to reality
that was based on science, developed by engineers, and primarily
practiced in factories. To be sure, the challenge of the frontier in
turn spurred the development at the American centers of technology
(Ferguson, 1979:7-14).

The conquest of the continent consumed most of the energy of the
Americans. Like Frederick Jackson Turner (1958) we are inclined to
think of this conquest as completed when the frontier ceased to exist
in 1890. But this is to take a merely extensive view of the matter.
In the American West, man's initial grip on the land was often
tenuous and hasty. It was through the rise of the industrial
technology that man took intensive possession of the land. Indeed,
we see the last stages of the process occurring around us now in the
West. This final subjection of nature and the land was still a
pioneer experience in the sense that it had few cultural antecedents
and obstacles to contend with. The conquest in its extensive and
intensive dimensions generated excitement and provided cohesion and
direction for the people.

It therefore escaped the general attention that no lasting ties
to the land were being established, that firm traditions of communal
living failed to grow up, that no focal points of celebration and
orientation were being taken up by the communities, that the sense of
responsibility for the land and for one another was weakly developed.[5] European culture seemed outmoded for the task of conquering the
continent and so was lost. The restlessness of the conquest
suppressed the very need for a new culture along traditional lines.

Despite these developments the technological culture of
domination and disengagement did not establish itself as the sole and
unquestioned approach to nature. As nature changed from an adversary
to a resource, the heroic tradition of the initial struggle lost its
foundation. But America had begun to understand itself in
distinction from Europe as a land of majestic natural forces. What
national character it had was shaped by the encounter with those
forces. To be sure, the first articulation and parlances of the
force of nature came from the Romantic movement in Europe. But it
only provided the initial spark (Nash, 1978:44-83). Wilderness is
nature in a more primal state than the nature of fields, pastures,

and vineyards. Wilderness is older than human memory; its beauty owes nothing to human work; its life is intricate and harmonious beyond human planning. Thus wilderness is a much more provocative challenge to human domination than groves and hedgerows which bespeak the hand of man. Nature in Europe is cultivated nature. Wilderness has been a faint memory for centuries.

Wilderness is a challenge both within and to the framework of technology. Technology is geared too meet challenges: to dam rivers, drain swamps, log forests, and mine coal. Wilderness areas, within this framework, appear as the last bastions yet to be taken by technology, the last areas where we should be able to cut, drill, and extract. At the very least these areas should be made available as recreational resources. But wilderness is a challenge also to the entire way of dealing with nature, i.e., to technology itself. In the controversies about the establishment of wilderness areas, the unspoken disagreement is always on how we should understand the challenge of nature, whether we should meet the challenge with domination or with respect.

We have noted that the conservationists have difficulty in speaking unequivocally on behalf of nature. They tend to slide into technological discourse. The key to this difficulty is that one cannot speak on behalf of nature without speaking about technology. One cannot defend wilderness on its own terms and at the same time adopt and sanction the terms of technology when speaking about everything outside the wilderness, about people, cities, and ways of life. And yet the challenge of wilderness in America continues to invigorate its supporters and to trouble its attackers. That is the uniqueness and strength of the American experience of nature. Its weakness is that it often remains in uncomprehending opposition to the technological culture. Because of this lack of comprehension, wilderness advocacy at times adopts unwittingly the framework of its adversaries, and when it resists that temptation, its criticisms of technology tend to become negative and sterile. The preservation of the world is in wildness only when the challenge of the wilderness is articulated and becomes fruitful in the midst of technology.

While the American experience with wilderness challenges the technological conception of nature, it provides no setting where an intimate relation between culture and nature had been worked out just prior to the rise of modern technology. Such a setting did exist in Europe, however, and since the transformative power of technology on reality is very uneven chronologically, such settings still prevailed at the beginning of this century. Here it pays to look closely, to see in one case and in detail how nature and culture were interwoven and how this texture was rent by the advance of technology. The case I want to consider is that of a wheelwright's shop just prior to its dissolution. A moving account has been given by George Sturt (1974), the last in a succession of wheelwrights.

Since the web of relations is so tight and manifold, it is difficult to present it in an abstract and summary way. But let us begin with those aspects in which the relation of man to nature is most singled out. As said before, the experience of cultivating the land was still alive at this time in England, and Sturt speaks repeatedly of "the age-old effort of colonising England" (Sturt, 1974:132). But colonizing he does not understand as conquering and subduing, but as an adaptation of man to the land, and he paraphrases it as the "age-long effort of Englishmen to get themselves close and ever closer into England" (Sturt, 1974:66). As man adjusts to the land, the land discloses itself to man. There is "a close relationship between the tree-clad country-side and the English who dwelt there." Sturt speaks of "the affection and the reverence bred of this" (Sturt, 1974:23). But it is impossible to abstract purely a man-nature relationship in the pretechnological setting. What takes the wheelwright into "sunny woodland solitudes," "into winter woods or along leafless hedgerows," and "across wet water-meadows in February" is the search for timber (Sturt, 1974:25). But "timber was far from being a prey, a helpless victim, to a machine," Sturt says and continues: "Rather it would lend its subtle virtues to the man who knew how to humour it: with him, as with an understanding friend, it would co-operate" (Sturt, 1974:45). This is a relationship not of domination, but of mastery. If the wheelwright, Sturt says elsewhere, "was really master of his timber, if he knew what he had already got in stock and also what was likely to be wanted in years to come, he kept a watch always for timber with special curves, suitable for hames, or shaft-braces, or waggon-heads, or hounds, or tailboard rails, or whatever else the tree-shape might suggest" (Sturt, 1974:31). Such respectful working with nature opens up dimensions that remain otherwise closed. "Under the plane (it is little used now)", Sturt says, "or under the axe (if it is all but obsolete) timber disclosed qualities hardly to be found otherwise" (Sturt, 1974:24). And elsewhere he says:

> With the wedges cleaving down between the clinging fibres--as he let out the wood-scent, listened to the tearing splitting sounds--the workman found his way into a part of our environment--felt the laws of woodland vitality--not otherwise visited or suspected (Sturt, 1974:192).

But again the intimacy of the wheelwright with nature did not stop with the materials, but embraced his entire world by way of the needs of his customers. Sturt puts it this way:

> And so we got curiously intimate with the peculiar needs of the neighborhood. In farm-waggon or dung-cart, barley-roller, plough, water-barrel or what not, the dimensions we chose, the curves we followed (and almost every piece of timber was curved) were imposed upon us by the nature of the soil in this or that farm, the gradient of this or that hill, the temper of this or that customer or his choice perhaps in horseflesh (Sturt, 1974:17-18).

And similarly he says in another place:

> The field, the farm-yard, the roads and hills, the stress of weather, the strength and shape of horses, the lifting power of men, all were factors which had determined in the old villages how the farm tackle must be made, of what timber and shape and of what dimensions, often to the sixteenth of an inch (Sturt, 1974:41).

This web of relations had, finally, its social aspects. It contained different guilds or groups, but no classes, i.e., divisions of people whose political and especially economic interests were opposed to one another (Laslett, 1965:25-52). The different groups had their character from their work and their relation to nature. In his search for timber, the wheelwright found not only trees, but also "country men of a shy type, good to meet" (Sturt, 1974:25). And back at his shop he was met by the carters, "a whole country-side of strong and good-tempered Englishmen. With the timber and the horses they seemed to bring the lonely woodlands, the far-off roads into the little town" (Sturt, 1974:28). The social network was sustained by fidelity, by wagons that were built to last a lifetime and that were carefully repaired when they had broken down (Sturt, 1974:30,43, 175-181). Prices were charged by tradition and not by calculation of costs and profits (Sturt, 1974:53,200). The tie between employer and employed was one of "kindly feeling" and as Sturt puts it, a relation of resourcefulness and trust (Sturt, 1974:53-55).

Sturt's account is remarkable not only for its portrayal of the strength and character of a pretechnological relation to nature. He is also painfully aware of the rise of technology and the destruction of the pretechnological setting. This process too becomes visible at the reference points of nature, materials, and social relations. Accelerated by the demands of the First World Ward, a "sort of greedy prostitution desecrated the ancient woods ...I resented it," Sturt says, "resented seeing the fair timber callously felled at the wrong time of year, cut too soon, not 'seasoned' at all" (Sturt, 1974). The conquest of nature was not confined to the treatment of the forests, but moved into the wheelwright's shop too, replacing skill with mechanical power which could "drive, with ruthless unintelligence, through every resistance" (Sturt, 1974:45). As said before, domination is not an end in itself, but serves to secure more radically the products of labor. Thus, as Sturt points out, "work was growing less interesting to the workman, although far more sure in its results" (Sturt, 1974:153). And domination provides more income for the purchase of commodities, but at the same time it disengages the worker from the world. This is Sturt's experience in the following passage:

> Of course wages are higher—many a workman to-day receives a larger income than I was able to get as 'profit' when I was an employer. But no higher wage, no income, will buy for men that satisfaction which of old—until machinery made drudges of them—streamed into their muscles all day long from close contact with iron, timber, clay, wind and wave, horse-strength (Sturt, 1974:201-2).

These transformations finally touched the social relations as well. "'The Men,'" Sturt says of his employees, "though still my friends, as I fancied, became machine 'hands'" (Sturt, 1974:201). The loss of skill went hand in hand with the loss of rustic village life, and the change in the living situation also upset the old social relations. Sturt, speaking of the changes in the life of one wheelwright in particular, says:

I was not in touch, through him, with the quiet dignified
country life of England and I was more of a capitalist.
Each of us had slipped a little nearer to the ignominious
class division of these present times--I to the employer's
side, he to the disregarded workman's (Sturt, 1975:113).

Sturt had an uncanny sense for the transformative power that
changed the face of his world. He recognized its concealment, the
semblance, that is, that technology was only a more efficient way of
doing what had been done throughout the ages (Sturt, 1974:154, 201).
And he recognized its radical novelty, the fact that technology
upsets the tradition from the ground up. The technological changes
forced him to introduce modern machines and take in a partner who
could supervise the new ways of working. "Neither my partner nor
myself," he says in retrospect, "realised at all that a new world
(newer than even America was to the Pilgrim Fathers) had begun even
then to form all around us" (Sturt, 1974:201). This agrees with the
point urged before that the effects of advancing technology were much
the same in both the ancient cultures of Europe and on the American
wilderness frontier. But the time has now come where technology no
longer advances irresistibly and unquestionably, and both the pretechnological settings of both Europe and America help us understand
our uneasiness about technology.

MAKING THE EXPERIENCE OF NATURE FRUITFUL

Though much is to be learned from Sturt's experiences in the
wheelwright's shop, I want to guard against a misunderstanding. As
far as I can tell, Sturt's case is typical of a wide range of
settings in Europe where modern technology and industry touched on
pretechnological culture and began to erode it. But I do not want to
base my main point on that thesis. Far less do I want to say that
every pretechnological setting is idyllic and preferable to the
technological culture. I rather want to urge that Sturt's account
can alert us to an experience that we all have had in our dealings
with the advances of technology. It is this: as technology
advances, our relation to nature, our experience with the things
about us, our work world, and our commerce with others are all
impoverished. While technology has undoubtedly liberated us from
much misery, it has also made us poorer in our engagement with the
world. The promise of enrichment that comes from technology has, on
the whole, not merely been empty, it has been misleading. It has
misled us into the expenditure of enormous ingenuity and energy which
has only yielded greater vacuity.
But the question remains how the experience of nature can be
fruitful in a technological society. Leo Marx has dealt with this
question at length and from a point of view which differs from the
one which has guided the preceding reflections. He has traced the
impact on the American experience of the intrusion of technology into
the natural landscape. And in particular he has examined the
attempts to reconcile the machine and the garden. He has looked at
biographies, fiction, and other literary documents from the beginning
of the republic to the first half of this century. The answer that

he gives to our question from this point of view is disheartening.
He finally puts it this way, speaking of the protagonists in American
fiction who have attempted to reconcile the machine with the garden.

> ..in the end the American hero is either dead or totally
> alienated from society, alone and powerless, like the
> evicted shepherd of Virgil's eclogue. And if, at the same
> time, he pays tribute to the image of a green landscape, it
> is likely to be ironic and bitter (Marx, 1964:364).

In Marx's account the symbol of technology is the railroad and
the locomotive which ruthlessly invade the countryside with their
tracks, noise, and disruption. This view of the matter is no longer
adequate for two reasons. Technology, we can now see, is much more
comprehensive and insinuating than the symbol of the locomotive has
it. The machinery of technology can still be obtrusive and disruptive as in stripmining or highway construction. But technology
shapes our lives mostly where its machinery is concealed and only its
commodities are apparent. An affluent suburb is seemingly the
incarnation of the pastoral garden that Marx's authors see threatened
by the incursion of the machine. And yet such a suburb is
technological through and through. It is a pretty display of
commodities resting on a concealed machinery. There is warmth, food,
cleanliness, entertainment, lawns, shrubs, and flowers, all of it
procured by underground utilities, cables, station wagons, chemical
fertilizers and weed killers, riding lawn mowers, seed tapes, and
underground sprinklers. The advanced technological setting is
characterized not by the violence of machinery, but by the disengagement and distraction of commodities.

The second way in which the relation of nature and technology
has changed regards a subtle, but important shift of balance. The
authors that Marx discusses still see nature as the primary context.
To be sure, technology defaces and threatens to destroy it. But they
see the machine in the garden and not the other way round. If we
recognize the pervasive and often stealthily transformative power of
technology, we come to see technology as the new orthodoxy, the
dominant character of reality. Nature in its pristine state now
consists of islands in an ocean of technology. This shift changes
the nature of wild areas. They now stand out as strictly extraordinary, and thus as a challenge to the ordinary ways of reality, i.e.,
to technology. A piece of land that was cut off from the ordinary
and dedicated to the extraordinary the Greeks called a temenos, a
temple. Similarly, the Romans encircled consecrated places and
called them praecincta (precincts). In these senses, our wilderness
areas are sacred precincts or holy places. In the experience of
wilderness we can begin to construct a non-technological relationship
with nature similar to the wheelwright's: a relation of respect,
affection and mastery rather than exploitation and dominance.

This should be understood as a sober and modest suggestion. I
do not advocate nature worship, and I am not even suggesting that
wilderness areas are finally more significant places than churches,
concert halls, or dinner tables. But they are perhaps initially more
important. Technology has insinuated itself into religion, art, and
family traditions, and, alas, into the wilderness experience also.

Still the wilderness as a focal point of political debate and as a place to be is the clearest counterposition to technology. If we are alive to the debilitating effects of technology, the wilderness is the place to regain strength.

The lesson to be learned there can best be understood against an expression that was a standard feature of the promise of technology when that promise was made most loudly in the middle of the 19th century (Marx, 1964:180-226, 194). Technology, so it was said, would annihilate time and space. This was meant, of course, as the procurement of the riches of the world, as the instantaneous and ubiquitous availability of all things. Today we are sensitive to the subtly destructive side of the annihilation of time and space, to the disorientation in a universe without time and space. In the wilderness, time and space are restored to us. Whereas by jet we can get anywhere on earth within the space of a day and night, a day's hike in the wilderness may take us no more than ten miles. But they will open up mountains and valleys, disclose forests and clearings; they will engage all our senses, step by step. Similarly we will not kill time with magazines and cocktails, but live through it, from the first dawn to the brightness of noon and the setting of the sun. As the darkness envelops and stills the mountains, the hiker will rest. The wilderness takes time, opens up space, and engages us.

We can accept the technological cast of ordinary reality if we can make room within it for engagement. The wilderness constitutes a clear place of engagement. But the lesson to be learned there will be of consequence only if it can be enacted elsewhere as well. We must make room in our lives for engagements with things. In a sense such engagements, like the islands of wilderness, are remnants of a pretechnological world also. But like the wild areas, they now contrast with the technological standard of living, and their engaging simplicity attains a new splendor. In a pretechnological world running is something that children would do and adults if they had to. But in a setting where driving, flying, and sitting are the standard modes of being in space, running becomes a splendid experience. It restores us to our full bodily existence, it allows us to take in space and feel the time. This is true analogously of a family meal, thoughtfully celebrated, or of music made in consort.

Through engagement we can make a start in adjusting technology to nature and culture without denying or fleeing from technology. The real problem, in fact, is not to start, since beginnings have been made everywhere, but to persist. Persistence is most threatened by the lingering force of the promise of technology. All of the social programs that command attention and occasional enthusiasm today promise more powerful and abundant means for the good life. The ends remain vague but are implied to be magnificent. In light of these grand if foggy prospects, the real things about us appear homely in their simplicity. It is only when we have penetrated the fog of the promise of technology and seen its central vacuity that the splendor of the simple becomes apparent.

If our lives are centered in engagement, it is possible to some extent to redeem the promise of technology. This can happen in several ways. Since engagement takes up space and time, there will be less room and time for commodities, and the most frivolous ones, we may hope, will disappear first. Surely the promise of technology is compromised badly when extraordinary expertise and ingenuity are expended to cater to our basest sides as when an enormous electronic industry is built up so that many can have libraries of pornographic videotapes. A second, redemptive step may occur when we consider the effect of engagement on the sounder technological commodities that will remain. To someone who is actively engaged in skiing, the Winter Olympics on television will not be merely a diversion which provides spectacular crashes and impressive injuries. He will rather appreciate the skill of the competitors, admire their dedication, and be inspired in his own efforts. And analogous points again hold for the musician who listens to records and for the family in which a tradition of simple meals goes out for dinner as a real occasion. The promise of technology, finally, is best answered in engagement itself. Here the time, security, and the instruments provided in part by technology are taken up in a way which constitutes a free and rich life.

In these ways we can begin to build the middle landscape of which the authors of the pastoral ideal have spoken, the landscape that is naturally placed between technology and the wilderness.

FOOTNOTES

1. Ferguson's confidence is not qualified either (Ferguson, 1979:23-24).

2. The population problem has of course been recognized since Malthus and in relation to it, a resource problem was always acknowledged.

3. For the late medieval tradition of the pastoral ideal see Huizinga (1954:128-138).

4. It gathered momentum from the end of the 18th to the middle of the 19th century and then reached its take-off point (cf. Marx, 1964:145-226).

5. For the contemporary result of these developments see Packard (1972) and Toffler (1974:7-181).

BIBLIOGRAPHY

Bacon, Francis. The New Organon and Related Writings. Fulton H. Anderson (ed.). New York: Liberal Arts Press, 1960.

Baier, Kurt and Rescher, Nicholas (eds.). Values and the Future, The Impact of Technological Change on American Values. New York: The Free Press, 1969.

Berry, Wendell. The Unsettling of America. San Francisco: Sierra Club Books, 1977.

Burke, John G. (ed.). The New Technology and Human Values. Belmont, California: Wadsworth, 1966.

Descartes, Rene. Discourse on Method. Lawrence J. Lafleur (tr.). New York: Liberal Arts Press, 1956.

Ferguson, Eugene S. "The American-ness of American Technology." Technology and Culture 20, 1 (January, 1979):3-24.

Fuller, R. Buckminster. Operating Manual for Spaceship Earth. New York: Pocket Books, 1969.

Huizinga, J. The Waning of the Middle Ages. Garden City, New York: Doubleday-Anchor, 1954.

Laslett, Peter. The World We Have Lost. New York: Scribner, 1965.

Leiss, William. The Domination of Nature. New York: G. Braziller Press, 1972.

Marx, Karl and Engels, Friedrich. Werke 3. Berlin: Institut fur Marxismus-Leninismus, 1959.

Marx, Leo. The Machine in the Garden. Technology and the Pastoral Ideal in America. New York: Oxford University Press, 1964.

Nash, Roderick. Wilderness and the American Mind, 2nd Ed. New Haven: Yale University Press, 1978.

Packard, Vance. A Nation of Strangers. New York: McKay, 1972.

Sibley, Mulford Q. Technology and Utopian Thought. Minneapolis: Burgess, 1971.

Socolow, Robert H. "Failures of Discourse: Obstacles to the Integration of Environmental Values into Natural Resource Policy." In When Values Conflict. Laurence H. Tribe, et al. (eds.). Cambridge, Mass.: Ballinger, 1976.

Stone, Christopher D. Should Trees Have Standing? Los Altos, California: W. Kaufman, 1974.

Stuart, Granville. Forty Years on the Frontier. Paul C. Phillips (ed.). Cleveland: Arthur H. Clark, 1925.

Sturt, George. The Wheelwright's Shop. Cambridge: Cambridge

University Press, 1974.

Toffler, Alvin. _Future Shock_. New York: Random House, 1974.

Tribe, Laurence. "Ways Not to Think About Plastic Trees: New Foundations for Environmental Law." _The Yale Law Journal_ 83, 7 (June 1974):1315-1348.

Turner, Frederick Jackson. _The Frontier in American History_. New York: Holt, 1958.

Walker, Charles R. (ed.). _Technology, Industry and Man. The Age of Acceleration_. New York: McGraw-Hill, 1968.

2
Social Organization and Environmental Destruction or Capitalism, Socialism, and the Environment

Thomas Michael Power

THE SOCIAL DETERMINANTS OF ECONOMIC WELL-BEING

Consumption and the Environment

In a basic sense, the primary source of environmental destruction (outside of warfare) lies in the pursuit of material goods and services to satisfy human beings' needs and desires. In the pursuit of these goods, we necessarily must manipulate the natural environment, for it is both the source of the raw materials and the recipient of the waste products produced. This is the basis for Pogo's often quoted assertion that the environmental enemy is "us" individually in our demand for various goods. Clearly the higher the level of demand for material goods, the more the natural environment has to be "used". High intensity consumption societies place ever increasing strains on that environment. Exponentially growing mass consumption presents the most serious long run threat to a stable, high quality natural environment.

Given the importance of production and consumption activity in threatening the natural environment, it is important to inquire into the determinants of consumption activity.

Most, especially economists, respond that this is a trivial topic to explore. We know why people seek high intensity consumption levels: insatiable human needs and desires cause our consumption activity and if the economy serves individual needs as it ought to, goods are produced to allow that consumption. Consumption is pursued because it adds to human well-being by satisfying previously unsatisfied needs. It is, we are told, that simple.

Consumption and Welfare

But the empirical literature on the role of material goods and services in determining human welfare is far from comforting. If one tries to determine, for instance, how the tripling of real family income since the 1930s or the doubling of real family income since the 1950s has affected our sense of well-being, very disturbing results are uncovered: there is no sign we judge ourselves to be better off as a result of these increases (Easterlin, 1973). The same result is found with respect to differences in perceived well-being in underdeveloped, developed, and over-developed countries like the U.S. (Kohr, 1977): despite our glittering affluence, no larger percentage of our population is "satisfied" or "happy" than in "poor" countries. Similarly, as large a percentage is seriously unsatisfied and unhappy (Easterlin, 1974).

Thus, even according to our own individual judgments, the outpouring of material goods has not had the positive impact on our well-being which economists and most of us simply assumed it would have. Yet in the process of producing and consuming those goods, enormous damage is done to the natural environment. Such a situation is clearly irrational: we destroy important natural resources but do not attain our objective in the process.

What can explain this national and almost worldwide commitment to such an irrational path? I will suggest that it is because we ignore the fact that well-being is socially, not individually, determined and that individual pursuit of well-being is self-defeating as well as environmentally destructive.

This may seem like a controversial or even radical assertion, but it is not really. Common sense and the experiences of everyday life confirm it. Suppose we stand in a crowd trying to see something and we individually try to improve our view by standing on our tiptoes. If all of us do the same, none of us see any better and all of us are made more uncomfortable. Individual pursuit of improved well-being makes us all worse off. This simple example can be repeated over and over again. In fact most of what we call manners, politeness, neighborliness, custom, moral standards, rules, and laws reflect this common-place realization: individuals single-mindedly pursuing their own well-being not only do not achieve it, in general, but make themselves and all of the rest of us worse off. For that reason we have always agreed to restrict ourselves so that something positive could in fact be accomplished.

The example of standing on tiptoes can be generalized and, for further illustrative purposes, divided into two different types of social limits on the individual pursuit of well-being: congestion and positional goods (Hersh, 1978; Scitovsky, 1976).

Congestion and Positional Goods

The way in which congestion limits our ability, as individuals, to benefit as much as we might have imagined from the use of goods which we own or activities in which we engage has been discussed extensively in the context of environmental problems. The overused "commons" is the aspect of environmental problems most focused on by economists.

If we all try to simultaneously speed to work in our private automobiles, we create a traffic jam which makes us all get to work slowly. If we all install air conditioners in our apartment houses, the hot exhaust raises the air temperature all of us have to face. If we all go hiking in the wilderness or rafting on the wild river to "escape it all", we escape nothing and destroy the wildness of those places. If we all burn wood to keep warm, we create a haze over our valleys which blocks the sunlight and leaves us cold and damp and in a permanent dusk. If we all move to rural areas to enjoy country living, none of us get country living.

Clearly for a broad range of activities, our individual enjoyment depends upon whether others simultaneously try to enjoy those activities too. The social context determines the welfare which results from the individual activity.

"Positional goods" are goods which are sought not just for the satisfaction their direct use gives but for the satisfaction which derives from the relative status which they confer on the owner. Early in this century Thorstein Veblen popularized the importance of the pursuit of status in consumption decisions and coined the phrase "conspicuous consumption" to describe this behavior (Veblen, 1972). The "keeping up with the Joneses" syndrome is familiar to all of us. It, too, reminds us that much consumption is carried out in competition for relative position or status.

That means that the satisfaction obtained from the good or activity is partially determined by how many others also obtain that good or engage in that activity. Again the social setting determines the level of welfare obtained. This applies not only to status or luxury goods but also to the definition of poverty. It has become increasingly clear to economists that poverty cannot be defined in terms of an absolute number of dollars of "necessary" income. To purchase basic food (soybeans), clothing (untailored cotton bags), and shelter (military barracks), only a tiny fraction of what we now define as a poverty level income would be necessary. But although that would be sufficient to sustain biological life and health, it would leave the recipients almost totally excluded from mainstream social and economic life and leave them dramatically stigmatized. Poverty, too, then, is a relative thing. It exists when individuals are excluded from primary social and economic life and do not have access to what the larger society defines as basic necessities. As survey research indicates, the larger society constantly expands what those basic necessities include as the level of general affluence rises. Thus how poor or rich we are depends not simply upon what goods and services we individually have access to, but upon what we have relative to the social median.

Maybe the example of college education will underline the problems created by the importance of positional goods. Getting a college education was seen by most of our parents as the ticket to a better job and economic security. For that reason they sought such an education for themselves and/or their children. But the value of a college education in attaining the desired relative economic status depended entirely on others not getting the same education. If all high school graduates go to college, going to college will not improve the average status of anyone. It provides a differential advantage and privileged access to jobs and income only if others do not go. Of course if others go and you do not, you are in real trouble. You have to go just to maintain average access to jobs and income. But that points out the net loss in welfare which competition for positional goods causes. It's very much like an arms race. We all struggle to obtain those goods to protect our status. But in the end almost none of us improve our status. The struggle, expenditure, and accompanying environmental damage do not improve the

average level of well-being, but simply maintain the status quo at an
enormous mutual cost. In that sense many of our consumption
expenditures are <u>maintenance costs</u> from which no collective benefit
is derived. In this situation what is needed, as in an arms race, is
an agreement among all the parties to scale down the level of
competition so that the costs are contained. Without that sort of
social agreement, we are all on a social treadmill pursuing goods and
services and destroying the environment, but not improving our
well-being.

Sources of Economic Well-Being

Rather than developing more counter-examples to the prevalent
assumption that individual consumption activities determine welfare,
let me offer some alternative general hypotheses about the sources of
economic well-being.

I would argue that welfare is primarily derived from <u>activities</u>
we engage in, not from "things" we come to possess. The degree of
satisfaction we derive from any activity, in turn, depends upon three
things (Gintis, 1972):

1. Our capacities to engage in, appreciate, and enjoy various
   activities. The larger society as well as we individually
   develop these capacities. That is partially what education is
   all about.
2. The social context in which the activity takes place. Congestion
   problems and positional "struggles" for status fit in here, but
   in addition the quality of social relations in our workplaces and
   communities are also important, as is the degree of participation
   and control permitted within our society.
3. The quantity, quality, and variety of material goods available to
   assist in the activity.

Here is where material goods come in, as a <u>means</u> not an end.
Our usual view of economic activity totally inverts this. We are
taught that one of our most important activities, work, is a
disutility grudgingly pursued in order to obtain the end of the
consumption or accumulation of physical goods. Work is viewed as a
means and what I have argued should be the ends, the pursuit of
quality in our activities, is ignored. On the other hand what should
be simply part of the means of pursuing welfare, accumulation and
consumption of material goods, is turned into the ultimate end.

This has disastrous social and environmental consequences. We
pursue material affluence at the expense of social development. The
material affluence does not improve our welfare because the social
context which allows us to derive satisfaction from our activities is
undermined or destroyed. Further, we degrade the quality of work so
badly that one of the primary sources of adult satisfaction, good
productive work, is destroyed. In the process, of course, the environment is mauled at an exponentially rising rate to produce the
goods which will provide us with no additional satisfaction. We
pointlessly attack the earth. In fact, with the satisfaction coming
from our jobs and communities declining, we focus all the more

desperately on the only available source of satisfaction, material
consumption, and go at it with increased frenzy.

SOCIAL ORGANIZATION AND ENVIRONMENTAL DESTRUCTION

If our economic well-being in a very basic sense is _socially_
determined but our economic system insists that economic well-being
is to be _individually_ pursued, one certainly might conclude that
there is something environmentally dangerous about that economic
system. This would not be a startlingly new conclusion. Many
Americans who have struggled with the seemingly limitless array of
serious environmental problems we face have come to suspect that
there may be something about our socioeconomic system which generates
or aggravates environmental destruction. Such suspicions that there
are _social_ sources of environmental destruction are regularly
attacked as naive. We are told that radically different social
systems, from the USSR to Japan to the U.S. to China, all face
similar environmental problems. Socialists and fascists seem to
pollute as much as plain ordinary capitalists do.

This latter point has been developed by academics in a theory or
observation which stresses the contemporary convergence between
different types of social systems, in particular between capitalist
and socialist systems (Tinbergen, 1961; Linnemann, 1974; Goldman,
1970; Prybyla, 1964; Millar, 1972). Centrally planned communist
regimes are experimenting with decentralization, the market, and
profit motivation, while capitalist countries are experimenting with
planning, welfare-state programs, and government co-ownership of
industry.

The message implicit in this convergence theory is very
conservative: there is no use in trying to change things fundamentally. Any social system is likely to be as bad as yours and it
might be worse. Better to stick to piecemeal, pragmatic corrections
and muddle through than to put energy into a hopelessly utopian
effort at social change, which in the end is likely to be bankrupt or
worse.

I want to deal directly with this conservative argument and
argue that our form of socio-economic organization, capitalism, _is_ an
important source of environmental destruction and that abandonment of
it for a non-capitalist or, as I will define it, socialist system, is
a prerequisite for environmental protection.

Defining Socialism

By "socialism" I mean what the ordinary language meaning of the
name implies: conscious social control of the primary determinants
of our well-being. This definition follows the ordinary language
meaning of "capitalism": the dominance of those who control capital,
capitalists, in socio-economic decision making. I emphatically do
not mean by socialism _state_ control of the economy or society. If
that is what socialism meant we would call it "statism" or "fascism"
instead. Clearly implicit in my definition of socialism is the
requirement that the system be radically and effectively democratic,

not just in the political sphere but in the economic sphere as well.

By any use of this simple definition, the Soviet Union and Eastern European Communist regimes are not socialist (Lerner, 1978:532; Harrington, 1976:175). In these countries there is no mechanism by which the vast majority of the population can exercise effective control over basic decisions. A small elite of Communist Party members control the means of production, do all the planning, hire the rest of the population, and direct almost all aspects of socio-economic life. This is quite similar to the facts of economic life under capitalism but to make matters worse in Soviet-type systems the democratic political system most western capitalist countries now have is missing. There is, within Soviet-type systems, no mechanism for the vast majority of the population to exercise social control. For that reason these countries can hardly be "socialist". "State capitalism", that is, a system where the state plays the role of the capitalist, might be a more descriptive title but most in this country would find it confusing. For that reason I will call such systems "state socialist" but wish to emphasize that despite the use of the word "socialist" they bear little semblance to what I and most Western socialists have in mind as a socialist form of social organization.

The similarities in environmental problems found in the state socialist countries and capitalist countries are tied to the similarities in social organization and goals. The Communist Party elites have organized production and consumption in a manner almost indistinguishable from that found in capitalist countries. The dominant goals embraced by the elites are also similar: as rapid as possible an expansion of the production of goods. In fact the Communist leadership has set up as an explicit goal "catching up" with Western Capitalist countries in the production of commodities. The historical reasons for the particular pattern of political economic development found in these state socialist countries lie beyond the scope of this paper. Charles Bettelheim's two volume work details the failure of a truly socialist form of social organization to emerge from the social upheaval and revolution in early twentieth century Russia (Bettelheim, 1976, 1979). What is important here is only that these societies also emphasize commodity production over satisfying productive human activity and define economic well-being heavily in individual terms. The narrow range of expression and autonomous social activity allowed also turns citizens strongly towards commodity consumption as the only source of satisfaction within their control.

The Social Consequences

The consequences of the individual definition and pursuit of well-being in a capitalist society are found in the deterioration of the social as well as the natural environment. If individuals are supposed to pursue actions primarily based on their own calculus of individual gain and loss; if all individuals are encouraged to ignore the social fabric of which they are a part, in hopes that an invisible hand of commercial competition will convert this random individual pursuit into a rational social system, the moral and cultural prerequisites for any human social existence will erode and in the end not even commercial activity will be possible.

People can live on top of one another in urban situations only if they consciously take into account the impact they have on others when they act. If they calculate only what is good for themselves in any given situation, they will be the ones who stand on their tiptoes in hopes of getting the advantage. There is no _individual_ reason not to. Each will try to take advantage of the other by ignoring some of the impacts they have on others. The collective impact of such behavior will be a suspicious, unfriendly, and predatory social environment where one has always to be on guard or on the attack. Some of our large urban areas have already taken on this character which, no doubt, is why people are fleeing them by the hundreds of thousands for smaller towns.

Again, we can live satisfying, productive lives with minimal destructive impact on our social and natural environment only if we recognize the social determinants of our individual well-being and abandon the individualistic myths and their extensions in the social organization we call capitalism. This prerequisite for a decent life—recognition of the inevitable social fabric of which we are all a part—is what I am calling "socialism".   As I emphasized above, this is almost the opposite of what we have been taught socialism means.

The struggle to rediscover, understand, and respect the social determinants of our individual well-being, the struggle to develop what I would call a socialist consciousness is a prerequisite for our individual and collective survival. If fear and hesitation born of our capitalist ideology succeeds in suppressing these social facts, I see no hope for reversing the current world-wide trends of social and natural destruction. We have to know and believe that alternatives are possible. It is for that reason that the concept of a non-capitalist or democratic socialist social system which is not merely a centralized statist construction of federal laws, regula- tions, and bureaucracy is crucial. It is also for that reason the conventional dichotomy which offers us only monopoly capitalism or authoritarian state socialism has to be rejected. What needs to be developed in its place is an understanding of how our individual welfares depend upon each other and the larger society. From that must develop the social mechanisms for taking account of that interdependence in a democratic manner. That is what socialism is all about (Gorz, 1980; Stretton, 1977). That is what an effective environmental movement must also be about.

BIBLIOGRAPHY

Albert, Michael and Hahnel, Robin. Unorthodox Marxism: An Essay on
    Capitalism, Socialism, and Revolution. Boston: South End
    Press, 1978.
Bettelheim, Charles. Class Struggles in the USSR: First Period,
    1917-1923. New York: Monthly Review Press: 1976.
_____. Class Struggles in the USSR, Volume II. New York:
    Monthly Review Press: 1979.
Easterlin, Richard A. "Does Money Buy Happiness?" Public Interest
    (Winter, 1973):3-10.
_____. "Does Economic Growth Improve the Human Lot? Some
    Empirical Evidence." In Nations and Households in Economic
    Growth, P.A. David and M. W. Reder (eds.). New York:
    Academic Press, 1974,89-125.
Gintis, Herb. "Consumer Behavior and the Concept of Sovereignty:
    Explanations of Social Decay." American Economic Review 10 (May,
    1972):267-278.
Goldman, Marshall I. "The Convergence of Environmental Disruption."
    Science 170, No. 3953 (2 October 1970):37-42. Reprinted in
    Comparative Economic Systems, Third Edition, Morris Bornstein
    (ed.). Homewood, Illinois: Irwin (1974),467-479.
Gorz, Andre. Ecology as Politics. Boston: South End Press, 1980.
Harrington, Michael. The Twilight of Capitalism. New York: Simon
    and Schuster, 1976.
Hirsh, Fred. The Social Limits to Growth. Cambridge, Mass.:
    University Press, 1978.
Illich, Ivan. Towards a History of Needs. New York: Pantheon,
    1978.
Kohr, Leopold. The Overdeveloped Nations: The Diseconomies of
    Scale. New York: Schocken, 1977.
Leiss, William. The Limits of Satisfaction: An Essay on the Problem
    of Needs and Commodities. Toronto: University of Toronto
    Press, 1976.
_____. "Needs, Exchanges, and the Fetishism of Objects." Canadian
    Journal of Political and Social Theory 2, No. 3 (Fall,
    1978):27-48.
Lerner, Michael. The New Socialist Revolution: An Introduction to
    Its Theory and Strategy. Delacorte Press, 1973. Reprinted in
    The Capitalist System. R. C. Edwards, et. al. (eds.).

Englewood Cliffs, N.J., 1975,532-54.

Linneman, H., Pronk, J. P., and Tinbergen, Jan. "Convergence of Economic Systems in East and West." In Comparative Economic Systems, Third Edition, Morris Bornstein (ed.). Homewood, Ill.: Irwin, 1974,493-510.

Millar, James R. "On the Theory and Measurement of Economic Convergence." Quarterly Review of Economics and Business 12, No. 1 (Spring, 1972):87-97. Reprinted in Comparative Economic Systems, Third Edition, Morris Bornstein (ed.). Homewood, Ill.: Irwin, 1974,481-499.

Prybyla, J. S. "The Convergence of Western and Communist Economic Systems: A Critical Estimate." Russian Review 23, No. 1 (Jan., 1964):3-17. Reprinted in Comparative Economic Systems, Revised Edition, Morris Bornstein (ed.). Homewood, Ill.: Irwin, 1969,442-453.

Rainwater, Lee. "Economic Inequality and the Credit Income Tax." Working Papers I, No. 1 (Spring, 1973):50-61.

Scitovsky, Tibor. The Joyless Economy: An Inquiry into Human Satisfaction and Consumer Dissatisfication. Fair Lawn, N.J.: Oxford University Press, 1976.

Schatz, Marshall. "Anarchism, Marxism and Liberalism." In Essential Works of Anarchism, M.S. Schatz (ed.). New York: Bantam Books, 1971.

Tinbergen, Jan. "Do Communist and Free Economies Show a Converging Pattern." Soviet Studies XII, No. 4 (April, 1961):333-41. Reprinted in Comparative Economic Systems, Revised Edition, Morris Bornstein (ed.). Homewood, Ill.: Irwin, 1969,432-441.

Veblen, Thorstein. The Theory of the Leisure Class. New York: Mentor, 1959.

Worthington, Richard, ed. Socialism and Ecology. Boston: South End Press, forthcoming.

3
The Logic of Resource Conservation: A Discussion of Our Responsibilities for the Future

Richard Barrett
Daniel Kemmis

One of the universal consequences of human activity is the exhaustion of vital natural resources. All over the world today we confront increasing scarcity of land, water, minerals, and energy. For some of us, the endless search for and exploitation of new resources mean that our lives, communities and landscapes are being irrevocably changed. And we must all consider how our decisions today either secure or jeopardize the futures of our children, grandchildren and even more remote generations.

The purpose of this paper is to discuss some of these issues. It is divided into two parts. In the first part we try to describe what some of the economic, political, and social effects of resource exhaustion are. In the second we discuss the responsibilities to the future such effects impose on us.

Our discussion of these issues draws on examples from both Latin America, and especially Mexico, and the State of Montana. These are areas in which we have special personal and professional interests, but their selection is not the result of that fact alone. Rather, it also reflects our conviction that there are important and instructive parallels in the experiences of communities, states, and nations all over the world. We are convinced that we have a great deal to learn from one another.

THE CONSEQUENCES OF EXHAUSTION

Suppliers

To turn to the issue, what are the implications of resource exhaustion? Consider first the situation of countries, states, or communities that supply resources In general, we are aware that resource development has a kind of natural life cycle. In Montana we call this cycle "boom and bust" and are unfortunately pretty familiar with its characteristics. "Boom," of course, refers to the period of rapid resource development that occurs because we discover a new deposit of the resource (this is what is happening in Mexico today, where discovered oil reserves have multiplied enormously), a new technology for recovering known deposits or transporting production to the market (of which ore concentration technologies and slurry pipelines are examples), or simply because the price rises enough to make exploitation desirable.

"Bust," on the other hand, occurs when the deposit is played out, or new technologies make alternative sources of supply more attractive, or prices for whatever reason fall enough to make further exploitation impossible.

From an economic perspective it is important to emphasize that both boom and bust are frequently essentially political processes in which physical availability of the resource -- either new discoveries or subsequent increasing scarcity or exhaustion -- may play a relatively minor role. It is true, of course, that increasing scarcity of resources helps to create the economic conditions conducive to both boom and bust. Increasing scarcity and rising costs of exploitation lead, simultaneously, to bust in some places and to the exploration, technical development, and rising prices that make new booms possible elsewhere. But this process is probably of minor importance in many of history's famous booms and busts. We suspect that over the short term, at any rate, both Montana's coal and Mexico's oil booms have less to do with physical exhaustion of energy resources, as inexorable as that process may be in the long run, than with decisions made in OPEC meetings, corporate boardrooms, Washington, Mexico, and Helena, Montana, the State's capital.

According to Celso-Furtado, the economic history of Brazil was marked by a series of boom and bust cycles in the production of sugar, minerals, coffee, and rubber. In almost every case, the collapse could be attributed to political and social rather than physical factors (Celso Furtado, 1963). Frank (1969) makes a similar point concerning Chile.

Whatever the source, what is the economic impact of a resource boom? One undeniable effect is that resource development can produce astoundingly rapid growth in income. In Mexico, for example, income generated by oil production has grown more rapidly than that from any other source. And by historical standards Mexico has had high growth rates in several sectors. The "gold rush" atmosphere surrounding Western energy development tells the same story here.

Except in an initial construction phase, however, resource booms do not seem to bring about comparable growth in employment. Even in Mexico and throughout the Third World, where unemployment is enormous by our standards, resource extraction and processing tends to employ lots of capital and relatively little labor.

It appears that this lack of employment creation is responsible for a third aspect of resource booms: namely that their benefits are often not widely distributed. This is true not only because of limited employment but also because windfalls often allow resource owners to capture a lion's share of the benefits. Concentrated ownership of resources is common and has often been made possible by purchases of resource rights or property before their economic value began to rise.

The effects of booms are not, of course, exclusively economic. They alter people's lives in other ways as well. There are often very far reaching changes in the social structure and the life style of the area affected. We use words like that so often that what they really mean may sometimes be lost on us. But during the great resource booms in the American West in the last century, the change in the social structure and the life style of Native Americans was drastic indeed. The effects on social structure and life style that occur with resource booms even now are in some ways comparable. This is particularly evident in those places around the world where resource development is in direct conflict with traditional cultures. An example can be found in the experience of the native people of the Amazon basin.[1] But it is also true of the American West. In Eastern Montana, coal development is replacing rural small town social structures with something entirely different and, in fact, one civilization with another. Very often when the extraction of a non-renewable resource replaces agriculture as the basis of the economy, the social conflicts that arise are very great indeed.

This is true partially because the attitudes of people involved in developing non-renewable resources may be very different from the attitudes of the "natives". One of the authors went to high school in Sidney, Montana which was then a small agricultural town. But it is no longer a small agricultural town, it is an oil boom town filled with hundreds and hundreds of people who would rather be anywhere else on earth but Sidney, who have no attachment to the land around them, who think it is the god-awfullest place they have ever seen. That pattern appears to characterize rapid expansion of an extractive industry.

The work force attracted to the mines or oil fields often comes from far away and leaves behind families, friends, and other ties. Viewing their stay as temporary, they establish few commitments to the new community. Thus oil field workers in the states of Chiapas and Tabasco in Mexico often spend what limited free time they have traveling to and from their home states or, if not traveling, trying to gain access to the limited number of telephone lines through which they can contact their families (Elman, 1979).

A second aspect of expansion is a whole range of environmental effects. In the case of Western coal mining, there is the danger of degradation of ground water and the land itself. If the coal is converted to some other energy form, there are large quantities of water used in the processing of the resource. The air is bound to be polluted. It is difficult to imagine rapid expansion of any extraction that doesn't involve effects like this. As we move closer to resource depletion in the future we will have to employ technically more and more advanced processes to get at what resources remain and the environmental consequences will become more and more far-reaching.

The consequences of the boom and bust cycle are of course not limited to the expansion phase. During the process of contraction, the economic base of the community obviously begins to shrink and to wither away. The question is whether there is any part of the economy capable of surviving that shrinking. Whether there is or not depends to a large extent on what has been done with the wealth that is being produced.

In Montana, and throughout the West, we have numerous examples of towns that were built up around resource extraction and died when that resource was exhausted. We can look at Montana's first two capitals, Bannack and Virginia City. They really no longer exist except as tourist attractions. Because Montana's copper deposits are playing out, the same thing is now happening to Anaconda and to a certain extent to Butte; we can expect the same thing to happen to Colstrip and Forsyth and Wibaux and to any number of energy boom towns in Eastern Montana. Had you walked through a Western ghost town when it was thriving, you may not have thought that its economy was vulnerable to the exhaustion of its resource base. You would have found that people in the town were doing all kinds of things besides, for example, gold mining. There were stores of all kinds, there were saloons, there were churches, there was a great variety of things going on. But it turned out that even though there were all kinds of other enterprises, it all really boiled down to the gold. When the mining stopped, so did everything else.

We often think of the inhabitants of gold towns as footloose single males with no real commitment to or investment in the community. Thus its collapse would be relatively unimportant. But in fact many people settled into the towns with an apparent conviction that they would stay permanently. They began to build a community life and future through schools, civic and cultural organizations, newspapers, and churches. All these were lost, of course, when the mines closed (Malone and Roeder, 1976:50-70).

In Eastern Montana we are now investing the proceeds of taxes on coal in schools, sewer systems, and other public activities. But this is not very much different from what was done with the gold towns. All we are doing is adding something to the superstructure, but nothing to the economic substructure, of those communities. When the economic resource base is gone the same thing will happen. No matter what we do with the superstructure, if we have not diversified the substructure of these communities, if we have not fostered other, non-extractive industries, then we can expect that the contraction phase will be as severe and destructive as it has been in the past.

The ghost town is, of course, far from an exclusively American institution. The history of some of the world's poorest nations and regions is full of examples of rapidly growing natural resource based industries which somehow failed to produce sound, self-sufficient economic structures. Brazil's recurrent booms, cited earlier, are examples. But Asia, Africa, and the rest of Latin America have had the same experience (Celso Furtado, 1968; Frank, 1969; Myint, 1965).

Consumers

The effects of resource exhaustion are not, of course, felt exclusively in the resource producing communities. On the contrary, the consumers of natural resources are also affected and in general are far more numerous than the people that supply them.[2] The science of economics recognized a couple of centuries ago that the depletion of certain kinds of resources served as limitations upon human activity and in particular on population growth and on the standard of living. This recognition has generally been associated with the British economist, Thomas Malthus. Malthusiansim has had its ups and downs in the past two centuries, but in the past decade something akin to it has again become the focus of those who have begun to pay attention to the limits to growth. That approach and that concern is typified by the work of the Club of Rome, which has attempted in a disciplined way to determine exactly what various limits to growth are and when those limits will come into play (Meadows, et al., 1972).

The approach of the Club of Rome was to build a large model of the world physical and economic system. The model incorporated interactions between industrial and agricultural production, resource use, pollution, and population growth. Its course through time could be projected by a computer and always led to the same result: world population and production would rise for some time and then in the 21st Century collapse disastrously as resource limits, pollution, and the unavailability of food took their toll. Collapse was always a rapid process.

The recognition of the limits to growth is perhaps one of the most important elements of public policy-making of our age. We believe that those who refuse to recognize the limits to growth are not capable of making effective public policy decisions. At the same time we recognize that there are those who can argue very persuasively against the approach of the Club of Rome and other modern day Malthusians.

No one can deny that any process dependent on resources cannot be sustained as those resources become increasingly scarce, least of all economists, who somewhat ambivalently claim Malthus as a founder of their discipline. But economists are ambivalent about Malthus because of the apparent failure of his predictions to materialize. And so they tend to attack modern Malthusianism as a repetition of errors committed in the early 19th Century. They argue specifically that the crisis of resource exhaustion has consistently been staved off by technical change. Eventually that which is exhaustible will be exhausted, but if technology can delay the eventuality long enough, it becomes unimportant.

Technological development has three aspects which economists emphasize.

First, technology makes the size of exhaustible resource reserves a variable. Obviously, we are in a better position to find reserves today with the help of satellites and other such marvels than when Malthus was around. For example, technological development has allowed us to go back to supposedly exhausted reserves of petroleum over and over again.

Second, technology makes us adaptable in substituting one kind of resource for another. The degree of adaptability is very important in determining the extent to which we can escape resource limitations. Many economists think that we are extremely adaptable. For example, two economists, on the basis of statistical measurement, have argued that only 10% of the difference in labor productivity in agriculture between industrial nations and the Third World is due to differences in the amount of land available to workers (Hayami and Ruttan, 1971:66). If this is true, it suggests we are very adaptable in overcoming the limitations of available land. Those who argue that our major energy crisis strategy should be improved conservation are also adaptability optimists. Technology, in their view, makes the substitution of solar energy and insulation for coal feasible and viable.

Finally, many economists argue that general technological progress over time is the largest single identifiable source of economic growth. This means that the production derived from all resources, natural, human, or manufactured has been rising over time. This increased efficiency of resource use has been outweighed by the enthusiasm for ever increasing production and the use of resources per person has consequently expanded greatly. But many economists argue that this general technical progress has made and will continue to make high levels of production and consumption possible.

RESPONSIBILITIES TO THE FUTURE

Resource depletion, then, bodes well for no one. Although we cannot agree on how soon or how severely, it threatens to limit our standard of living and perhaps threaten life itself. And as we try to maintain supplies of vital resources we tear up the earth and create and destroy communities with little regard for the people living in them. But given that exhaustion is inevitable at some point, what can we do about it? What is the proper response of resource users or producers who can look forward and see these results coming? Surely ceasing to use the resource is not the appropriate response. That simply mimics the effects of exhaustion itself and does it sooner, rather than later. What can we do? What are our responsibilities in this dilemma? We are going to discuss two possible solutions.

Conservation

The first is that although stopping the use of the resource may not be a viable alternative, slowing down the rate of depletion is. Slowing down is important because it buys time and time is important in the process of resource depletion.

Although we are not all aware of it, one of the things that we are actually depleting along with copper and oil and coal is time itself. This is because as we go through the activities of the world, we gradually, but steadily and inevitably, render finite stocks of energy and resources unavailable for continued use. This unusability is called entropy. Because of it, there is only so much time for human activity of the type we have known. How much depends on how fast we go through these activities.[3] Thus the decisions that we make now of how fast to use up resources, in a sense also decide how much time, as well as resources, are left for future generations. By slowing the rate of resource depletion we buy time in the sense that we make it available for future generations.

But time is also very important in this context in a couple of other ways. First of all, one of the key elements in the limits to growth argument is that growth is exponential in nature. If resource use is growing at the rate of, say, 6%, that growth continuously compounds and therefore becomes more and more rapid all the time.[4] One thing that this means is that all effects that we have attributed to resource extraction and depletion come at us much faster all the time. It is difficult enough to adjust to those changes without having them come at us faster all the time. In order to try to stop that from happening it is essential that we slow down the rate of growth.

The third sense in which it is important for us to slow down the rate of growth arises from the fact that the change itself is not only disruptive to communities and to the environment, but also to the human psyche. It seems likely that human beings as a species are adapted to dealing with change at a limited pace, but have a very difficult time in dealing with the enormously rapid changes of our era. Faced with change too rapid to be assimilated, humans react in a variety of ways. One current manifestation is the recent turn to the conservatism of the New Right and the Moral Majority. We believe this conservatism reflects a new approach to time: a desire to turn it back upon itself. Things have "gotten out of hand" and in desperation people choose what is impossible: to go backward in time. That is not an available option. But neither can we continue to rush ahead at the rate that we are going now. And so, somehow we have to begin to fashion some creative solution somewhere in between.

But agreement on this point is not universal. There are those who dispute the necessity of conserving natural resources, of slowing the current rate of use. The same critics of the Club of Rome who feel that technology can greatly reduce resource constraints also feel that it can bring the pace of resource exhaustion within manageable limits.

As we have pointed out, all of the complex computer models of the world system that include resource constraints show collapse occurring very suddenly after a period of ostensibly sustainable and untroubled growth. The designers of these models have tried to account for the effects of technological development by starting their simulations under technically more favorable conditions: with land _twice_ as productive as it actually is, with _twice_ the natural resources that currently exist, and so forth. The results, however, are always the same; collapse is only slightly delayed.

Economists and other critics have attacked this approach on two grounds. One is that to represent technological change as a once and for all doubling of land productivity or resource availability ignores what they believe to be its continuous character. Historically in the United States, acreage yields double about every 40 years. If we wish to predict what will happen in the future to agricultural production and represent technical change in the process by a doubling of initial productivity levels, we are assuming in effect that the historical pace of technical change will continue for forty years and then stop all together. Although this may be reasonable, the authors of the Club of Rome report have done little to justify it.

A second reason for attacking the world system models is that they fail to provide for the adaptability which has been displayed historically in substituting one resource for another. We have already talked about this earlier.

The result of accounting for technology in the way that economists think it operates is to push collapse of the world system beyond the time horizon of the models (Nordhaus, 1973:1180-83). Indeed it may never happen at all. For economists what all this means is that pressures brought about by resource exhaustion will not

happen so fast or so unexpectedly that we cannot cope with them.
Deliberate efforts to slow down resource use are not needed.

Replacing Lost Resources

Even if we slow down the pace of resource use and at that slower
pace can cope successfully with the hardships brought on by
exhaustion, we still face a fundamental problem. Given that resources are gifts of nature, are we not under some sort of obligation
to share them with future generations? Or if we use them up, should
we not attempt to replace them with something of equal value we can
leave our children?
     At one level, of course, this may be utterly hopeless. If we
accept the notion of entropy, usable energy and resources and hence
the time span of human existence are limited and finite. Every time
we change a natural resource into any kind of a man-made resource we
increase the level of entropy and hasten the time when human activity
is no longer possible on the face of the earth. Entropy grows
whether or not we engage in that kind of transformation, but every
such transformation has the actual effect of decreasing what is left
of available energy.
     Economically, on the other hand, there seems to be little
question that we can replace used up resources with something of
equal value. Regardless of the system we use to assign values to
things, there must be some quantity of hospitals, or art museums, or
schools or factories producing useful things that the community
considers as valuable as, say, 1,000 tons of coal. Thus the question
is not can we replace lost resources with something of equal value,
but will we? It seems that there might be two reasons why we will
not.
     The first is that we are simply ungenerous. We who are alive
today own, either collectively or privately, everything we think has
economic value. In theory, we can use it all up if we want (limited
only by unavailability of time to consume that fast). But the record
in that regard is good. For several centuries now we have used the
productive capacity we have in excess of our subsistence needs to add
to the store of productive resources that we pass on to future
generations. We have not usually plundered our patrimony. Whether
this is the result of generosity or, say, the forces of accumulation
working on capitalists in the struggle to survive, is unclear. But
the result is clear.
     Another reason that we might not replace used up resources with
something of equal value is that we consistently underestimate what
resources will be worth to future generations and overestimate the
value of what we plan to replace them with. The fact of the matter
is that as economic creatures making decisions about how fast to use
up resources, we consistently and systematically undervalue the
importance of those resources to future generations. Human beings,
as a matter of course, would rather have a dollar now than a dollar
in the future; and there is a very simple reason for that. Any
particular human being knows that he has a better chance of being
here to spend the dollar now than he does at any particular time in
the future. Because of this and other uncertainties about the

future, we consistently discount it. Indeed, when it comes to making economic decisions, we discount the future very sharply beyond our own particular generation. The lives of people in the future are never going to be as important to us as purely economic actors as are those lives going to be to the people themselves. That is an economic fact of life. What it means is that if we are going to make decisions about how fast to use up resources, those decisions must be made by people who actively take account of the future in their political decisions rather than simply making economic decisions.

Now, there is another sense in which the transformation of resources into something that is man-made leads to problems. Even if it were possible to take a resource and turn it into something that was somehow permanently of an equal value, the question remains: Who is it that gets the benefit of what is transformed? Even if the resource itself, in some sense, belongs to everybody, it is usually the case that whatever it is transformed into belongs to some particular people. How is it that a resource which in some important sense belongs to the earth rather than to any individual person, comes to be transformed into something that belongs to a particular person?

Let us go back again a few centuries in economic thought, this time to a political scientist rather than an economist but one who was also interested in economic questions. John Locke suggested that the only legitimate way that anybody could take something out of the common store and make it his own was by mixing his or her labor with it. That very rarely happens in the kind of resource extraction that we have been discussing, at least not in the Lockean sense. In order to draw a contrast we can cite two different experiences in the mining of coal in Eastern Montana. One is the experience of the Peabody Coal Company, which, through a whole series of legal manipulations has found itself in control of ton after ton of coal in Eastern Montana which it is free transform into whatever form of wealth it wishes. The other is the experience of one of the authors while growing up on a farm in Eastern Montana. Each winter his family would hitch horses to a sleigh and drive four or five miles to an underground coal mine under a section of state-owned land. All the neighbors would gather there and spend the day mining coal and then take it back and have it to heat their houses for the winter. It seems that that kind of activity and that kind of mixing of labor with the resource does create a property in that resource that is defensible. If somebody from a future generation came along and asked "What are you doing?", you would be able to do a pretty good job of explaining what you were doing, namely that you were keeping yourself alive. On the other hand, if the State of Montana had come along and attempted to impose a severance tax on that load of coal it would have met with a great deal of justified resistance. But Peabody or Decker Coal Company takes an electric drag line and with each scoop mines enough coal to have heated a family home for twenty winters and does that hour after hour after hour. If somebody from a future generation asked them "What are you doing to my coal?", the answer would be less obvious. At the same time the State would be justified in taking the position that at least some of the coal belonged to the future and should be taxed to assure the future had something to replace the coal.

In trying to guess at the future value of things, exhaustible resources have two values peculiar to them which rarely receive economic expression. First, many people value a wholeness and integrity in the natural world which is clearly inconsistent with the exhaustion of resources. The most obvious example is wilderness. Although the simple existence of wilderness may have a value to people greater than that of the gas, or oil lying beneath it, the simple fact is that there are markets where we can express our willingness to pay for the latter but not the former.

The second unmarketable value we may place on stocks of exhaustible natural resources is that they allow us choices. When we have used up our coal we will have destroyed an option for future generations. The option itself has value but again there is no market in which we can express our willingness to pay for it.

The idea of unmarketable values leads to the third sense in which we can ask the questions of whether it is possible to replace exhausted resources with something of equal value. This is the social sense. As we go through the disruptive processes of resource exploitation and exhaustion, is it possible to maintain or even enhance the social life of the surrounding community?

In some respects, the evidence from Mexico is not good. Oil development has led to rapid urbanization, the displacement of existing agricultural communities, corruption, the creation of a large force of transient laborers, and the temporary dissolution of the work force along union and skill lines (Elman, 1979). It remains to be seen whether the economic benefits of oil development will be great enough, pervasive enough, and widely distributed enough to justify these costs.

It is important in thinking about this problem to avoid being romantic about the social life being sacrificed in the name of resource development. We tend to think of non-industrial society as "unspoiled," "idyllic," "simple," and so forth. The image that comes to mind is that of the contented peasant living close to nature and enjoying its abundance. That image is false in some respects. Rural populations may have a social life that has many satisfactions, but it also involves extreme inequality of economic and political power, disease, malnutrition, and futures without the opportunity for personal growth or change.

CONCLUSION

Despite all these difficulties, most nations, states and communities faced with the destruction of their natural patrimonies are trying to some degree to defend them. The defense is imperfect: we see the future with uncertainty, respect its interests begrudgingly, and must work with a bewildering variety of policies, laws, taxes, plans, and regulations whose effects we may not fully understand. But even ghost towns and abandoned mines and fields may yield guideposts to that uncertain future.

FOOTNOTES

1.   This experience is described by Ronald Erickson in his paper in this volume.

2.   This obviously accounts for the conflict between consumers and producers.   Users of electric energy in, say, the Midwest, may be indifferent to the impact of coal mining on Montana as long as electricity stays cheap.   In the resulting dispute, Montanans may feel themselves to be, and are, seriously outnumbered.

3.   Herman Daly's paper is this volume further elaborates the implications of entropy.   The only form of energy not subject to entropic decay is solar.

4.   A simple numerical example can dramatize this point.   If at current rates of use we have a fifty year supply of, say, petroleum and our use is growing at 6% per year, then in ten years the remaining stock will last 21.8 years at the rate of use then prevailing.   Thus a problem that appears to lie safely in the distant future leaps much closer.   Continued growth would, of course, cause the situation to continue to worsen.

BIBLIOGRAPHY

Daly, Herman E. (ed.). Toward a Steady State Economy. San Francisco: W. H. Freeman and Company, 1973.

Elman, Richard. "Boom Time in Tabasco." Geo, 1 (August 1979):6-31.

Frank, Andre Gunder. Capitalism and Underdevelopment in Latin America. New York: Modern Reader, 1969.

Fuller, Robert. The Rising Cost of Living on a Small Planet. New York: Worldwatch Institute, 1980.

Furtado, Celso. The Economic Growth of Brazil. Berkeley: University of California Press, 1968.

Hayami, Yujiro and Ruttan, Vernon. Agricultural Development: An International Perspective. Baltimore: Johns Hopkins Press, 1971.

Howe, Charles W. Natural Resource Economics. New York: John Wiley and Sons, 1979.

Kapp, K. William. The Social Costs of Private Enterprise. New York: Schocken Books, 1971.

Malone, Michael P. and Roeder, Richard B. Montana: A History of Two Centuries. Seattle: University of Washington Press, 1976.

Marglin, Stephen A. "The Social Rate of Discount and the Optimal Rate of Investment." Quarterly Journal of Economics 77 (1963):95-110.

Meadows, Donella H., et al. The Limits to Growth. New York: Universe Books, 1972.

Myint, Hla. The Economics of the Developing Countries. New York: Praeger, 1965.

Nordhaus, William. "World Dynamics: Measuremeent Without Data." Economic Journal, 83 (December 1973):1156-83.

Pigou, A. C. The Economics of Welfare. London: Macmillan, 1920.

Sen, A. K. "On Optimising the Rate of Saving." Economic Journal, 71, 283 (1961):479-496.

Western Analysis, Inc. Capital Formation and Development Finance in Montana. Helena: Western Analysis, Inc., 1980.

4
Man the Beneficiary?: A Planetary Perspective on the Logic of Wildlife Preservation

Thomas H. Birch

> The ancients left rice for mice, and did not light lamps out of pity for moths. These thoughts of theirs are the operation point of humanity in life. Lacking this, a man is a mere earthen, wooden body. Kojisei

> We shall never fully understand nature (or ourselves) and certainly never respect it, until we dissociate the wild from the notion of usability. John Fowles[1]

Should we, the human species, preserve wild land, and preserve it on a worldwide scale? If so, should we preserve it for the benefit of the human species, or essentially for some other reasons? What are the real reasons for preserving wild land? I shall suggest that these reasons are not well understood even in the preservationist community, either in the United States or abroad, and shall then indicate what some of the real reasons for such preservation are.

OBLIGATIONS AND USABILITY IN OUR RELATIONS WITH NATURE

Those who are concerned to preserve wildlands feel an <u>obligation</u> to nature to leave at least some of nature alone, so it can be free to be itself. They feel the same sort of obligation to persons. They feel an <u>obligation</u> not to impose their own will, their human ideals, on the whole of nature. They feel that ethics require that, like the ancients to whom Kojisei refers, humans should leave food, and habitat, and space for all the beings of the non-human world, from mice to elk to plants to rocks.

Wildland preservationists see that the idea of a moral community, with some beings in, and the rest out, with some beings <u>persons</u> and the rest mere <u>things</u> to be <u>used</u> by persons in whatever ways persons may wish, is a bogus and unethical idea. They see that all beings, humans and non-humans, belong to the moral-ecological 'community'. They see that all beings ought to be respected, as John Rodman has put it, "for having their own existence, their own character and potentialities, their own forms of excellence, their own integrity, their own grandeur" (Rodman, 1977:94).

Preservationists find, as Henry Beston eloquently expresses the matter:

> ..the animal shall not be measured by man. In a world older and more complete than ours they move finished and complete, gifted with extensions of the senses we have lost or never attained, living by voices we shall never hear. They are not brethren, they are not underlings; they are other nations, caught with ourselves in the net of life and time, fellow prisoners of the splendour and travail of the earth (quoted by Rodman, 1977:94).

Black Elk speaks of "all the nations that have roots or legs or wings." There are also nations of rocks, moving slowly from the mountains, down, to become soil, the basis of life.

Let us consider the rocks. Let us consider rocks with a view toward discovering something about the ethics of our relationship with them. If we are to see the real reasons for preserving wild land, it is important to think about the ethics of relating with rocks, primarily because offhand, as products of modern culture, we are apt to believe that when it comes to rocks there are no ethics at all. Thinking seriously about rocks can help free us from the grip of our homocentric ethos and expand the horizons of our ethical conceptions.

There are countless billions of small rocks, and there are larger rocks, for example, the Rock of Gibraltar or the great pinnacles and spires and summits of the Bitterroot Range. Rocks are very powerful. After all, they literally support us all. Perhaps even more important, rocks can "speak" to us, in the sense that we can learn from them. I am not saying that rocks can speak English, or Swahili, or that they can feel, or are conscious in even the most dim of all possible ways. Rocks are paradigmatically non-conscious beings. But rocks can talk to us in the sense that we can learn things from relating with them. We then put into words and actions what we learn. That is how rocks can be teachers. It is because they are so totally _different_ from us, so _other_, so mute, so paradigmatically opaque, that they are often good teachers.

Some of the most important things I have learned about ethics have come from relating with rocks, from climbing them, from walking across fields and streambeds of them, from dodging them, from having them fall and explode next to me, from getting hit by them, from seeing them and hearing them in streams and lakes, from taking shelter among them, from throwing them, from gathering them on beaches, from fondling them, from building with them, and so forth. I like to think that rocks broke the grip of my own egoism and my homocentricity, and of my own acculturation toward solipsism.

The most important thing we learn from rocks is the inadequacy, even the absurdity, of a homocentric, human- centered, usability approach to nature, to the non-human, and to other humans as well. We learn this because, once we have noticed the existence of rocks, we soon see that there are just too many rocks to use. How could we use them all? There are too many of them, and too many shapes, sizes, types. Think of the _possibilities_ in the field of rock taxonomy. The possibilities are obviously infinite, as in all other cases, of course. With appropriate apologies to the science of geology, we may say that our rock taxonomy has only scratched the surface. Why is our rock taxonomy still so limited and unimaginative? Because we do not have any conceivable <u>desire</u> to use them all. Most of the rocks are just <u>there</u>, on their own, ignored by our interestedness.

Of course we have been using rocks for millions of years. Along with sticks they have been our primary tools since before our species got up onto its hind feet. So it is not that we do not use them. In fact, we ought to use them, <u>have to</u> use them, to cooperate in the business of building life and civilization. And they tell us, and we learn, that it is often appropriate to use them, to work with them. How beautiful rocks are in walls, in gardens, in fireplaces! How well they hold and radiate heat!

However, if we think of rocks only in terms of their usability, we fail to understand them and cannot relate with them properly nor learn very much from them. This is because to relate with a rock, or with any other being, only in terms of its/her/his usability is to deny the otherness, the self-integrity, the separate identity, of the other being, whether that other being is a person, place, animal, plant, or thing, like a rock. It is relationships with others as such, as they are in themselves, apart from their usability, that save us from the predicament of egocentricity and solipsism. Such relationships enable us to learn and understand, and love; in a word, to live, to be quickened with the powers of life, both as individuals and as a species.

As it is with rocks, so it is with nature as a whole. Most of nature is just not useful to humans. The millions of species of living things that humans are now in the process of destroying (cf. Eckholm, 1978) have no known use, and it is unlikely that they ever could. This is true in spite of the very many new uses for things that we might come to find or to rediscover. Still, most of nature would not be useful. Because it is not useful, our attitude is one of thorough-going disregard. Our attention and our ethical consideration become narrowly focused by our interests on what we think is useful, and we forget about the rest. We do not even see the rest anymore, and we can no longer learn anything. We act as if we already know everything that is worth knowing. We no longer relate with nature as nature is in itself.

When we approach nature only in terms of its usability our attitude toward things is primarily one of assessment of their utility for the fulfillment of our desires.[2] We use things to get what we need and want. When they are related to in this way, things become mere objects and mere means toward our ends or values. Furthermore, in order to ensure that they behave so as to fulfill our desires, or maximize the realization of our values, we try to enslave them, dominate and conquer them, manage them. We thus strive to become technological beings, and masters of the earth. However, the master cannot relate to the slave as the slave really is, but only in terms of what he desires the slave to be. Characteristics of the slave that do not contribute to the slave's utility for the realization of the master's desires are ignored or eradicated. The master thus comes to relate only with his own idea of what the other,

the slave, should be. This is, in fact, the master's goal, success
for his imperialism. Thus the master comes in reality to relate only
with himself. If the intended slave becomes recalcitrant, the master
finds himself either at war with the intended slave, as many scholars
have alleged in the case of humanity and nature (cf. Nasr, 1968), or
the master finds himself in a state of despair because nature, the
intended slave, seems to refuse to give him what he wants, such as
happiness, somehow (anyhow) defined. In contrast, if we knowingly
let nature be its wild self we can be freed from the possibility of
such despair.

Because it leads us to try to enslave nature, the usability
approach to nature leads us to a loss of contact with nature. Either
the intended slave 'goes into hiding' or is destroyed by war; or
because what is disregarded is often destroyed out of negligence,
many non-useful attributes of the slave, of nature, are eradicated
out of neglect. At best, the usability approach to nature as slave
causes us to ignore much of nature, and because it is ignored much of
nature is simply lost to active human life, out of ignorance of its
very existence. Usability leads us away from a condition of living
relationship with nature and into an egocentric and ultimately
solipsistic condition of absolute alienation, which amounts to the
state of death.

Humans are also a part of nature, and humans too are wild at the
core. The usability approach to nature comes home to roost with a
vengeance, because usability comes to define our approach to the
other members of our own species and finally to ourselves. Usability
causes us to treat other nations, other races, the other sex, other
individuals, and even ourselves, as mere objects to be used for the
fulfillment of our desires. When this is done we cut ourselves out
of the possibility of living relationship with other people, and even
ourselves. Then we find ourselves dead and alone, out of the world,
exhausted, and no longer open to the empowering energies which come
from living relationships with others, as others.

Others are always wild to us. This is because their mystery,
their residual autonomy or freedom, their ineluctable unpredictabili-
ty, the unmitigable contingency of any relationship with them, all
these and more characteristics of wildness, constitute the otherness
of both humans and non-humans. Herein lies the importance and the
necessity for consciously preserving wildness and wilderness land.
The question of our relationship to nature centers on the question of
preserving, or saving, wild, wilderness land. Wild land is the heart
and marrow of nature, both as nature exists separate from and other
than human beings, and also as we humans exist as participants in
nature, ourselves fused into wildness at the center of our being.

VIEWING WILDLANDS AS A RESOURCE

However, our modern, technological, usability oriented culture
does not think of wildlands in this way. In the United States
designated wilderness has recently come to be thought of as a
resource.[3] Of the five major multiple uses of National Forest land
only timber production is prohibited in designated wilderness.
Wilderness resource uses are wildlife habitat, watershed protection,

recreation, and forage for commercial livestock production. Mining is also permitted. Wilderness in national parks is thought of as a resource to be used for recreation, wildlife, and watershed protection.

In construing wilderness as a resource we are absorbing it into the mode of usability. It has been a significant accomplishment to provoke agencies and politicians to recognize wildlands and wilderness even as a resource. Although there are some serious difficulties in thinking of wilderness as a resource, even as a resource in its own right and apart from its multiple uses, recognizing it as a resource in either of these ways is an improvement over not attending to it at all. For now resource managers are stimulated to include wilderness in their managerial calculations, whereas in the past it has been generally ignored.

Areas of wild land have been set aside for preservation in Canada, Australia, New Zealand, Sweden, in East Africa, in India, in the Soviet Union, in South America, and elsewhere. But a worldwide survey of reasons given for wild land preservation shows that these reasons are primarily utilitarian, cast in the mode of usability, and homocentric. With a very few exceptions the modern world justifies wildland preservation in terms of the benefits accruing to humanity. Consequently, if no arguments demonstrate a clear excess of benefits over costs from leaving land wild, then it becomes almost obligatory, in the prevailing mode of thought, to develop that land, to "get it into production."

Recent attempts to further wild land preservation at the international level are characterized by this essentially homocentric thinking. Thus wild land areas are included among UNESCO's Biosphere Reserves in order to serve as necessary controls to measure the increasing impact of civilization on the natural environment (Stankey, 1978:22-23). The goal is to ensure proper management of such naturally provided benefits as solar energy generation, waste recycling, and climate for the whole of "spaceship earth." Notice that to conceive of the earth as a "spaceship," as a vehicle, is to think of it in utilitarian terms, as a means to be used for the fulfillment of human desires. The earth itself becomes merely a vehicle, taking us toward a state as rich as possible in satisfactions. One cannot help but wonder where (we cannot say "where on earth"), as well as what, this state might be. Thinking of the earth primarily as a spaceship thus quickly degenerates into a reductio ad absurdum of the usability approach to the earth.

In proposing a system of preserved natural areas to be. called "The World Heritage Trust" (at the Second World Conference on National Parks in 1972) Russell Train argued that such a system

> is merely an extension of the concept of national parks....We now recognize that there are certain areas of such universal natural, cultural, or historic interest that they belong to the heritage of the entire world. Their preservation and sound management are important to the inspirational, educational, and recreation welfare of the peoples of the world, to scientific progress, and to the economic advancement of the country in which they lodge (quoted by Stankey, 1978:20).

Train's appeal is to human welfare. Land preserved under the aegis of a World Heritage Trust would be used to improve human welfare. That is the rationale.

The same homocentric thinking provides the justification for creating the world system of Biosphere Reserves. To date there are 144 biosphere reserves in 35 countries (Stankey, 1978:23). The rationale for this program is summed up by George Stankey:

> The program is a response to a recognized need to provide a system of reserves that can meet scientific, economic, educational, cultural, and recreational needs. Such areas are essential for many kinds of scientific investigations of ecosystems. They serve as baselines against which change is measured and they frequently constitute important gene pools (Stankey, 1978:22-23).

The purposes of the system of world biosphere reserves are to benefit man. This is especially clear in the case of furthering the scientific research that is necessary to manage the "spaceship earth" in order to protect and improve human welfare. There is no talk about anything like preserving natural areas in order to fulfill an obligation to leave nature free. The areas are to be preserved in order to be used for scientific purposes and the benefit of humanity. (I shall discuss gene pools below.)

The prevailing mode of justification for wild land preservation in terms of resource values affords only the most tenuous protection for wild land. As human populations and needs, both genuine and putative, increase, the pressure to develop all remaining resources tends to become overwhelming. Wild lands, especially if they contain any commercially exploitable resources, are viewed as land wasted, and become the first and easy targets of development interests.[4]

A PHILOSOPHICAL ALTERNATIVE TO USABILITY

Although the prevailing homocentric, usability ethos of our time may seem to offer the only available framework for justifying wild land preservation, there is an alternative tradition. In ethical philosophy the central and broadest division between types of ethical theories is between teleological and deontological theories. The theories that underlie and rationalize the prevailing usability approach to nature are teleological, as in the case of various forms of utilitarianism. For a radical alternative to this approach it is most fruitful to explore the deontological tradition in philosophical ethics. The deontological tradition is the older ethical tradition. It is the tradition of primary, pre-technological peoples. It is the tradition of Taosim, and in fact of all the great world religions, including Judeo-Christianity, although I shall not argue that now. In the modern world the deontological approach is the minority tradition.

The deontological tradition holds that obligations, "oughts," are the primary stuff of genuine ethicality and are the source of values, and that, in the final analysis, human values are of secondary concern when it comes to the tough business of judging what we ought to be doing. It puts "oughts" first, and allows that sometimes what we ought to do is not what we think would be the most valuable, or desirable, thing to do. It even allows the possibility that the human species ought not to survive, if, for example, it continues to behave unethically toward nature. We can feel the power of that moral possibility as we view the results of our war on the natural environment.

A philosophically precise explication of "deontological" is provided by John Rawls:

> ..a deontological theory [is] one that either does not specify the good independently from the right, or does not interpret the right as maximizing the good. (It should be noted that deontological theories are defined as non-teleo-logical ones, not as views that characterize the rightness of institutions and acts independently from their conse-quences. All ethical doctrines worth our attention take consequences into account in judging rightness. One which did not would simply be irrational, crazy) (Rawls, 1971:30).

The deontological tradition is perhaps most readily understood in contrast with the teleological tradition: "For teleologists, notably UTILITARIANS, our only duties have reference to ends and are to produce value, or perhaps to distribute it in certain ways." For deontologists, "duty is prior to value, and at least some of our duties, such as promise-keeping, are independent of values" (Lacey, 1976:60).[5]

In the case of wild land preservation the deontological view requires that our fundamental concern is whether we ought to preserve a piece of land. This cannot be decided solely or ultimately in homocentric terms even though, of course, we have to make the judgment. The reason why our culture finds the deontological perspective implausible, insofar as we can even understand it, is that modern technological culture is almost exclusively usability oriented (is utilitarian or teleological), and we are very deeply indoctrinated into this usability approach.

Because of this indoctrination, we tend to believe unreflective-ly that our obligations to others, to both land and people are a function of the values that can be realized out of the various sorts of relationships. We tend to assume this teleological mode of ethical thought uncritically and are so imbued with it that we can hardly conceive of the deontological alternative. So, in our culture we find it not simply implausible, but very nearly unintelligible, and even 'irrational', that our obligations to others, including non-humans, could be anything but those actions that would maximize human value and minimize dis-value. Because of our indoctrination into this sort of teleological, usability theory of ethics, we find it difficult to see even the possibility that our obligations to nature and other humans can, and must, be rationally determined in another way, in the terms of different conceptional priorities. From the alternative, and nearly forgotten, deontological perspective, the central priority in ethics is to discover what it behooves us to do, what we must do, what is binding upon us to do, what we ought to do,

and try to do that.[6] Really, this is not anything new. What our
culture has forgotten is that this can be done rationally without
placing the central priority on values. We all know and acknowledge
that the main business of ethics is the ascertainment and fulfillment
of obligations. The deontological tradition simply insists that we
take this knowledge seriously, make it our first priority, and act
accordingly. The overall point is that the deontological ethical
knowledge of the primacy of obligation has not been lost, even in
modern cultures that seem to subsume, and trivialize, it into the
rhetoric of value.

Deontological reasoning about our obligations to land and people
lives as the minority tradition in our technological world. Many of
the pleas for wilderness in the United States are deontological, and
many of the arguments for wilderness, while they are not explicitly
deontological, can be given deontological reformulations. That is,
we can make explicit the deeper, but implicit, deontological
arguments that underlie much talk about why we should save wildlands.
Furthermore, the deontological mode of thought can be seen working in
some Native American thought and action, such as the creation of a
sacred reserve in the upper Jocko-Rattlesnake area on the Flathead
Reservation in Montana.

A deontological justification for wildland preservation is not
to be equated with 'biocentricism' as this is often, but incorrectly,
understood at the popular level.[7] 'Biocentric' arguments of this
confused variety tend to result from and to enforce an alienation of
humans from wildlands. Thus they tend to reduce wild areas to the
status of museum pieces, to be observed, but not to be lived together
with. This hands-off, no-use approach is not the only alternative to
usability. To "use" things is not necessarily to approach them in
the terms of usability. It is, after all, the living relationship
with things and land, which necessarily involves their use, that is a
source of creativity and creation insofar as we humans participate in
it.

It could be said that technological culture necessarily
relegates all creativity to the museum. A museum, or an area of wild
land conceived as a museum piece, is a mausoleum of creativity, where
past but dead examples of creativity are to be viewed as interesting
relics, as it were, but where the processes of creation are no longer
to be participated in. The adequate deontological view accommodates
and encourages creativity and continuous creation, and human
participation in it. It seeks to articulate a new-old rationality
that accepts as a basic premise the fact that life originates from
relationships, of self with others, of humans with the radical
otherness of wild nature. It recognizes that the continuation of the
possibility of relationships logically requires the continuing
existence of the relata, the persons-things that are related, the
continuing existence of both humans and wild land. It sees that
therefore humans are obligated to save wild land. Reality requires
it. The continuance of the world requires it.[8]

In Heidegger's view, to save land is to set it free to be itself
on its own terms regardless of our human interests:

Savings does not only snatch something from a danger. To
save really means to set something free into its own

presencing. Saving the earth does not master the earth and
does not subjugate it, which is merely one step from
spoliation (Heidegger, 1971:150).

In the "saving" of wild land we preserve our humanity, our very
ethical being. We are obligated to "leave wild rice for the mice"
and not to burn the lamps of our technological culture in every
corner of the night. We are obligated to "save" wild land, to leave
some of it alone to be itself. We know this in the deepest sense of
knowing, in our bones, at our core, because our own core is itself
wild. We are part of the "green chaos," and the "green chaos" is a
part of us. [9]

A developed deontological rationale can provide the rational
basis for strong wildland preservation in a manner that would be
transculturally plausible, and which would encourage a modern, living
synthesis of a reformed and appropriately technological civilization
with its wild pre-technological sources. [10]

PHILOSOPHICAL PERSPECTIVES ON ARGUMENTS FOR WILDERNESS

Let us now consider four of the main sorts of arguments for
preserving wilderness: (1) the gene bank argument, (2) economic
arguments, (3) recreational or re-creational arguments, and (4) the
land ethic argument.

In the world of real politics, in Congressional hearings, and in
international attempts to preserve wildlands, these arguments are
given usability formulations. What I wish to suggest is that in
reality these political formulations have a deeper, deontological,
and therefore genuinely ethical, foundation. When we are forced by
political realities to argue for wildlands in the mode of usability,
we can do so with the confidence that we are 'coming from', or
standing on, another place or ground. The articulation of this
deeper and ethically more solid ground could give us the transculturally plausible rationale for truly effective preservation of wilderness. Let us now turn to indicating, first, the usability, and,
second, the alternative deontological formulation of these four sorts
of arguments for wilderness preservation. [11]

Gene Bank Arguments

Usability Formulation: The gene bank argument stresses the need
for genetic diversity and richness to maintain a healthy ecosystem,
one that is less susceptible to catastrophe than near monocultures,
and one that is capable of recovery from catastrophes, such as ice
ages, or massive crop failures. The technological mind is aware of
the importance of a continuingly healthy ecosystem for human
survival, and therefore this argument has significant effect in
modern cultures. Often the further point is made that we need to
preserve a rich gene pool because it has been, and should continue to
be, a source of extremely valuable and useful commodities and
medicines, such as penicillin, "the tonics and barks that brace
mankind," as Thoreau put it. These are good arguments, but they do

not express what is at stake at a deep ethical level.

Deontological Formulation: In a relationship with another, whether the other is a person or nature itself, it is ethically mandatory to 'save' the other, that is, to let the other be itself/himself/herself.   That   is   respect.   This does not entail having no impact, or effect, or influence on the other.   That   would be an absurd algorithm for an alienation from nature that would entail species suicide. But the requirement of carefulness about our influences and impacts on others is entailed, as well as a general policy of 'touching lightly', or minimizing unnecessary impact.

Without respect, as for example in the attempt to dominate another, there can ultimately be no relationship, for the self-integrity, the other-identity, of the other is destroyed. Do we, are we to, avoid destroying the possibility of relationships for our own sakes, for our own individual and species fulfillment, or for *its* sake, that is, for the sake of the relationship, and thus, for the sake of the world? From the deontological perspective we are to avoid destroying relationship for *its* sake, not ours. Of course we too benefit, because such preservation is what makes fulfillment possible, but that is not the most fundamental reason for engaging in the attempts at preservation in which we ought to engage.

In arguing for gene banks one is arguing for the opportunity for nature to be itself, and for the opportunity of the world of living relationship of humans with nature to continue.

Economic Arguments

Usability Formulation: Economic arguments for wilderness are constructed to show that in terms of costs and benefits it is more lucrative for society to leave a piece of land wild and undeveloped than it would be to develop it. The classic here is Krutilla and Fisher (1975). Such arguments have usually been constructed in terms of recreational versus commodity production dollars. But as the scope, subtlety, and power of economic analysis grow, they could be conceived ever so broadly (Tribe, 1974:1317ff.; 1973). We might even devise plausible ways to analyze the economic values of genetic diversity, of wild, spontaneous mutative processes, and perhaps even of the felicitous versus infelicitous probabilities of the intervention of unknown ecological factors, thereby factoring in the unknown into our managerial calculations.

Deontological Formulation: Ethically sound economic arguments for preserving wildlands can be developed in the framework of what we might call a pre-and-post-technological economics. Such a "new" economics must return from being the "science of the production, distribution, and consumption of goods, or the material welfare of mankind" to what economics is originally all about, which is the business of proper and ethical management of our household, our earth household, and of ourselves as members of the earth household.[12] What follows is an attempt at reconceptualizing economic arguments for wild land preservation on a deontological basis.[13]

Economics is the science of managing the household.   Our households, however, do not and cannot function in a vacuum, apart from what is outside of them. A household is not an island.   A household extends to and includes its neighborhood, its larger community, and the rural and wild lands that surround it. A household has ties with all that surrounds it and that informs it with meanings. Thus the wildlands about us come into our homes. They are internally related to us. They are an essential part of our household. Wild lands are thus a part of our economy.

A primary economics, concerned with managing the total household, must deal with all the ingredients. It must manage wildlands as essential ingredients in the properly functioning home. One first principle of managing a household has to be the care and preservation and maintenance of the essential ingredients. A sound economics requires caring for, cherishing, preserving our wildlands.

A household, as a true home, is composed of people, animals, and things, in a harmonious, continuing, dynamic, and mutually supporting system of relationships. Humans, like parents, are responsible for maintaining and furthering the household. Other beings are necessary parts of the whole, and make their own contributions. In order for them to do this, humans must take the responsibility to encourage them in their otherness, to keep them free to be themselves, in contrast to dominating them with overly strict controls that would enslave them and thereby diminish them to some present idea of what they ought to be.

Good parents provide guidelines for their children to develop their own capacities so they can make their own new contributions to household and community. Their new contributions are the result of a cultivated capacity to respond to what lies outside the immediate understanding and present institutions of the household and community. Flexibility, growth, and aliveness are the result, in contrast to stagnation, alienation, loss of touch with reality, and death.

Things and wildlands must be managed in the same way as children, to encourage and sponsor their liberation, so that they can "speak" to children and parents. Things and wildlands are infinitely rich and complex. We never know all that they can mean and inspire in their relationship with us. If we can let ourselves let them do it, things serve as a constant source of fresh ideas and inspirations, many of which are highly practical, many of which are simply beautiful and cause for celebration. This is the basic and essential way that wildlands enter into our households and communities. They are necessary as sources to keep our households dynamic and alive, and they are necessary as a constant reminder of our need always to stay in touch with our sources.

One must be alert to the danger of misconstruing this attempt at a deontological reconceptualization of economic arguments for wildland preservation. Because economics, including the above suggested deontological economics, is concerned with managing the household, it would be easy to misread the reconceptualization offered here along usability lines. Such a mistake would involve seeing wildlands as extrinsically, or instrumentally, valuable to the household. Then, of course, wildlands become in principle dispensable, when some other means is found to serve the same function, or make the same contribution to the good of the household. The argument found here, however, intentionally says nothing about the extrinsic (or intrinsic) value of wildlands. Rather, the household

is construed on the model of climax ecosystems. Wild lands are
reconceived as essential ingredients, internally related to everything that constitutes the household, so that without their
contribution there simply can be no complete household at all. Thus
nothing could be substituted for them. The conclusion of this line
of argument, then, is that wildlands must be managed in a way that
allows them to keep playing their essential roles, to make their
essential contributions to the overall proper functioning of the
whole household. The best way to so manage them is to preserve them.

Recreational or Re-creational Argument

Usability Formulation: From the usability, utilitarian, and
political point of view the argument for the recreational value of
wild lands is seen as a case of special interest pleading. Although
it is usually argued that wilderness recreation would be good for
anyone and that keeping it available is good for society at large,
still in the overall resource crunch a mere form of recreation must
be given short-shrift, and it is. Simulations of the 'wilderness
experience' may also be offered. The argument that wild land
recreation has a deeper meaning, as it does, than forms of mere
recreation, that the wilderness re-creates the human spirit, even
that it is important psychologically for the mental health of some
productive members of society, is construed as a special case of the
broader recreation argument just given, or as the interest of an
'odd-ball' religious consciousness. The political effectiveness of
recreation arguments thus turns out to be strictly a function of the
political power of the interest groups that espouse them. Society
will respond to these arguments in proportion to the power behind
them, and in terms of what can be 'afforded'.

Deontological Formulation: Wilderness recreation affords humans
an opportunity to make contact and establish ties with nature as
nature is in itself. The fundamental relationship with powers and
forces greater than anything human can be re-established. The result
of this re-creative. Humans can learn again, what technological
culture tries to extirpate from our understanding, that there is a
way of placing ourselves in the world that opens us to instruction
from the powers that guide us, that provide the gifts of meaning and
of life itself, and on which whatever meaning our lives can have is
originally and finally grounded. Thus recreation and re-creation
arguments are not special interest pleading. Rather, they are meant
to maintain the possibility of live and full and ethical participation in the world with continuing contact with our sources. They are
directed toward the preservation of the 'world', and preserving this
'world' includes preserving the possibility for ethical human
participation in it.

Land Ethic Argument

Usability Formulation: The land ethic, as from Leopold (1949),
is co-opted and corrupted by the usability approach, by the political
and technological mind. Morality is reduced to a value, 'moral

value', to be sought and promoted only insofar as it contributes to
the maximum of value over dis-value, as in Findlay (1961).

An ethic that is adequate to the land will have to foster the
integrity of all beings, not humans exclusively. The overall
integrity of the biosphere is its central concern. It must allow and
encourage all beings to be free. Thus it must allow for the
integrity of nature, and of the things of nature, wildlife and
ecosystems, and even rocks. Since wildness is essential to the
integrity of nature, a land ethic requires humans to save wildlands,
and not just a token amount of wildlands, but at least enough to keep
nature free, however the quantity is to be determined. Contact with
wildlands is necessary, or at least highly instrumental, in winning a
populace over to the land ethical point of view.

When we ask from the usability point of view why there is really
any need for a widespread adoption of a land ethic, the answer must
be that it is in our collective interest to adopt a land ethic. The
question about adopting a land ethic becomes a question of utility.
The argument is now that an ethical approach must be furthered for
other purposes, in order to get people to behave in a manner that
will avert ecological catastrophe. The argument has become
contingent upon the sociological hypothesis (which seems to be true)
that the adoption of a land ethic would be a technique that would
facilitate human survival. From being wilderness advocates we are
transformed into social engineers. Adopting a land ethic becomes
something worth doing only insofar as it is an efficacious technique
for the realization of other ends. However, the possibility is now
open that there might be 'better ways' of promoting these ends
(perhaps more totalitarian ways). Even so, this is still a good
usability, utilitarian argument. And of course if a genuine land
ethic were generally and truly adopted, then the ethical, and
deontological, battle would be won.[14]

Deontological Formulation: It is not primarily because it might
promote other ends that we wish to see a land ethic adopted. It is
not for such technological reasons, not primarily because it would be
useful. It is because it would be right, true to the world and to
our place as humans in the world.

To argue for a land ethic is not to argue for anything that has
direct bearing on the question of what is in the collective best
interest of humans, although it is, incidentally and fortunately, in
our interest to place ourselves properly and ethically in the world.
Arguing for a land ethic is arguing for an ethical stance in the
world. There cannot be a non-ethical, usability, justification of
land ethical action that still allows the ethical stance to remain
basic, for then something else would be more basic. One sees the
necessity of land-ethical action, which is sensitive to wild nature
as well as to humanity, only when his understanding of the world and
man's place in it forces him to see it. The usability view of the
world and man's place simply will not allow an ultimate place for
deontological ethical considerations. However, once we have
struggled through our training in the usability perspective, to a
different and accurate understanding, a land-ethical stance becomes
mandatory.

Thus wilderness preservation is necessary because it is a necessary part of the broader battle against the domination and destruction of the world, of humans and nature in continuous creative relationship, by technology and the usability approach. That is the real meaning of trying to save wild land—to try and save the world. That is also why the attempt to preserve wildlands is one of the most deeply revolutionary acts possible in the modern world. It strikes at the heart of usability and our domination by technological thought.

SUMMARY

In summary, I have been suggesting that there is an alternative to the prevailing usability arguments for wildland preservation and that this alternative deontological tradition and perspective, which now does seem, sometimes, to be rising from disregard into popular consciousness, can provide us with good ethical reasons for saving wilderness on a worldwide scale. This is primarily because, on this alternative deontological basis, preserving wilderness is no longer something to be done to satisfy any special human interest, or any human interest at all, but because it is a universal human obligation.

In conclusion, however, I wish to raise another problem, a problem of practical international politics and practical ethics. Thoreau writes

> If I knew for a certainty that a man was coming to my house with the conscious design of doing me good, I should run for my life...for fear that I should get some of his good done to me...If...we would indeed restore mankind...let us first be as simple and well as Nature ourselves, dispel the clouds which hang over our own brows, and take up a little life into our pores. Do not stay to be an over-seer of the poor, but endeavor to become one of the worthies of the world (Thoreau:332).

Other peoples, especially those of the Third World, should indeed be wary of the Russell Trains and David Browers and "Sierra Clubbers" who want to "do them good" by saving their wildlands. The wilderness preservation movement does seem to be largely a product of the privileged American middle class. Here is the source of the land ethic that recommends saving wildlands of all types all around the world. Could this be a 'recreational imperialism'? Could this be no more than a desire on the part of jet setters, who can afford it and have plenty to eat, to create more playgrounds—no matter how high-sounding the ethical talk behind it?

The point is that saving wildlands throughout the world must begin at home. I do not mean that we should merely set a good example by preserving lots of wilderness in the United States, although we should do that. The fact that the ethical concern for wild nature has arisen primarily in the American affluent classes does not invalidate the concern or the ethical soundness of the concern. What does tend to invalidate it is not practicing what we preach by not being ethical 'worthies', to use Thoreau's term,

ourselves, as a culture and as individuals. To become worthy we not
only have to abandon our usability approach to nature, but also must
abandon the kind of life that has such a heavy impact on nature, and
on other peoples. We can begin to do this by encouraging urban
self-sufficiency, by eliminating the consumerism that pervades
ourselves and our culture, by freeing ourselves from the victimiza-
tion by desire that discolors our own lives and our own culture.

In the end, of course, wilderness preservation begins with each
of us as individuals. When our own lives are improving, when as a
culture of individuals seeking seriously to minimize our impact on
nature we do evidence in our practice what we preach about preserving
wild land, then other cultures will find our ethical example
plausible, and may seek to follow it.

Virtually every culture contributes to the progress of ethical
consciousness. Because of the great potential for communication that
the modern world affords, a genuine exchange and reciprocity of
ethical understanding has become possible. In its imperialistic
approach to the North American continent, Western culture re-discov-
ered the ethical need for respect for wild nature, and it discovered
the consequent ethical necessity of wilderness preservation as a
practice to embody this respect. Now the Western adventure in
imperialism over nature and other peoples is coming to its end. Thus
there is increasing reason to believe that this ethical discovery,
which is corroborated in manifold diverse ways throughout world
cultures, will become in fact a living contribution to the ethical
consciousness and practices of the world.

FOOTNOTES

1. These quotes by way of a preface are from Kojisei (Blyth, 1949:72) and Fowles (1979:54).

2. This paragraph intentionally oversimplifies complicated matters. For example, we can have desires to fulfill obligations and use things to fulfill such desires. We can also simply use things to fulfill obligations, even obligations that we do not really desire to fulfill, and so forth.

3. Perhaps the leading spokesman for the recognition of wilderness as a resource has been Mr. William Moore, formerly of the United States Forest Service. Although the same can be alleged for all resource values, Mr. Moore does insist that wilderness is a very special resource. He is correct insofar as it is proper to construe wilderness as a resource at all. The philosophical difficulty is, very simply, that since wilderness is really the source of resources, it is a "category mistake" to call it a resource. It is unfortunately a mistake that has serious practical consequences for the allocation and management of wildlands. For to construe wilderness as a resource is to subsume it under the rubric of the technological-utilitarian ethic, and then to treat it accordingly as one among many resource values. The logic is the same as the teleological subsumption of Moral Value, in ethics, into the realm of other values, into "the kingdom of ends." See, for example, Findlay (1961).

4. Witness the intensifying pressure on wildland and wilderness sanctioned by Secretary of Interior Watt and the present administration in the United States.

5. To say that one's ethical theory is deontological is thus really to say little more than that it is non-teleological. Very much is still left open. Perhaps the central reason that deontological theories have been held in low esteem by many modern philosophers is that there has often been a tendency among deontologists, a tendency from which Kant himself is not immune, to sanction the a priori deduction of particular moral judgments, in rigid oblivion to the vagaries, the indefiniteness, and the infinite richness of specific circumstances and situations. Such a tendency is 'moralistic' in the bad sense. But a deontological approach to ethics does not have to involve such unacceptable practices. In fact, any such insensitivity to circumstance and situation would itself be in violation of one of the basic principles of an adequate deontological ethics, viz., the requirement of perceptiveness, of seeing, and consequently of eschewing the blinders of a priori formalism. Blind ethical judgments cannot be fully ethical because their justifiability would be chiefly a matter of luck or accident.

6. In what we might call original necessity, in, for example, early Greek consciousness and perhaps in that of most primary,

pre-technological peoples, as well as in our own moral experience, moral necessity is not distinguished from causal necessity. There is just one undifferentiated, yet at times ambivalent necessity. The possibility of successful human transcendence of the moral-causal laws of the world (moira) is not considered real. For humans to attempt such an unreality is considered exceedingly dangerous (the hubris of the Greek tragedies) both to themselves and to the fabric of all things. All imbalances created by such attempts are inevitably, and often brutally, rectified. Perhaps a deep belief in these pre-technological concepts, a belief still held unconsciously by modern man, can explain the profound uneasiness, and even guilt, that modern man feels about his apparent technological domination of nature, especially as he sees the radical ecological imbalances this domination creates.

Phenomenologically, that is, in terms of individual human experience, necessities originate undifferentiated into causal or moral necessity. We simply feel, see, know, that something has to be, must be, done, regardless of its later categorization. In its emphasis on the primacy of obligation in moral experience the deontological tradition is more true to the ingredient of undifferentiated necessity that is so essentially characteristic of moral experience, both phenomenologically and historically, than is the teleological tradition. Mere values, when excised from the context of their origination, do not have the aura of necessity about them that obligations have, and consequently it becomes plausible to say, for example, that the values in the field or 'firmament' of value can be identified by a disinterested, or 'impersonal", wishing (cf. Findlay, 1961). The sense of urgency about doing what is necessitated by experience and circumstance is lost in the teleological account. Values are simply there, arbitrary and indifferent, as possible goals to pursue. In contrast, the deontological tradition, in insisting on the primary of obligation, acknowledges and makes systematic space for the urgency, the compulsion, the full-blown necessity felt in moral experience, as it is born out of relationships with others.

With the emergence of ecological consciousness we can see the beginnings of a new synthesis of causal and moral necessity, now a conscious synthesis. This promises to be one of the main features of post-technological ethical consciousness. It will be a recovering of important ethical knowledge into a contemporary idiom (and it will legitimize fundamental aspects of much third world ethical thought, especially that of many so-called 'primitive' peoples). False ethical practices, especially toward the environment, stemming from the technological mind's confused notion that the differentiation between moral and causal necessity warrants a thorough-going divorce between them, a confused notion that has acted as one of the warrants for humans to behave as if they were not a part of nature, will have to be abandoned. A continuous acknowledgement of the close link between moral and causal necessity will be re-instituted in personal and social practice.

7. Aldo Leopold's biocentric land ethic (Leopold, 1949:224-25) includes humans as an integral part of the biosystem. What Wendell Berry has aptly called the "terrarium syndrome" (Berry, 1977:28) is a

common misunderstanding of Leopold's biocentricism, a misunderstanding that is symptomatic of our culture's alienation from nature.

8. Although we do, and ought to, have an interest, or desire, to preserve the possibility of relationships, to preserve the world, our obligation to do this (even to have the interest) cannot be reduced to having the interest, as many current forms of teleological ethics would require.

9. The "green chaos" is John Fowles' expression (Fowles, 1979).

10. Perhaps the pivotal reason why a deontological rationale for wild land preservation would be plausible transculturally is that arguments flowing from it would truly transcend the parochialism, and in many cases the imperialism, of special cultural and national interests.

11. The argument sketches or characterizations offered here, as well as the overall analysis, should be viewed as exoteric and programmatic.

12. The expression "earth household" comes from Gary Snyder (1957).

13. The work of E.F. Schumacher, for example (1973 and 1979), makes many important suggestions for beginning this job of reconceptualizing economic theory and practice. However, the trap of the entrenched teleological and utilitarian mode of thought and speech is difficult to avoid, and even Schumacher's "Buddhist Economics" seems to fall into it.

14. In this manner, because he places such a high and strong value on ethicality or moral value, even John Stuart Mill turns out, if the logic of his thought is closely pursued, to be more a deontologist than he is a strict utilitarian. Of course, his primary focus is on one and only one deontological principle, the principle of utility, and he himself does not explicitly carry through the logic of his classical ethicality to its deontological conclusion.

BIBLIOGRAPHY

Berry, Wendell. The Unsettling of America. San Francisco: Sierra Club Books, 1977.

Blyth, R. H. Haiku. Vol. 1, Eastern Culture. Tokyo: Hokuseido, 1949.

Eckholm, Erick. Disappearing Species: The Social Challenge. Washington, D.C.: The Worldwatch Institute, Worldwatch Paper 22, July 1978.

Findlay, J. N. Values and Intentions. London: Allen and Unwin, 1961.

Fowles, John. "Seeing Nature Whole." Harper's 259, 1554 (November 1979):49 ff.

Heidegger, Martin. Poetry, Language and Thought. New York: Harper and Row, 1971.

Hendee, John C., Stankey, George H., and Lucas, Robert C. Wilderness Management. Washington, D.C.: United States Department of Agriculture Forest Service, Miscellaneous Publication No. 1365, 1977.

Krutilla, John V. and Fisher, Anthony C. The Economics of Natural Environments. Baltimore: Johns Hopkins, 1975.

Lacey, A. R. A Dictionary of Philosophy. London: Routledge and K. Paul, 1976.

Leopold, Aldo. A Sand County Almanac. New York: Oxford, 1949.

Nash, Roderick. Nature in World Development: Patterns in the Preservation of Scenic and Outdoor Recreation Resources. Rockefeller Foundation Working Paper, March 1978.

Nasr, S. H. The Encounter of Man and Nature. London: George Allen and Unwin, 1968.

Rawls, John. A Theory of Justice. Cambridge, Mass.: Harvard University Press, 1971.

Rodman, John. "The Liberation of Nature." Inquiry 20, 1 (Spring 1977).

Schumacher, E. F. Small Is Beautiful. New York: Harper and Row, 1973.

_____. Good Work. New York: Harper and Row, 1979.

Snyder, Gary. Earth Households. New York: New Directions, 1957.

Stankey, George. "Wilderness Concepts and Management: An International Perspective." In Wilderness Management in Australia, R. W. Robertson, P. Davey and A. Davey (eds.).

Canberra: School   of   Applied   Science,   College   of   Advanced
Education, 1981.   i.-5;Thoreau, H. D.   Walden and "Walking".   In
The   Portable   Thoreau,   Carl   Bode,   (ed.).   New York: Viking,
1975.

Tribe, Laurence.   "Ways   Not   to   Think   About   Plastic   Trees: New
Foundations   for   Environmental Law." The Yale Law Journal 83, 7
(June 1974):1315-1348.

_____.   "Technology Assessment and the Fourth Discontinuity: The
Limits   of   Instrumental   Rationality."   Southern California Law
Review 46, 3 (June 1973):617-660.

5
Three Visions
of the Economic Process

Herman E. Daly

> In practice we all start our own research from the work of our predecessors, that is, we hardly ever start from scratch. But suppose we did start from scratch, what are the steps we should have to take? Obviously, in order to be able to posit to ourselves any problems at all, we should first have to visualize a distinct set of coherent phenomena as a worth-while object of our analytic effort. In other words, analytic effort is of necessity preceded by a preanalytic cognitive act that supplies the raw material for the analytic effort. In this book, this preanalytic cognitive act will be called Vision. It is interesting to note that vision of this kind not only must precede historically the emergence of analytic effort in any field but also may re-enter the history of every established science each time somebody teaches us to <u>see</u> things in a light of which the source is not to be found in the facts, methods, and results of the pre-existing state of the science (Schumpeter 1954:41).

Schumpeter's notion of a "preanalytic vision" corresponds precisely to Thomas Kuhn's concept of a "paradigm." Schumpeter's recognition that in practice we hardly ever start from scratch but instead build on the work of our predecessors is precisely equivalent to Kuhn's (1962) concept of "normal science" as the cumulative building on the past within the framework of a shared paradigm. Schumpeter's further observation that vision may re-enter the history of any established field whenever someone teaches us to see things in an entirely new light is precisely the same idea as Kuhn's "paradigm shifts" that occur in periods of revolutionary science.

I take it for granted that paradigms or visions are necessary, real and of fundamental importance in all sciences, as has been convincingly argued by Schumpeter, Kuhn, Michael Polanyi (1962), and others.

I want to argue that economics is currently in a state of revolutionary science in which vision is re-entering the history of our discipline and will eventually lead to a paradigm shift. I suggest that there are currently three visions which are vying for the honor of becoming the new paradigm which will guide and unify a new epoch of normal science. These three visions of the economic process may be labeled as follows: (1) the standard vision expounded in the economic theories of markets, growth, and stability; (2) the physical limits to growth vision, and (3) the steady-state vision.

Since these are pre-analytic visions I will represent them in terms of three simple pictures and discuss only their most fundamental characteristics. It is impossible to arrive at a preanalytic vision by analysis. Analysis can elaborate the vision, but vision is the starting point, not the result of analysis. Starting from scratch is something we hardly ever do, so the attempt is unfamiliar and will require a conscious effort to assume a naive state of mind. I will proceed as follows: First the standard growth economist's vision will be presented and subjected to cross-examination by the physicist (one who holds the physical limits vision); second, the physical limit-to-growth vision will be presented and subjected to cross-examination by the economist; third, a steady-state synthesis will be presented and submitted for cross-examination by the reader.

VISION I: STANDARD GROWTH ECONOMICS

In the standard vision, the economic process is conceived of as a circular flow of value between families and firms in an isolated system. Families spend money to buy the goods firms produce and firms spend money to buy the factors (land, labor and capital) families own and that are needed in production. This is represented in Figure 1. In this figure money flows clockwise in payment for real things (goods and factors) flowing counter clockwise.[1]

The focus in this vision is on two decision-making units: firms and families. The firms, the producing units, seek to maximize profits, while the families, the consuming units, seek to maximize utility or the benefit derived from consumption. The theory of the firm and the theory of the consumer explain the formation of supply and demand in the product and factor markets, which explains the formation of prices, which in turn explains allocation of resources and distribution of income. Microeconomics elaborates these themes.

Macroeconomics also originates in this vision because the aggregate circular flow of value, measured at product prices is national product, and when measured at factor prices it is national income. Moreover, the value of national product is equal to the value of national income[2] even though the physical embodiments of value are totally different physical flows in each case. The "soul" of value becomes reincarnated in a different physical embodiment every time it passes through firms or households. The value flow keeps circulating, while the physical flow is at best totally abstracted from, and at worst presumed to continue in a circular flow just like value. The entire principles course is an analytical elaboration of this basic vision, and intermediate and advanced courses in both micro and macro economics are usually further elaborations. It is indeed a dominant and powerful vision, and one

can learn much from it. I would not want to forget it or erase it
from the textbooks.   But it does cause problems.   It conceals from
view some fundamental truths which nowadays cry out for explicit
recognition.

FIGURE 1

STANDARD VISION

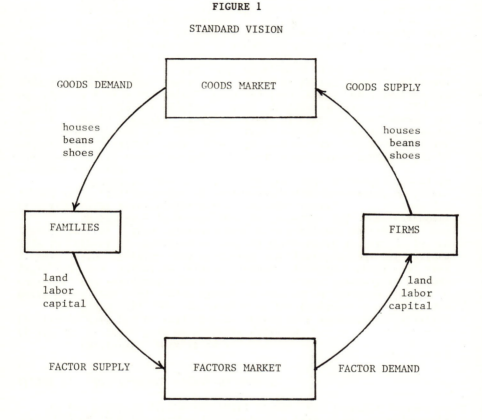

Specifically, the standard vision conceals all relationships of
the economic process with its environment. An isolated system has no
relationships with its environment. Therefore one cannot speak of
depletion or pollution of the environment, nor relate them in any way
to economic activity. Any consideration of the interrelationship of
the economy and its environment, the ecosystem, is ruled out from the
very beginning. It is hard to overstate the importance of this
simple fact, an importance insisted upon by Georgescu-Roegen who has
observed that our adherence to this vision is a reflection of
economists' devotion to a mechanistic epistemology even after the
mechanistic paradigm has been abandoned by physics.   As Georgescu-Roegen says:

> In this representation the economic process neither induces any qualitative change nor is affected by the qualitative change of the environment into which it is anchored. It is an isolated, self-contained and ahistorical process - a circular flow between production and consumption with no outlets and no inlets, as the elementary textbooks depict it (Georgescu-Roegen, 1971:2).

To avoid confusion let us note that the Principles texts do speak of outlets ("leakages") and inlets ("injections") into the circular flow of value. But these are leakages and injections of purchasing power, not of matter and energy. Furthermore the whole object of policy is to make total injections (investment, government spending, and exports) equal to total leakages (savings, taxes, and imports) at some desired magnitude of the circular flow of value.

The main problem with the standard vision is the macroeconomic interpretation in which growth becomes the overriding goal. To elucidate this problem let us imagine that the standard economist is being cross-examined by a physicist who wants to understand Figure I.

Physicist: Since economic growth seems to be the major goal of all nations, please explain to me how economic growth is represented in this diagram.

Economist: Economic growth is simply an increasing volume of the circular flow of value, measured either as national income or national product, usually corrected for inflation, sometimes corrected for population growth also.

Physicist: When the flow of value increases do the physical flows of matter and energy in which this value is embodied also have to increase, or can value increase with the physical flows remaining constant?

Economist: Well, conceptually one could imagine a growing value flow embodied in a constant physical flow as a result of qualitative improvement - but as a practical matter we cannot measure qualitative change and do in fact measure only quantitative change, so, yes, economic growth as we measure it does require an increasing flow of matter and energy.

Physicist: Very well then, where does it come from? How does the additional matter and energy embodied in the additional commodities break into this circular flow?

Economist: Why it comes from additional factors of production. To produce more shoes, houses, beans and haircuts requires more land, labor and capital.

Physicist: Wait a minute. The laborer and the capital equipment do not become physically a part of the shoe. They are simply agents that transform something else into a shoe. And land does not become a part of the shoe either since there is just as much land after the shoe is made as there was before! So you still haven't told me where the extra matter and energy come from.

Economist: A mere question of terminology. When economists say "land" they mean to include the flow of resources, matter and energy, from the land, as well as mere space.

Physicist: Strange usage (it is usually best to represent different things by different names), but let that pass. I see from your diagram that "land-including-resources" originates in Families.

How can that be? Do you imagine that families reproduce resources like they reproduce laborers?

Economist: Of course not, families own the resources and when resource prices rise they have an incentive to supply more. That is where it comes from! That is how the market solves problems of scarcity.

Physicist: You mean that ownership and incentive (mere social conventions) can create the matter and energy required to expand the circular flow of value?

Economist: Of course, haven't you heard of "supply side economics"? If you want more of something subsidize it, if you want less of something tax it.

Physicist: I see, we want more rich people, so we subsidize them, and fewer poor people, so we tax them. Brilliant! But this is beside the point. Have you ever heard of creation ex nihilo and perpetual motion? Your diagram is false even without growth. Even a constant circular flow of matter and energy is impossible because of entropy. Your vision is wrong because it contradicts physical laws, and furthermore it rules out any consideration of depletion and pollution as necessary consequences of economic activity.

Economist: Hold on now, read the title of Chapter 43 of my latest text, "The Economics of Depletion, Pollution, Crime, Marriage, Divorce, Racial Discrimination and Drug Addiction."

Physicist: Sure, but that is Chapter 43, the customary lame attempt at trendy relevance that your publisher insists on. Not only is Chapter 43 unrelated to Chapter One's basic vision, it is, as I have said, totally contradictory to that diagram. To include depletion and pollution (forget Crime, Divorce, etc.) in your analysis the environment must be present in your preanalytic vision, which means that your vision cannot be that of an isolated system.

Economist: OK. Our vision is not perfect. But even you physicists have had to abandon your vision of a mechanistic universe. If you are so smart give me a better paradigm.

Physicist: Here it is . . . . .

VISION II: THE PHYSICAL LIMITS TO GROWTH

In the physical limits-to-growth vision, the economic process is conceived of as a uni-directional, entropic flow of matter and energy through an open subsystem, the economy, within a closed total system, the environment. There are no closed circular flows of either matter-energy or value. In fact there are no values at all. There is matter, energy, and entropy. The economy, consisting of stocks of human bodies and artifacts, is an open sub-system which receives a continuous flow of low entropy matter-energy from the environment while returning a continuous flow of high entropy matter-energy back to the environment. Small amounts of matter passing through the economic subsystem may be recycled through again, rather than being lost in unusable form in the environment. This is not true of energy. The flows embodied in this view of economic activity are represented in Figure 2.[3]

The total environment or ecosystem, in its turn, is a finite closed system, which means that it imports and exports only energy – not matter. Since the environment is finite and the economy is a subsystem of the environment it is immediately obvious that physical growth in stocks cannot be a long-run norm. Could physical growth in the flow of throughput be a long-run norm? No, for two reasons. First a growing throughput with a given stock implies a shorter turnover period of the stock – i.e., a shorter life expectancy for both people and artifacts. There is certainly a lower limit to life expectancy and durability. Also a more rapid throughput means more depletion and pollution of the finite environment. So for neither stocks nor flows can growth be the norm. Standard growth economics involves a fundamental error.

Cross-examination is now in order.

Economist: Your way of seeing the economy is interesting as far as it goes. Physical growth in stocks and flows are indeed limited by finitude and entropy. But there is a problem with your picture. The final output of the economic process as you depict it is high entropy or waste matter and energy. In a strictly physical view the economy is just a big machine for converting useful raw materials into useless waste. Hardly an intelligent activity! And precisely because of this purposelessness there is nothing to your picture to tell us how big the economy should be. Granted that continual growth is impossible it is important to know whether we should cease growing at twice the present level, or whether we should have stopped at half the present scale. Your paradigm cannot even consider such a question because in physics you have no criterion of value.

Unless you go beyond mere matter and energy and introduce the idea of satisfaction of human wants and enjoyment of life, which for short we may call service, then you are stuck with a correct but trivial vision of the economy. It is easy to be rigorously correct if you are willing to be trivial.

Physicist: I'll admit that what you say makes me uneasy. But I read somewhere that some ecologists have developed an "embodied theory of value." If we can identify the energy embodied in a commodity with its value or price, then we could have a purely objective physical criterion of value and could then specify the optimum size of stocks as that for which embodied energy is greatest – or something like that.

Economist: It won't work, and for the same reasons that Marx's labor theory of value doesn't work. Of course you are free to try it and see how far you get. But I suggest we are better off with dualism than with a forced reductionist monism. Let's keep your physical limits vision, but add to it a value dimension rather than try to reduce value to a physical magnitude, as in the energy theory of value.

FIGURE 2

LIMITS TO GROWTH VISION

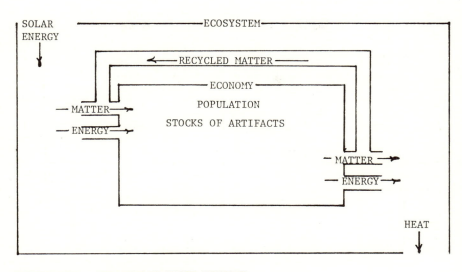

VISION III: THE STEADY-STATE ECONOMY

In the steady state view the economy again is an open system maintained by an entropic flow of matter and energy from and back to the environment. The stocks of population and artifacts making up the economy, however, are held at a constant level such that the throughput required to maintain them is sustainable and the service (or provision of well-being) derived from both the economy and ecosystem is maximized. These relationships are depicted in Figure 3.

The steady-state paradigm is simply an elaboration of the physical limits-to-growth paradigm. It subtracts nothing, but it adds a criterion of value, namely the satisfaction of wants or enjoyment of life, called service for short. That stock of artifacts and size of population for which total service is a maximum is the stock which we should strive to maintain in a steady state. By maximizing service we mean maximizing service over the long run, which implies that the optimum level of stocks be sustainable. Otherwise short run maximization of service only for the present could lead to overshoot and collapse.

We have two sources of service: service rendered by the stocks of artifacts and people, i.e. the economy; and service rendered directly by the environment or ecosystem. The stock is physically maintained by the throughput which depletes and pollutes the environment. (The throughput is not a circular flow. Although it begins and ends with the environment, the same matter and energy is not directly recycled. The same materials may ultimately be recycled after being reconstituted by biogeochemical processes, but not 100%,

and of course energy is not recycled at all.) A larger stock provides
additional service and requires additional throughput for production
and maintenance. The additional throughput implies more depletion
and pollution of the ecosystem, which in turn, beyond some point,
implies disruption of ecological systems and consequent reduction in
natural ecosystem services. These natural services are often of a
"public goods" nature[4] and include the benefits derived from such
things as: climate, soils, quality of air and water, nutrient
cycles, waste disposal, pollination of crops, and the library of
genetic information which is the basis for future coevolution of all
species. We could not begin to replace these natural services with
comparable economic services on the scale required, even if we had
the technical know-how, which in most cases we do not. Yet we are
quite capable of disrupting these services with the side effects of
powerful technologies designed to increase economic growth and the
economic component of total service. The current rate of species
extinction, due largely to the takeover of habitats to fuel
continuing economic growth, cannot possibly avoid weakening the
structure of spaceship earth, perhaps fatally, if allowed to continue
very long. It requires very little imagination to conceive of the
possibility that a gain in economic service might be purchased at too
high a price in terms of natural services sacrificed. Beyond some
level the growing throughput required to support the growing stock
could provide losses of ecosystem services that are more valuable
than the extra economic service that was rendered by the extra stock.

In sum, the stock should not grow beyond the point where its
marginal cost (in terms of sacrificed natural services) is just equal
to its marginal benefits (in terms of extra economic services). A
more elementary application of economic logic is hard to imagine.
Yet the implication is profound: beyond some point so-called
"economic growth" becomes anti-economic in that it costs more than it
is worth. The limits-to-growth paradigm made clear the physical
limits to growth, but without showing where growth should stop. The
steady-state paradigm simply adds a criterion of value by which costs
and benefits of growth can be compared, and says to stop where
marginal cost equals marginal benefit. By contrast the standard
growth paradigm never compares costs and benefits at all at the macro
level. It simply adds up all value flows (costs plus benefits) to
arrive at its aggregate circular flow of value, which is simply an
index of gross economic activity, and provides no criterion
whatsoever for determining an optimal level of activity.

The only kind of growth that can perhaps continue indefinitely
is purely qualitative growth, that is improvement or development
which allows more service to be derived from the same sized stock, as
old artifacts are replaced with new qualitatively superior artifacts.
But as we noted in connection with the standard paradigm, pure
qualitative improvement is not included in the usual measures of
economic growth. The steady-state paradigm does not rule out
qualitative improvement or development. It does rule out continuing
quantitative physical growth, and consequently economic growth as it
is conventionally measured.

FIGURE 3

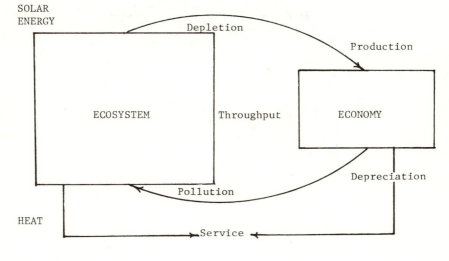

STEADY STATE VISION

SOLAR ENERGY

Depletion

Production

ECOSYSTEM   Throughput   ECONOMY

Depreciation

Pollution

HEAT

Service

The goal of optimizing the size of the stock (maximizing the sum of natural and economic services) may well remain beyond our capacity for measurement. For now, and perhaps for the indefinite future, "satisficing" rather than maximizing may represent the most reasonable mode of behavior. By "satisficing" I mean seeking an acceptable or satisfactory and sustainable level of stock rather than that precise level for which total service is a maximum. Given some satisfactory level of stock, the service it yields should be maximized and the throughput required for its maintenance should be minimized. Alternatively the problem could be stated as satisficing the throughput (according to ecological and ethical criteria) and then maximizing both the physical stock maintained per unit of throughput and the service yielded per unit of stock. This way of framing the problem is probably more operational, but applying the satisficing criterion to stocks has the conceptual advantage of highlighting the nature of throughput as a cost, i.e. something to be reduced whenever possible. In the second formulation the steady-state view would require a different behavior mode for each of the three basic magnitudes: (1) Stock would be satisficed, on the basis of ethical criteria of sufficiency and ecological criteria of sustainability, (2) Service would be maximized, given the stock, (3) Throughput would be minimized, given the stock. The standard growth vision has trouble with (1) and (3).

Satisficing may be preferred to maximizing for yet another reason. Even if measurement of cost and benefits were perfect it is not likely that the cost function (ecosystem services sacrificed) would be well-behaved. Marginal costs are not likely to be monotonically increasing. There is no human rationality operating in the physical environment that would ensure that the least important ecosystem services are always sacrificed first. There are also discontinuities due to threshold effects. Yet a further problem in valuation lies in the public goods nature of most ecosystem services which rules out the competitive market as a measuring device. Thus the careful equating of cost and benefit at the margin required by optimization is probably not operationally feasible, and the quest for an optimum level rather than a sufficient and sustainable level is probably an _ignis fatuus_.

In the analytical elaboration of the steady-state vision I suggest that economics, ecology, and ethics must be combined. Specifically, the determination of what is a sufficient and sustainable level of stocks (or of throughput) is a question whose answer requires a great deal of ecological knowledge and ethical clarification of basic values. But given a sufficient and sustainable physical stock, certainly economics comes into its own in the complementary problems of maximizing the service yielded by the stock and minimizing the throughput required to maintain the stock in a steady state, or the closest feasible approximation thereto.

I submit that the "raw material for the analytic effort" of economists, to borrow Schumpeter's phrase, should be the steady-state vision. Cross-examination and elaboration of that vision are now very much needed.

FOOTNOTES

1. The ideas represented in Figure 1 can be found elaborated in any standard introductory economics text. See, for example, McConnell (1981)

2. This is true because one component of national income, profit, is _defined_ as the difference between national product and the other components of income. If this difference is negative, the result is losses rather than profits.

3. Perhaps the best known elaboration of the argument that there are physical limits to growth is that of Meadows, _et al_ (1972).

4. Public goods are those that no matter how valuable do not command a price on private markets. This is because the benefits they produce can be enjoyed without paying for them.

BIBLIOGRAPHY

Daly, Herman. _Steady State Economics_. San Francisco: W. H.
     Freeman, Co., 1977.
Georgescu-Roegen, Nicholas. _The Entropy Law and the Economic
     Process_. Cambridge: Harvard University Press, 1971.
Kuhn, Thomas. _The Structure of Scientific Revolutions_. Chicago:
     University of Chicago Press, 1962.
McConnell, Campbell. _Economics_. 8th Edition. New York:
     McGraw-Hill, 1981.
Meadows, Donella H., _et al_. _The Limits to Growth_. New York:
     Universe Books, 1977.
Polanyi, Michael. _The Republic of Science, Its Political and
     Economic Theory_. Chicago: Roosevelt University, 1962.
Schumpeter, Joseph. _History of Economic Analysis_. New York: Oxford
     University Press, 1954.

6
War, Peace and the Environment

Paul Gordon Lauren

The subject of war, peace, and the environment is fundamentally different from all other topics discussed throughout this book. In every single chapter presented thus far and in those that will follow, environmental destruction is either unwanted or accidental. In this subject, it is deliberate.

In times of peace environmental concern focuses upon those matters with which we are familiar: industrial output and development, economic growth and employment, agricultural production and the "Green Revolution," technological diffusion, energy generation and consumption, land and water use, mining and conservation, resource scarcity and population growth, and strategies for combating pollution, among many others. In all of these areas the harm wreaked upon our Planet Earth comes about as an unfortunate consequence. Few people deliberately desire erosion, melt-downs at nuclear plants, pollution of their air and water, destruction of forests and agricultural land by development, depletion of unrenewable resources, birth defects from chemical wastes, desertification, and general contamination. These consequences occur not because people want them, but because they simply desire other things more. They want the security of jobs, the comfort of homes and heat, the convenience of automobiles, the supply of food and electricity, and the luxury of consumer goods. Most people obviously would prefer to have all of the benefits of modern society without the costs of environmental destruction if they could. Harm to the environment in all of these cases is either unwanted or accidental.

In one particular area, however, such environmental devastation is precisely, and shockingly, the desired objective. This is the matter of warfare. Here, deliberate and conscious efforts are made to render the environment uninhabitable to plant, animal, and human life.

The potential of deliberate destruction of the environment in this regard is overwhelming and, by comparison, can easily render other environmental concerns nearly insignificant. Whether or not this conscious destruction occurs or not is a question of war and peace—the fundamental question of international relations. Consequently, no book dealing with international environmental issues would be complete without a discussion of war, peace, and the environment, however unpleasant it might be.

HISTORICAL TRENDS IN WAR AND PEACE

The complex relationship between war, peace, and the environment can be understood best by being seen first within the context of history. Man's experience throughout the ages demonstrates that war is society's supreme act of violence. It kills people and maims others for life. It destroys property, homes, factories, farms, and livestock. It places extreme stress upon political, social, and economic institutions. It restricts civil liberties and individual rights. It is expensive, for soldiers, weapons, and ammunition cost money. Moreover, it frequently helps to destroy man's belief in himself, in his goodness, and in his ability to control his own actions. With all of these incredible costs of time, effort, lives, property, finances, values, and psychological well-being, one might conclude that humans would not go to war. It would seem that the benefits of fighting would never be able to outweigh the losses. One would think, therefore, that the history of the world would show very few wars or that violence is an aberration, an exception to the rule of peace and harmony.

Unfortunately, this is not the case. If we look back over the span of human experience we are forced to the conclusion that war is one of the most common features of history. Men have fought ever since their first existence. They have killed each other, wounded each other, stolen each other's lands and wealth, and constantly sought newer and better ways of improving their chances for victory at the expense of their opponents. This has happened for centuries of time.

Faced with this fact, we might like to take psychological refuge in thinking that we are different. That is, from time to time we are inclined to believe that we must be more civilized than all of those who have preceded us. From time to time there is even some evidence that we do hold in higher regard such civilized attributes as pity, compassion, remorse, intelligence, and a respect for the customs and values of people different from ourselves. Nevertheless, the fact remains that in the twentieth century--our own century--we have killed more than seventy million of our fellowmen. Moreover, we have killed them on purpose, in war. Since 1900 more men and women have been killed than in any other comparable period in all human history (Rooney, 1971). Regardless of time or place, however, certain patterns or trends have emerged, all of which have been accelerated by modern weapons attacking Planet Earth.

In the first place, throughout history warfare has been overwhelmingly influenced by the state of technological development. Weapons are tools or machines of destruction (Brodie and Brodie, 1973). For this reason, they are highly dependent upon the sophistication of technology. Increasingly, as the state of technological advancement proceeds, weapons become much more destructive. A primitive level can produce only clubs, bows and arrows, spears, and slings that propel stones. These simple devices can kill relatively few people and certainly are incapable of inflicting any serious damage upon the environment. Another stage of development made possible by the Industrial Revolution produces rifles, machine guns, accurate artillery pieces, and armored tanks. Yet another quantum level of sophisticated technology creates missiles with multiple independently targetable warheads, hunter-killer satellites, computer-directed and laser-guided weapons, and various devices capable of destroying much of life and the environment as we know it.

A second trend invovles the <u>duration</u> <u>of</u> <u>battles</u>. Throughout history armed conflicts and their immediate effects have become increasingly longer. During most of recorded history, battles lasted only a few hours. Whatever transpired on a particular plain or battlefield from whenever the sun came up in the morning to whenever it set on the same day determined the course of events and was recorded forever in history books. With the advent of the Industrial Revolution in particular, this began to change as nations found themselves capable of sustained fighting for weeks, months, or even years as evidenced by the wars of 1914-1918 and 1939-1945. The advent of modern weapons capable of envionmental havoc can prolong the direct effects of battles for generations.

In addition, during the course of historical experience the <u>size</u> <u>and</u> <u>extent</u> <u>of</u> <u>battlefields</u> have grown. For long periods of time battlefields encompassed only the confines of whatever could be seen with the naked eye. The famous Battle of Hastings, for instance, transpired along the downward slope of a single hill and transformed the course of English history. The Battle of Waterloo similarly took place in a very confined amount of space. In our own twentieth century, battlefields have extended in a very real sense over the continents, as evidenced by the First and Second World Wars. Environmental weapons of today can expand this size and extent even further to wherever the oceans flow and wherever the winds blow irrespective of national boundaries.

Another trend in warfare concerns the <u>nature</u> <u>of</u> <u>the</u> <u>victims</u> of armed struggle. In the more distant past, the immediate victims of warfare were armed combatants. Opposing armies of men assembled on the field of battle for combat. They confronted each other face to face in hand-to-hand struggle. Civilians--women, children, and the elderly--were seldom touched and, if so, generally by accident. Through time, this distinction between combatants and civilians began to change dramatically, particularly with the advent of air power and guerilla warfare, as evidenced by the saturation bombing of the Second World War and incidents like My Lai in Vietnam. Weapons against the environment accelerate this process even further, for radiation or chemical and biological agents make no distinction between combatants and civilians, nor do they discriminate on the basis of age, race, sex, or place of national origin.

Finally, there is the historical trend of <u>peace</u>. Ever since men have fought and tried to kill each other, others have attempted to eliminate war completely or to limit its destructiveness. Fearful of the consequences of armed conflict and desiring to create a better life for themselves, men and women throughout history have worked for peace. Despite the difficulties and the agonizing choices of this action, as will be discussed at the conclusion of this chapter, efforts at peace hopefully will continue in the future as they surely must.

Every one of these major historical trends in war and peace has been accelerated by the development of modern weapons capable of massive destruction against Planet Earth and its environment, as we shall now see.

ENVIRONMENTAL MANIPULATION AND DESTRUCTION

Man's attempts at environmental manipulation and destruction in military conflict are not new. From time immemorial combatants have sought to use or abuse the natural environment against their opponents. Ancient man, for example, employed fire on occasion against enemies to burn buildings, deny escape, destroy crops, and kill (Lohs, 1973; Fisher, 1946). In destroying Carthage in 146 B.C. the Romans sowed the soil with salt to prevent cultivation (McClintock, 1974:5). Accounts of medieval warfare, among others, tell of armies in desperation sending the carcasses of dead animals flying over the walls of strongholds by means of catapults to spread disease (Batten, 1960; Derbes, 1966; Rosebury, 1960; Kokatnur, 1948). During some of the religious wars in Europe, armies poisoned the wells of their enemies. Moreover, in defense against the attack from Napoleon, the Russians adopted a "scorched-earth policy" designed to deny food, shelter, and comfort to the French soldiers.

In all of these instances and others in the past, however, the destruction remained very restricted and limited in terms of space or geographical area, time, and the extent of effect. These limitations of the past have increasingly disappeared to the point where even observers without hyperbole now use adjectives like "catastrophic" and "irreversible" to describe the effect. Limits and restrictions of earlier ages have disappeared because of our unwillingness to refrain from further development and use of modern weapons.

Several years ago in a very influential book analyzing the relationship between weapons and foreign policy, Henry Kissinger made the following observation:

> In Greek mythology, Nemesis, the goddess of fate, sometimes punished man by fulfilling his wishes too completely. It has remained for the nuclear age to experience the full irony of this penalty. Throughout history, humanity has suffered from a shortage of power and has concentrated all of its efforts on developing new sources and special applications of it. It would have seemed unbelievable even fifty years ago that there could ever be an excess of power, that everything would depend on the ability to use it subtly and with discrimination.
>
> Yet this is precisely the challenge of the nuclear age. Ever since the end of the second World War brought us not the peace we sought so earnestly, but an uneasy armistice, we have responded by what can best be described as a flight into technology: by devising ever more fearful weapons (Kissinger, 1957:3).

The result of this "flight into technology" and this "curse of Nemesis" can be seen in a number of different kinds of weapons specifically designed to destroy people and entire ecosystems in "ecocide" (Barnaby, 1976, 1975; SIPRI, 1979, 1977; Westing, 1974; Falk, 1973; New York Times, 1970).

Nuclear Weapons

From the beginning of time until 1945, the world did not know our present fear of nuclear weapons. As a result of the so-called "Battle of the Drawing Boards" during the Second World War, when scientists of different countries raced against each other to discover the secrets of the atom for military purposes, two bombs were dropped on Hiroshima and Nagasaki and opened an era in warfare. By today's standards, these first two bombs were miniscule. Their heat, blast, and shock effects stunned the world, but what made them radically different from conventional explosives --and what separates nuclear weapons from all others--was the radioactive material produced at detonation.

Nuclear explosions emit various forms of radiation. These include high energy gamma rays originating in the atomic nuclei, alpha and beta particles, and neutrons. The amount of radiation is enormous and would prove immediately lethal for a large part of the population that might survive other effects of the explosion.

In addition, the detonation produces large quantities of fission products, analagous to the familiar nuclear power plant wastes, which are themselves highly and persistently radioactive. The gamma ray activity, for example, of only two ounces of fission products from a small one-kiloton yield explosion is equal to that of approximately 30,000 tons of radium. These products, which take the form of small particles, can be deadly not simply for minutes, days, or weeks--as with previous weapons in history--but for years and even centuries. For example, the half-life (or time required for the radioactivity of a given element to decay to half of its initial value) of the isotope plutonium-239 is 24,000 years. These radioactive particles condense around all the pulverized earth and other debris produced by the explosion and are sucked up into a mushroom-shaped cloud. Within a short time, gravity, wind, and weather begin to make these materials fall back to earth. The result is known as fallout (Defense Preparedness Agency, 1974; Edvarson, 1975:209-210; Glasstone and Dolan, 1977:1-63).

It is this deadly fallout, with its associated radioactivity which decays over a long period of time, that presents the main source of residual nuclear radiation. The extent and nature of the contamination can range between wide extremes, from close-in battlefields to global proportions. The actual situation is determined by a combination of circumstances associated with the design of the weapon, energy yield, height of the explosion, nature of the surface beneath the point of burst, and the prevailing meteorological conditions. From the first 15-megaton device tested at Bikini Atoll in the Pacific, for example, the fallout caused, in the words of one United States Department of Defense publication, "substantial contamination over an area of more than 7,000 square miles" (Glasstone and Dolan, 1977:37). Other radiation can be worse, for those radioactive particles initially carried up into the troposphere have a mean resident time there of about one month, and are typically deposited over miles of space in a band roughly at the explosion latitude. The material injected into the stratosphere has a longer resident period, ranging from one to five years, and could be spread throughout the hemisphere in which the explosion takes place (Edvarson, 1975:209-210; United Nations, 1972).

Exposure caused by external radiation from particles in the air or deposited on the ground can result in thermal burns, ataxia (loss of motor control), immunologic and hematological disorders, epilation (hair loss) and death. Internal radiation can be caused by eating or breathing contaminated materials such as those dangerously passing into the food chain from plants to man. The results of this exposure can range from death to leukemia, thyroid abnormalities, bone nerosis, or genetic damage to the reproductive organs—thus causing damage not only to the living but also to the as yet unborn (Glasstone and Dolan, 1977:541-627).

One of the most dangerous sources of such radiation upon the environment is that presented by strategic nuclear weapons, or those launched from great distances and capable of inflicting massive damage over a large front. These weapons have yields in the range from one to ten megatons of explosive power (one megaton equals one million tons of TNT). In other words, they have fifty to five hundred times the yield of the original bombs employed against Japan. Although we have avoided using these awesome weapons in warfare since their development, over one thousand have been detonated for testing in peacetime, including many atmospheric tests (Westing, 1978:93). Those who possess the giant's share of these weapons, of course, are the superpowers of the Cold War. By one recent count of total megatonnage, the United States possessed two thousand megatons, while the Soviet Union possessed over sixteen thousand megatons of explosive power (The Economist, 1980:35-38). In this situation, the expression "overkill" hardly does justice to the reality.

Tactical nuclear weapons, or those used in local theaters, present yet another source of radiation. In particular there is the new enhanced radiation device known popularly as "the neutron bomb." It is a low- yield weapon ranging from one-half to one kiloton that emits far more fast, or high energy, neutrons than other fission munitions. This kind of device is designed not to destroy inanimate objects but rather to kill the living (Jarvis, 1977; Der Spiegel, 1978). Within a radius of 1,000 yards, a minimum of three thousand rads of radiation (one rad is the maximum recommended dose for medical x-rays) would be emitted, causing human incapacitation within five minutes and death within four to six days. Within a radius of 1400 yards the fatality rate is estimated to be approximately 50 percent. The same single weapon also would cause great damage to diverse biota and ecological systems, ranging from mammals and birds, to vegetation, down to microorganisms (Westing, 1978). The extent of envionmental damage with such weapons, therefore, is severe. In the words of one author, nuclear weapons provide the potential for "ecological catastrophe" unprecedented in the history of the world (McClintock, 1974:27-38).

Biological and Chemical Weapons

Another major category of modern weapons capable of causing great environmental damange to Planet Earth is that of biological and chemical agents (Holmberg, 1975; Ambrose, 1974; SIPRI, 1973; United Nations, 1969; Hersh, 1968). In the twentieth century

absolutely amazing strides have been made in understanding molecular
biology, toxicology, organic compounds, and hundreds upon hundreds of
health-related fields. This acquired knowledge has been used to heal
the sick, cure disease, and comfort the ill—and to kill plant,
animal, and human life.

     Biological agents are designed to spread rapidly highly
infectious diseases among an opponent's troops and population,
causing symptoms ranging from nausea to violent headaches, from
temporary blindness to acute conjunctivitis, or from retinal hemor-
rrhage to death.   The standard microorganisms selected for germ
warfare include bacterial diseases such as plague and anthrax,
rickettisial diseases such as Q-fever and encephalomyelitis, and
anticrop fungal diseases such as rice blast and potato blight
(Holmberg, 1975). Once released, however, these agents are highly
unpredictable and uncontrollable, and unable to discriminate between
friend and foe, or even between men and other forms of life. As one
scientific adviser writing in a medical journal observes:

> Everything that breathes in the exposed areas has an
> opportunity to be exposed to the agent. This will involve
> vast numbers of mammals, birds, reptiles, amphibians, and
> insects.   Various natural history surveys have indicated
> surprising numbers of wildlife inhabiting each square mile
> of countryside. It is possible that many species would be
> exposed to an agent for the first time in their
> evolutionary history. We have no knowledge of the range of
> susceptibilities of these many species of wildlife to
> specific microorganisms, particularly through the respira-
> tory route of administration of infectious aerosols.   What
> would be the consequence? Would new and unused zoonotic
> foci of endemic disease be established?   Would it create
> the basis for possible genetic evolution of microorganisms
> in new directions with changes in virulence for some
> species?   Would it create public health and environmental
> problems that are unique and beyond our present experience?
> (cited in Hersh, 1968, 82-83).

     Due to these unanswerable questions and the frightening nature
of biological agents, as evidenced in small part by the Biological
Warfare Convention of 1972 (Kristopherson, 1975:244; U.S. Congress,
Senate, 1974), most attention is directed instead toward chemical
warfare.   The advances in modern chemistry have actually been
employed in military conflict on several occasions during the
twentieth century. Combatants suffered the consequences of various
gases during the First World War, the Italian-Ethiopian War, the
Second World War in China, and the Vietnam War. Any number of secret
tests of chemicals were conducted on an unsuspecting American public
during the 1950s (Easton, 1980).   Most recently, funds have been
appropriated in the United States to produce binary weapons which
combine dangerous chemicals in flight on their way to the intended
target and, in the words of one Army spokesman, produce "a hell of an
effective weapon on the battlefield" (Bernstein, 1981).

Early chemical agents included chlorine gas, phosgene, and mustard gas, which cause death, skin blistering, and any number of mutagenic, teratogenic, and carcinogenic effects. Today neurotoxicants, or nerve gases, like Tabun, Sarin, and VX gas are all heavily stockpiled. Their purpose is to inhibit the relay of nerve impulses within part of the nervous system, between nerve endings and body organs. The eventual result of their use can be death due to paralysis of respiratory muscles and/or inhibition of the respiratory centers in the central nervous system (Bernstein, 1981; Chapman, 1980; Bay, 1979; Holmberg, 1975).

Herbicides are among the most recently manufactured and used chemical agents in warfare. Their purpose is the defoliation of trees that might provide cover for enemy troops and the destruction of crops that might provide food for an opponent. These include the so-called "Rainbow of Death" compounds of Agent Orange (2,4-D plus 2,4,5-T), Agent Blue (cacodylic acid), and Agent White (picloram). Each is designed to consciously exploit the toxic effects of chemicals upon plants for purposes of military conflict (Holmberg, 1975; SIPRI, 1975; McCarthy, 1969). They were sprayed from the air over great areas of forest and cropland during the Vietnam War, particularly from 1966 through 1969 (SIPRI, 1976; Westing, 1975; Neilands, 1972; McConnell, 1970; Perry, 1968). Throughout this period, nearly five million acres of land received herbicidal "treatment". This easily achieved the immediate military objectives: the forests were destroyed and the crops of rice, banana, sweet potato, and papaya ruined. The damage did not stop there, however. Nutrient-rich leaves dropped, causing impoverishment of the local ecosystems. The invasion of tenacious weed species followed the destruction of extant vegetation. Deprived of its habitat of food and shelter, wildlife perished. Soil erosion resulted, as did subsequent laterization, or hardening of the soil when exposed to the elements. The destruction of mangrove forests similarly destroyed the breeding grounds for offshore fish and crustaceans. In some cases, this devastation of active biotic communities will require generations to correct. Moreover, the health effects of such chemical warfare are currently being suffered by both user and victim alike who were exposed to the herbicides (Time, 1981; Woollacott, 1980).

Most recently, press reports indicate the use of chemical warfare by Soviet troops against the insurgents in parts of Afghanistan. It is well known that the Soviet Union stockpiles enormous quantities of chemical and biological agents (Chapman, 1980; The Times, 1978) and, indeed, in the process of manufacturing and testing has suffered from accidents. During the spring of 1979, for example, the Soviets experienced a bacteriological warfare disaster. An explosion from a plant in the Urals accidentally released the I-21 strain of anthrax into the air. Vaccination proved to be ineffective, more than one thousand people died, topsoil was stripped from the swath of the infestation, and dirt in the nearby village was paved over with asphalt (New York Times, 1980; U.S. Congress, House, 1980).

Environmental and Geophysical Weapons

Modern technology can destroy Planet Earth not only through the damage and devastation that it causes during fighting, but also through the use of actual environmental and geophysical weapons (Carter, 1979; Goldblat, 1977, 1975; Jasani, 1975; Granville, 1975; Barnaby, 1975; Hampson, 1974; MacDonald, 1968). For many centuries men sought to control the environment and its natural processes for their own purposes. Primitive man attempted magic, prayers, and even sacrifices to deities to start or stop storms, floods, fires, and other events. Today scientific knowledge is used to effect certain geophysical modifications in fact. These can be employed for peaceful purposes such as assisting in agricultural production or airport visibility. But, like so many other discoveries and improved technologies, they also can be utilized for combat objectives of deliberate destruction.

In the last several years a great deal of attention, research, and development has centered upon the possibility of using environmental and geophysical weapons to manipulate the biota, lithosphere, hydrosphere, and atmosphere for overt military purposes (U.S. Congress, Senate, 1976, 1974, 1973, 1972; Weiss, 1975; Seshagiri, 1977; Sullivan, 1975; Cohn, 1972; Purrett, 1972; McClintock, 1974:51-62). The result is popularly known as "weather war."

Our planet is a very complex physical and chemical system. The complexity arises particularly from the fact that it is a dynamic system. The phenomena of weather and climate result from the interaction of processes which range from those on a large scale, like the air circulation around the globe caused by the differences in radiation arriving from the sun in equatorial and polar regions, to small-scale processes, such as the exchanges of water molecules on the surfaces of minute drops or on ice crystals in clouds. Since considerable amounts of energy are required to modify weather conditions by altering the global processes, scientists have instead studied ways of changing the microphysical processes (Jasani, 1975). These modifications are achieved by introducing materials such as water droplets, dry ice, solid CO , silver and lead iodide, or liquid propane.

If experiments with weather modifications prove successful, there are a number of military applications that could be developed. Rain, for example, could be used to inhibit mobility, block transportation routes and troop movements, and produce floods. Fog and clouds could be dispersed to make targets open to visual attack. Lightning storms could be created by increasing corona discharge to start fires and destroy communications. Tornadoes and hurricanes could be produced or directed to cause high winds, heavy rains, and storm tides to destroy ports, fleets, and airfields. Serious studies have further examined the possibilities of generating tsunami, or tidal waves, on the oceans to destroy low-lying areas and surface fleets; of spreading a monomolecular layer of oil on oceans and lakes to prevent evaporation in order to cause storms and crop failures; of stimulating volcanic eruptions and earthquakes to destroy military bases and strategic facilities; of creating "holes" in the ozone layer to destroy life not under protection; and of melting polar ice caps to produce flooding and the destruction of coastal areas (Carter, 1979; Goldblat, 1977; Jasani, 1975; McClintock, 1974:51-61).

Although many of these proposals are highly improbable and very speculative for the near future, others clearly are not. The whole phenomenon of geophysical weapons has been taken seriously enough by the world community that several international conferences have been held to create an environmental warfare convention dealing with weather modification (Carter, 1979; U.S. Congress, Senate, Executive Documents, 1978; U.S. Congress, House, 1975; Canada, 1975; Goldblat, 1977). In fact, the United States practiced weather war in Vietnam from 1967 to 1972 with more than two thousand classified missions to seed clouds in order to intensify and prolong the annual rainy season (Shapley, 1974; Norman, 1974; Ognibene, 1972; Hersh, 1972; Greenberg, 1972). The purpose was to render the Ho Chi Minh trail sufficiently muddy to make it impassable. It also resulted in floods, erosion, toxicity to living things from the cloud-seeding agents themselves, and an increase in water-dependent insects, including disease vectors (SIPRI, 1976: 55-58; Westing, 1975).

PEACE AND THE FUTURE

The result of the development of modern weapons with nuclear, biological and chemical, environmental, and geophysical capabilities has been a vast acceleration in all of the major historical trends in war. The potential now exists for technology to become increasingly and staggeringly destructive against Plant Earth, for battles and their effects to last infinitely longer than at any time in the past, for battlefields to expand to a size and scope that know few boundaries, and for the number of victims in military conflict to reach catastrophic proportions with no distinction made between combatant and civilian or, at times, even between friend and foe. The potential also exists for an acceleration in the historical trend for peace.

With a growing realization that for the first time in history man possesses the capability to destroy much of life and the environment as we know it, there is increasingly an urgent concern about the necessity for peace. Agreement upon the desire for peace is nearly universal, and those of any number of different political and philosophical persuasions can accept this premise. The problem thus comes about not from diverse opinions about abstract goals, but rather from the vastly different approaches toward the means of achieving peace. This is well illustrated by a contrast encapsulated in a scene occurring on Easter Sunday 1981, at the gates of Malmstrom Air Force Base, Great Falls, Montana. Placards carried by men and women protesting the presence of Minuteman missiles at the base carried the inscription, "Peace," while guards in uniform barring trespass stood before a large sign reading "Peace is Our Profession." Both groups could readily reach a consensus upon the necessity for peace, but they could hardly agree on the means toward that end. Their dilemma--and ours--is that throughout history those pursuing the trend of peace have been forced to choose between essentially three alternatives.

The first of these is peace through deterrence, or peace through strength. The Air Force guards at the missile base believed that in order to secure peace for the future it is necessary to be strong enough to deter a war initiated by an opponent. This is accomplished by convincing an adversary in advance that the costs and risks of launching an attack will be unacceptable and will never be outweighed by any potential advantages that might be gained by armed conflict. Proponents of this position argue this is ending wars before they even begin, that weakness has tempted aggression in history, and, consequently, that the surest way to invite a war is to unilaterally disarm.

The second major approach toward peace is that of pacifism. Those persons gathered outside the locked gates of the base and drawing attention to the missiles believed that war is best eliminated by removing weapons. One can hardly conduct military campaigns and cause devastation without the means of fighting. People cannot struggle in armed combat unless they possess the tools to do so. To restrain international tensions, to stop the insanely escalating arms race, and to achieve peace, proponents of this argument maintain, it is therefore necessary to take the first step by completely disarming and eliminating existing stockpiles of weapons destruction.

The third choice is that of peace through arms control, or by means of negotiated settlement for the limitation and/or reduction of weapons. The achievement of peace requires practical solutions to difficult problems rather than rhetoric or unfounded idealism. Those who support this alternative therefore argue that the advantages of strength cannot be simply dismissed, but that deterrence alone only breeds greater insecurity. Similarly, they maintain that unilateral disarmament rests on the dangerous assumption that opponents will reciprocate by laying down their arms as well, but that unless someone is willing to risk a first step toward reduction of weapons escalation will continue unabated. Arms control seeks to combine the best features of the other two approaches while at the same time avoiding their worst faults.

Each of these alternatives for achieving peace is accompanied by enormous complications and dangers. The actual decision of selection, however, cannot be avoided in an age when the potential losses are so great. To be effective, we must understand the choices, know the facts regardless of how unpleasant they might be, and think about the unthinkable. As one recent editorial concluded (The Economist, 1980, 10):

> The whole subject of preventing nuclear war combines the obscurity of higher mathematics with the ugliness of horror fiction. This leads many people to say that the best way of avoiding the unthinkable is not to think about it. They are wrong. It is the unthinkable we must think about, and then act intelligently upon the thinking.

That is what this chapter is all about.

BIBLIOGRAPHY

Ambrose, J. T. "Insects in Warfare." _Army_ 24 (1974):33-38.
". . .And a Plea to Ban 'Ecocide.'" _New York Times_. 26 February
1970.
Anderson, J. "Air Force Turns Rainmaker in Laos." _Washington Post_.
18 March 1971.
Bainton, Roland. _Christian Attitudes Toward War and Peace_.
Nashville: Abingdon, 1960.
Barnaby, Frank. "Environmental Warfare." _Bulletin of Atomic
Scientists_ 32 (1976):36-43.
_____. "The Spread of the Capability to do Violence--An
Introduction to Environmental Warfare." _Ambio_ 4 (1975):
178-185.
Batten, J. K. "Chemical Warfare in History." _Armed Forces Chemical
Journal_ (now _National Defense_) 14 (1960):16-17, 32.
Bay, Charles. "The Other Gas Crisis--Chemical Weapons." _Parameters:
Journal of the U.S. Army War College_ 9 (September 1979):70-80.
Bernstein, Peter. "U.S. Aims to Perfect Chemical Weaponry."
Newhouse News Service. 17 June 1981.
Bjornerstedt, R. _et al_. _Napalm and Other Incendiary Weapons and All
Aspects of Their Possible Use_. New York: United Nations, 1973.
Brodie, Bernard and Brodie, Fawn. _From Crossbow to H-Bomb: The
Evolution of the Weapons and Tactics of Warfare_. Bloomington:
Indiana University Press, 1973 ed.
Canada. "Suggested Preliminary Approach to Considering the
Possibility of Concluding a Convention on the Prohibition of
Environmental Modification for Military or Other Hostile
Purposes." Document #CCD/463, Conference of the Committee on
Disarmament, Geneva, 1975.
Carter, Luther. "Environmental Warfare Treaty." _Science_ 205 (17
August 1979): 674.
Chapman, Betty. "Chemical Warfare: The Dirty Weapon." _National
Defense_ (June 1980):33-37.
Cohn, V. "Weather War: A Gathering Storm." _Washington Post_. 2 July
1972.
Commoner, B. _Science and Survival_. New York: Viking, 1966.
Defense Civil Preparedness Agency. _Radiological Defense_.
Washington, D.C.: Department of Defense, 1974.

Derbes, V. J. "DeMussis and the Great Plague of 1348: A Forgotten Episode of Bacteriological Warfare." Journal of the American Medical Association 196 (1966):59-62.

Easton, Nina. "Chemical Warfare Tested on U.S. Cities." Baltimore Sun, as cited in The Missoulian [Missoula, Montana]. 17 August 1980.

Edvarson, Kay. "Radioecological Aspects of Nuclear Warfare." Ambio 4 (1975):209-210.

Falk, Richard. "Environmental Warfare and Ecocide." Bulletin of Peace Proposals 4 (1973):1-17.

Federov, E. K. "Disarmament in the Field of Geophysical Weapons." Scientific World 19 (1975):49-54.

Fisher, G. J. B. Incendiary Warfare. New York: McGraw-Hill, 1946.

"Forgotten Warriors." Time. 13 July 1981.

Fothergill, L. D. "Some Ecological and Epidemiological Concepts in Anti-personnel Biological Warfare." Military Medicine 128 (1963):132-134.

Glasstone, S. and Dolan, P. The Effects of Nuclear Weapons. 3rd Edition. Washington, D.C.: Department of Defense and Department of Energy, 1977.

Goldblat, J. "Environmental Warfare Convention: How Meaningful Is It?" Ambio 6 (1977):216-221.

_____. "Prohibition of Environmental Warfare." Ambio 4 (1975):186-190.

Granville, Pierre. "Perspectives de le Guerre Meteorologique et Geophysique." Defense Nationale 31 (1975):125-140.

Greenberg, D. S. "Vietnam Rainmaking: A Chronicle of DoD's Snowjob." Science and Government Report 2 (1972):1, 4.

Hampson, J. "Photochemical War on the Atmosphere." Nature (1974):189-191.

Hersh, S. Chemical and Biological Warfare. New York: Bobbs-Merrill, 1968.

_____. "Rainmaking Is Used As Weapon By U.S." New York Times. 3 July 1972, 4 July 1972, 9 July 1972.

Holmberg, Bo. "Biological Aspects of Chemical and Biological Weapons." Ambio 4 (1975):211-215.

"It Has to Deter." The Economist. 16 August 1980.

Jarvis, Jeff. "Neutron Bomb: The People Killer." San Francisco Examiner. 3 July 1977.

Jasani, B. M. "Environmental Modifications: New Weapons of War?" Ambio 4 (1975):191-198.

Kilko, G. "Report on the Destruction of Dikes: Holland 1944-45 and Korea 1953." In J. Duffett (ed.), Against the Crime of Silence. Flanders, N. J.: O'Hare Books, 1968.

Kissinger, Henry. Nuclear Weapons and Foreign Policy. New York: Harper and Brothers, 1957.

Kokatnur, V. R. "Chemical Warfare in Ancient India." Journal of Chemical Education 25 (1948):268-272.

Kristopherson, L. (ed.). "Selection of Documents ... Pertaining to War and the Environment." Ambio 4 (1975):234-244.

Lohs, K. "Fire as a Means of Warfare." Scientific World 17 (1973):18.

Lumsden, Malvern. "'Conventional' War and Human Ecology." Ambio 4
    (1975):223-228.
MacDonald, G. J. F. "Geophysical Warfare: How to Wreck the
    Environment." In N. Calder (ed.), Unless Peace Comes: A
    Scientific Forecast of New Weapons. New York: Viking Press,
    1968.
McCarthy, R. D. Ultimate Folly: War by Pestilence, Asphyxiation,
    and Defoliation. New York: Knopf, 1969.
McClintock, Michael et al. Air, Water, Earth, Fire: The Impact of
    the Military on World Environmental Order. San Francisco:
    Sierra Club, 1974.
McConnell, Arthur. "Operation Ranch Hand." Air University Review.
    January-February, 1970.
"NATO and the Warsaw Pact." The Economist. 9 August 1980.
Neilands, J. B. et al. Harvest of Death: Chemical Warfare in
    Vietnam and Cambodia. New York: Free Press, 1972.
"New War Germs 'Bred in Russia.'" The Times [London]. 31 January
    1978.
"Nicht humaner als Giftgas." Der Spiegel. 10 April 1978.
Norman, C. "Pentagon Admits Vietnam Rainmaking." Nature 249
    (1974):402.
Ognibene, P. J. "Making War with the Weather." New Republic 167
    (1972):12-14.
Perry, T. O. "Vietnam: Truths of Defoliation." Science 160
    (1968):601.
Purrett, L. A. "Weather Modification as a Future Weapon." Science
    News 101 (1972):254-255.
Red Cross, International Committee of the. Weapons That May Cause
    Unneccessary Suffering or Have Indiscriminate Effects. Geneva:
    International Committee of the Red Cross, 1973.
Ritchie, D. J. "Reds May Use Lightning as Weapon." Missiles and
    Rockets 5 (1959):13-14.
Rooney, Andrew. "An Essay on War." Chicago: Britannica Educational
    Corporation, 1971.
Rosebury, T. "Biological Warfare: Some Historical Considerations."
    Bulletin of Atomic Scientists 16 (1960):227-236.
Schneider, M. M. "Gegen den militarishchen Missbrauch der Umwelt."
    Deutsche Aussenpolitik 21 (1976):578-601.
Seshagiri, Narasimhiah. The Weather Weapon. New Delhi: NBT, 1977.
Shapley, D. "Rainmaking: Rumored Use Over Laos Alarms Experts,
    Scientists." Science 176 (1972):1216-1220.
_____. "Technology in Vietnam: Fire Storm Project Fizzled Out."
    Science 177 (1972):239-2441.
_____. "Weather Warfare: Pentagon Concedes 7-Year Vietnam
    Effort." Science 184 (1974):1059-1061.
Stewart, O. C. "Fire as the First Great Force Employed by Man." In
    W. L. Thomas, Jr. (ed.), Man's Role in Changing the Face of
    the Earth. Chicago: University of Chicago Press, 1956.
Stockholm International Peace Research Institute. Chemical
    Disarmament: New Weapons for Old. Stockholm: Almqvist &
    Wiksell, 1975.
_____. Ecological Consequences of the Second Indochina War.
    Stockholm: SIPRI, 1976.

_____. Law of War and Dubious Weapons. Stockholm: SIPRI, 1976.
_____. The Problem of Chemical and Biological Warfare: A Study of the Historical, Technical, Military, Legal, and Political Aspects of CBW, and Possible Disarmament Measures. Six volumes. Stockholm: Almqvist & Wiksell, 1973.
_____. Warfare in a Fragile World, Military Impact on the Human Environment. Stockholm: SIPRI, 1979.
_____. Weapons of Mass Destruction and the Environment. London: Taylor and Francis, 1977.
Studer, T. A. "Weather Modification in Support of Military Operations." Air University Review 20 (1968-1969):44-50.
Sullivan, W. "Ozone Depletion Seen as a War Tool." New York Times. 28 February 1975.
Thorsson, I. "Disarmament Negotiations: What are They Doing for the Environment?" Ambio 4 (1975):199-202.
"Toll Is Put at 1,000 in Soviet Accident." New York Times 16 July 1980.
United Nations, Secretary General. Chemical and Bacteriological (Biological) Weapons and the Effects of Their Possible Use. New York: United Nations, 1969.
_____. Ionizing Radiation: Levels and Effects. New York: United Nations, 1972.
U.S. Central Intelligence Agency. A Study of Climatological Research as It Pertains to Intelligence Problems. Washington, D.C.: CIA, 1974.
U.S. Congress, House, Committee on International Relations. "Prohibition of Weather Modification as a Weapon of War." 94th Congress, 1st Session, 29 July 1975.
_____. House, Select Committee on Intelligence. "The Sverdlovsk Incident." 96th Congress, 2nd Session, 29 May 1980.
_____. Senate, Executive Documents. "Convention on the Prohibition of Military or Any Other Hostile Use of Environmental Modification Techniques." 95th Congress, 2nd Session, 22 September 1978.
_____. Senate, Senate Armed Services Committee. "Fiscal Year 1974 Authorization for Military Procurement, Research, and Development ..." 93rd Congress, 1st Session, April and May 1973.
_____. Senate, Senate Foreign Relations Committee. "The Geneva Protocol of 1925." 92nd Congress, 1st Session, March 1971.
_____. Senate, Senate Foreign Relations Committee. "Prohibiting Environmental Modification as a Weapon of War." 93rd Congress, 1st Session, Report No. 93-270, 25 June 1973.
_____. Senate, Senate Foreign Relations Committee. "Prohibiting Hostile Use of Environmental Modification Techniques." 94th Congress, 2nd Session, 21 January 1976.
_____. Senate, Senate Foreign Relations Committee. "Prohibiting Military Weather Modification." 92nd Congress, 2nd Session, 26-27 July 1972.
_____. Senate, Senate Foreign Relations Committee. "Prohibition of Chemical and Biological Weapons." 93rd Congress, 2nd Session, 10 December 1974.
_____. Senate, Senate Foreign Relations Committee. "The United Nations Environment Program Participation Act of 1973." 93rd Congress, 1st Session, Report No. 93-196, 5 June 1973.

_____. Senate, Senate Foreign Relations Committee. "Weather
    Modification." 93rd Congress, 2nd Session, 25 January and 20
    March 1974.
U.S. Department of Agriculture, Forest Service. _Forest_ _Fire_ _as_ _a_
    Military _Weapon_. Washington, D.C.: USDA, Forest Service, 1970.
Weiss, E. B. "Weather Control: An Instrument for War?" _Survival_ 16
    (1975):64-68.
Westing, Arthur. "Environmental Consequences of the Second Indochina
    War: A Case Study." _Ambio_ (1975):216-222.
_____. "Neutron Bombs and the Environment."
_____. "Proscription of Ecocide: Arms Control and the
    Environment." _Bulletin_ _of_ _Atomic_ _Scientists_ 30 (1974):24-27.
    Ambio 7 (1978):93-97.
Whiteside, Thomas. _The_ _Withering_ _Rain_. New York: Dutton, 1971.
Woollacott, Martin. "Victims of an Orange Rain." _The_ _Guardian_.   19
    May 1980.
Wurtz, R. H. "War and the Living Environment." _Nuclear_ _Information_
    (now _Environment_) 5 (1963):1-20.

Part II

Latin America

7
Environmental Consequences of the Development of the Amazon

Ronald E. Erickson

WHY FOCUS ON THE AMAZON?

In the 1970s the Brazilian government decided to build a series of highways across and around the Amazon basin. Their decision, and similar development decisions by the other nations which share that basin, could affect all of us--everyone on the planet. That is because certain human actions <u>do</u> have global consequences. The development of the Amazon may be one of those actions, and for that reason alone it's worth looking at.

But even if the environmental and human consequences of opening up the Amazon are confined to that region and affect only the people, cultures, plants and animals that live there, to study the situation is worth our time. Such study might lead us to act on behalf of the area--public pressure from the international community has already made some difference in the Amazon. Or, we might simply choose to focus on the Amazon because of our concerns for issues nearer home. That is, developments there may serve as a mirror for what we do here. The mirror may be distorted and distant, but in it we could see ourselves as well as those who live there.

PHYSICAL AND BIOLOGICAL CONTEXT--THE AMAZON BASIN

The physical and biological magnitude of the Amazon River and the basin it drains dwarfs all comparable river systems. A few numbers and facts are illustrative:

1. The basin is three-fourths the size of the contiguous United States.
2. One seventh of the planet's river water flows to the ocean through the basin, with over a thousand tributaries flowing into its 4000-mile course.
3. The Mississippi at Vicksburg is 70 feet deep and a third of a mile wide. The Amazon at Obidos is 1-1/2 miles wide and 200 feet deep.
4. A thousand miles from the river's mouth, Manaus is a port for ocean vessels which could continue another 1300 miles upstream.

⌐e elevational drop of the Amazon in 2,300 miles is only 300 feet.
. The basin occupies 35% of the South American continent.
7. The millions of species which coexist there make it the richest biological resource area in the world.

We would not expect a land area as large as that just described to be simple ecologically, and it is not. There is a valid generality, though, which is crucial to understanding the environmental consequences of the basin's development: despite its enormous size and apparent fertility, the "tropical wet forest is ecologically a desert covered by trees" (Goodland, 1975:47). Why is this so? Simply because Amazonia is very old geologically (70 million years). Over 70% of its soils (yellow, red or red yellow latosols) are derived from Pliocene sediments deposited in an inland sea. They are deeply weathered and low in nutrients, and the apparent fertility of the area is based on finely tuned nutrient cycling mechanisms. For example, nutrients are passed to living tree roots by micorrhizal fungi which abstract these nutrients directly from dead organic litter on the forest floor (Stark, 1971:177).

That doesn't mean that all soils are infertile. In fact, 2% of the basin is flood plain (verzea), enriched yearly and highly productive. Up to 10% or so,[1] separated in pockets throughout the region, is probably capable of sustainable agriculture.

HISTORICAL CONTEXT

It is also useful to reflect briefly on Brazilian and Amazonian history and its effect on the current development pattern.[2]

Brazil was first claimed by the Portugese under the provisions of the Treaty of Tordesillas. This treaty divided the Western Hemisphere into Spanish and Portugese areas of domination along a line running between the poles and lying 370 leagues west of the Cape Verde Islands. Drafted in considerable geographic ignorance, the treaty accorded the largest and richest share of the South American continent to Spain and thus failed to resolve territorial disputes between the colonial powers. Portugese settlement efforts soon violated the treaty and the Portugese subsequently extended Brazilian boundaries westward into all the bordering Spanish territories, especially in the Amazon. Portugese de facto claims were legitimized in the Treaty of Madrid in 1750, and the westward expansion continued under both the Portugese and, following independence, Brazilian governments. A series of border conflicts and treaties established the current borders of Brazil. These are depicted in Map 1.

Brazilian expansion to the west was facilitated by geography. The relief of the Amazon basin made penetration of the upper Amazon relatively easy, while Peru, Colombia and Ecuador had to cross the Andes in order to colonize their claims on the basin.

To quantify the last point, 40% of Columbia lies in the Amazon basin, but only 1% of its population resides there. The figures for Peru (46% and 9%) and Ecuador (18% and 2%) show the same pattern, though Peru has aggressively and successfully colonized their section

FIGURE 1

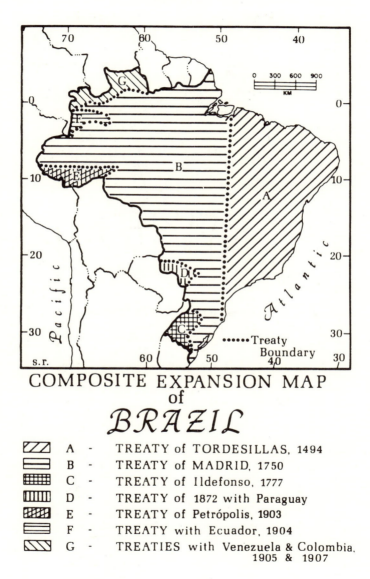

COMPOSITE EXPANSION MAP
of
BRAZIL

▨	A -	TREATY of TORDESILLAS, 1494
▤	B -	TREATY of MADRID, 1750
▦	C -	TREATY of Ildefonso, 1777
▥	D -	TREATY of 1872 with Paraguay
▨	E -	TREATY of Petrópolis, 1903
▤	F -	TREATY with Ecuador, 1904
▧	G -	TREATIES with Venezuela & Colombia, 1905 & 1907

Source: Wagley (1974)

of the basin in recent years (Wagley, 1974:45). Even Brazil, with
its relatively easy access, has found it difficult to keep a large
population in the Amazon. Distance from both national and international markets has inhibited economic activity and settlement.
Despite these difficulties, however, Brazilian expansion has left it
bordering all the nations of South America except Ecuador and Chile.

Westward expansion has continued in Brazil since the early
sixteenth century. Thus when one reads that one of the major reasons
for the highway into the Amazon is for "national defense", the
natural, incredulous response ("Brazil is afraid of Bolivia?") has to
be softened. Brazil is simply adhering to its historical pattern.

WHY HIGHWAYS?

Map 2 shows the extent of the Brazilian Amazon highway
system—about 13,500 kilometers of roads through the jungle. Highway
building is the cornerstone of the Brazilian effort to develop the
basin, an effort driven not only by considerations of national
defense, but by the need to resolve other pressing national problems.

One of these problems is the conditions prevailing in the
"Northeast", the region of Brazil located on the section of the
continent that bulges toward Africa. The Northeast is overpopulated
and subject to frequent droughts. A third of its children die of
starvation or disease in the first year of life. Its hungry people
flock to the south, to the big cities of Rio de Janeiro, Sao Paulo
and Brasilia, looking for work. One of the official reasons for
highways and development was to provide a place for Northeasterners.
Until recently, Brazil considered itself vastly underpopulated—
pointing always to the sparsely populated Amazon region as proof that
the frontier still existed.

A third reason to develop the Amazon is to search for physical
resources—that is, there is a dimension to development plans which
surpasses the need to find work and land for people. Brazil is
desperately short of resources. The only oil in the Amazon is one
river basin too far (in Peru) and Brazil finds itself importing 85%
of its petroleum (de Carvalho, 1981:6). In order to meet balance of
payments deficits, there is a clear trend toward exporting food and
non-food agricultural crops. To meet the demand for energy
resources, land is taken from food production in order to grow coffee
for export or casava for alcohol fuels. Meanwhile, Brazil continues
to import foods—$900 million worth of rice, beans and meat in 1979.
Developmental hopes for Amazonia thus include agricultural crops but
non-renewable resources—iron, aluminum ore (bauxite), manganese, and
tin—also provide a major attraction (Goodland, 1975:113).

Finally, the Amazon may be developed to exploit another
potentially renewable resource: hydropower. One scheme would have
flooded much of the basin with a series of "Great Lakes"—the largest
twice the size of Lake Superior, and large enough to be visible from
the moon—or a dam with 50 times the capacity of Aswan on the Nile
(Mitchell, 1979:68-69). Such grandiose schemes fade with the
building of highways, but hydropower potential distant from major
cities may still attract such heavy power users as uranium enrichment
plants.

FIGURE 2

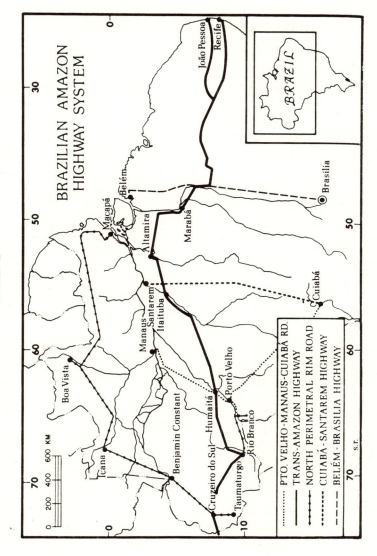

BRAZILIAN AMAZON
HIGHWAY SYSTEM

.... PTO. VELHO-MANAUS-CUIABÁ RD.
———— TRANS-AMAZON HIGHWAY
—•—•— NORTH PERIMETRAL RIM ROAD
- - - - - CUIABÁ-SANTAREM HIGHWAY
– – – – BELÉM-BRASILIA HIGHWAY

Source: Wagley (1974)

The importance of the search for resources is reflected in the following statement by an Amazonian businessman:

> Why must we develop Amazonia? To insure that its boundless resources are firmly established as Brazilian. What means are we using? The government is offering generous fiscal incentives to private enterprise. Are we succeeding? Spectacularly! We just signed major mineral exploration agreements with U.S. Steel and Alcoa (Katzman, 1976:445).

It is to the question of the success of the effort of the Amazon that we now turn.

HAS DEVELOPMENT BEEN SUCCESSFUL?

The answer to the question depends on which of the goals is being considered and on the time frame of the one who answers. As a major drain for population pressure, the scheme has clearly failed. An elaborate plan in 1973 for the land along the highway called for (Goodland, 1975:25):

1. Agricultural plots of 250 acres per family with narrow frontage on the highway. 50% of the plot was to be left in forest.
2. "Agrovilas" every 10 kilometers with 48-64 houses and an elementary school.
3. An "agropolis" every 50 kilometers with 500 houses, a high school, and various stores and small businesses.
4. A "ruropolis" every 150 kilometers with a population of 50,000.

The plan was linear, exact and absurd and, since only about 7% of the soils along the highway are fertile, never had a chance. Government hopes for crops have faded. Most settlers cannot survive economically, and soon plant pasture grass and raise cattle—or more likely, sell out to large ranches which raise more cattle. Costs of cattle raising are much less than costs of raising crops (where fertilizers are a necessity) and government subsidies (e.g. saving 50% on income taxes) encourage large companies such as Volkswagen (350,000 acres in the state of Para) into cattle raising ventures. Meanwhile, the fraction of families from the Northeast settling in the Amazon is insignificant. Of 1.3 million families in the Northeast with insufficient employment, about 4,000 had moved to Amazonia by 1975.

For the short term there have been successes for individuals and for firms. For individuals the frontier still constitutes a rural alternative to urban migration or starvation (Gross, 1979:112) and some have found better lives in the Amazon than they were accustomed to elsewhere.

The highways, by dramatically reducing transport costs to major national markets, have made some small scale production possible.

An individual economic success story related by Richard Bourne (Bourne, 1978:176) is illustrative.[3] Fernando Goncalves de Sousa fishes an Amazonian tributary near Humaita (see Map 2) using a large refrigerated boat and several small canoes. Fish which would bring

only $0.38/kilo in Humaita sell for $1.90 in Sao Paul, 1,500 miles to
the south, and the road between Porto Velho and Cuiaba allows direct
truck travel to Sao Paulo at a cost of only $0.19/kilo. Thus the
highway raises net revenue from fishing by over 300%.

The promise of natural resource exploitation has also been at
least partially realized. Tin and manganese production from the
Amazon have increased substantially (Bourne, 1978:142) and the
world's largest iron ore deposit awaits production sometime in the
1980s. However the old economic problem--distance from markets--
remains, and for their exploitation to be profitable, resource
deposits must be much more substantial in Amazonas than elsewhere in
Brazil.

But the hope of opening the Amazon to settlement by small scale
farmers has proven false. Soil infertility and rapid declines in
yield following settlement, the prohibitive costs of fertilizers and
other inputs, distance from markets, and the economics of cattle
raising have meant that large scale cattle ranching, rather than
farming, is the predominant activity in the basin. The ranches are
very large and land ownership extremely concentrated. In Matto
Grosso, the _average_ ranch size is 60,000 acres, and one worker for
every 4,000 acres is common. Only .7% of the holdings control 46% of
the land, and in Para the figures are similar (Kirby, 1976:122).

Though clearing trees for cattle is the major direction of
development in the Amazon, large scale plantations and industrial
development also are occurring. The mammoth sized Jari[4] project,
about to be described, is unique but it deserves attention both
because its size leads to regional impacts and because it has been
spoken of as a "model" for future development.

As with so many features of the Amazon basin, it is the
magnitude of the Jari development which first demands our attention.
Consider the following numbers: an area between 3,860 and 14,670
square miles (the latter area is about the size of Holland); a new
city of 7,000 inhabitants; 40,000 workers; 150,000 acres of cleared
forest on high ground planted in monoculture of _Gmelina_ _aborea_ (an
Asian tree known for its rapid growth); 35,000 acres planned (10,000
planted) of rice on the flood plain; a 750 ton/day pulp mill in
operation and a larger plant planned for 1983; a major saw mill for
tropical hardwoods with a 6,000 cubic meter capacity; 4,800
kilometers of new roads; a 46 kilometer wood burning railway; and a
50 megawatt wood burning power plant. Other monoculture crops are
planned (e.g. teak, manioc for use in preparing alcohol for fuel)
and a kaolin mine is in production.

Economically, it's not clear that the system works. Daniel
Ludwig, an 83-year-old American tanker billionaire, has spent more
than 600 million dollars on the enterprise, and has threatened that
he will close down the operation unless he gets more help from the
Brazilian government (_Economist_, 1980:100).

Not only is the Jari development questionable economically, its
operation raises numerous environmental questions. We will turn to
those questions in the next section where we will see that despite
the size of Jari, ecological problems associated with Amazonian
development dwarf any single scheme.

..it should be stressed that the debate today is not

whether or not the Amazon Basin will soon become a major source of food for a hungry world, but whether or not the region will survive the coming onslaught of development without an ecological collapse, or at least a permanent cutback of productive capacity (Eckholm, 1976:149).

ENVIRONMENTAL CONSEQUENCES

Possible environmental consequences from the development of the Amazon stem mainly from deforestation. The magnitude of that deforestation is great, but difficult to measure with certainty. Thus, according to Campbell, satellite data indicates that "62,000 square miles of the Brazilian Amazon rain forest were destroyed by pell mell development in 1975....At this rate, in 30 years the forest will be gone" (Campbell, 1977:106). Mosaic reports a somewhat lower loss rate[5] of 50 acres per minute (Mosaic, 1979:11). The effects of deforestation may be global or local.

Global Effects on Climate

Could Brazilian decisions on developing the Amazon affect global climate? Perhaps. All the evidence is not in and scientists who have studied the question differ in their conclusions. Let us look briefly at the controversy.

There are two ways by which humans may change global climate inadvertently. First, thermal pollution originating from the burning of any fuel-fossil or nuclear--could affect climate if excessively high rates of use continue into the next century. Second, increasing amounts of carbon dioxide emitted into the atmosphere could lead to a global "greenhouse effect" which would increase temperatures--slowly at first--but by as much as 3 plus or minus 1.5 degrees Centigrade by the middle of the next century (U.S. Department of Energy, 1980:3). While a 3 degree Centigrade (about 6 degrees Fahrenheit) temperature change may seem small, its effects would be dramatic. Most significantly it could lead to major shifts in agricultural zones and declines in world food producing capacity.

Most of the concern over carbon dioxide comes from global burning of fossil fuels. During the '60s and '70s fossil fuel use increased rapidly (about 4% per year) while measured carbon dioxide levels increased by about half that amount each year (U.S. Department of Energy, 1980:3).

Brazil and other countries with tropical forests enter the picture because excessive deforestation does two things at once. First, it immediately decreases the photosynthesis sink for carbon dioxide--and depending upon the nature of the crops (and their success) may take away a long term sink as well. Second, deforestation always adds carbon dioxide to the atmosphere through the burning of slash and underbrush. More may be added by further combustion depending upon whether most of the wood is burned, turned into lumber, or converted into pulp.

Whether or not deforestation will lead to climatic change will depend to some extent on the amount of land deforested and the amount of carbon dioxide released from such deforestation relative to the amount already released from other sources. Fossil fuel combustion adds about 5 billion metric tons of carbon dioxide to the atmosphere each year. Estimates for yearly carbon dioxide release from the clearing of tropical forests varies widely from, for example, 600 million (Wong, 1979:210) to 3.5 billion metric tons (Woodwell, et. al., 1978:145). Even the lower figure would imply that total release is more than 10% higher with deforestation than without. Thus, while the implications of increasing carbon dioxide concentrations are not completely known, there can be little doubt that deforestation contributes substantially to the process.

Local Effects on Climate

Besides the direct effects that deforestation might have, there is a secondary set of regional effects which may also alter global climate.

It's been shown that half the rainfall which reaches the Andes arises from evapotranspiration in the forests to the east (Saltari, 1978:206). That is, rain moves westward, falling on the forest. The forest re-releases that moisture through transpiration and evaporation, clouds reform and rain occurs again further westward. It is known that shrubs and pasture grass offer much less evapotranspiration than forests. Thus deforestation may alter local rainfall patterns and affect global climate through minor changes in monsoon lines (the shift would be southward and disastrous for some areas). But whether it does or not, there will clearly be ecological changes within the region. Evapotranspiration now leads to some rainfall even in the dry season. Without forests, the region can expect increased rain splash erosion, rapid runoff, attenuation of the dry season, high floods in the rainy season, and dry waterways in the dry season (Sioli, 1975:287). In fact there is some evidence that increased flooding in the rainy season in Peru has occurred since deforestation began upstream (Gentry, 1980:1354).

Species Loss

Clearing the Amazon leads to a second problem of global dimensions and concern. Of the 16 million square kilometers of tropical forests which existed less than a century ago, only about 9 million remain. Those tropical forests contain about two thirds of all the 4.5 million plant and animal species which the planet possesses. Some scientists claim that these numbers are much too conservative--that there may be 10 million species and that over eighty percent are in the tropics (Myers, 1979:14-24).

It's difficult to overestimate the richness of life in the Amazon--examples may be better than pages of statistics.

1. A single hectare of forest near Manaus contains 235 tree species (a temperate zone forest might contain 10).
2. Amazonia has 1800 species of birds--more than any comparable area in the world.
3. The basin similarly has the richest fish fauna in the world with 2000 identified species versus 1000 in the Congo and 250 in the Mississippi.

Of course the people who deforest tropical lands do not do so in order to exterminate species--but habitat destruction leads to species destruction as an inevitable consequence. If we accept the 4.5 million species estimate for the world, then as tropical habitat disappears, 2.5 million of these may become extinct before they become known. As a single example of the extinction process, consider the diking of the Amazon flood plain. It has recently been discovered that a symbiotic relationship exists between some 200 species of fish and trees in the 40,000 square miles of the basin which is flooded annually. During high water, fish feed in the forest on the seed and fruits of trees and then disperse those seeds elsewhere. Man depends on those fish (three fourths of which come from the flood plain forest) for protein. Now those flood plains are being diked, with an inevitable loss of fish, tree species and food (Maugh, 1981:1151).

Why is the loss of species important? A number of reasons, usually centering on the benefits of species diversity to man, have been suggested.

One of these stems from the fact that plants are an important source of food. Indeed 20 plants produce 90% of all our food, 3,000 are edible and it is estimated that 80,000 could be used. While the security of the food supply is threatened by plant diseases and pests, genetic diversity in food plants permits the evolution and development of resistant strains and thus reduces human vulnerability to widespread crop losses. Narrowing the pool of genes from which such strains can be drawn limits the range of possible adaptations and increases vulnerability.

This problem does not lie entirely in the future. The United States, for example, already has a dearth of native crop germ plasms. Thus, in 1973, the Department of Agriculture could write: "the situation is serious, potentially dangerous to the welfare of the nation, and appears to be getting worse rather than better" (Myers, 1979:63).

The use of plant and animal species for pharmaceutical products provides a second utilitarian rationale for saving species. At least 40% of the prescriptions in the United States contain a drug of natural origin, and plant medicinals are valued at over three billion dollars (Myers, 1979:68). Most of these drugs originate in tropical forests, and there is a comprehensive effort to inventory rain forest species. Ghillean T. Prance of the New York Botanical Garden reports on the exceptional number of new species collected on one expedition in the Amazon: "The largest number came from an endangered area along a new north-south highway linking Santanem on the Amazon River with Cuiaba..." (Mosaic, 1979:13). Several plants from the Amazon have yielded insect repellents, and there are hopes for finding sources of drugs for difficult-to-cure diseases (one

recent example is an effective agent for leukemia found in the
tropical periwinkle from Madagascar).

As a final example, Amazon Indians gave France the bark from a
vine they use in a contraceptive preparation. Initial tests on the
substance confirm what native people understand of its utility
(Mosaic, 1979:13).

Species diversity is also said to benefit humanity for aesthetic
reasons and because it allows for greater scientific understanding of
life. But the essence of the anthropocentric, utilitarian rationale
for saving species is that "the first principle of intelligent
tinkering is to save all of the parts."[6]

Snyder also argues the non-anthropocentric case for saving
species: "Diversity provides life with the capacity for a multitude
of adaptations and responses to long-range changes on the planet.
The possibility remains that at some future time another evolutionary
line might carry the development of consciousness to clearer levels
than our family of upright primates" (Snyder, 1974:103).

Other Problems

In addition to problems of a global nature, the disturbance of
fragile tropical ecosystems leads to a host of other environmental
and economic problems. Soils have been mentioned earlier, but more
observations are pertinent.

Some of the lateritic soils of the Amazon simply turn to a hard
red brick-like clay after clearing occurs. Most soils, however,
change first into poor pasture land, then into a scrub savanna. The
process appears to be irreversible, and was shown to occur a half
century ago in Brazil (near Belem) and in Venezuela. Cattle raising
works, but declines from 2-3 animals per hectare to less than 1 per
hectare have occurred in 4-5 years (Kirby, 1976:105).

The development at Jari illustrates several regionalized local
environmental problems. Monocultures invite pests. That was shown
to be the case in the Amazon as long ago as the early 1930s, when the
Henry Ford rubber plantation succumbed to South American leaf blight
(Goodland, 1975:19). Jari's tree plantations have shown susceptibility to pests, too. One insect infestation defoliated 750 acres of
Gmelina in 1974, and a killing fungus began to appear in several
areas in 1976. Even more disturbing is the fact that Jari plans 6-10
year rotations for Gmelina (6 years for pulp, 10 years for lumber),
but has so little data on soil nutrients that it is not even certain
whether the cycle can continue for many years. It's been shown that
in sandy soils trees begin senescence after seven years and at such
sites, other varieties of trees are being planted (Fearnside,
1980:152).

The rice plantations bear heavily twice a year. Because the
paddies are in the flood plain, one would expect that annual flooding
would replenish nutrients. However, a series of dikes assures that
the land is "mined" of its nutrients and it is expected that nitrogen
fertilizer loads will have to double by 1982. Weed problems haven't
been serious yet, but wild red rice found in neighboring Guiana is
known to have destroyed 70-80% of rice crops in Italy. Weed
invasions will inevitably lead to higher demands for herbicides or

result in loss of yield.

In addition to these problems, which potentially threaten the
sustainability of Jari, there are a number of external environmental
impacts associated with the development. According to Fearnside and
Rankin, these include (Fearnside, 1980:154):

1. Water pollution from the pulp mill and from the heavy use of
    pesticides and herbicides in agricultural areas;
2. Loss of breeding sites for riverine fish species due to diking of
    the flood plain.
3. Siltation of the river from the use of heavy machinery in forest
    clearing.
4. Loss of ecosystems and the unique species which live in them.

Finally, new health problems arise with clearing of the canopy
along stream banks. These cleared areas are excellent habitat for
planorbid snails, which are vectors of human schistosomiasis (Sioli,
1975:283). The problem would not be widespread normally because
Amazonian waters are naturally acidic, inhibiting snail population
growth. However, official agricultural policy calls for liming of
fields, which will lead to neutralized waters, and prime habitat for
the disease bearing snails (Goodland, 1975:51).

THE LOSS OF CULTURES

The Amazon basin was populated well before the Portugese and
Spanish arrived. Estimates of the native population are guesses at
best, but Goodland speculates that the number of native inhabitants
dropped precipitously from 1,000,000 in 1500 to 500,000 in 1940 and
50,000 in 1975 (Goodland, 1975:64).

While expansion into the Amazon has decimated the native
population, the government denies that it has followed a policy of
deliberate extermination. Thus in 1970 Interior Minister General
Costa Cavalcante formally rejected "the accusation that the Brazilian
Government has at any moment practiced genocide against our Indians.... The policy of the Government of Brazil is one of gradual
integration" (Akwesane, 1974:8). Official policy and action on the
ground differ, and a 7,000 page report to the Brazilian Congress in
1968 documented machine gunning, strychnined sugar and other horrors
(Goodland, 1975:63). Since then, the highway network has moved
inexorably through lands formerly assigned as Indian.

The loss of life in the Amazon has two very different
dimensions. For the short term it can be measured in strictly
personal, human terms—people are dying, sometimes cruelly, sometimes
from white man's diseases. For the long term, it's the loss of
cultures which matters. In addition to the loss of people guessed at
above, consider this data: in 1900 there were 230 tribal groups, by
1957 there were 143, and now there is information on only 109 and
half of these are represented by only a few hundred individuals
(Goodland, 1975:64).

While the government may not sanction genocide as a national policy, it does encourage the extinction of cultures. Thus, according to Interior Minister Reis,

> This is a promise that I can firmly make: We will assume a policy of integrating the indigenous population into Brazilian society in the shortest time possible....We believe that the ideals of preserving the indigenous population within its 'natural habitat' are very nice ideals, but unrealistic (Akwesane, 1974:8).

It is not certain how long our species has been in this hemisphere—but it is safe to say that Amazonian native cultures have developed and evolved to live within their environments over several thousand years. Clearly, they learned how to live in a fragile land. It is not obvious that the Brazilian drive toward monoculture—agricultural and human—can do as well.

REMEDIES: TREATIES AND CHANGE

The issues raised in this paper are not new. Brazilians—in and out of government—have considered them and argued about them. They have admitted mistakes in the past, and Brazil has in fact led the Amazon basin countries in talking about the problem. The eight countries which share the basin signed a treaty in July, 1978, in which they promise to pay more attention than in the past to the ecological dangers inherent in the unbridled exploitation of the basin (Bond, 1978:64). However, the 28 articles of the treaty include such "ecological" ideas as promotion of tourism, development of transportation and promotion of joint research. One commentator has noted: "The question in the minds of some observers is whether there will be anything left for the scientists to study" (Schroeder, 1979:17).

The small but vocal environmental community in Brazil does not see any current government treaties or actions as sufficient. A recent interview of Jose Lutzenberger (a leader of the Brazilian environmental movement) places the problem in a long range perspective:

> <u>Many people today say that environmental concern is an elitist hobby and that it distracts attention from Brazil's more pressing problems of poverty and injustice, which require rapid growth for their solution. How do you answer these people?</u>
>
> I say that on the contrary it is the growth mythology that has allowed us to put off questions of distributive justice. As long as faith in the myth of eternal growth of the cake persists, we can say that those with the smallest proportional slices are getting better off absolutely even if not relatively, and that they should patiently wait for the cake to grow bigger before we redivide it more fairly, because premature redistribution would hurt the poor by slowing down the rate of growth of the cake. Simple people

believe this. Today in Brazil we are constructing a
consumer society for 20 million people on the backs of the
other 80 million or more.

But, when we finally realize that the cake is not
growing and cannot continue growing, and that in fact it is
even shrinking, then no longer will we be able to avoid
facing up to the demands for at least minimum justice in
the distribution of income. For this reason the myth of
perpetual growth is assiduously maintained by those who no
longer believe it themselves, but find it in their
interests that everyone else should believe it. Ecological
concern and social justice are as inseparable as are the
two faces of a coin (Daly, 1981:23).

MIRRORS

As an "outsider" I see Brazil as a mirror—a series of distorted
and distant reflections of our past and continuing mistakes. The
reader has probably already noted many of these. I will list just
three.

The Frontier. Not only is the Amazon seen as a limitless
frontier, but its conquest (and the language used for such
exploitation is almost always in military idiom) involves the
destruction of native peoples. The native peoples of Brazil, like
our native Americans, have been under assault for generations, but
the mirror is distorted in time. New technology—the road built by
machete, bulldozer and radar—has changed the pace of destruction.

Another of our mistakes is being repeated on the Amazonian
frontier. We believed that the arid west could be treated similarly
to the fertile plains of the midwest, assigned 160 acres as a
"farmable" unit for homesteaders—then watched the deep plowed soil
blow away and homesteaders head for new frontiers. In the Amazon,
the ecological situation differs, but the lack of understanding of
the difference in cultivation techniques remains the same—and it is
doubtful if 250-acre homesteads will survive.

Technical Solutions. There is a tendency to seek solutions to
complex problems through technology, without due consideration to
social or environmental consequences. The clearest example of this
in Brazil is the decision to "solve" their energy problem by using
biomass to produce alcohol to fuel their automobiles. But only a
small percentage of Brazilians drive cars, and the land that used to
grow beans for food for those who don't need automobiles becomes the
fuel source for those who do. Our energy policy is comparably
nearsighted.

Monocultures. Brazil is following the lead of the United States
devoting more and more land to monocultures. Such agricultural
practices demand excessive amounts of fertilizers and pesticides—
which in turn demand more energy sources, deplete the soils of
nutrients, and breed more and more resistant strains of insects.

History is a great teacher but one that is frequently ignored.
The future of the Amazon, and perhaps of many of the world's people,
requires that its lessons be heeded.

FOOTNOTES

1. Exact figures for soil fertility are still unavailable, though satellite data has proven useful. Kirby suggests that "4% of soils in Brazilian Amazonia are of moderate to high fertility." (Kirby, 1976:106).

2. This paper deals mainly with the Brazilian Amazon. For other Amazonian countries, see Kirby (1976) and Hiraoka (1980).

3. Bourne's book is not only the most readable single source on Amazonian development, it is the most even-handed. Many of the sources used for this paper were written by environmental scientists or others who had a specific point of view. Bourne's journalistic, unbiased account is all the more powerful because, in the end, he shares the concern over the effects of the "Assault".

4. Jari is Jari Forestal e Agropecuaria, Ltda. and is located west of Jari River. (See Map 2. The Jari River flows from the north into the Amazon just east of the eastern-most river on the map.)

5. The rate of deforestation reported by Campbell (62,000 square miles/year) implies that the forest is being destroyed at the rate of 75 acres/minute.

6. The statement is attributed to Wendell Berry, and its beauty lies in the fact that it can be applied both to species and to the past, which can be thought of as a "parts bin" for the future.

BIBLIOGRAPHY

"A Policy of Genocide." Akwesane Notes. International Congress of
     Americanists. Mexico City (Sept. 1974):8-10.
Bond, R. D. "Venezuela, Brazil and the Amazon Basin." Orbis 22
     (1978):635-651.
Bourne, R. Assault on the Amazon. London: Victor Golanz, Ltd.,
     1978.
Campbell, R. "A Timely Reprieve or a Death Sentence for the Amazon."
     Smithsonian 8, 7 (Oct., 1977):100-110.
"Crossroads for Tropical Biology." Mosaic 10, 3 (May/June
     1979):10-18.
Daly, Herman. "Brazil's Leading Environmentalist." Not Man Apart
     (March, 1981):12, 13, 23.
de Carvalho, Arnoldo. "Brazil Continues the Rapid Development of Its
     Alcohol Program." Energy (1981):6.
Eckholm, Erik P. Losing Ground. New York: W. W. Norton and Co.,
     Inc., 1976.
Fearnside, Philip M., and Rankin, Judy M. "Jari and Development in
     the Brazilian Amazon." Interciencia 5 (1980):146-156.
Gentry, A. H. and Lopez-Parodi, J. "Deforestation and Increased
     Flooding of the Upper Amazon." Science 210 (1980):1354-1356.
Goodland, R. J. A., and Irwin, H. S. Amazon Jungle: Green Hell to
     Red Desert? New York: Elsevier Scientific Publishing Co.,
     1975.
Gross, A. R. "Getting to the Frontier." Journal of Development
     Studies 16 (1979):99-112.
Hiraoka, Mario. "Settlement and Development of the Upper Amazon:
     The East Bolivian Example." Journal of Developing Areas 14
     (1980):327-347.
Katzman, M. T. "Paradoxes of Amazonian Development in a
     'Resource-Starved' World." Journal of Developing Areas 10
     (1976):445-460.
Kirby, J. M. "Agricultural Land-Use and the Settlement of
     Amazonia." Pacific Viewpoint 17 (1976):105-131.
Maugh, T. H.,II. "A Fish in the Bush is Worth..." Science 211
     (1981):1151.
Mitchell, J. G. "The Man Who Would Dam the Amazon." Audubon 81
     (March 1979):64-80.
Myers, Norman. The Sinking Ark. Oxford, England: Pergamon Press,

1979.

"Public Hostility for a Private Fief." _Economist_ 276 (1980):100-101.

Saltari, Eneas; Marques, Jose; and Molion, Luiz Carlos B. "Origin and Distribution of Rain in the Amazon Basin." _Interciencia_ 3 (1978):206.

Schroeder, R. C. "Woodman Spare that Tree." _Americas_ 31 (1979):17-18.

Sioli, H. "Tropical Rivers as Expressions of Their Terrestrial Environments." In _Ecological Studies II - Tropical Ecological Systems_. F. B. Golley and E. Medina (eds.). New York: Springer-Verlag, Inc., 1975, 275-288.

Smith, Nigel J. H. "Colonization Lessons from a Tropical Forest." _Science_ 214 (November 13, 1981):755-761.

Snyder, G. "Energy is Eternal Delight." In _Turtle Island_. New Directions Publishing Corporation, 1974.

Stark, N. "Nutrient Cycling II. Nutrient Distribution in Amazonian Vegetation." _Tropical Ecology_ 12 (1971)177-201.

U. S. Department of Energy, Carbon Dioxide Effects Research and Assessment Program. _Carbon Dioxide Research Progress Report, Fiscal Year 1979_. April, 1980. DOE/EV-0071.

Wagley, C. _Man in the Amazon_. Gainesville, Florida: The University Presses of Florida, 1974.

Wong, C. S. "Atmospheric Input of Carbon Dioxide from Forest Fires." _Science_ 200 (April 13, 1979):197-200.

_____. "Carbon Input to the Atmosphere from Forest Fires." _Science_ 294 (April 13, 1979):209-210.

Woodwell, G. M.; Whittaker, R. H.; Reenens, W. A.; Likens, G. E.; Delwicke, C. C.; and Botkin, D. B. "The Biota and the World Carbon Budget." _Science_ 199 (1978):141-146.

8
Dirt, Water, International Development, and Resource Security

Chris Field

INTRODUCTION

Our world has problems aplenty. War, nuclear weapons, and political and economic repression and instability all urgently require attention and pose problems that seem difficult to resolve. But overshadowing all of these is the vast gap in human welfare that now exists between the "developed" and the "less developed" countries. Most of the earth's people are desperately poor, and unless we manage peaceful technological and distributional changes, global inequality will grow in the future.

Standing in the way of human and social development, however, is the endangered condition of the resource base upon which such development ultimately depends. For the truth is that the efforts of the world's people to survive today, let alone to feed, clothe and shelter expanded numbers in the future, are producing losses of soil, vegetation, water, habitat, and species of animals and plants which are essential to human survival. Any objective view of future economic development must recognize that with the loss of dirt, water, and genetic material, any kind of increase in agricultural productivity becomes a formidable agronomic and social challenge. And without first securing the food supply, further development seems impossible. My view is then that our <u>major</u> global problem is environmental, for it is only from the continued good functioning of the biosphere that any future societies will be supplied. In simpler terms: today's greatly accelerated impoverishment of life is our most basic problem. Extinction of kinds of plants and animals, mainly through destruction of their habitats, is an irreversible loss. A social, as well as obviously biological loss, this diminishment of the potential of life on earth is not a kind of pollution for which we can find a set of control strategies and technical repair fixes once the political will to do so becomes established. Biotic simplification is pervasive and fundamental, both global and local. Its consequences are far more serious than exhaustion of oil or mineral deposits, more significant to social continuity than ideological differences.

The roots of this developmental tragedy lie in an extensive unprecedented devegetation of the world's wet and dry tropics wrought by millions of desperately poor people scrabbling for a living from

marginal, eroded or unimproved lands. The people struggling to
survive today are mostly poor, insecure, underemployed and politically powerless. Perhaps there are over 780 million whom the World Bank
calls the "absolute poor" (IBRD, The World Bank, 1980:33). Most of
these people can be characterized as members of transitional agrarian
societies forced by a desperate search for subsistence into an
abandonment of traditional production methods and constraints on land
usages. However, the resulting accelerated destruction of habitat
with the consequent losses of soils and biota are also caused by
externally stimulated commercial and industrial development efforts.
With the exception of some big cats, meat animals, and whales, trends
toward extinction are not the result of conscious, deliberate species
exploitation. Today, most of the disappearing species are going as a
by-product of the changes in soil and water conditions that accompany
intense subsistence exploitation and "development" of natural
resources as defined by industrial societies.

When one considers the degraded environmental conditions of the
marginal lands which are now the only recourse of vast numbers of
rural poor and landless, it is not at all surprising that cause and
consequence of poverty follow close upon each other. Unlimited human
poverty literally devours its last hope, the natural resource base.
It is mostly the poor who starve, are malnourished and illiterate.
Millions must suffer the scarcities of firewood and scrounge food or
housing materials from their immediate environments. As runoff is
increased by devegetation, and as the springs or streams dry up in
season, it is the poor who must walk further, suffer from drinking
contaminated water, and lose their crops to drought, flood or
erosion. And, in the desperation of feeding children and attempting
to retain some elements of social dignity, their redoubled efforts
usually succeed in a more complete destruction of a meagre patrimony.
As the best land becomes preempted for the advantages of urban and
international commercial exchange, and subsistence processes exhaust
the resources of the countryside, the desperation turns inward to
stimulate the institutions of social control. Often the military
state flourishes.

However misconstrued, misapplied, or rationalized sincere
international developmental efforts may be today, it seems reasonable
to wish that they enhance, not limit, opportunities for ethical
social choice. Such a hope clearly implies that preservation of the
environmental basis of a society's subsistence is morally imperative.
It seems obvious that impoverishment of the biosphere reduces
opportunities to create and sustain the societies which could
practice, develop, and transmit civilization. It is doubtful that
our own civilized values--such as individual freedom of expression
and association, accompanied by perceptible improvement of social
equity in opportunity and justice--can survive without a sufficiency
of those goods required to satisfy basic human needs. Along with the
fundamental air, water, food, shelter and health, one must include
space, community identity, work, and aesthetic satisfactions as
essential dimensions of human development. When the environmental
endowment of a place--or the world--becomes abused to diminishment or
degradation of its biotic productivity, less satisfaction of these
basic needs is possible over the time needed for a group to establish
a history and transmit civilization. Without local control and

maintenance of an adequately functioning resource base to provide food, it seems very doubtful that any society or nation could have the independence required to make essentially moral kinds of social choices possible. In a society reduced to competitive struggle for the necessities of animal survival, there is less opportunity for fulfillment of the individual human potential.

Although our American passion for economic development has many self-satisfying and moralistic overtones, its dominant commercial materialistic core is drawn from a western history of colonial piracy and technical superiority, fed by the abundant resources of a "New World". Nevertheless, the industrial system requires interdependence based on global trade. It has also become evident in our time that global environmental health will be an essential element in the maintenance of societies both numerous and diverse enough to make ideologies significant.

THE CASE OF COSTA RICA

The situation of Costa Rica illustrates the process in which "development" leads to environmental degradation and ultimately threatens to destroy itself. This delightful country is a hopeful spot in an unhappy and dismal neighborhood. Whatever problems it has are worse in Nicaragua, El Salvador or Panama. Costa Rica has a reputation as a kind of tropical Switzerland; an agrarian democracy on its way to becoming a middle- income, industrialized paradox. There is no formal standing army. Thirty to forty percent of the national budget is spent on education. The 1978 per capita GNP was about $1,540. From 1960 to 1977 the economy grew at 3.3 percent per year (IBRD, 1980:111). Population growth was down to 2.5% and declining. There is a well nourished, educated, and for Central America, a numerous middle class. The population is just over two million in a territory a bit larger than Denmark but smaller than West Virginia. Although short on mineral and fuel resources, Costa Rica has considerable potential abundance. Ecologically new, relatively fertile volcanic soils are not yet everywhere degraded. From the wet tropical forests of its northeastern Caribbean shore over central mountain ranges to the semi-arid valley of the northwest, Costa Rica holds an extraordinary diversity of bioclimates and forest communities.[1]

Costa Rica is far ahead of any Hispanic American country in its tangible support of conservation. Following on the accomplishments of President Daniel Oduber, who greatly enlarged the National Park system and added the 290 square kilometer Corcovado Lowland Rainforest Park, in 1978 President Rodrigo Carazo committed his government to a: "Broad, aggressive, and coordinated program for conservation and rational use of renewable natural resources." His explanation was:

> Costa Rica is approaching the point of no return with regard to the management of its natural resources ...traveling through the interior of the country, especially in the dry season it is possible to observe that vast areas have been completely cut over, burned, and are suffering

from the effects of the cancer of erosion. The most
lamentable part of this picture is the obvious instability
and poverty of the rural communities, the reduction in the
potential for productivity of the soil, and the loss of
options for uses having greater economic and social
benefits (U.S.A.I.D., 1979: 17).

Fine presidential words, fulfillment of which, in spite of noble
intentions and solid accomplishment so far, runs beyond the
institutional and fiscal capacity of the country. In The Sinking
Ark, Norman Myers points out that the Corcovado Park effort alone is
comparable to the United States having raised 1.7 billion dollars to
set aside a park the size of West Virginia, taking into account the
relative wealth, population and territory of the two countries
(Myers, 1979:147). If one counts all the forest and indigenous
reserves, Costa Rica has attempted to protect 11% of its national
territory.

Deforestation: Causes

Although Costa Rica has the oldest (1942) government supervised
forestry program in Latin America, the destruction of forests is
widely perceived to be the most important national environmental
problem. 1978 estimates put the remnant virgin forest cover at about
35 percent of the national territory, but most of it is on poorly
drained lands or very steep slopes (Albertin, 1978:1). It has been
estimated that only 17 percent of the land area of the country is
virgin forest capable of being commercially and continuously
exploited (Albertin, 1978:21).
    Studies of the forest industry forecast deficits in domestic
roundwood and woodfiber within a decade. Although there has been
experimentation with exotics and native species for many years, only
about 1,000 hectares of plantations are functioning (Albertin,
1978:1). The idea of reforestation is popular, but sufficient
nurseries, seedlings, programs, and financing are hard to find. The
Government has neither the cadastral records or survey to resolve,
nor the money to pay off, the competing claims to land reserved.
Even though they are conscious of the consequences of deforestation
in loss of hydroelectric potential, increased costs of domestic and
industrial water, and increasing welfare load, the several government
agencies seem unable to resolve their overlapping responsibilities to
support both the enforcement of laws and the development of knowledge
needed to rationally manage the resources. Costa Rica has an
association, ASCONA, a nascent Sierra Club, devoted to environmental
education. They understand that without a broadly accepted and
understood land ethic it will eventually be politically impossible to
protect the "abstract" values which parks and reserves represent
(personal interviews, 1978).
    Meanwhile, back at the ranches, the pasturelands and beef cattle
of Central America have doubled in the last 25 years and it is this
rapid growth of the cattle industry that ultimately drives the
process of deforestation forward. Costa Rica had about 900,000
cattle in 1960; now there are about two million head (Myers,

1979:145).   Costa   Rica   exports   about 45 million kilos of beef per
year; over half to the USA. Our Meat Importers Council says that
most goes into processed products and convenience foods. In 1976 we
imported 675,522 metric tons of beef;   431,781   from Australia/New
Zealand,   roughly   33   thousand   from Brazil, 18 from Mexico, 22 from
Nicaragua, 25 from Costa Rica, 18 from Honduras, and 15 from
Guatemala.

As beef production in Costa Rica doubled during the 1960s, per
capita   domestic   consumption   dropped by 26 percent to 8 kg per year
(Myers, 1979:145). Similar drops are noted in Guatemala, Honduras,
and El Salvador. In Forest to Pasture: Development or Destruction?,
James Parsons has written the most succinct explanation:

> Why, in the face of malnutrition and   underconsumption
> of protein is Central America so enthusiastically exporting
> it (beef), and to one of the best fed nations on earth?
> Quite clearly because it is profitable to do so—it brings
> in much needed foreign exchange. But also because stock
> raising is an activity congenial to the latin value system.
> Ganadero like Caballero is a term of respect.   It carries
> prestige and it implies an attractive way of life that is
> relatively easily entered. With price ceilings imposed on
> most basic commodities it has not been attractive to the
> small farmer to intensify his efforts to produce rice,
> maize, beans, or yuca. And the market for traditional
> export crops such as coffee, bananas, and sugar has been
> notoriously fickle and unreliable.
>
> With beef it has been another matter, especially since
> the opening of the U.S. market some 20 years ago. Profits
> have been good and the risks low. Moreover, grass is the
> easiest of crops to grow. It takes less resources in
> capital and management to develop pasture than to intensify
> cropping efforts... and it is simply easier, requiring
> less work and effort. In some cases the shift to cattle
> may reflect a desire to avoid labor problems or perhaps a
> recognition that the tired land has been pushed to the
> limit and needs a rest. In the drive to diversify exports,
> governments have encouraged an expanding cattle industry,
> and international agencies have given further support.
> Especially decisive has been the availability of low-cost
> credit.   In Costa Rica nearly half of all agricultural
> credit in recent years has been to the livestock industry
> (Parsons, 1976:126).

Another commentator, George Guess, cited the 1973 census and
some AID-IDB-IBRD studies to note that ..."the distinguishing
characteristic is lack of majority access to both agricultural land
and credit." "The degree of majority access is indicated by the
following figures: 63.7% of agro-export and beef cattle farms are
larger than 200 hectares, occupy 90.3% of the area in [such]
production, receive 88.2% of total agricultural credit allocations,
and produce 71% of the total agro-export output [coffee, bananas,
cacao, beef]." "The agricultural sector provides 65% of total export
earnings and about 35% of all employment opportunities." "Small

farmers received 73% of the number of loans, but only 18% of the money" (Guess, 1978:599-611). Myers found that the Costa Rican beef industry was dominated by 2,134 ranchers holding an average of 750 hectares each to control 51% of the land in use (Myers, 1979:145).

Along with the dramatic increases in beef production and growth in value of coffee, cacao and sugar output, there appears to be some concentration of land into large units. Most observers agree that the distribution of land ownership in Costa Rica is not as badly skewed in favor of the larger units as it is in most of Latin America. As space for the traditional colonizer or small to medium agriculturist becomes filled, exhausted, or put to pasture, the political pressures for agrarian reforms can only increase. From data offered by George Guess it appears that during the 1963 to 1973 decade the number of small farms (0.2 to 10 hectares) grew from 52.7% to 57.6% of the total units. But, during that period the area occupied by such farms declined from 4.8% to 3.9% of the total. Over the same period farms and ranches of over 200 hectares also became more numerous (from 3% to 3.5% of the number) and grew to occupy 54.4% of the area in agriculture (Guess, 1978:599-611).

As part of these changes in agriculture Costa Rica is at the threshold of having to cope with an explosive growth of a rural landless class. Although the causes of rural poverty are complex and not to be attributed solely to land quality or tenurial access, it is apparent that landlessness is becoming a significant element in the structure of Costa Rican society. Drawing on the 1973 census, Richard Kreitman states "The non-farm rural poor are the largest poverty group in the country, comprising 23.3% of the national population, 37.5% of the rural population...and 61.6% of the rural poor" (Kreitman, 1976:96). Samuel Daines, commenting on Kreitman and the same data notes "...in Costa Rica there are significant numbers of poor farms in the 10-20 hectare size. Poverty is not simply a question of gross farm size..." (Daines, 1976:26). The rural poor are not only those with very small or no holdings, but also those without title or whose title is questionable. Of such "landless farms", Daines reports that 68.5% are poor. Compared to farming for export or domestic consumption, the beef cattle industry offers few jobs or seasonal employment to rural people. Conventional wisdom in Costa Rica holds that a minimum of 60 hectares is needed for a subsistence cattle ranching operation. Out on the forest edge, the pioneer fringe, most squatters now struggle and fail. After a few years of subsistence cropping they sell their doubtful rights or titles to the more powerful class. Or, they fulfill their contract by planting grass at the end of three years and move out, usually into steeper and more marginal forest. The dream of independence, food security, and landowners status which the existence of forested expanses made plausible and which by tradition supported a measure of social stability, is no longer.

Costa Rica is forcing the transformation from agrarian democracy to urban-industrial society. In the process values and structures have to change. The social consequences of rural against urban wage differentials and the migrations of poor to the cities are now somewhat offset by the Asignaciones Familiares, a set of sales tax financed public health, nutrition, and welfare programs. Although the birth rates are high but declining and malnutrition and begging are rare, it remains true that education, social service, and food supply distribution policies all reflect the biases of an urban society. The quality of all the above is substantially less in rural areas (personal observations, 1978, 1968).

It is apparent that landholdings for beef production have grown larger as subsistence plots have been both displaced and become smaller. Traditional Hispanic cultural aspirations, export market opportunities and government policies supported by international assistance programs have combined to drive the Costa Rican pioneer farmer through the forests to the mountaintops and into the swamps as well as the cities.

Consequences

Let us return to the physical consequences of forest removal. Leave aside the potential sources of drugs, dyes, fibers, pesticides, foods, knowledge, beauty, and pleasure lost forever when habitats are destroyed. Let us recognize, let us finally learn that "...over and over the history of development in the tropics has shown the belief that the soils of luxurious tropical forest would yield a succession of rich crops to be a cruel illusion" (Parsons, 1976:127). On the other hand, we lack data to demonstrate conclusively that conversion to grass always causes serious reduction of nutrients and degradation of soil structure. Few nutrient flow studies of various cropping combinations for tropical land use strategies exist. Now that most of the aboriginal systems of shifting forest agriculture are gone, we have few models and experiments to test. It is apparent, however, that most of the nutrient stock of humid tropical forest sites is bound in the biomass. Converted to ash in the clearing process, leaching and runoff take the nutrients beyond the reach of most crops and shallow rooted grasses (Parsons, 1976:127). In addition, on sites with dry seasons, soil temperatures are greatly increased. Loss of organic matter and reduced water holding capacity in some soils usually so favors grass or erosion that either continued cropping or forest succession to replacement could become unlikely. Without careful management of stocking rates, fire, moisture, and fertility levels, most grasses either thin out or become woody under trampling, soil compaction and erosion. Invasion by woody growth, rejected by cattle for impalatability, may require burning, hand weeding or other costly treatments. Soil chemistry changes as water levels rise following loss of forest transpiration. Pugging by cattle, soil creep and landslides also usually reduce potential productivity. Such physical changes to the real underpinnings of the production processes that support an economy cannot proceed for long without forcing adjustments in social structure. Sometimes technological innovation, substitution of resources, or expansion of trading relationships has made cultural continuity possible. But, for a basically agrarian society there is no possible long term substitution of the complex which soil, water, climate and place represent. That physical--environmental--condition is the fundamental basis for societal construction and continuity.

It is likely that under some seasonal rainfall patterns with very porous volcanic soils and well managed grass cover, a ranching or dairy economy could return net energy gains. A few individuals are attempting to develop more stable agro-ecosystems. Besides Costa Rica's shaded coffee system, an example of the kind of agro-forestry which might be developed to a sustained yield is the alder-and-pasture dairy farming found on the slopes of Mt. Poas. The trees host nitrogen fixing bacteria, make timber, and shade the grazing cows below. But few agricultural techniques now used in Costa Rica or in other parts of the American humid tropics maximize biologic productivity. Neither are they all physically or economically sustainable for much more than a generation's time with current levels of high quality energy inputs. The challenge to tropical development is one which requires more knowledge of social and physical system interaction. The present techniques of simplification and extraction or the apparent short run advantages of scale and export will not sustain self-sufficiency, whether that be in food, social identity, technology, or power to influence the terms of trade.

Thus, even though there still are bright spots of hope, Costa Rica is following the path of industrial concentration and simplification of agriculture which will eventually stumble to the same prospects of hunger and terror which is the lot of their quasi-totalitarian neighbors.

Environmental and social costs--whether they be in reduced present productivity, or in postponed repair and construction and maintenancee--are being put forward, debited to a now disenfranchised future society which although surely more numerous, is not likely to be better informed, organized, or rich enough in energy to better afford conservative restraint and careful experimentation.

In the past, man has been able to improvise and innovate brilliantly under conditions of resource abundance and substitutability. It is not thermo-dynamically probable that we will soon discover--or invent--some technical breakthrough comparable to the agricultural revolution which brought us this last 25 thousand years or so. We are now and will remain necessarily dependent on the living relationships between organisms, water, and minerals.

CONCLUSION

Basic economic security in diversity and stability of food supply could contribute to a real development. A better than contemporary biologic adaptation might give us time to develop societal structures which might use freedom for the making of ethical decisions. Instead of the world view which postulates an obligate competitive struggle against nature, one based on bio-technological cooperation will prove essential to physical and civilizational survival. Our competitive models of society and economic relations lead to ever larger scale resource exploitation, resulting in cycles of growth and environmental degradation. The stresses of this destruction lead to war, revolution, envy, disease, population declines and losses of cultural continuity. Some security in food and space are essential human needs. But, so also are contexts in which the creative potential of our restless minds could grasp and enjoy a measure of freedom. Historically, conditions of massive suffering and widespread deprivation are not those under which humanity has grown in grace and accomplishment. Totalitarian controlled and centralized large social experiments have also contributed to human suffering. Massive global environmental degradation seems likely now, as in the past, to be accompanied by restriction of alternatives, losses of freedoms, and by cultural decadence. In the context of a biologically impoverished future, reconstruction of human civilization would seem to be a greater challenge than that of conserving what now remains.

FOOTNOTES

1. Over 8000 plant species have been recorded. The "La Selva" forest reserve of 730 hectares has 320 tree species, 42 fish, 394 birds, 104 mammals (63 bats), 76 reptiles, 46 amphibians, and 143 kinds of butterflies. The country has 758 bird species only 138 of which are migrants. That is more than North America north of the Tropic of Cancer (Myers, 1979:142).

BIBLIOGRAPHY

Albertin, Waldemar. A Review of Some Environmental and Natural Resource Problems and Possible Solutions in the Areas of Forestry, National Parks and Reserves, and Fish and Wildlife in Costa Rica. Unpublished manuscript. USAID Mission, San Jose, Costa Rica. March 5, 1978.

Daines, Samuel. "Analysis of the Rural Poor." In Costa Rica Agriculture Sector Assessment Working Papers. A report to USAID, Costa Rica, prepared by Samuel F. Daines. Washington, D.C., December, 1976.

Guess, George. "Narrowing the Base of Costa Rican Democracy." Development and Change 9 (1978):599-611.

Kreitman, Richard. "Rural Poor Profile." In Costa Rica Agriculture Sector Assessment Working Papers. A report to USAID, Costa Rica prepared by Samuel R. Daines. Washington, D.C., December 1976, 885-126.

Myers, Norman. The Sinking Ark. New York: Pergamon Press, 1979.

Parsons, James. "Forest to Pasture: Development or Destruction?" Revista de Biologia Tropical 24, Supl. 1 (1976):121-138.

United States Agency for International Development. Environmental and Natural Resource Management in Developing Countries. A Report to Congress I. Washington, D.C.: Department of State, February, 1979.

The World Bank. World Development Report 1980. New York: Oxford University Press, 1980.

Part III

Europe

9
Energy and Environment in Scandanavia

John Duffield

> The consumption of fuel in our day is so terribly large; it is perpetually increasing, and prices are rising so fast, that many are beginning to believe the long-standing and oft-repeated prophesies of an imminent general shortage of this indispensable commodity.
>
> Christian Olufsen[1](Copenhagen, 1811),
> Professor at the Classen Institute
> for Agriculture

INTRODUCTION

The topic of this paper is energy and environment in Scandinavia and, in the Scandinavian tradition, what I have pulled together is a bit of a smorgasbord. The aim is to shed some light on U.S. energy policies and problems through a comparative analysis. The specific choice of issues and examples is determined in part by the special concerns of Montana and the Rocky Mountain West. Since mine is the only paper in this volume dealing explicitly with energy, I will begin with some general considerations on the connection between energy and environment. The next section is a factual comparison of overall energy use in the U.S., Sweden, and Norway. Included here is a varied collection of Scandinavian innovations in the area of shelter and energy. Next, energy policies are examined to explain both energy use patterns and the level of innovation. Lastly I will briefly explore the relevance of the Scandinavian energy experience for our culture.

ENERGY AND ENVIRONMENT

Energy conversion and extraction are perhaps the major causes of environmental disruption in the world today. The underdeveloped and developed countries differ, however, in patterns of energy use and attendant environmental consequences.

Typically, the underdeveloped countries still rely mainly on renewables. In India, for example, firewood and animal power supply 71% of all energy sources (Lockeretz, 1977:563). As populations exceed the capacity of a given region to produce food and fuel, the major long-run impact has been on the destruction of soil resources. Several other papers in this volume describe the massive deforestation and erosion associated with the search for firewood and expanded food production in Nepal, Costa Rica, and Brazil.

By contrast, the energy problem for developed countries is dependence on rapidly depleting reserves of fossil fuels. Past, present, and future "recoverable" world oil reserves total 2 trillion barrels (Carter, 1976). About 40% of proved reserves has already been consumed. It is likely that within four generations, the bulk of the world's oil supply, created over hundreds of millions of years, will be gone. In addition, the combustion and extraction of these fuels has a substantial environmental impact, mainly on air and water resources. In the United States, for example, airborne emissions of sulfur dioxide, particulates, carbon monoxide, and oxides of nitrogen are largely from energy conversion by utilities, households, and automobiles (Dorfman, 1977:71). Energy conversion impacts are diverse, however, ranging from the destruction of aquafers through stripmining on the Great Plains to oil spills in the Arctic. The nuclear option is beset by the same basic problems: finite uranium supplies plus unsolved long-run environmental problems, especially in waste storage.

Contrary to the direction indicated by these general findings, the current U.S. policy is to expand production of domestic fossil fuels and increase support for the nuclear industry. At the heart of this policy lies an apparent faith in new technology and its ability to wring still more resources from the earth's crust while keeping environmental impacts from destroying the biosphere. This faith has a long intellectual history in America, as the following quotation suggests:

> We leave it to the Political Arithmetician to compute, how much Money will be sav'd to a Country, by its spending two thirds less of Fuel; how much Labour sav'd in Cutting and Carriage of it; ... and to Physicians to say, how much healthier thick built Towns and Cities will be, now half suffocated with sulphury Smoke, when so much less of that Smoke shall be made, and the Air breath'd by the Inhabitants be consequently so much purer (Franklin, 1744:32).

This statement (advertisement!) is from Benjamin Franklin's An Account of the New Invented Pennsylvania Fireplaces. But Franklin's optimism, however appropriate in 18th century Philadelphia, is mistaken in another time and place. In Missoula, Montana 236 years later, a doubling of wood consumption in the last few years (burned in Franklin-type stoves) has led to violations of all federal and state ambient air standards for particulates. While this situation is, of course, calling forth new wood combustion technology, the point is that for any given technology only some finite level of consumption is compatible with the carrying capacity of the environment. This is unarguably true for what may well be the ultimate constraint on fossil fuel conversion: global carbon dioxide levels and the long-term impact on climate through the greenhouse effect (Laurmann, 1979).

In the short-term, the effects of some technologies have been not to eliminate but to shift the problem from one environmental media to another or from local to global areas. A good example of both phenomena is the very widespread use of tall stacks to reduce the impact of fossil fuel combustion on local airsheds. The result has been the long range transport of sulfur and nitric oxides to more distant areas where they are precipitated as acid rain.

Ironically, while Scandinavian countries have been world leaders in the control of pollution, acid rain has had a heavy impact on the water resources of these countries. This is largely due to being downwind from European and British industrial centers, the high precipitation induced by the peninsular mountain ranges, and the inert nature of the rock and soil, which provide poor buffering or "neutralization" of acid rain.

A recent article in <u>Scientific American</u> (Likens, 1979) noted that more than 70% of the sulfur in the atmosphere over Southern Sweden is from human activity and 77% is believed to originate from sources outside Sweden. Similarly, in Southern Norway the coastal mountains elevate the moist and sulfur-laden air masses from Great Britain, resulting in a very high annual deposition. Instead of the nearly neutral rains of clean atmospheres, precipitation in North Western Europe is now a dilute solution of sulfuric and nitric acids. In the most extreme example yet, recorded in Scotland in 1974, a rain had the same acidity as vinegar (Likens, 1979).

The effect of this acid rain is by now well-documented in Scandinavia. Jensen (1972) has shown that a gradual increase in acidity has eliminated the brown trout and salmon populations in many rivers and lakes in Southern Norway. Eggs and fingerlings of trout and salmon are most susceptible, so that recruitment stops entirely before kills of mature fish can be observed. Historical statistics on the best 79 salmon rivers show that outside the South, most are as productive as they were 80 years ago. But for example, nine rivers in the southernmost two counties produced 81,000 kg of salmon in 1885, 11,000 kg in 1925, but only 1,650 kg in 1968 (Jensen, 1972:224).

While the meteorological data and level of analysis in the U.S. lags behind that in Scandinavia, it is reported that the Northeastern U.S. (especially in the Adirondacks) is suffering a similar loss of fish populations (Wright, 1976; Likens, 1979).

Acid rain has become a cause of concern in the Rocky Mountain West because of the potential levels of sulfur emissions associated with development of western coal. At present there is no promise of a simple "technical fix" for sulfur emissions. A recent study by the Brookhaven National Lab (Morris, 1979) examined eight alternative coal-based ways of supplying the space and hot water needs of a hypothetical 1.1 million dwelling city for one year. The analysis included direct combustion of coal, synthetic gas, synthetic oil, and fluidized bed combustion. The sulfur dioxide emissions varied across technologies by a factor of 4:1; but even the best on sulfuric oxide grounds (Lurgi process synthetic gas) would result in emissions of

8,000 tons/year (Morris, 1979:659).
     Acid rain is only one highly visible example of the many impacts
of energy conversion on this planet's life-support system. The long
term solution is to reach an equilibrium between energy consumption
and local and regional renewable energy flows. For the underdeveloped countries, with per capita consumption already limited   to
renewables   at   near subsistence levels, this probably implies
population control. For the developed countries, what is needed   is
both a transition from fossil fuels and a reduction of per capita
energy consumption.
     Within the developed countries, the U.S.   stands out as an
energy over-consumer. With only 5% of the world population, we
account for one-third of both annual world oil and annual world total
energy consumption (Lovins, 1977). At least one view from outside
the U.S. is that the United States, "through extravagant patterns of
energy consumption and the withholding of domestic energy supplies,
more and more is identified as the world's number one energy problem"
(Noreng, 1979:325). The remainder of this paper will briefly outline
the potential in the United States for a transition from what Daly
calls our "geophysical capital consumption economy" to one based on
permanent solar income (Daly, 1979). A comprehensive survey of this
issue would entail a major study of alternative technologies, end
uses, and costs, such as the recent analysis by the Solar Energy
Research Institute (SERI, 1981). The approach here will be to
illustrate our aggregate potential for conservation and renewables by
examining energy use and policy in the Scandinavian countries.

ENERGY USE IN SCANDINAVIA

     Scandinavia is of particular interest for a comparative analysis
because in many ways it is more like the United States than any other
world region. Aside from ethnic ties and general cultural values,
there are parallels in terms of standard of living, population
density, climate, and composition of national output.   These basic
similarities make differences in energy use all the more striking.
As Schipper (1978) has noted, there are two main differences: what
is used and how much.
     The key fact is that Scandinavia is the most oil dependent area
in the world, with petroleum comprising about 65% of all energy
sources for the region. Except for Norway, all of this oil is
imported, and the Scandinavian economies are consequently very
vulnerable to supply disruption. By contrast, about 25% of U.S.
energy end use is dependent on imported oil. Within the Scandinavian
group, Denmark, Sweden, and Finland are the "have nots" with only
very modest domestic fuel resources (Schipper, 1978). Norway is the
best endowed, with the largest per capita hydro-electric base in the
world, in addition to recent discoveries of large North Sea oil
reserves. Iceland has geothermal resources. By comparison, the U.S.
is richly endowed with a wide variety of energy resources.
     The other major difference lies in how much energy is used.   As
illustrated in Figure 1, the U.S. consumes approximately twice as
much energy as Sweden, Denmark, Norway, and Finland but with about
the same or only slightly higher standard of living. This suggests

that high levels of energy consumption in the U.S. are not the inevitable consequence of a high standard of living and that the potential for conservation is much greater than it is generally thought to be.

Given the compelling environmental and national security-related reasons for cutting U.S. energy consumption, it is worthwhile to briefly focus on a U.S.-Sweden comparison.

FIGURE 1

Energy Consumption Per Unit of GNP

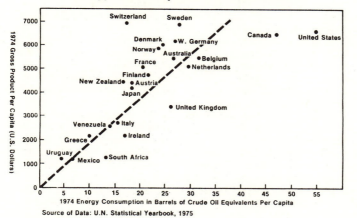

Source of Data: U.N. Statistical Yearbook, 1975

Source: Carter (1977)

U.S. AND SWEDISH ENERGY USE COMPARISON

Within Scandinavia, Sweden is the country that is the most like the U.S. As noted, Figure 1 indicates that Sweden uses about half as much energy per capita as the U.S. to maintain a comparable standard of living. The specific index in Figure 1 is per capita income. Schipper (1976) has undertaken a careful and exhaustive survey of other indexes of social well-being (such as doctors per 1,000 of population, live births, etc.) that generally indicates the average Swede is at least as well (if not better) off than the average American. Another major similarity is population density. The U.S. and Sweden are almost identical in this regard, with all the rest of Europe (and Asia) about five times as densely populated. The importance of population density is mainly for analysis of energy use in transportation. Within the U.S., for example, gasoline consumption per household varies from 864 gallons in densely populated New York to 2,222 gallons in Wyoming (Green, 1979:191). In addition to population density, the composition of Swedish national output is comparable in terms of the mix of energy intensive industries (whereas comparisons of the U.S. to the bank and watch economy of Switzerland on the one hand [see Figure 1] or steel-dominated Luxembourg on the other would be misleading).

Because of these similarities, the major differences in energy use between the two countries has to do with intensity of use and efficiency. For example, about 40% of the total per capita energy consumption difference between the two countries is in the transportation sector. We use passenger cars much more intensely (about 9,050 miles per capita U.S. versus 5,050 in Sweden) and our cars are much less efficient (13.7 miles per gallon versus 24.0)(derived Schipper, 1976:1003). The net result is we use about four times as much energy per capita for personal auto transportation. Part of the difference in intensity of automobile use is attributable to much greater reliance on railway and bus transportation in Sweden. The basic reason for our much lower mileage, however, is simple physics: our cars average 3,740 pounds in weight versus 2,420 for Sweden! While it may look like a move to the Stone Age to some, it is not inconceivable that we might be just as happy driving cars that weigh only one ton instead of two. In the process we could conserve substantial amounts of energy.

Schipper (1976) provides a similar very methodical analysis of every end-use of energy. Of particular interest is residential space heat. In a climate that is approximately twice as severe as our own (as measured by degree days of heating load), the Swedes heat their homes with 25% less energy per capita than in the U.S. (Schipper, 1976:1004). This is equivalent to heating a home in a Juneau, Alaska climate with less energy than it takes to heat a home in Seattle. Schipper has shown that this is almost entirely due to relative insulation levels (rather than average size of homes or the single family/multi-family mix). This was accomplished in Sweden by instituting higher building standards requiring greater insulation or "R" value in walls and ceilings.

INNOVATIONS IN ENERGY AND SHELTER

The discussion to this point has been limited to a comparison of aggregate historical statistics. The future potential for energy conservation and substitution is better indicated by examining innovations. By way of example (a similar analysis could be undertaken for any of the end-uses of energy), several Scandinavian innovations in energy and shelter will be briefly explored.

One general approach is to look for community rather than individual solutions. At present about 25% of Sweden's population participate in district heating systems which generally employ waste heat from thermal electric plants (Karkheck, 1977). Indeed, as early as 1971, 35% of Sweden's fuel-based electricity came from combined electric heat systems (Schipper, 1976:1007). The effect of utilizing "waste" heat in district heating is to raise the overall thermal efficiency of the fuel used in electric generating plants from about 35% for typical U.S. plants to 70% to 85% for Swedish plants (Lind,

1979:16). There are also associated environmental benefits: thermal pollution is avoided and lower overall air pollution levels are achieved. Hogstrum (1975) found that Swedish communities with a significant share of space heat from district heating stations had sulfur dioxide levels averaging one-half that of other communities of similar size.

Another community scale approach to space heat which Scandinavians have been pioneering is annual storage. The problem in Sweden (and in many parts of the United States) is the seasonal imbalance of load and solar flux: hot summer sun and freezing dark winters. The U.S. approach has been to oversize solar collector areas to better capture what winter sun is available. An alternative is to build such massive thermal storage that one can capture the summer warmth and have it last into winter. The cost of such massive storage can be overcome by building community-scale water storage ponds. A project is currently underway in Studsvik, Sweden with a 52 foot diameter and 20 foot deep pit (Margen, 1978:24). Solar collectors float on top of the pond all summer and heat the water, which is circulated to heat homes in the winter.

Another innovation, which has been around Norway for centuries (and is just being discovered in the U.S.) is earth sheltered homes, which include the torvtak (sod-roofed buildings) and gammes (A-frame structures with the peak exposed for light and ventilation). On the torvtak, Roger Hyde writes "A sloppy, leaking thin wood roof when covered with 4 to 5 inches of dirt and a healthy crop of grass becomes a model of strength and insulation" (Hyde, 1979:74). Hyde also has some interesting observations on the energetics of the Norwegian barn (hay/insulation above, cows below) and hillside farm.

The ultimate in current architectural experiments is to put these design concepts (thermal mass, solar energy, insulation, earth-sheltering) together in a 100% self-sufficient home. One of the early prototypes is the Zero Energy House, built in Lyngby, Denmark in 1973 (Besant, 1979). The main features of the building are very well insulated, double-stud walls and ceilings (15" and 11" of fiberglass or R52 and R39, respectively) and a large active solar system (Korsgaard, 1978). The overall heat loss is about 2.8 BTU per square foot of floor space per degree day (or about 30% of even the Swedish average heat loss for the early 70s reported by Schipper). The house is so tight and well insulated that about 10% of the annual heating load is met by the body heat of the people living in it.

Currently many of these design innovations are finding their way into the U.S. housing market. A contractor in Butte, Montana working with low-cost designs developed by the National Center for Appropriate Technology, is currently building houses that match the performance of the Danish Zero Energy House. The basic point here is that the technology is already available to attain substantial and cost-effective (Duffield, 1980) reductions in energy consumption for residential space heat.

130

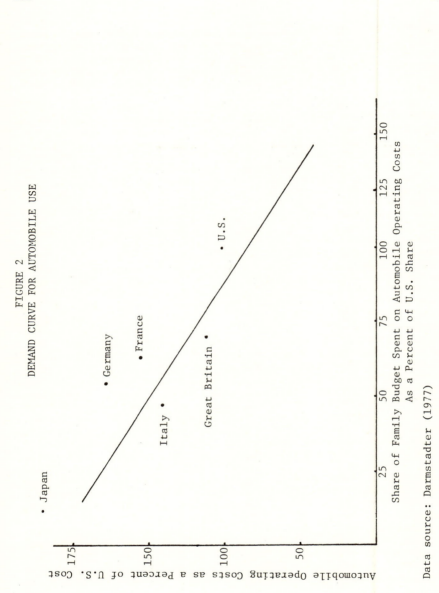

FIGURE 2

DEMAND CURVE FOR AUTOMOBILE USE

Share of Family Budget Spent on Automobile Operating Costs
As a Percent of U.S. Share

Data source: Darmstadter (1977)

SCANDINAVIAN ENERGY POLICY

All this raises an interesting question: Why are the Scandinavians (and perhaps the Swedes in particular) so innovative and energy efficient? One hypothesis might be that they are an enlightened and socially conscious group of people. However, as Darmstadter (1977) has shown, then, judging by per capita energy use, so are the Japanese, West Germans, etc. -- in fact just about every culture where energy prices are high! It is no surprise to economists to see a strong inverse correlation between average price and per capita consumption. Figure 2 is a crude illustration of such a relationship between prices and per capita consumption using observations from a number of developed countries. (The true price/ consumption relationship would need to be corrected for other effects such as income, and the price and availability of substitutes.) At the time that Schipper did his study in Sweden (in 1974) gasoline was $1.16 per gallon in Sweden, or almost triple the price of $.45 per gallon in the U.S. Based on the relationship indicated in Figure 2, prices probably go a long way toward explaining the U.S.-Swedish difference in overall energy use.

The preceding example emphasizes the importance of the market as an allocative device. We are of course now experiencing similar price effects on gasoline consumption in the U.S. The major difference in Sweden is, however, that very high energy prices have been in part the result of conscious government policy. For the $1.16 gas price in 1974, $.68 or two-thirds was a government tax (Schipper, 1976:1010). One need only think back to 1974 (or now) to imagine the political feasibility of tripling U.S. gas prices with a tax! In fact, we went the opposite direction with price controls, which had the effect of increasing our import dependence. Certainly part of the motivation for the much more aggressive Swedish policy is the greater dependence on foreign energy sources. Not only the Arab embargo of 1973-74, but the Suez crisis of 1956, had a major effect on the energy policies of Sweden and the other import dependent Scandinavian countries.

The Swedish gas tax is perhaps typical of the general focus of Scandinavian energy policy on energy end use, as opposed to the supply/production orientation of U.S. policy. The remainder of this section consists of an overview of Danish, Swedish, and Norwegian energy policy issues, with an eye toward gleaning some lessons for the U.S. and the Rocky Mountain West.

Perhaps the outstanding example of the use of government policy to alter energy use patterns is Denmark. The motivation is that this small country is more dependent on imports of energy than any other industrialized country. Only 2% of Denmark's energy requirements are met from domestic sources; the other 98% consists almost entirely of oil and a small amount of coal imported from Poland (Janssen, 1977:1). Typical of Danish regulations are the high registration fees the government imposes to discourage the use of large, gas-guzzling cars. According to Janssen (1977), to get a license plate Danes must pay a fee of 105% of the first $2,500 of a car's price and 180% of the remainder. At best, this is like getting one car for the price of two! In addition, there is a graduated tax on weight that is paid every six months; on large cars this tax can

exceed $400.   As a result, Janssen observes that "The message gets
through: even in sophisticated Copenhagen, people stare at an aging,
grey Buick, distinguished only by its bulk" (Janssen, 1977:16).
Danish policy on other end-uses is similarly restrictive;   for
example, a recent building code bans air conditioners in all new
houses. By comparison, one might recall the fate of former President
Carter's (much more modest) "gas guzzler" tax proposed for the U.S.

While controls of end-use are more typical in Scandinavia than
the U.S., there are also some interesting policy issues on the supply
side. A good example of this is the Swedish nuclear debate.   Since
the 1950s, motivated by its incredibly high imported oil dependence
(around 70%), Sweden has been pursuing the dream of the peaceful
atom.   In fact, it has the largest per capita civilian reactor
program in the world. In a country with literally no fossil fuels,
Sweden's low grade uranium ore deposits are much larger than the
combined reserves of Western Europe and perhaps constitute 15% of
world supply (Abrahamson, 1979:30).   The reactor program has been
almost entirely home-based, with the development of a unique Swedish
nuclear industry and technology. There was smooth sailing until the
nuclear debate moved to Sweden in the early 1970s.   While the
government's expectation was that more information would quiet fears,
in fact public discontent grew. In September 1976, the ruling Social
Democratic Party in Sweden's stable political system was voted out
for the first non-Socialist government in 44 years.   The new prime
minister's major platform had been an ethically-based opposition to
nuclear power. However, the nuclear debate has continued, with a
focus on waste storage.   The twists and turns of politics since
include the new prime minister resigning in September 1978 over the
approval of a new reactor, the minority liberal government approving
that reactor in a blatant sacrifice of scientific data to political
convenience, and--following the Three Mile Island accident--a call
for a national referendum on nuclear development.

The main differences between U.S. and Swedish nuclear policy
are: (a) the focus on storage of wastes as opposed to proliferation
or the threat of nuclear war; (b) the Swedish belief that citizens
must participate in the energy decisions, and not leave them to
technicians. Much of the literature on Sweden supports this basic
point.   After the crucial 1976 election that ended 44 years of rule
by the Socialists, the new government formed an energy commission to
formulate policy.   Realizing the resource imbalance in interested
parties, it has given about $42,000 to Friends of the Earth to
prepare its case and another $20,000 to a Swedish environmental
coalition (James, 1978). However, the sobering similarity to the
U.S. is the political muscle evidenced by the Swedish nuclear
industry.

Given the substantial political power of major energy suppliers
on both sides of the Atlantic, the lack of a domestic oil and gas
industry (and lobby) in Sweden makes the other arm of their energy
policy--conservation and solar--of particular interest. In an
important government study, Solar Sweden (Johansson and Steen, 1977),
the authors developed a future energy supply system for total
national self-sufficiency in about 35 years, even allowing for
doubling of output. An important feature of the supply projection is
that biomass conversion is expected to provide a very large

proportion (61%) of the total. Some of the biomass is forest waste, but about 80% is expected to come from a fast-growing species of willow and poplar in large energy plantations. The land use impact would be substantial, since such plantations would require about 2.9 million hectares or 6% to 7% of Sweden's land area. This is equivalent to the percent of the area in agriculture but substantially less than that occupied by pulp and paper forests (23 million hectares)(Johansson and Steen, 1978). Photovoltaic solar cells and windpower will provide for growth in electricity consumption beyond the current hydroelectric capacity. Approximately 70% of the spaceheating needs will be met by annual storage solar heating, with the remainder supplied by biomass. Direct solar will be about 21% of projected supplies in the year 2015, biomass 61%, and hydro and wind about 18%.

Solar Sweden is a concrete example of the "soft path" alternative described at a more general level by Amory Lovins (1971). It will be of great interest to follow the extent to which Sweden actually employs the solar alternative. The difference with the U.S. is again, that there is no substantial domestic fossil fuel industry (oil and coal) and lobby to dominate the energy policy debate. This is an obvious contrast to the U.S., where serious government support for a soft path approach is not being manifested.

NORWAY AND THE AMERICAN NORTHWEST

While we have been pursuing the analogy of Sweden and the U.S., there is perhaps an even stronger analogy between Norway and Montana and other states of the Northwest. The abundance of natural scenery, concern for the environment, and relatively low population densities are part of this. However, the main similarity is Norway's North Sea oil and Montana's coal fields. Exploitation of these energy resources raises additional policy issues.

Ultimate recoverable reserves in the North Sea are estimated to be at least 50 billion barrels (Eckbo, 1979:91). North Sea proven reserves (about 1/3 Norwegian and 2/3 British) are 13 billion barrels or 30% of all the world supply. By comparison, U.S. recoverable reserves are about 30 billion barrels. Importantly, in the political context, North Sea oil is 50% of the proven reserves for all of Europe (Eckbo, 1979). When oil drilling began in the North Sea in 1964, most observers were pessimistic; one U.S. petroleum geologist "offered to personally drink all oil found on the Norwegian Continental Shelf" (Morse, 1977). As yet there is still no exploration in the northern two-thirds of the Shelf; some estimates are that Norwegian ultimate reserves may be second only to those of Saudi Arabia and the U.S.S.R. This is pretty heady stuff for a small country of less than 4 million people. And as can be expected, as reserve estimates grow so does Western Europe's impatience for the imports.

In a similar way, the U.S. is eyeing the vast coal reserves of the Northern Great Plains. Montana alone has 24% of total U.S. deep and strippable coal, roughly 108 trillion tons and, more importantly, almost all of that is low sulfur coal constituting 50% of U.S. low sulfur coal reserves (Hibbard, 1979). Given the overwhelming

magnitude of these resources relative to the regional economies, both
Montana and Norway have been following a go-slow or conservationist
attitude.   This is evidenced in Norway by very limited leasing to
date and in Montana by a 35% coal tax (far higher than any other
state in the union)(Hibbard, 1979:159).   For both areas, a key
consideration includes the socioeconomics and environmental impact of
rapid development.
     Obviously, it is somewhat easier for Norway as an independent
nation to keep the world more or less at arm's length.   An
interesting political problem for them is balancing their interests
between OPEC and the West.   In many ways their interests are becoming
more akin to those of the OPEC nations, as symbolized by an OPEC
meeting in Oslo in 1978 (Noreng, 1979).   Further symbolic of this is
their refusal to accept full membership in the International Energy
Association (IEA), the consumer cartel formed by the U.S. in 1974 to
counter OPEC.   To date Norway has even resisted any formal agreement
with neighboring Sweden.   Hambraeus has noted:

> It (Norway) has a good bartering position toward Sweden and
> there are counter demands that Sweden provide either
> electricity from nuclear power stations, forest products,
> or industrial equipment in exchange for an agreement on oil
> imports...(Hambraeus, 1977:434).

The U.S. is in a somewhat similar situation vis-a-vis Mexico and
Canada, as has been recently pointed out by Oystein Noreng (1979).
With Mexico the bargaining issues may be immigration and industrial
exports.
     Another aspect of North Sea development is Norway's creation (in
1972) of Statoil, a state owned entity to refine, distribute, and
market Norway's petroleum products.   As yet there has been no
comprehensive assessment of this venture in the economics literature.
However, Morse (1977) in an article entitled "Second Decade for
Norwegian Oil -- Second Thoughts?", raises some of the standard
market organization issues of efficiency and political control.
There may be an interesting lesson here for U.S. energy policy,
where the approach in leasing and development of federal off-shore
oil and Montana coal is entirely market oriented.
     Another strong analogy between Montana and both Sweden and
Norway is the abundance of hydropower, and the associated
environmental conflicts.   Norway derives a world high 43% of its
total energy from hydroelectric generators, while for Sweden it is
20% (Schipper, 1978).   Norway is the only nation in the world whose
electric generation is near 100% hydro (Kober and Vinjar, 1978).
Montana is quite similar, with the Montana Power Company system being
79% hydro in 1975 (Duffield, 1977).   However, with the four
coal-fired Colstrip plants, hydro's share in Montana generation will
decline rapidly to about one-third by 1990.   At present, development
of new hydro sites in all three areas is constrained by environmental
impacts.   Presently in Montana one can observe the debate over the
Libby Reregulating Dam and the Corps of Engineers studies on the
Flathead River.

Hydroelectric development in any area often entails the loss of important agricultural, wildlife, historical and scenic resources. For example, the Northern Lights rural electric coop has an application currently pending for a hydro development at the unique Kootenai Falls site in Northwest Montana.   Similarly for Sweden Hambraeus observes:

> The conflict between hydroelectric exploitation and the preservation of unspoiled nature is long-standing in Sweden (Hambraeus, 1979:436).

In fact, both Sweden and Norway (Kober, 1978) have recently reserved from development 10 to 15% of their total potential hydro capacity. However, new developments are still going forward. In May 1979 the Norwegian parliament authorized the construction of a 400 foot dam on the Alta River (Europe's richest salmon river) at Savtso, the largest canyon in northern Europe (Brown, 1981:12). The nineteen mile long reservoir would flood the village of Masi, the largest original remaining Lapp community. The development would also impact reindeer calving and migration, destroy agricultural lands, and   reduce fisheries.   All of these are crucial to the traditional nomadic life of the Lapps.   In July 1979 and again in January 1981, more than 15,000 people demonstrated at construction sites to halt the development (Brown, 1981:12). After police action against the demonstrators, hunger strikes and international pressure, construction was halted in March 1981 for a high court review of the issue. While not on the same scale, the Kootenai Falls project in Montana is encountering similar resistance from both environmentalists and native people.   Pat Lefthand of the Kootenai Tribe has said that a Kootenai Falls dam would impact the spiritual life of the tribe: "We didn't pick the site.   The spirits picked the site for us. The Supreme Being does not guarantee an alternative site" (Dudko, 1980:1).

As a generalization, in both Montana and Norway, the response to projected energy shortages is basically to augment existing energy sources rather than promote conservation or the development of alternative renewable sources.   The extent of public resistance to any of these is a measure of unevaluated environmental and cultural costs.   As we push into increasingly costly and marginal sites for all these sources, the basic underlying phenomenon being encountered is the finite nature of both geological and renewable energy flows. It appears that the time has come for a shift in emphasis to demand-side policy (conservation) and exploration of other renewable technologies.

CONCLUSION

Having pulled together this somewhat eclectic survey of energy and environment in Scandinavia, what are the basic lessons for the U.S.? The key theme is that the Scandinavian countries are beset by energy and environmental problems that are very similar to ours but in general more extreme, either in extent or timing. In a way, these nations seem to be a bellwether for us, and chart a course through

the coming scarcity that we may well have to follow. The major U.S.
energy problem at present is certainly import dependence. However,
our dependence is minor compared to that faced by Denmark or Sweden.
These countries provide a good example of what strong government
policies (working in part through the market) can accomplish.   A
basic conclusion is that we should be optimistic about the technical
feasibility of conservation and the use of renewables.

On the environmental side, however, the message is somewhat more
pessimistic.   First, the impact of acid raid in Norway is a
frightening example of the global nature of pollution and of man's
ability to wipe out entire biotic communities.   Secondly, the
political conflicts between preservation of the natural world and
economic development, exemplified by nuclear waste storage in Sweden
and hydro-development in Norway, are just as present and real as in
the U.S.   Their resolution appears to be handled with more debate,
but with no less a power struggle or absence of grace than in the
U.S.

Much of what we can learn here is due to the Scandinavian states
being sovereign nations.   Their problems differ and so will their
solutions.   This diversity and independence provides us with
experiences and evidence that are missing in the more or less
homogeneous United States. For example, the Norwegian experiment
with Statoil should be of considerable interest to the Western
coal-producing states. Similarly, discovering the full potential of
solar energy and other renewables may require both the incentive of
very high import dependence and the lack of a domestic fossil fuel
lobby.   If current U.S.   energy policy is any indication, we will
have to look abroad for a serious exploration of a long-term energy
solution.

                                   FOOTNOTES

[1] Quoted in the <u>Scandinavian Review</u>, Vol.   66, No.   3 (Sept.
1978), page 68.

137

BIBLIOGRAPHY

Abrahamson, Dean. "Sweden Debates the Peaceful Atom." The Bulletin of the Atomic Scientists 35, 9 (November, 1979).
Besant, Robert, and Dumont, R. S. "Comparison of 100 Percent Solar Heated Residences Using Active Solar Collection Systems." Solar Energy 22, 5 (1979):451-454.
Brown, Tony. "Scandinavian Natives Fight for Their Homeland." Not Man Apart II, 6 (June, 1981):12-13.
Carter, J. "Origins of the U.S. Energy Problems." The National Energy Plan. Washington, D.C.: U. S. Government Printing Office, 29 April 1977, 1-23.
Daly, Herman E. "On Thinking About Future Energy Requirements." In Supporting Paper 5, Sociopolitical Effects of Energy Use and Policy, a Study of Nuclear and Alternative Energy Systems. Washington, D.C. National Academy of Sciences, 1979.
Darmstadter, Joel. How Industrial Societies Use Energy: A Comparative Analysis. Baltimore: Johns Hopkins Press, 1977.
Dorfman, R. Environmental Economics, 2nd Edition. New York: Norton, 1977.
Dudko, Robert. "Packed House Discusses Kootenai Falls Project." Missoulian 107, 78 (July 30, 1980):1-2.
Duffield, John. "Future Prices of Electricity in Montana." Montana Energy Advisory Council, 1977.
Duffield, John. "Passive Solar Economics and Ethics." Proceedings of the Fifth National Passive Solar Conference (American Section of the International Solar Energy Society), 1980.
Eckbo, Paul L. "Perspectives on North Sea Oil." Annual Review of Energy 4 (1979):71-98.
Franklin, Benjamin. An Account of the New Invented Pennsylvania Fireplaces. Philadephia, 1974.
Greene, David L. "State Differences in the Demand for Gasoline: An Econometric Analysis." Energy Systems and Policy 3, 2 (1979):191-212.
Hambraeus, Gunnar and Stillesjo, Stattan. "Perspectives on Energy in Sweden." Annual Review of Energy 2 (1977):417-453.
Hibbard, W. R. "Policies and Constraints for Major Expansion of U.S. Coal Production and Utilization." Annual Review of Energy 4 (1979):147-173.
Hogstrum, Ulf. "District Heating: Air Pollution in Swedish Communities." Ambio 4, 3 (1975):120-25.
Hyde, Roger. "Going Underground in Arctic Norway." The Co-Evolution Quarterly (Summer, 1979):70-77.
James, Peter. "Energy Planning in Sweden." Town and Country Planning 46 (1978):263-265.
Janssen, Richard F. "Whittling Waste: Denmark Shows How Frugality, Invention, Can Cut Energy Use." The Wall Street Journal 57, 249 (October 4, 1977):1, 16.

Jensen, K. W. and Snekvik, E. "Low pH Valves Wipe Out Salmon and Trout Populations in Southern-most Norway." Ambio 1, 6 (Dec. 1972):223-225.

Johansson, Thomas B. and Steen, Peter. Solar Sweden. Stockholm: Secretariat for Futures Studies, 1977.

Joskow, Paul. "America's Many Energy Futures - a Review of Energy Future, Energy: the Next Twenty Years, and Energy in America's Future." Bell Journal of Economics II, 1 (1980):377-398.

Karkheck, J. et al. "Prospects for district heating in the United States." Science 195 (March 11, 1977):948-55.

Kober, Kjell and Vinjar, Asbjorn. "Cascades to Kilowatts." Scandinavian Review 66, 3 (Sept. 78):36-39.

Korsgaard, Vagn. "The Zero Energy House." Scandinavian Review, 66, 3 (1978):21-24.

Laurmann, J. A. "Market Penetration Characteristics for Energy Production and Atmospheric Carbon Dioxide Growth." Science 205 (31 August 1919):896-898.

Likens, Gene E. et al. "Acid Rain." Scientific American 4 (October 1979):43-51.

Lind, C. E. "District Heating in Sweden, 1972-1977." Energy Policy 7, 1 (1979):74-76.

Lockeretz, William. Agriculture and Energy. New York: Academic Press, 1977.

Lovins, Amory. Soft Energy Paths. Cambridge: Ballinger, 1977.

Margen, Peter. "A Central System for Annual Solar Heat." Solar Age 3, 10 (1978):22-26.

Morris, S. C. et al. "Coal Conversion Technologies: Some Health and Environmental Effects." Science 206 (9 Nov. 1979):654-662.

Morse, Randy G. "Second Decade for Norwegian Oil - Second Thoughts?" Scandinavian Review 65, 1 (1977):24-31.

Noreng, Oystein. "Friends or Fellow Travelers? The Relationship of Non-OPEC Exporters with OPEC." Journal of Energy and Development 4, 2 (Spring, 1979):313-335.

Schipper, Lee. "Lessons from Scandinavia." Scandinavian Review 66, 3 (September, 1978):7-16.

Schipper, Lee and Lichtenberg, Allan J. "Efficient Energy Use and Well-Being: The Swedish Example." Science 194, 4269 (1976):1001-1013.

Solar Energy Research Institute. Report on Building a Sustainable Future. Washington, D. C.: U. S. House of Representatives, Committee on Energy and Commerce, Committee Print 97-K, 97th Congress, 1st Session, April, 1981.

Stobaugh, Robert and Yergin, Daniel. Energy Future. New York: Ballantine Books, 1979.

Wright, Richard and Gjessing, Egil T. "Acid Precipitation: Changes in the Chemical Composition of Lakes." Ambio 5, 5-6 (1976):219-223.

10
International Environmental Protection at the Regional Level: Western and Eastern Europe

Forest L. Grieves

INTRODUCTION

Since the "Age of Environmental Concern" burst upon the world a scant decade ago--if the modern wave of environmental crisis literature and the landmark 1972 United Nations Conference on the Human Environment may be regarded as initial milestones in this new "Age"--the nation-states have been groping for the technical and organizational means for managing the environment. In spite of the modern wave of concern for environmental degradation (a concern which many environmentalists fear has already begun to wane), serious observers of environmental affairs are well aware that environmental problems as well as concern for solving them have been developing for some time. Although "the Environment" appears to be an "overnight" issue, it in fact is not. Successful management of the human environment will not be accomplished overnight either.

The 1972 United Nations Conference on the Human Environment itself rapidly demonstrated the "reality" of the problems involved in international management. The Swedish Ambassador to the United Nations who proposed an international conference on the environment and conveyed his government's willingness to host the conference in Stockholm, concluded his remarks on the environmental threat to mankind by saying: "There are many issues on which the members of the United Nations are divided. On the issue now before the General Assembly we are hopefully all united" (S. Johnson, 1972:742). When the Conference subsequently convened in Stockholm, its slogan of "Only One Earth" did not obscure the fact that nearly 150 United Nations members were decidedly disunited, not only concerning the scope of environmental problems but also about what to do to solve them. Although the "environment" achieved recognition as an "issue" at Stockholm, its salience has been clearly circumscribed by the competition of widely-differing national ideologies, economic systems and foreign policies.

Alternative forms of environmental management are certainly needed. If universal efforts at environmental protection are hampered within the United Nations, are the prospects at the regional level perhaps more promising, especially given the features of geographical compactness, the smaller number of states involved, and the presumed more intimate understanding of shared local problems?

This study briefly reviews the current environmental regulatory efforts of six European regional organizations in western and eastern Europe: the European Communities, the North Atlantic Treaty Organization, the Council of Europe, the Organization for Economic Cooperation and Development, the United National Economic Commission for Europe and the Council for Mutual Economic Assistance. The purpose of examining the work of these six organizations is to assess the value of regionalism as an approach to international environmental protection. The European regional situation is an interesting test of the ability of nation-states to manage their natural environments. At least three interrelated features of the European region solicit the scholar's interest.

First, while environmental management is first and foremost a national issue, it has obvious international dimensions. Europe as a continent represents a concentration of the world's great industrial nations (who are also the great polluters) with a complex pattern of transnational environmental problems. These countries are a major portion of George Kennan's "club" of advanced, industrialized states with the resources and technology to reverse and control the environmental degradation they caused (Kennan, 1970:401-413).

Second, Europe's compactness and rich history of spawning various international organizations would appear to set the stage for regional environmental management. In a world in which regional organizations now account for over 2/3 of the nearly 300 existing intergovernmental organizations, one study notes that most international environmental problems occur at the regional level (Bishop and Munro, 1972:348), while another, assessing post-Stockholm institutional change, concludes:

> On no aspect of the debate on future international institutional arrangements has there been such widespread agreement as that the great bulk of intergovernmental cooperation to deal with environmental problems must occur at the regional level (B. Johnson, 1972:283).

Third, while a regional environmental approach in Europe avoided two of the divisive factors that were present at the UN's Stockholm Conference (North/South politics and the "abstractness" of universalism), it focuses directly on a third—the ideological division that splits not only eastern and western Europe, but in a larger sense also the world.

With the qualification of certain supranational aspects within the European Communities, all of the six European organizations are intergovernmental, meaning that unanimity is a usual requirement for agreement among sovereign, independent, equal nation-states. In such situations the lowest common denominator of agreement generally prevails. If Europe can't cooperate, with all that they seem to have in common, what future prospects are there for international environmental protection?

EUROPE'S ENVIRONMENT

     In spite of its romantic image, Europe is badly polluted. By
way of example, one estimate of West German air pollution places
total yearly emissions at 4 million tons of sulfur dioxide, 8 million
tons of carbon monoxide, 2 million tons of hydrocarbons, 4 million
tons of dust particles, plus a host of other pollutants (Beinhauer,
1978:89). Some 450 million cubic yards of refuse are produced
annually in West Germany which, if spread evenly, would cover this
Oregon-size country with a 5.5 inch layer of garbage. If piled in
one place this yearly garbage would produce a mountain the height of
the Zugspitze (9,718 ft.), Germany's highest mountain (Tatsachen uber
Deutschland, 1978:257). And figures circulated by the German
Government in 1978 produced the conclusion that the "pollution of the
Rhine, from which 8 million inhabitants of the Federal Republic and
the Netherlands obtain their drinking water, is 20 times higher than
in 1949" (Tatsachen uber Deutschland, 1978:253).
     West Germany's internal environmental situation appears in one
form or another all over Europe, but West Germany's situation also
dramatizes the transnational dimensions of European pollution problems. The Rhine receives pollutants from the chemical industry in
Basel (Switzerland), from potash mines in Alsace (France) and from
various sources in Luxembourg and in Lorraine (France) via the Saar,
Moselle and Sauer rivers. Pollution from East Germany (salts and
other poorly degradable substances from the mining industry in
Thuringia) enters West Germany via the Ulster, Werra and Elbe rivers.
This kind of transfrontier pollution tends to be passed on. The Elbe
River, for example, empties into the North Sea. The West German
National Fisheries Institute in Hamburg, reporting on sick fish they
had found in the North Sea with rotting fins and numerous tumors,
noted that much of the lower Elbe was already dead, with the German
Bight and North Sea not far behind (German Tribune, 1980:8).
     Eastern Europe and the Soviet Union are no exception to the
apparently universal rule that economic and industrial development
produce pollution. Russian scientists, for example, noted in the
1930s a decreased growth rate in Moscow's trees and attributed it to
the widespread pollution that began with the first Five-Year Plan.
By the 1940s there was evidence of the withering of local pines in
the Moscow area.
     Industrial pollution has had a heavy impact in such widespread
areas as the Ural Mountains, Polish Silesia, Czech Sudentenland, the
Angara-Baikal area in Siberia and East Germany's Saxony. Air
pollution is corroding historic buildings in the beautiful city of
Prague. The city of Leningrad, situated in a swampy area of northern
Russia between the Gulf of Finland and the large expanse of Lake
Ladoga, hardly boasts one of the world's better climates under the
best of circumstances. The heavy, low-hanging clouds common to this
heavily industrialized area trap all manner of airborne pollutants.
Residents suffer from a high rate of respiratory ailments, headaches,
nausea, dizziness, eye irritation, and disturbances of the central
nervous system.
     The water systems also suffer from pollution. The Danube,
Volga, Dnieper and Don rivers have been damaged, as have a host of
lesser known waterways. The Baltic and Black Seas are badly polluted

in various respects, while damage to the Caspian Sea has endangered
the favorite Russian delicacy--caviar. Heavy agricultural withdraw-
als of water have also had an impact. With the present rate of water
loss, it has been estimated that the Aral Sea will be a dry salt
marsh by the year 2000. Known world-wide for its depth and pure
water, the Soviet Union's Lake Baikal has been threatened by the
lumbering industry and pulp mills (Grieves, 1978:25-30). The
dimensions of environmental problems in Europe leave little doubt as
to the potential importance of international cooperation, and the
regional organizations represent perhaps the most important immediate
framework for that cooperation.

EUROPEAN COMMUNITIES

Three European communities are potential vehicles for regional
environmental cooperation. The European Coal and Steel Community
(ECSC), the European Economic Community (EEC), and the European
Atomic Energy Community (EURATOM) were created by separate treaties,
each conveying supranatural powers within specified limits to new
international institutions representing a common western European
political and economic future.[1] A merger treaty in 1967 produced
common European Community (EC) institutions--a Council of Ministers,
a Commission, a Court of Justice, and a European Parliament.[2]
Institutional interaction, within the context of the treaties, may
result in binding directives issued to the ten western European
member states.[3]
Europe's pollution problems are now well known. Newspaper
articles describing the still beautiful Rhine River as an "800-Mile-
Long International Sewer" are common examples of an environmental
awareness that did not exist at the time the European Communities
were being launched. And since their creation predates these
concerns, the Community treaties provide only a vague basis for
dealing with environmental problems as they are perceived today.
Nevertheless, the Communities are under pressure to deal with
environmental problems, not only because of the real threat environmental decay poses for a decent human existence on the planet, but
because of the threat to the organizational purpose of the
Communities themselves, namely economic integration (other EC
problems are discussed in Ungerer, 1981:107-120). Individual nations
within the Communities will ultimately have to evolve their own
environmental standards (a process that is already underway) if
Community-wide standards cannot be produced. A common market area
based upon free economic competition could be seriously distorted by
differing national environmental requirements restricting access to
national markets.
The three Communities are not without legal authority to act in
the environmental area, although that authority is widely scattered
and in part only obliquely supported by treaty text. A great deal
depends on the _political_ commitment to interpret, develop, and use
whatever mandate can be deduced from the treaties.
The EURATOM Treaty devotes a whole chapter (Ch. III, Arts.
30-39) to the protection of worker and public health from radiation
danger, and the Commission is given a role in the formulation of

"basic standards" of radiation protection. These standards become binding upon the ten Community members upon final approval by the Council of Ministers. An unusual feature of EURATOM is its ability to penetrate some areas of national domestic jurisdiction. It has, for example, a right of access to national atomic installations to examine the national monitoring devices which Member States are required to operate. Although EURATOM has been criticized for internal red tape and slowness in keeping up with nuclear developments, its "environmental" mandate is perhaps the most explicit of the three treaties (Dickstein, 1974:444). Under the European Coal and Steel Community Treaty, Article 55 obliges the Community to encourage research concerning coal and steel, as well as workers' safety in these industries. There is, however, no reference to the management of the natural environment.

The European Economic Community Treaty, in spite of a lack of explicit concern for environmental affairs similar to that of the other two treaties, seems nevertheless to have provided the most far-reaching basis upon which to build Community environmental policy. In July 1971, the Commission first proposed that the Council of Ministers fill the lacunae in the Treaty regarding Community environmental authority by adopting a comprehensive environmental management program. As a basis for Community action, Articles 2, 100 and 235 of the EEC Treaty were cited.

Article 2 of the EEC Treaty gives the Community general responsibility for such areas as promoting a harmonious development of economic activities and raising the standard of living. Article 100 (Articles 101 and 102 are also relevant here) gives the Community a structured role in issuing directives to reduce dissimilarities in national legislative and administrative provisions affecting the operation of the Common Market, the intent of which is to prevent trade distortions due to differing national laws (e.g., national environmental laws). Article 23 provides for Community action to achieve one of the objectives of the Community in cases where the Treaty has not provided a mandate. This latter article was never intended to be an open grant of power to the Community and has been applied restrictively in past practice.[4]

Amending the three Community treaties to provide a clear and comprehensive mandate for Community action in the environmental area is a logical and necessary step advocated regularly by observers of European environmental politics.[5] The political will seems present for the time being, however, to proceed on the basis of current authority perceived in the treaties. Following responses to its initial proposal on the environment, the Commission adopted and submitted to the Council the Community Programme Concerning the Environment. The Commission noted in summary:

> The protection and improvement of the environment are therefore already included in the Communities' tasks. They are explicitly or implicitly included in their aims.... The Commission will give greater attention to the aspects of protection and improvement of the environment in implementation of the provisions of the Treaties and will endeavor to ensure that the preparation of its proposals in

the various fields is accompanied by an assessment of the
consequences of the envisaged or proposed measures on the
quality of life (Bulletin, 1972:16).

The Community and its organs have undertaken an ambitious
environmental program in the First and Second Action Programmes on
the Environment, stressed a "polluter pays" principle, and put forth
an impressive number of regulations, directives, recommendations, and
resolutions concerning pollution control, environmental improvement,
and international actions by the Community. Nevertheless, the
national "political will" that supports the Community environmental
effort, while commendable, is still modest, and the Community's
environmental effort would clearly be enhanced by the solidification
of that "will" in new treaty text. Failure to solidify the "will"
can only raise doubts about the "will" itself.

Two Community actions of interest have been the continuing
efforts to express the Community's environmental viewpoints within
other international organizations with environmental programs (such
as the UN's Environmental Programme), and the halting efforts to
establish formal relations with Eastern Europe's Council for Mutual
Economic Assistance.

NATO

None of the other European regional organizations possess quite
the institutional muscle of the European Communities, but that fact
has hardly slackened at least their formal attention to environmental
matters. The North Atlantic Treaty Organization (NATO) has attracted
critical scrutiny and sparked controversy by its organizational entry
into the environmental field in 1969.[6]

President Richard Nixon proposed on April 10, 1969, that NATO
"explore ways in which the experience and resources of the Western
nations could most effectively be marshalled toward the quality of
life of our peoples" (Remarks, 1969:5). He also noted that "the
industrial nations share no challenge more urgent than that of
bringing 20th century man and his environment to terms with one
another—of making the world fit for man, and helping man learn how
to remain in harmony with his rapidly changing world" (Remarks,
1969:7).

The Nixon initiative resulted in the creation by the NATO
Foreign Ministers of the Committee on the Challenges of Modern
Society (CCMS), which is responsible for examining ways to improve
the environment of NATO states. NATO's environmental role has been
called its "Third Dimension," adding to the alliance's military and
political functions (Huntley, 1971:6-7). Article 2 of the North
Atlantic Treaty, however, already gives the alliance a broad mandate
for civil cooperation:

The Parties will contribute toward the further development of peaceful and friendly international relations by
strengthening their free institutions, by bringing about a
better understanding of the principles upon which these
institutions are founded, and by promoting conditions of

stability and well-being. They will seek to eliminate conflict in their international economic policies and will encourage economic collaboration between any or all of them.

The North Atlantic Council, NATO'S governing body, created a Committee of Three on Non-Military Cooperation in May of 1956. The recommendations of that Committee resulted in the creation of a number of specialized committees and the undertaking of new programs in cultural, economic, scientific and other areas of "non-military" cooperation. NATO'S environmental "Third Dimension" would seem to be a natural extension of this kind of activity.

CCMS is charged to pay due regard to the aims of the NATO alliance and is not to undertake executive action or engage in research itself. Rather, its concern is to stimulate action by member states via two basic concepts. First is the idea of the pilot country, which involves a country (possibly in association with others) taking responsibility for the study of a particular environmental problem. The pilot country plans, pays for, reports on, and tries to implement the results of its study. Second, it is hoped these efforts will result in the formulation of government policy and legislation. This hope rests in large measure on the fact that a NATO pilot country has put its prestige and resources on the line before its allies in seeking a solution to an environmental problem of presumably both national and international interest and relevance. To date there have been pilot studies in such areas as coastal water and air pollution, disposal of hazardous substances, transportation issues, health care, disaster assistance, and energy (see United States Environmental Protection Agency, 1979 and Von Ward et al., 1979:12-17 and 1980:17-19).

Critics have been skeptical of NATO's environmental role on several grounds. For example, in spite of the mandate of Article 2 of the North Atlantic Treaty, NATO is still primarily a military alliance. That feature carries with it at least three implications: (a) the NATO countries are linked by politico-military considerations and do not always share common environmental problems; (b) while NATO stands in a position of rivalry with the Warsaw Pact, member countries of both alliances do share such problems and (c) the European neutrals and other nonmembers with an environmental stake in the region represented by NATO would appear to be generally excluded from participation in its activities. This is so although over 20 nations worldwide, including Sweden and the Soviet Union, have participated in one form or another in the pilot studies; see Von Ward et al., 1980:18.

Another area of skepticism regarding NATO's environmental role concerns the feeling in some quarters that the new undertaking represents an American ploy to revitalize NATO and reassert sagging American leadership in the Western alliance. While American support has been strong, the European response to NATO's new role has often been tepid.

One observer suggests that NATO's specific environmental mission is unclear, posing the obvious problem of overlap with other organizations. Perhaps more significant, however, is his interesting observation that there is no special NATO mandate to investigate the environmental effects of the military. In that regard, he writes:

> No other organization in the world treats this issue,
> and no other organization is better suited to investigate
> it. NATO is the world's largest military block and NATO
> countries border on three oceans and possess territories
> with environments ranging from arctic to tropical.   The
> alliance has an unparalleled opportunity to study such
> problems as the environmental impact of military exercises
> and installations, the disposal of ship- and shore-genera-
> ted military wastes, and the pollution caused by military
> aircraft.   Yet, today, NATO does not even require its
> contractors to put out environmental impact statements
> (Kyba, 1974:260).

Whatever problems may be apparent in NATO's emergence as a
vehicle for environmental activity, the alliance also possesses
certain strengths. For one thing, the organization appears able (in
spite of the unanimity rule that typifies intergovernmental organizations) to stimulate at least some action on the environmental front.
If one accepts the view that environmental management is an urgent
matter, then perhaps the specific forum for action is not as
immediately crucial as the action itself.   As one writer notes:
"Governments such as the United States which perceive this urgency
should perhaps act where they are most accustomed to find compliance,
in this case through a regional security pact" (Doran, 1973:669).

This "action" issue has also been addressed by Russell Train,
former Administrator of the U.S. Environmental Protection Agency and
U.S. Representative to NATO's Committee on the Challenges of Modern
Society.   He feels in general that international organizations
dealing with the environment have not been properly integrated with
domestic policy-making processes and that while such organizations
have been effective in facilitating the exchange of technical
information, domestic policymakers have been too busy with national
matters to devote time to documents circulated by international
organizations (Train, 1974:168).

NATO emerges, Train argues, as a strong agent for linking
national and international policy, particularly given the tradition
of scientific and other cooperation developed under Article 2 of the
North Atlantic Treaty. He notes further:

> But this spirit of cooperation among the Atlantic
> Community nations is not the only positive attribute of
> NATO. NATO has certain other specific characteristics not
> found in most international organizations: (1) it is
> action oriented and geared to rapid results; (2) it is the
> political expression of the most vital ties between Europe
> and North America; (3) it is thus able to command the
> attention and response of governments at a high level
> (Train, 1974:171).

Few would claim that NATO has not been effective in stimulating
national action concerning environmental problems. The pilot country
technique seems generally to be eliciting a favorable response from

observers and has even served in a modest way to reinvolve France, NATO's perennial reluctant ally, in the work of the organization. The basic issue, however, of whether or not NATO is the most appropriate organization for an environmental undertaking continues to be a matter of dispute.

COUNCIL OF EUROPE

The Council of Europe is Western Europe's most broadly based political assembly--going beyond the customs union of the three European Communities yet without the military implications of NATO.[7] It is a quasi-parliamentary organization devoted to encouraging political, economic, and social cooperation among its members, and it has been a consistent symbol of the notion of "European" unity. The Council has no supranational power; rather, it has been primarily a forum for political discussion. The Council may make recommendations to member governments. During the nearly 30 years of its existence, the Council has submitted an impressive number of draft conventions (covering such areas as patents, social security, university admissions, human rights, extradition, and peaceful settlement of disputes) to member governments for ratification--many of which have been approved.

According to Sten Renborg, the Council of Europe's Director of Environmental and Local Authorities, the Council has been concerned in a general way with problems of man's adaptation to his environment since the organization's creation in 1949 (Renborg, 1973:42). It was not until 1961, however, that the Council's Consultative Assembly recommended "... that a permanent system of co-operation in the sphere of nature conservation in Europe be set up in the Council of Europe" (European Committee, 1974:1). As a result of that recommendation a committee of experts was established in December, 1962, which is now called the European Committee for the Conservation of Nature and Natural Resources.

Initial environmental emphasis by this new Committee was placed on wildlife and landscape protection, but by the mid-1960s its concerns became more diverse as the world became more aware of the broader dimensions of environmental problems. The activity of the European Committee falls into four general areas: (1) conservation of nature and natural resources; (2) water problems; (3) air pollution; and (4) ministerial conferences.

The European Committee's work in the conservation area has concerned the protection of nature parks, reserves, and highly sensitive natural environments; the study of flora, fauna, and pesticides; and information, education, and training programs intended to influence public opinion. A highpoint in the public opinion campaign was the proclamation by the Council of Europe of 1970 as "European Conservation Year" (ECY), inaugurated by a European Conference of representatives of all associations concerned in one way or another with the environment.

In the area of water problems, the European Committee has conducted a series of studies and made recommendations to the Committee of Ministers of the Council of Europe concerning water pollution and general water management. Similar activities have been

undertaken regarding national and transfrontier air pollution.   Part
of the public information and education work of the European
Committee has been to urge the convening of a European ministerial
conference as well as to stimulate other international environmental
meetings. One notable result was the convening of the first European
Ministerial Conference on the Environment in Vienna from March 28 to
30, 1973.

The Council of Europe is a forum that brings together national
government leaders, parliamentarians and representatives of local
government in Europe. The prestige derived from its membership, the
exchange of ideas at the intergovernmental level, and the ability to
make recommendations and publicize ideas all enhance the Council's
potential as a vehicle for environmental management. On the other
hand, the Council has no direct authority in the environmental or any
other area. Referring to the European Water Charter (1968) and the
Declaration of Principles of Air Pollution Control (1968), two
results of Council of Europe activity, Sten Renborg notes: "While
these two texts do not commit governments to taking specific
measures, they do represent a consensus on the broad policies to be
pursued by them" (Renborg, 1973:45).

All of the European regional organizations appear to be groping
for a suitable environmental role. At the 1973 European Ministerial
Conference on the Environment, for example, some national delegations
felt that the Council of Europe at most should be concerned with
nature conservation. In their view, questions regarding industry and
society—questions with economic and technical implications—would be
more appropriately handled by the European Communities or OECD
(Parliamentary Assembly, 1975:23). At the close of that Conferrence,
however, the Ministers expressed satisfaction with the Council's
contributions to environmental policy in Europe, confirmed their
resolve to support the UN Action Plan for the Human Environment, and
recommended that the Council of Europe encourage exchanges of
information to avoid duplication of work and attempt to define
individual rights and responsibilities regarding Europe's environment
(Parliamentary Assembly, 1975:23-24).

OECD

The Organization for Economic Cooperation and Development (OECD)
is a regional economic organization established in 1961 to replace
the Organization for European Economic Cooperation (OEEC), which had
been created in 1948 to coordinate common action among Marshall Plan
recipient countries recovering from World War II. OECD is primarily
concerned with the promotion of free trade and economic growth among
23 nations of the industrialized West, as well as coordinating
Western aid to the developing countries.[8]

The basic organ of OECD is a Council, composed of all the Member
States, which is served by a Secretary-General and his staff. Under
Article 5 of the OECD Convention the Organization may (a) make
decisions binding upon the Members, (b) make recommendations to
Members, and (c) enter into agreements with Members, nonmember
states, and international organizations.[9] Article 6, however, makes
it clear that no Member can be bound without its consent, although

decisions may apply provisionally to Members who do accept them.

Several specialized committees have been established to serve the Organization, one of which is the Environment Committee set up in 1970. According to Hilliard Roderick, the Director of the OECD Environment Directorate, "the object of the Committee and the Directorate of the international secretariat that serves it is to help Governments make decisions on environmental policy" (Roderick, 1973:75).

The Environment Committee's mandate gives it responsibility in four general areas for:

1. investigating the problems of preserving or improving man's environment, with particular reference to their economic and trade implications;
2. reviewing and confronting actions taken or proposed in Member countries in the field of environment together with their economic and trade implications;
3. proposing solutions for environmental problems that would as far as possible take account of all relevant factors including cost effectiveness;
4. ensuring that the results of environmental investigations can be effectively utilized in the wider framework of the Organization's work on economic policy and social development (Roderick, 1973:75).

On May 26, 1972, the OECD Council (meeting at the Ministerial level) adopted several guiding principles for environmental policy. They accepted the "polluter pays" principle followed by the European Communities and attempted to establish guidelines regarding environmental standards.[10] Other guiding principles treated nondiscrimination between imports and domestic products as well as the establishment of common procedures for checking whether products conform to environmental standards.

The OECD would appear to be a most promising forum for regional environmental cooperation. It includes all of the prominent states of the industrialized West, which engage additionally in a high level of economic interaction. OECD includes all of the NATO members as well as all of the members of the European Communities. The Commission of the European Communities is even represented at the OECD by a Permanent Delegation which attends meetings and takes part in the work of the Organization.[11]

On the other hand, OECD remains an intergovernmental organization. Its ability to cooperate is perhaps diluted both by its large and geographically dispersed membership as well as by the fact that the economic foundations of the Organization do not necessarily support political agreement. This latter point was prominently displayed at the time of the 1973-74 oil embargo by the Organization of Petroleum Exporting Countries (OPEC).

The industrialized OECD countries were highly vulnerable to OPEC "petroleum diplomacy." Although OECD had been active for some time in reviewing common energy problems (there were even several committees reviewing oil and other energy issues), its unanimity rule and lack of agreement among prominent members thwarted a coordinated response to the oil embargo.

ECONOMIC COMMISSION FOR EUROPE

The United Nations Economic Commission for Europe (ECE) joins 34 European countries (including the United States and Canada) in a region-wide agency for: (a) the promotion of international trade; (b) scientific and technological cooperation; (c) policymaking aimed at long-term economic growth; and (d) the improvement of the environment.[12]

The ECE offers several advantages from the standpoint of regional environmental management. Operating under the Economic and Social Council of the United Nations, ECE provides a structural point of contact between regional activity and universal objectives. ECE is also part of a network of regional organizations in that four other U.N. Economic Commissions are concerned with Latin America, Asia and the Pacific, Western Asia, and Africa. Because the other four Commissions serve largely the developing world, however, their perception of environmental problems is somewhat different from that of ECE. Other advantages of ECE are that it includes most of the industrial states (and presumably the major polluters) as well as provides a regional forum for both East and West Europe. Expanded geographical unity also enhances environmental coherency.

The expanded size of ECE relative to the other European organizations also has the disadvantage of diminishing the lowest common denominator of agreement so basic to intergovernmental organizations. As is customary with such organs, ECE's powers are limited to research, consultation, and recommendations to the member governments, and its operations require unanimous consent by the membership.

The Commission has been a vehicle for international environmental cooperation longer than any other United Nations' body (see United Nations, Economic Commission for Europe, 1978). Water pollution problems have been before the ECE's Inland Transport Committee since the 1950s. ECE interest expanded in 1968 to the entire area of water management under a new Committee on Water Problems. The Committee on Housing, Building and Planning has been concerned with problems of human settlements since the 1950s, while the Coal Committee took up air pollution in 1963.

By the mid-1960s emphasis shifted away from the sectoral (water, air, soil, etc.) approach to environmental problems and concentrated instead on overall coordinated approaches. In that vein, the ECE decided in 1967 to convene a meeting of senior national officials to make a comprehensive study of European regional environmental problems. Held in Prague in 1971, the meeting was unique in including delegates from both East and West (United Nations, Economic Commission for Europe, 1971; a summary of the symposium can be found in Stein, 1972:118-123). An important part of the preliminaries for the Prague meeting included the preparation by each country of a background study of its major environmental problems as well as a description of the national machinery for handling the problems. Although the studies were quickly out-of-date as many countries undertook to modify their national machinery in light of their own studies, the review process itself made the Prague meeting something of a success even before it convened. Though no earth-shaking substantive results came from the Prague meeting, the process itself was significant and helped pave the way for the subsequent UN Conference on the Human Environment in 1972.

Prior to the Prague Symposium, the ECE created a new body--the Senior Advisers to ECE Governments on Environmental Problems--whose responsibilities cover the broad policy aspects of environmental questions. The Senior Advisers provide:

> ... a means for Member Governments to exchange their experience and consult with one another on their environmental policy plans and intentions, to study the various options and methods open to them, to sponsor joint studies on matters of common concern, and to give a lead for the development of policies and projects which aim to protect and improve the environment (United Nations, Economic Commission for Europe, 1975:17).

At the Annual Session of the ECE held in Geneva, a new program of work for the period 1977-1981 was adopted with emphasis on energy, environment and trade (Bulletin, 1977:58).

CMEA

The Council for Mutual Economic Assistance (CMEA or Comecon) currently joins ten socialist bloc states into a loose economic organization that began as a response to the Marshall Plan for European recovery and to initial projects for West European unity following World War II.[13]

Like the European Communities, CMEA was not initially concerned with environmental problems. The organization was founded in 1949 with a general goal of increasing economic cooperation among the member states, but a basic organizational statute did not exist until 1959.[14]

Article I of the 1959 statute commits the member states to economic and technical progress, cooperation, and respect for sovereign equality. CMEA has four principal organs: the Session of the Council, the Executive Committee, a Secretariat, and twenty-two Permanent Commissions. In addition to these four principal organs, various other standing bodies have been created, many of which are significantly involved in environmental issues. CMEA and its organs have no power of enforcement; it is clearly not a supranational organization.

Perhaps the most potentially significant dimension of modern CMEA activity, however, was the adoption at the 25th Session in Bucharest (July, 1971) of the Comprehensive Program of Socialist Economic Integration.[15] The Comprehensive Program commits the member countries to international coordination in the harmonizing of national legal rules and institutions. Flowing from that beginning, the 31st Session of CMEA in 1977 endorsed a program for coordinating the CMEA countries' economic plans for 1981-1985 (Faddeyev, 1977:54). Western Europe's Economic Community has of course been experimenting with integration via the harmonization of national laws and other forms of coordinated undertakings. It remains to be seen whether the centralized state planning practiced in the socialist bloc states will prove a more effective integrative process. Much depends on the commitment of the Soviet Union to the process, Eastern European resistance to perceived Soviet hegemony, and the institutional evolution of CMEA itself.

A Polish writer, commenting on the joint planning effort, makes the following assessment:

> In the formation of the socialist countries' economic relations, international planning operates in tandem with domestic planning; this process is based on the unity of state interests as expressed in national plans and international interests as expressed in international assignments.
> International planning among CMEA countries does not mean that any supranational body has to be set up; joint planning, which applies to a relatively small number of industry sub-units or individual types of goods, is carried out by CMEA agencies, international economic organizations dealing with single industries and international associations, combines or enterprises, on both a bilateral and a multilateral basis. The system of representation in international organizations and the practice of requiring prior agreement on the areas and scale of international planning ensure that each partner's national interests are respected (Marszalik, 1976:5).

The aspects of central planning and coordination would appear to make CMEA a strong vehicle for dealing with environmental problems. The CMEA member countries are certainly aware of the environmental challenge, which is as much in evidence in Eastern as in Western Europe. The socialist bloc press is full of articles and commentary on environmental issues, periodic government communiques and statements by public officials make it clear that environmental issues are a regular agenda item, and there is even evidence of environmental interest-group activity.

At the operational level, CMEA as a regional organization has been active for some time in the environmental area. Work has been going on within CMEA since 1962 on the protection of water resources. A report was submitted by CMEA in 1971 to the United Nations Economic Commission for Europe Environmental Symposium in Prague that reviewed the environmental work of CMEA standing commissions (United Nations, Economic Commission for Europe, 1971:320). The adoption of the 1971 Comprehensive Program provided a strong basis for CMEA environmental cooperation. In 1973 the Council for Environmental Protection and Improvement was created under the CMEA Committee for Scientific and Technical Cooperation, both agencies having been spawned by the momentum of the Comprehensive Program.

Council efforts have focused on stimulating and coordinating environmental research on the implementation of research results and on promoting an awareness of the strong relationship between national planning and environmental protection.

EAST-WEST COOPERATION

CMEA has attempted to establish ties with other regional organizations within Europe, although it has no authority to engage in external negotiations without the direct cooperation of its member states. CMEA has been attempting since 1973 to establish ties with the European Communities. The 1975 Helsinki Conference on Security and Cooperation in Europe (CSCE) called for economic, scientific, technical, and environmental cooperation and a 1977 CMEA proposal urged official relations between CMEA and EEC in these areas.

For its part, the European Community has had mixed feelings about formal relations with CMEA. There have been of course bi-lateral environmental agreements as well as cooperation through the Economic Commission for Europe--an organ which holds a great deal of promise for East/West environmental cooperation.[16] European Community/CMEA environmental relations, however, seem to hold out the promise of cooperation at the "action" level.

On the general theme of relations between the two organizations, however, certain factors have inhibited "normalizing" relations with CMEA. First, the differing _national_ policies in both East and West have complicated negotiations, as has concern over the hegemony of the Soviet Union. Second, as a matter of international law the European Community members may sign treaties as a unit; CMEA members may not. There has been a fear in some quarters that Western pressures to cause CMEA to negotiate as a unit might strengthen the hegemonial role of the Soviet Union within the organization. Third, from a practical _trading_ standpoint (the _raison d'etre_ of these organizations is after all _economic_), there are important problems concerning the flow of trade and whether either side sees any important benefit (or burden) in expanding dealings with the other (Franzmeyer, 1977:9-17). Fourth, the Community has been concerned with the _full_ implementation of the agreement produced by the CSCE in Helsinki. As Wilhem Haferkamp, Vice-President of the EC Commission, noted during discussions in Moscow in 1978 that attempted to establish working relations between the two organizations:

> The Community has firmly advocated the complete implementation by all signatories of all the provisions of the Final Act of the Conference on Security and Cooperation. As is well known, the Community as such took an active part in drafting this important document. However, the results of that Conference have unfortunately not been reflected in all fields, and in particular in our relations. The present state of relations between the Community and individual CMEA countries, as well as with CMEA itself, is not helpful to the process of detente.... It is not sufficient to speak in favour of detente. Appropriate action is needed....Today, 111 countries maintain diplomatic relations with the Community. The fact that this is not yet so in the case of our immediate neighbors, is an anachronism (_Bulletin_, 1978:11-12; see also the arguments by Lebahn, 1980:147-165).

A Hungarian observer notes that it would be an illusion, under present circumstances, to expect smooth development of East/West economic relations, although all-European cooperation is most promising in non-ideological areas such as environmental protection (Hedri, 1979:291-298). This view, while persuasive, returns us to the kind of optimism regarding environmental cooperation that preceded the 1972 UN Conference in Stockholm.

One persistent suggestion regarding East/West environmental cooperation has been to work through the UN's Economic Commission for Europe (ECE). ECE has a long and respected record in environmental work, although its role is associated primarily with studies, symposia, information exchange and similar activities. These efforts should not be overlooked—indeed they should be strengthened. Shifting the focus of environmental activity from one forum to another might occasionally be of organizational or tactical value, but it cannot obscure in the long run basic facts of political or economic disagreement—neither between East and West nor among the members of either camp.

The main point to note, however, is that successful environmental management will depend ultimately not so much upon specific organizational structures as upon a common vision of a decent human existence, the development and sophistication of the scientific technology necessary for providing a clean environment, and most significantly upon the political commitment to cooperate.

OBSERVATIONS

While the foregoing pages offer an overview of the environmental activities and techniques of six European regional organizations, they do not necessarily provide a clear picture of regionalism as an approach to international environmental protection.

At least two difficulties hamper evaluation, not only of regional but also of universal environmental activity. First, there are no real standards. Determined conservationists are apt to regard any environmental achievements short of a return to the Garden of Eden as failures while hard-bitten industrialists might perceive the lowering of pollution levels by a modest percentage as realistic progress. Hence one's evaluation of the European organizations hinges in large measure on his frame of reference. A second difficulty stems from the often near-romantic attachment observers tend to develop vis-a-vis international organizations. Neither the perception of the environment as an "international" issue nor the wide range of international organizational efforts to evolve international environmental law should obscure the fact that the "environment" is also a national problem, intimately linked with national sovereignty and domestic politics (see Wilson, 1974, and Grieves, 1972). National determination to make international organizations work will in large part be measured by domestic environmental determination, although participation in an international organization may stimulate and aid national environmental efforts.

The prospects for future regional environmental management would appear strong because of the large number of regional organizations worldwide wide and their ability to focus on local problems. On the other hand, the "smooth functioning" of intergovernmental organizations is always hampered by problems of national sovereignty. Because of their intergovernmental nature, the European regional organizations have generally been involved in essentially investigative and advisory undertakings. The only organizations to go much beyond this level of activity have been the European Communities, whose supranational aura allows for some intervention into national affairs. But one should not automatically conclude that this feature provides an advantage for policymaking. One study points out, for example, that the United Kingdom is much more disposed to see OECD as "a more politically realistic and flexible forum than the EEC and without any of the politically sensitive 'loss of sovereignty' and 'supra-national' overtones of the latter" (Woodliffe, 1975:541).

As time passes, the European regional organizations may move away from "studies" and attempt to become more "action-oriented." Such a process, which is already to some extent underway, could be enhanced by a growing sense of environmental standards, national understanding of environmental problems, and a continuing interaction between national governments and regional organizations.

Two areas that will require the attention of observers interested in the European regional experiments are the effects of the organizational activity and the problem of duplication. Crucial to a true assessment of regionalism is a judgment regarding the effect of the entire effort on the coherent evolution of environmental rules and ultimately on environmental problems themselves. The question of duplication challenges us to decide what to make of the rather haphazard creation and entry of myriad overlapping international bodies (both regional and universal) into the environmental area. One is torn between support on one hand for virtually any attempt to manage the environment and on the other fear that such a multiplicity of effort might be counterproductive and self-defeating.

Perhaps an interim judgment can be passed upon the European organizations. Former United Nations Secretary-General, U Thant, made the following observation regarding the environmental efforts of the Economic Commission for Europe:

> Change is overtaking many quarters nowadays. Those countries which were first touched by the Industrial Revolution are now confronted with new problems. And this is happening before this revolution has even reached many of the less developed countries of the world. Economic growth is beginning to encounter questioning and resistance in the affluent societies and will have to submit to new social and even ecological criteria. It was timely, therefore, that the concern of your Commission should have extended to these new areas. The ECE may turn out to be one of the most sensitive barometers of new currents in economic and social thinking (U Thant, 1971:4).

In a broader context, Mr. Thant's remarks represent a fair assessment of all the European regional efforts at international environmental protection.

FOOTNOTES

*European research for this study was aided in various phases by
the German Academic Exchange Service, the Fulbright Commission, and
the Alexander von Humboldt Foundation. Professor Jurgen Domes,
Universitat des Saarlands, kindly provided work facilities for the
conduct of the research in West Germany. Some of the materials used
in this study are derived from Grieves, Spring, 1978, pp. 309-331,
and are used with the kind permission of the Editor.

1. ECSC Treaty, 261 U.N.T.S. 140 (1957); EEC Treaty, 298
U.N.T.S. 3 (1958); EURATOM Treaty, 298 U.N.T.S. 167 (1958).

2. Official French text in _Journal Officiel des Communautes
Europennes_, No. 2 (1967):2.

3. Belgium, Denmark, France, Greece, Italy, Luxembourg, the
Netherlands, Republic of Ireland, United Kingdom, and West Germany.

4. Community environmental authority could also be potentially
linked with such other Community powers in the EEC Treaty as
agricultural policy (Art. 43), transport policy (Art. 75), social
policy (Arts. 117-118), or the negotiation of Community agreements
with non-member states or international organizations (Arts.
228-231). A thorough examination of possible Treaty authority is
offered by Behrens (1976).

5. See for example Burhenne and Schoenbaum (1973:494-503); Bungarten (1976); or Behrens (1976). Comprehensive and specific treaty
text revisions have been proposed by Grabitz and Sasse (1977).

6. The 15 NATO member countries are: Belgium, Canada, Denmark,
France, Germany (Federal Republic), Greece, Iceland, Italy, Luxem-
bourg, Netherlands, Norway, Portugal, Turkey, United Kingdom and the
United States.

7. The eighteen-nation membership includes Austria, Belgium,
Cyprus, Denmark, France, Germany (Federal Republic), Greece, Iceland,
Ireland, Italy, Luxembourg, Malta, the Netherlands, Norway, Sweden,
Switzerland, Turkey and the United Kingdom.

8. Full membership includes Australia, Austria, Belgium, Canada,
Denmark, Finland, France, Germany (Federal Republic), Greece,
Iceland, Ireland, Italy, Japan, Luxembourg, Netherlands, Norway,
Portugal, Spain, Sweden, Switzerland, Turkey, United Kingdom and the
United States. Yugoslavia and New Zealand have qualified membership
status.

9. T.I.A.S. No. 4891, entered into force September 30, 1961.

10. Both the Council of Europe and OECD, however, have taken the
position that transfrontier pollution problems should as far as

possible be handled at the domestic level. See McCaffrey (1977:56).

11. See Supplementary Protocol to the OECD Convetion, T.I.A.S.
No. 4891, entered into force September 30, 1961. See also ECSC
Treaty, Article 93; EEC Treaty, Articles 116 and 231;   and EURATOM
Treaty, Article 201.

12. The 34 member countries are Albania, Austria, Belgium,
Bulgaria, Byelorussian SSR, Canada, Czechoslovakia, Cyprus, Denmark,
Germany (Democratic Republic), Germany (Federal Republic), Finland,
France, Greece, Hungary, Iceland, Ireland, Italy, Luxembourg, Malta,
Netherlands, Norway, Poland, Portugal, Romania, Spain, Sweden,
Switzerland, Turkey, Ukrainian SSR, USSR, United Kingdom, United
States and Yugoslavia.

13. The current CMEA members are Bulgaria, Cuba, Czechoslovakia,
East Germany, Hungary, Mongolia, Poland, Romania, USSR and Vietnam.
Yugoslavia has participated since 1964 in matters of mutual interest.
North Korea and the People's Republic of Yemen send observers.
Cooperation agreements have been concluded with Finland (1973), Iraq
(1975) and Mexico (1975).

14. The Communique issued by CMEA's founders is reprinted in
Keesing's Contemporary Archives, VII, 976 B (1949). The 1959 CMEA
Statute can be found in Peaslee, International Governmental
Organizations: Constitutional Documents, Rev. 2nd Ed., Vol. I.
The Hague: Martinus Nijhoff, 1961, 332-338.

15. Full original text appears in Economicheskaia Gazeta, Moscow
(August, 1971):33.   English translation is available in Soviet and
Eastern European Foreign Trade (Fall-Winter, 1971-1972): 187.

16. The range of East/West cooperation is discussed in Fullenbach
(1977).   Both EEC and CMEA, incidently, have observer status at the
UN and advisory status in the UN's ECE.

Behrens, Fritz. Rechtsgrundlagen der Umweltpolitik der Europaischen
    Gemeinschaften. Berlin: Erich Schmidt Verlag, 1976.
Beinhauer, Hagen. "The Fight Against Pollution." In Meet Germany.
    17th rev. ed. Hamburg: Atlantik-Brucke, 1978,89-93.
Bishop, Amasa S. and Munro, Robert D. "The Regional Economic
    Commissions and Environmental Problems." International
    Organizations, XXVI, 2 (Spring, 1972):348-371.
Bulletin of the European Communities. Supp. 5 (1972):16; Supp. 5
    (1975):11-12; Supp. 4 (1977):58.
Bungarten, Harald H. Die Umweltpolitik der Europaischen
    Gemeinschaft. Bonn: Europa Verlag, 1976.
Burhenne, Wolfgang E. and Schoenbaum, Thomas J. "The European
    Community and Management of the Environment: A Dilemma."
    Natural Resources Journal, XIII, 3 (July, 1973):494-503.
"Communique on the 31st Session of the Council for Mutual Economic
    Aid." Current Digest of the Soviet Press. XXIX (July 20,
    1977):8.
Dickstein, H. L. "National Environmental Hazards and International
    Law." International and Comparative Law Quarterly , XXIII, 2
    (April, 1974):426-446.
Doran, Charles F. "Can NATO Defend the Environment?" Environmental
    Affairs, II, 4 (Spring, 1973):667-684.
Erhardt, Carl A. "EEC and CMEA Tediously Nearing Each Other."
    Aussenpolitik, XXVIII, 2 (1977):162-177.
European Committee for the Conservation of Nature and Natural
    Resources, Council of Europe. Council of Europe Activities
    Relating to the Natural Environment. Strassbourg, 20 May 1974,
    CE/Nat/Centre (74) 8.
Faddeyev, N. V. "CMEA: Deepening Integration Among Members."
    Reprints from the Soviet Press, XXV, 7 (October 15, 1977):54-59.
Franzmeyer, Fritz. "Zum Stand der wirtschaftpolitischen Beziehungen
    zwischen RGW and EG." Europa-Archiv, XXXII, 1 (January 10,
    1977):9-17.
Fullenbach, Josef. Umweltschutz Awischen Ost und West. Bonn:
    Europa Union Verlag, 1977.
German Tribune. February 17, 1980:8.
Grabitz, Eberhard and Sasse, Christoph. Competence of the European
    Communities for Environmental Policy: Proposal for an Amendment
    to the Treaty of Rome. Berlin: Erich Schmidt Verlag, 1977.
Grieves, Forest. "Environmental Regulation in the Soviet Bloc
    Countries." Montana Business Quarterly, XVI, 2 (Summer,
    1978):25-30.
_____. "International Law and the Environmental Issue." Environ-
    mental Protection." International Lawyer, XII, 2 (Spring,
    1978:209-331.
_____. "Regional Efforts at International Environmental
    Protection." International Lawyer, XII, 2 (Spring,
    1978):209-331.
Hedri, Gabriella Izik. "Gedanken uber mogliche Beziehungen zwischen
    RGW un EG." Europa-Archiv, XXXIV, 10 (May 25, 1979):291-298.

Huntley, James R. Man's Environment and the Atlantic Alliance.
    Brussels: NATO Information Service, June, 1971.
International Herald Tribune. December 11, 1978:7.
Johnson, Brian. "The United Nations' Institutional Response to
    Stockholm: A Case Study in the International Politics of
    Institutional Change." International Organization, XXVI, 2
    (Spring, 1972):255-301.
Johnson, Stanley. "Stockholm 1972." New Statesman, June 2,1972:742.
Kennan, George. "To Prevent a World Wasteland." Foreign Affairs,
    XLVIII, 3 (April, 1970):401-413.
Kommission der Europaischen Gemeinschaften. Erste Mitteilung der
    Kommission uber die Politik der Gemeinschaft auf dem Gebiet des
    Umweltschutzes. Brussel, 22 July 1971, Dok. SEK (71) 2616.
Kyba, Patrick. "CCMS: The Environmental Connection." International
    Journal, XXIX, 2 (Spring, 1974):256-267.
Lebahn, Axel. "Alternatives in EC-CMEA Relations." Aussenpolitik,
    XXXI, 2 (1980):147-165.
Marszalik. A. "Joint Planning is a New Form of Cooperation Among
    CMEA Member Countries." Current Digest of the Soviet Press,
    XXVIII (November 3, 1976):5.
McCaffrey, Stephen C. "Pollution of Shared Natural Resources: Legal
    and Trade Implications." American Society of International Law
    Proceedings (1977):56-61.
Parliamentary Assembly, Council of Europe. Report on the Environment
    Policy in Europe in 1973-1974. Strassbourg, 15 January 1975,
    Doc. 3530.
"Remarks of the President at the Commemorative Session of the North
    Atlantic Council, Departmental Auditorium, Washington, D.C., on
    April 10, 1969." Release of the Office of the White House Press
    Secretary.
Renborg, Sten. "Environment Protection Work in the Council of
    Europe." European Yearbook 1971, XIX. The Hague: Martinus
    Nijhoff, 1973,42-51.
Roderick, Hilliard. "The Work of OECD in the Protection of the
    Environment." European Yearbook 1971, XIX. The Hague: Martinus
    Nijhoff, 1973,75-80.
Stein, Robert E. "The ECE Symposium on Problems Relating to
    Environment." American Journal of International Law, LXVI, 1
    (January, 1972):118-123.
Tatscachen uber Deutschland. Auflage fur das Presse- und
    Informationsamt der Bundesregierung. Gutersloh: Bertelsmann
    Lexikon Verlag, 1978.
Thant, U. Address by the Secretary-General of the United Nations to
    the Twenty-Sixth Session of the Economic Commission for Europe.
    April, 1971. U.N. Document E/5001, Annex 1.
Train, Russell E. "A New Approach to International Environmmental
    Cooperation: The NATO Committee on the Challenges of Modern
    Society." Kansas Law Review, XXII, 2 (Winter, 1974):1167-191.
Ungerer, Werner. "Problems of the European Community."
    Aussenpolitik, XXXII, 2 (1981):107-120.
United Nations, Economic Commission for Europe. ECE: A Key to
    Economic Co-operation. New York, 1975. U.N. Doc., INF/ECE/1/-
    75.

_____. ECE Symposium on Problems Relating to Environment. Prague, May 2-15, 1971. U.N. Doc. ST/ECE/ENV/1.

_____. Three Decades of the United Nations Economic Commission for Europe. New York, 1978. U.N. Doc. E/ECE/962.

United States Environmental Protection Agency. CCMS: The First Decade. A Report to Commemorate the Tenth Anniversary of the NATO Committee on the Challenges of Modern Society. Washington, D.C.: Environmental Protection Agency, October, 1979.

Von Ward, Paul et al. "Ten Years of CCMS--The Record and the Future." Part 1 in NATO Review, XXVII, 6 (December, 1979):12-17, and Part 2 in NATO Review, XXVIII, 1 (February, 1980):17-19.

Willrich, Mason and Conant, Melvin A. "The International Energy Agency: An Interpretation and Assessment." American Journal of International Law, LXXI, 2 (April, 1977):199-223.

Wilson, Clifton. "Environmental Policy and International Law." In Stuart S. Nagel (ed.), Environmental Politics. New York: Praeger Publishers, 1974,103-123.

Woodliffe, J. C. "A New Dimension to International Co-operation: The OECD International Energy Agreement." International and Comparative Law Quarterly, XXIV, 3 (July, 1975):525-541.

11
The Environment and Socialism: The Soviet Model

Michael Kupilik

This paper is an examination of the institutional process of environmental degradation in the Soviet Union. My thesis is that the Soviets have built environmental destruction into their system by the way they have structured their institutions and that this structure is independent of the existence of socialism.

The paper consists of three parts. In the first part, I examine Soviet perceptions of Western attitudes toward environmental problems and contrast these perceptions with Soviets' official position on these issues. Secondly, I shall outline actual Soviet performance in the environmental area and third, try to explain the institutional factors which cause actual performance to differ so radically from the official position.

This paper is <u>not</u> meant to be a comparison of environmental problems in the United States and the Soviet Union; but, of course, such comparisons are impossible to totally avoid.

SOVIET ATTITUDES TOWARD THE ENVIRONMENT

<u>Soviet Perceptions of Western Attitudes Toward the Environment</u>

In Soviet writing on environmental subjects, a common perception of Western attitudes emerges.[1] The attitudes that the Soviets believe Western writers have in common are:

1. The contention that the ecological crisis is inevitable.
2. The virtual denial of the social causes of the impending ecological crisis.
3. An appeal for austerity in consumption and a cutback in economic and technological development.

Thus the Soviets see the writings of many Western environmentalists as pessimistic and hold that bourgeois scientists find it increasingly difficult to reconcile the needs of society with the spirit of private enterprise. This is particularly true of questions about the relationship of society with nature and the disposal of its wealth, bestowed on all and for the benefit of all.

The Soviets believe that mankind today holds capitalism and colonialism primarily responsible for the rapacious exploitation of natural resources and for damages to the habitat of mankind as a whole. They further believe that the capitalist nations can do nothing to alleviate this situation for two reasons. First, they regard the views of Western environmentalists as seriously limited by the class to which they belong and by a general inability to explain the processes governing world development from a socioeconomic aspect. Second, and more important, they believe that policy makers and analysts restrict their ability to act by making a fetish of the processes of scientific and technological development as phenomena which cannot be controlled by man (Ananichev, 1976:18).

The Official Soviet Position

The official position of the Soviet authorities on environmental problems is based, theoretically, on the writings of Marx, Engels, and Lenin. But to lend ideological purity to the official position, it was necessary for Soviet academicians to meticulously reread these writers. Academician/Philosopher Pyotr Kapitsa expresses the ideological base by stating: "The problem of the man-nature relationship holds a conspicuous place in the classics of Marxism-Leninism. Marx and Engels regarded the communist rebuilding of society as a guarantee of harmony in the man-nature relationship" (Kapitsa, 1977:12). Kapitsa's interpretation of Marx and Engels, however, seems strained. Concern for the environment plays a minimal role in the writings of Marx and Lenin, and a somewhat greater one in Engels'. The current Soviet position on the environment is therefore not to be found in the works of any of these three (Goldman, 1972:13).

This position instead is basically grounded on the belief that socialism can eliminate all environmental problems. This belief is based on two points. These are that (1) socialist production will eliminate the incentive to pollute and (2) central planning will eliminate waste of natural resources and environmental disruption.

Consider point one. Western economists from Pigou to the present have maintained that many environmental problems are due to what are called externalities, or situations in which the private costs of production are smaller than its social costs. Since in a market economy the firm does not bear the social costs of pollution, there is no incentive not to pollute. The Soviets maintain that since, under socialism, society owns the firms, all costs are made internal to the firm and therefore the production process and the environment will be in harmony. Since society at large manages firms, it will not allow them to create unwanted pollution. Unlike the individual capitalist, society under socialism has both the means and incentive to sacrifice profits to maintain environmental quality.

Not only is socialism thought to effectively "internalize" production costs, but in addition central planning will guarantee sound use of the environment and its resources. To quote academician Nikolai Semonov:

The Soviet Union has been able to implement the Marxist-Leninist principles. The experience of the Soviet Union shows that socialist society is able not only to define its development goals and forecast its future but also make concrete plans for a relatively long period ahead. These naturally take into account the quality of the environment, the reserves and location of natural resources. Planning and forecasting development for several decades ahead, however, requires a comprehensive analysis of all the aspects of interaction between society and the natural environment, particularly with reference to major projects for reshaping nature. Introduction of new methods of using natural resources as well as the process of growing urbanization [are factors] (Semonov, 1977:72).

This faith in scientific planning has an interesting result. Namely, the Soviets believe that growth and technology are means of solving, rather than creating, environmental problems. Bourgeois scholars, on the other hand, are thought to believe that technology and economic growth are the chief factors likely to cause a worldwide ecological crisis. Such "technology pessimism" is believed to deliberately obscure the main culprit of the environmental crisis, which is not growth nor change but capitalism itself. The Soviet position is that technology and growth in a socialist setting is harmonizing between man and nature.

To illustrate the application of the Soviet position to an environmental problem, let us consider Ananichev's analysis of population growth in his _Environment: International Aspects_:

With the growth of the earth's population and its demands, on the one hand, and the near exhaustion of many resources, on the other, some bourgeois scholars hasten to raise the question as to whether too many people live on the planet. In whatever disguise they present their arguments and conclusions, this cynical and unhumanistic question runs through a large number of works published in the West on the environment (Ananichev, 1976:16).

Thus Ananichev sees some Western writers viewing the population problem as one of scarcity and distribution: with resources fixed, how many people can the earth support? Ananichev obviously disagrees with this approach. Technology can liberate us from resource constraints that currently appear absolute. To quote Ananichev further:

There may be, indeed, some "limits to growth" of the population in space and in time, within which the earth's population of so many thousand million can exist. But how can this number be determined? A figure that seems reasonable today may change drastically tomorrow in view of scientific and technological progress. What criteria should be applied to defining this number?....In fact no answer need be given, since the question is pointless for the developing mankind (Ananichev, 1976:17).[2]

This then is the Soviet perception of the West and its own official position. Soviet analysts acknowledge some environmental problems but consider them short-run dislocations best solved by continued socialist development (growth) and increased use of technology. They also point with pride to their environmental laws. And indeed, the Soviet Union was the first nation to pass a modern set of laws, starting as early as the late 1950s, which were comprehensive in setting maximum permissible levels of pollution and in strictly requiring anti-pollution devices. We shall consider these laws further below, but first we turn to a description of environmental realities in the Soviet Union.

ENVIRONMENTAL REALITY IN THE SOVIET UNION

If it were only a question of ideology or of hearts being in the right places, there would be no environmental disruption in the USSR. That should be evident from the official position or by examining Soviet environmental law. However, the environmental record of the Soviet Union is no better and in many ways worse than the record in the West. In order to examine the Soviet record, I divide the problem of the environment into three main aspects: pollution, waste of natural resources, and disruption of the environment. In this section I give examples of Soviet performance in each of these areas which I believe are representative of a much more widespread problem. Examples are more dramatic but less precise than statistics. Anyone wishing such information, however, can refer to the bibliography.

Pollution

Probably the best example of environmental pollution in the Soviet Union is the famous case of Lake Baikal. Lake Baikal is unique. Estimated to be 25-30 million years old, it is probably the oldest lake in the world. It is fed by 336 rivers but drained by only one, the Angara, which flows north for 2,500 miles to the Arctic Sea. The lake's water changes every 200-300 years. This rate of turnover is slow when compared, for example, to Lake Michigan, which changes every 100. Thus, if you put something into Baikal, it will stay there. It is the deepest lake in the world at 5,346 feet. It covers 12,200 square miles and contains 5,520 cubic miles of water, making it the largest body of fresh water on earth. Indeed, 2.5% of all the earth's fresh water is in Lake Baikal. And fresh is the way to describe the water (or at least it was). Its mineral content is 50 to 25% lower than that of most other freshwater bodies. Over 1,200 living organisms have been catalogued in the area, of which 708 are found nowhere else. This includes 30,000 nerpa, the world's only freshwater seal (Goldman, 1972:179-80).

Lake Baikal is situated in Siberia near huge stands of forests. So, it is understandable that sooner or later it would catch the attention of officials in the timber, paper and wood working ministry. Beginning in the 1950s about 50 factories were built along the Selenga River, which supplies half of Lake Baikal's water. These included meat-packing plants and lumber mills. Only one plant in five treated their waste before it was discharged raw into the Selenga. Most of these factories were located near the city of Ulan Ude which, as of 1974, also emptied its sewage untreated into the Selenga (Kelley, et al., 1976:178). The lake of course showed the effects of such activities. For example, from 1945 to 1957 the catch of omul, the lake's major commercial fish, fell 55% (Goldman, 1972:182).

Then things got worse. Starting in 1957 a decision was made to bring industry directly to the shores of the lake. Plans were drawn up for the construction of paper and pulp mills and a cellulose fiber plant. It was ministry officials who were directly responsible for the initial proposals to exploit Baikal's unmatched resources. But in response to public outcry both domestic and international, the Supreme Soviet passed a number of tough environmental laws to protect Baikal specifically. However, these laws were poorly enforced by local officials and a number of industries continued to receive exceptions.

Nevertheless, the Soviets claim to have saved Lake Baikal in an example of how well their system works. Their claim is in doubt, however, and in 1974, the Soviet authorities refused to permit a visiting team of American environmentalists to inspect the five worst polluting factories in Ulan Ude (Kelley, et al., 1976:177).

Further doubt is cast on Soviet claims by Boris Komorov:

> For more than fifteen years public attention has been focused on the southern part of Baikal. Not long ago, for example, the construction of a close water-circulating system at the Selenginskii paper and pulp combine was ballyhooed as a great achievement since with it (supposedly) the combine will not pollute the lake. Yet at the same time, plans were being drafted at secret institutes for the construction of lead and zinc mines, a concentrating mill, a thermoelectric station, and a large settlement with roads and other facilities on the Kholodnaia River. Construction is now in full swing. The complex should be ready for operation by 1980. Sewage and atmospheric discharges for all the nonferrous metallurgy works are among the most ecologically harmful. Even after treatments they will undoubtedly do more harm to Baikal than the effluents from the Baikal paper and pulp combine. Compared to sewage waters containing heavy metals, the runoffs from the Baikal combine will probably seem like harmless fizz-water (Komorov, 1980:14).

Although Lake Baikal may be unique, its story is not. An example is the pollution of the Donets Basin by chemical plants and air pollution in general, especially in cities other than Moscow.

In the late 1950s the Soviets established strict standards for many pollutants. These standards were specified in levels of maximum permissible concentration (MPC).[3] Ten cities were reported with pollution levels of one hundred MPC's, one hundred with levels of ten MPC's and over one thousand with pollution levels of five MPC's (Komorov, 1980:21).

Constant exposure to concentrations of 25 MPC's and above is dangerous not only to the living but also to their potential offspring. Experiments conducted by the M. Pinigin Clear Air Laboratory showed that after 500 hours of exposure to an atmosphere containing 20 MPC's of sulphur dioxide, the sex cells of white mice were permanently damaged (Komorov, 1980:21).

Nevertheless, The Bulletin on the Problems of Environmental Pollution, published for use by a select group of specialists and ministry officials, reports severe levels of air pollution in the country. Pollution exceeds the permissible maxima and reaches levels considered hazardous to human health. In this regard, concentrations in excess of 25, of 10 to 15, and of 5 MPC's are considered to be at "extremely hazardous," "immediately threatening" and "warning" levels respectively.

Waste of Natural Resources

One of the most interesting cases of waste of a natural resource occurred along the Black Sea shore. Due to its geographical location, the Black Sea is the prime tourist region of the Soviet Union. There are more warm days there than at any other seaside resort in the country, and along its shores are located such famous attractions as Sochi, Yalta, Sukhumi, and Odessa. Sochi was Stalin's cold weather haven, and Khrushchev built a vacation home at Cape Pitsunda. A range of mountains protects these areas from some of the more violent storms of the continent (Goldman, 1972:156).

Soviet planners were quick to exploit the area's recreational resources and in the late 1930s began large scale construction of hotels and resort accommodations along its shores. Later one of the first jet airports in the Soviet Union was built near Cape Pitsunda (Goldman, 1972:160).

Most of the Black Sea shoreline which was developed for recreation consists of a narrow strip set off by a range of steep hills. To provide the concrete and other materials needed for construction, the contractors used the pebbles and sand located along the beach. These materials would whet the appetite of any cement maker. Because they were free for the taking and easily available and because obtaining other construction materials would involve the extra expense of transportation over the mountains, local contractors used them heavily. During the period 1945-57, 40 million cubic yards of sand and gravel were mined for construction purposes (Kramer, 1979:896).

Thus, the beach was mined to build beach resorts, as well as the roads, railroads, seaports, and city buildings. The development of the area also led to an increase in the demand for electricity which was met by the construction of numerous dams along the mountain streams. These dams curbed the flow of silt and gravel from the mountains to the river mouths at the sea.

A disaster was in the making. The sand and gravel had previously acted as a buffer against the force of the waves, a force which has been measured at 4 to 12 tons per square meter. Without the beach and the replenishing from the rivers the sea ate away what was left of the shoreline and then started in on the land. Whole sections of roads and some of the resorts fell into the sea. The Soviets are currently trucking sand across the mountains and dumping it into the sea in an attempt to halt the process (Kramer, 1979:897).

Pollution is also ruining the Black Sea coast. As reported in the Soviet publication Nature 1980, "The entire resort area along the Black Sea from Odessa to Batumi is highly polluted with oil. In all regions—Kherson, Yalta, Sevastopol, Gelendzhik, Tuapse, Pitsunda, and Sukhumi—the coastal waters contain 10 to 12 MPC's of oil. And in addition there is about the same level of phenol. Bacterial contamination has also reached dangerous levels at most resorts" (Komorov, 1980:37).

There are other problems. Currently in Uzbekistan there are approximately 25,000 artesian wells in use. Of these wells about 20 percent were installed without valves or taps and since they cannot be closed an estimated 100 million cubic meters of water are lost yearly. The wasted water forms lakes and ponds around the wells (Komorov, 1980:53).

Indeed, water is probably the best single example of waste of a natural resource in the Soviet Union. For example, a Soviet steel firm uses up to 764 tons of water to produce one ton of steel. One very efficient French firm uses one ton of water for one ton of steel. Even the best Soviet firms use 25 tons of water for one ton of steel. There are also cases of the Soviets pumping fresh water into oil wells instead of using stratal water (Komorov, 1980:40).

Disruption of the Environment

Finally, agricultural, mineral, and industrial development has seriously disrupted the fragile environments of the Soviet steppes, Siberia, and the far North.

A well known example is the Virgin Lands project. Launched during the regime of Nikita Krushchev, this was a program to plow up the steppes and plant corn with the hope of making the Soviet Union self sufficient in providing food for the population. Unfortunately this process exposed to the wind the thin layer of top soil characteristic of the area. The result was to begin the creation of a Soviet version of the dust bowl. Corn production failed and the program was stopped with, and largely responsible for, the removal of Khrushchev in 1964. You could say that Khrushchev truly stepped into trouble.

Probably the best current example of disruption of the environment is the result of development of Siberia and the far North. Most of this area lies north of the permafrost line and contains plains, forests, mountain ranges, rivers and lakes, all on a gigantic scale. Because of climate and the permafrost, natural resource development is difficult and the ecosystem extremely delicate. Great care must be taken when developing such an area, and indeed, there must be limits on the degree to which it can be developed at all. Komorov gives us an interesting example of the care that is being taken:

Rivers large and small in Siberia and the North are being mercilessly mutilated by gold dredges. Picturesque and fertile valleys are being turned into dumps of gravel and

shingle, and for hundreds of kilometers along their courses
the water is white or brown with roiled sand and silt.
Even the simplest species of fish cannot survive in such
water. Gold miners work not only along the river beds.
The steep banks, which they have eroded, have become the
source of slippages and slides that clog streams and
rivulets. All gold mining enterprises discharge unfiltered
wastes. The lack of ceremony of the gold miners is easily
explained: gold is a 'strategic product.' A few years ago,
at a meeting of the Magadan Regional Committee of the CPSU,
one of the country's high-ranking officials...suspended all
the environmental protection laws in those areas where gold
was mined (Komorov, 1980:116).

BASIC CAUSES FOR SOVIET ENVIRONMENTAL PROBLEMS

It is clear that the official Soviet position on environmental
quality and Soviet performance differ markedly. It is my thesis that
this division between ideology and reality arises in the operation of
the plan at the managerial level. I do not mean to imply that the
managers in the Soviet Union are inherently evil people who purpose-
fully ruin the environment. On the contrary, they are professionals
who follow as they should the signals they receive from the
Politburo, the central planning agency, and their respective
ministries.
The Soviet hierarchy, however, seems to say one thing and signal
another. These signals usually are contained within the plan or in
the way the authorities allow the plan to be executed. These signals
can be viewed as the incentives the central authorities provide
either to induce or to force the managers into a course of action.
As we shall see the incentives do not provide for responsible
ecological behavior. Indeed, the opposite is true.
I believe that there are three major institutional factors which
incite this dysfunctional behavior. These factors are not inherent
in socialism and exist in the Soviet Union because of the particular
preferences of the decision makers, which in the Soviet Union means
the Politburo. Let us examine these factors.

Emphasis on Rapid Economic Growth

In a country where it is generally agreed that economic growth
must be accelerated in order to overtake more advanced countries, the
attack on nature is usually pursued with more intensity. The Soviets
have designed a system that places maximum emphasis on increasing
production. Everything else is of secondary importance. This is
reflected in practice as well as spirit. Recall the gold mining
example in the previous section. Another example of growth at all
cost is that of Yasnaya Polyana, Tolstoy's old country home, a place
surrounded by a beautiful forest. In 1955 a coal gasification plant
was built about a mile from the estate. Then, as part of a campaign
to develop and expand the chemical industry, a urea plant was added.
As soon as the plans were announced, local residents began to protest

that the fumes from the factory would harm the trees. As I. Fedorova, the Chief agronomist of the estate said: "Just as conservationists at Lake Baikal are now being reassured so we agronomists were told that the chemical factory would cause no damage..." (Goldman, 1972:63). The plant was made operational, the trees began to die. There were more protests. A commission was established by the Council of Ministers but as Fedorova later explained:

> The special commission has closed down, but now it appears that already new work has begun—the work of the chemical combine. The tactics of predators are always the same. First they promise to save, guard, preserve in full splendor and even expand the threated object. But after the damage occurs, then they plead the importance of the higher governmental priorities. Now the managers rationalize their damage with statements like "Think of it—3 pine trees have been killed. What is more important for our government—3 pine trees or a kapron plant?" (Goldman, 1972:63).

It is quite clear that in the Soviet Union a higher priority is given growth than in safeguarding the environment.

The Price System

Working from a Marxist ideological base, the Soviets have constructed an administered price system. This means that for the planned sector of the economy prices are set by the state planning agency and not established by markets. It has been shown by Lange and Taylor that it is theoretically possible to establish a set of administered prices in a socialist economy which are efficient, market clearing prices (Lange and Taylor, 1964). There is also no reason why these prices could not include the social as well as private costs of production. In practice, however, almost no effort is made in the Soviet Union to assign such social costs when figuring prices. Consequently, the Soviet factory manager has no incentive to clean up his pollution himself since he views the pollution as costless. Thus, as described above, the managers of construction along the shores of the Black Sea treated gravel as costless when its use in fact entailed significant social losses.

A second and equally serious problem with the Soviet pricing system concerns the lack of pricing, or, at best, the underpricing of natural resources. This problem stems from Marxist ideology. Recall the discussion on the use of water. A number of academicians have tried to convince the Soviet government that the price of water should reflect the fact that it is scarce. Scarcity requires that resources be used with the recognition that they have valuable alternative uses and should, as well, be conserved for the future. But at the level of the Central Committee of the Communist Party, scarcity pricing is absolutely rejected. The reason given is that such pricing "would contradict the principles of a socialist economy," in which the value of a thing is determined by the social labor needed to produce it (Komorov, 1980:40). Since labor has not produced the water in rivers and lakes, it follows that water, or any natural resource, belongs to the state and should be provided free to any authorized user. Thus, in effect, state enterprises have been able to treat the country's resources as free goods. The result is overuse.

Another example is found in the mining industry. Soviet rates of recovery are unusually low. The economist I. W. Sukotin reported rates of recovery of 40 to 50% on the extraction of coal, oil, potassium and natural gas. Another critic complains that there is a higher zinc, lead and copper content in the abandoned slag of the non-ferrous metallurgical industry in Kazakhstan than there is in the mines presently being worked (Goldman, 1972:48). Such waste is only to be expected when the mine operator has no need to worry about a careful sifting of his ore. It is hard to dispute the logic of such an approach. The raw material is free, but the mine worker is not. Therefore, the mine operator seeks to obtain as much output per laborer as he possibly can. Under the circumstances since the material in the ground is free to him, he will simply move on to another part of his mine deposit or to a new mine where the ore content is higher and/or more accessible. We see the institutional framework failing to create any incentives to conserve on the use of natural resources.

Success Indicators

Until 1965, the success indicator for a Soviet manager was fulfillment of the plan (or even better, in some cases, over-fulfillment). Successful completion of the plan was rewarded with a bonus accounting, in some cases, for 60% of a manager's salary (Gregory and Stuart, 1981:189). After 1966, the bonus formulae were amended to encourage some cost reductions and the maintenance of quality of output. However, as we saw above, costs of environmental damage are usually not taken into account (Kramer, 1979:896). This means that in the reward system for plant managers the primary success indicator remains fulfillment of the plan. Concern for the environment, especially if it would raise costs or, what is worse, cut physical production, is not rewarded. The factory manager thus is extremely reluctant to divert any of his investment funds away from production toward conservation or pollution abatement. To do so would probably reduce his bonus.

This attitude is reflected in a discussion with a plant official reported by Vladimir Soloukhin in _A Walk in Rural Russia_. The factory manager says:

> If the factory did not carry out its obligation according to plan, there would be recriminations—someone might even lose his job. But if the filter were not made, no great harm would be done, no inquiries would be made, no one would notice. The fish would disappear? The people would fall ill because of the water? Well, in the first place, it is never certain what is the cause of people falling ill. Our job is production according to the plan (Goldman, 1972:69).

Komorov recounts a similar case observed by an expert on forest legislation:

> I try to keep a cold heart in law suits on the destruction of forests. You can't get involved in them. Five years ago I was at the giant forest station near Krasnoiarsk. I saw a whole city on the river bank. Huge cedars several arm lengths in circumference, larches, and firs lay in piles without end. And all this just lay there because the railroad had not provided freight cars. But that wasn't all. The railroad had not provided enough cars for one, two, even three years, and the forestry trust had known before hand that there would be too few cars. Nevertheless each year more and more trees were felled. The trust had its plan. Dozens of acres of wonderful cedar taiga were uprooted, with a semi-desert left in their wake--and for this the state received rotten wood. Not even lumber (Komorov, 1980:69, emphasis added).

If the reward system does not provide incentives for concern for the environment then the other alternative is to force responsible behavior by a punishment system. We have mentioned a set of environmental laws which Marshall Goldman characterizes as "perfection itself" (Goldman, 1972:22). Regrettably, it is perfection only on paper. The Soviet emphasis on legal formalities appears to rest on a form of self-deception in which it is believed that the passing of environmental laws is all that is necessary to induce compliance. The problem here is one of enforcement. A good example is Lake Baikal. The first potentially effective law regulating the quality of Lake Baikal was passed in May 1960. It soon became apparent that no one was paying any attention to the law. A new law was passed by the Council of Ministers in February 1969. This also seemed to have little effect. So a third law was passed in September 1971 (Kelley, et al., 1976:175-77). This time it was signed not only by the Council of Ministers but by the Central Committee of the Soviet Communist Party as well. The involvement of the Central Committee was presumably intended to show the seriousness of the issue.

Even when the laws are enforced, the punishment is too weak to be effective. When the matter is treated as a non-criminal act, the administrative penalities are hardly very intimidating. The fines range from 5 to 200 rubles. In U.S. currency, the average fine is around $120 (Goldman, 1972:35). When this is weighed against the reward to achieving the output plan, it is hard to see how these fines could affect behavior of the manager at all.

Even if the act is considered criminal and handled under the criminal code with stiff fines (jail sentences are all but unknown), the law may not serve as a deterrent. The fines levied in these cases are usually paid for out of the enterprise fund. Under these circumstances the plant manager may actually gain by polluting since it may help achieve the plan. Academician Armand, one of the Soviet Union's most respected ecologists, reports that funds to pay the fines were frequently included in the financial plan of the enterprise at the beginning of the year (Goldman, 1972:35).

The Soviets are beginning to realize their system of laws has had little effect. One well-known Soviet jurist had the following to say about them:

> The practical implementation of the laws on nature conservation and, above all, the application of punitive measures are characterized by the following. First, punitive measures are not applied to the fullest. Second, they are applied unjustly. Third, in the vast majority of cases they are not applied at all. Too often these measures—a fine or rarely a suspended prison sentence—are not commensurate with the magnitude of the harm done to nature; they are much lighter. Too often a punitive measure lacks any moral force, since it is not the real culprit who sits in the dock but someone who has carried out illegal orders. Both the judge and the defendant know this, and the trial is turned into a game. Everyone knows that a factor's attitude toward the environment depends heavily on instructions from the industrial section of the local party district or municipal committee, on their need to produce a plan at any given price. However, a district committee gives its instructions in such a way that there is no law under which it can be construed to be accountable (Komorov, 1980:67).

Soviet environmental law may be a model piece of legislation, but it will not serve as an incentive not to destroy the environment until it is enforced.[4]

SUMMARY

The Soviets claim that socialist production will solve any long-run environmental problem. This will occur through the internalization of all costs of production and the efficiency of central planning for both short and long-run time periods. In this system growth and technology are tools which solve environmental problems. These tools are in the control of mankind, not *vice versa*.

Examination of the Soviet record, however, reveals a significant difference between theory and reality. This divergence was explained by the existence of institutional factors which are independent of socialism. These factors are the Soviet emphasis on growth, its reliance on prices that do not reflect the costs of pollution or the scarcity of resources, and its system of rewards and punishments for managers.

FOOTNOTES

1. Because expression is tightly controlled in the Soviet Union, published writing tends to reflect a single position on most issues. Thus is makes sense to talk about "the" Soviet view even though specific individuals may differ from it. When conflict does emerge in the press, it is typically indicative of more fundamental disagreements on the issue within the Communist Party. See the essay by Philip Maloney in this volume.

2. Soviet bloc opposition to population control evident, for example, at the United Nations conferences on population and food, follow from this analysis.

3. MPC--maximum permissible concentration--is a standard for the content of toxic substances in the air, water, etc. In the air it is expressed in milligrams per cubic meter. For example, the Soviet standard for the concentration of carbon monoxide (CO) is 1 mg/cu m for a daily average and 3 mg/cu m for a spot test.

4. For a further discussion of enforcement of environmental laws see Gustafson (1978).

174

BIBLIOGRAPHY

Ananichev, K. Environment: International Aspects. Moscow: Progress Publishers, 1976.

Bogdanov, B. "The Economics of Environmental Decay." Ekonomika selskogo Khozyaystva, No. 2, February 1970. Reprinted in translation in Current Digest of the Soviet Press 22,19(June 9,1970):6-9.

Bonin, John P. "On Soviet Managerial Incentive Structures." Southern Economic Journal 42,3(January 1976):490-495

Communist Party of the Soviet Union. "The Central Committee of the CPSU and the Council of Ministers of the USSR on the Intensification of Nature Conservation and Improved Utilisation of Natural Resources". In Society and the Environment: A Soviet View. Moscow: Progress Publishers, 1977,148-152.

Davitaya, Feofan. "Changes in the Atmosphere and Some Problems of Its Protection." In Society and the Environment: A Soviet View. Moscow: Progress Publishers, 1977,99-110.

Dienes, Leslie and Shabad, Theodore. The Soviet Energy System: Resource Use and Policies. Washington: V. H. Winston and Sons, 1979.

Ellman, Michael. Planning Problems in the USSR. London: Cambridge University Press, 1973.

Enloe, Cynthia. The Politics of Pollution in a Comparative Perspective: Ecology and Power in Four Nations. New York: David McKay Company, Inc., 1975.

Fyodorov, Yevgeny and Novik, Ilya. "Ecological Aspects of Social Progress." In Society and the Environment: A Soviet View. Moscow: Progress Publishers, 1977,37-55.

Gerasimov, Innokenty. "Man, Society, and the Geographic Environment." In Society and the Environment: A Soviet View. Moscow: Progress Publishers, 1977,25-36.

Goldman, Marshall I. The Spoils of Progress: Environmental Pollution in the Soviet Union. Cambridge, Mass.: The MIT Press, 1972.

_____. "Pollution Comes to the USSR." In Soviet Economic Prospects for the Seventies. Washington, D.C.: United States Congress, Joint Economic Committee, 1973, 56-70.

_____. "The Convergence of Environmental Disruption." Science, 170(October 2, 1970):37-42.

_____. "Externalities and the Race for Economic growth in the USSR: Will the Environment Ever Win?" Journal of Political Economy, 80,2(1972):314-327.

Gustafson, Thane. "The New Soviet Environmental Program: Do the Soviets Really Mean Business?" Public Policy 26, 3(Summer 1978):455-476.

Houck, Oliver A. "Lenin's Trees." Audubon (March 1980):104-119.

Kapitsa, Pytor. "Our Home, the Planet Earth." In Society and the Environment: A Soviet View. Moscow: Progress Publishers, 1977,9-14.

Kelley, Donald, et al. The Economic Superpowers and the Environment. San Francisco: W. H. Freeman and Company, 1976.

Khachaturov, T. "Economic Problems of Ecology." Voprosy ekonomiki 6, (1978):3-14. Reprinted in translation in The Soviet Review 20 (Fall 1979):81-100.

Komarov, B. Destruction of Nature in the Soviet Union. White Plains, New York: M. E. Sharpe, Inc., 1980.

Kovda, Viktor. "Land Resources and the Prospects for Their Use." Society and the Environment: A Soviet View. Moscow: Progress Publishers, 1977,111-125.

Kramer, J. M. "Prices and the Conservation of Natural Resources in the Soviet Union." Soviet Studies 24 (January 1973):364-373.

_____. "Environmental Problems in the USSR: The Divergence of Theory and Practice." Journal of Politics 36 (November 1974):886-899.

Leeman, Wayne A. "Bonus Formula and Soviet Managerial Performance." Southern Economic Journal 36 (April, 1970):434-445.

Mandell, William. "The Soviet Ecology Movement." Science and Society 36, 4 (Winter 1972):385-416.

Oldak, Pavel. "The Environment and Social Production." In Society and the Environment: A Soviet View. Moscow: Progress Publishers, 1977, 56-68.

Papp, Daniel S. "Soviet Scarcity: The Response of a Socialist State." Social Science Quarterly 57, 2 (September 1976):350-363.

Pryde, Phillip. "Protection and Restoration of Surfaced Mined Land in the Soviet Union." In Environmental Misuse in the Soviet Union, Fred Singleton (ed.). New York: Praeger, 1976, 60-74.

_____. Conservation in the Soviet Union. London: Cambridge University Press, 1972.

Shabad, Theodore. "Communist Environmentalism." Problems in Communism 28 (May 1979), 64-67.

Taga, Leonore. "Externalities in a Command Society." In Environmental Misuse in the Soviet Union, Fred Singleton (ed.). New York: Praeger, 1976, 75-100.

Volgyes, Ivan. Environmental Deterioration in the Soviet Union and Eastern Europe. New York: Praeger, 1974.

Weitzman, M. L. "The New Soviet Incentive Model." The Bell Journal of Economics 7,1 (Spring, 1976):251-257.

12
Socialist Growth and Nature –
A Literary Perspective

Philip Maloney

INTRODUCTION

Unlike the other papers in this volume, this entry does not deal with specific cases of environmental disruption. Rather, this essay is concerned with the reflection of environmental problems in literature and how literature serves to transmit certain values, which in turn help to form our judgments concerning such things as nature in general and environmental degradation in particular.

Literature has always served to reflect the interests of authors and to present opinions on all kinds of matters. Russian literature in particular has always been concerned with social, political, and philosophical questions, despite the fact that both under the Tsars and the Soviets, a controlled press and censorship of artistic literature have been the rule rather than the exception. One has to remember that Party politics have been either outlawed or kept to a minimum, and that philosophy, at least in the universities, had been reduced to either a study of prescribed religious dogma under the Tsars or, after the Revolution, confined to a stultifying interpretation of Marxism.

With philosophy and politics closely controlled, literature became an outlet for political and philosophical ideas. Although artistic literature--fiction, etc.,--was and is censored, it is possible for a clever writer to slip in a point of view and not rouse the suspicions of the censor. This was certainly the case under the Tsars; the Soviet censorship, however, is more rigorous and writers are not as able to maneuver as they were before the advent of Stalinist efficiency. Recent developments, however, indicate a continuation of the pre-Revolutionary tradition as samizdat literature makes the rounds in the Soviet Union and as unapproved fiction is sent to the West for illegal publication.[1]

THE CLASSICAL TRADITION

In addition to this heritage of social concern, Russian literature has carried on the general traditions of Western culture and civilization. The legacy of classical antiquity underlies many, if not most, of our beliefs and assumptions concerning contemporary

reality. The traditional fundamental components of Western civilization—the Judeo-Christian religious tradition, Greek philosophy and
political theory, and the Roman concept of law—have been passed on
to posterity through the study of various aspects of classical
civilization, especially through literature, and, even more importantly, through the influence of these components upon Europe and its
various philosophical systems and vernacular literatures (cf.
Highet, 1949).

One of the most important ideas which has derived from ancient
Greece is respect for the earth and the environment. Ancient Greek
philosophy considered earth to be maternal, nurturing life through
food and plants and receiving human bodies at the end of life (Wheelwright, 1966:20).

Another prevalent theme in Greek philosophy is the theory that
man is a microcosm of the intelligible and sensible world. Empedocles, a predecessor of Plato and Aristotle, is credited with
originating this idea, although traces of it are found in even
earlier works.

Concerning the teaching of Empedocles, Guthrie writes:

> There is a certain community uniting us not only with each
> other and with the gods but even with brute creation.
> There is in fact one breath pervading the whole cosmos like
> soul, and uniting us with them (Guthrie,1962,I:278).

Empedocles believed that all elements of nature—animal,
vegetable, and mineral—share a kinship, including the transmigration
of souls. The Greek philosopher claimed to have been a fish, a bird,
and a bush at other times (Wheelwright, 1966:141).

Democritus posited a more precise relationship between man and
nature. Building on the base of previous philosophers, Democritus
taught that the cosmic order is divine and that insofar as man's
internal life is kosmios (orderly), man shares in this divine order
(Wheelwright, 1966:184).

Plato also ascribed divinity to the cosmos, citing the
harmonious subordination of the parts within the whole as evidence
for this belief. In Timaeus, Plato (1952:448) asserts his belief
that the universe is living and that it shares a kinship with all
living things.

The microcosmic view of man, developed from philosopher to
philosopher in ancient Greece and then passed on to European
civilization, can be summed up as follows: (1) the entire universe
is animated; (2) all parts of the universe are related in the
harmonious relationship of parts within a divine whole; (3) there is
a kinship of all nature.

The microcosmic view of man—man as an integral part of
nature—has survived in many forms, although refined and limited by
the Judeo-Christian tradition of monotheism. Even in this century
the French philosopher and scientist Pierre Teilhard de Chardin,
operating from a traditional religious base, attempted to balance the
Christian emphasis on spirit by weaving a philosophy of matter and
nature which harkens back to Greek philosophy (cf. Teilhard de
Chardin, 1962, 1964).

The microcosmic view of man is an archetypal idea of Western Civilization and recurs throughout literature. John Donne (1966:25), the English metaphysical poet, states in verse, "yea plants, yea stones detest and love." Shakespeare, along with many other authors, employed a variation on this theme by sometimes matching human moods or deeds with corresponding events in the realm of nature--for example, the fury of King Lear and the fury of the elements (cf. Curry, 1937). In Russian folklore trees droop with sadness or the weather is bad as some evil deed is performed, while the sun shines and the trees stand upright when good deeds are portrayed. Happiness and sadness are also echoed in natural phenomena. Finally, a parallel is drawn between the moral goodness of man and the abundance of unspoiled nature with the inference that both can be diminished.

Friedrich Engels was apparently a believer in the microcosmic view of man. Engels, a close collaborator of Karl Marx, was appalled at the thought that man could attempt to conquer nature and not believe or understand that dire consequences could ensue.

> Let us not, however, be very hopeful about our human conquest over nature. For each such victory, nature manages to take her revenge. Each of these victories, it is true, has in the first place the consequences on which we counted, but in the second and third phase...there are quite different, unforeseen effects which only too often cancel out the significance of the first (Goldman, 1972:15).

Engels cites examples of people in Greece, Mesopotamia, and Asia Minor destroying forests to obtain farm land and unknowingly removing the collecting centers and reservoirs of moisture, thus paving the way for the present devastated condition of those countries. After other examples of the same nature, Engels draws an interesting conclusion:

> Thus at every step we are reminded that we by no means rule over nature like a conqueror over a foreign people, like someone standing outside nature--but that we, with flesh, blood, and brain, belong to nature and exist in its midst, and that our mastery over it consists in the fact that we have the advantage over all other beings of being able to know and correctly apply its laws (Goldman, 1972:15).

THE PRE-REVOLUTIONARY RUSSIAN TRADITION

Russian literature, in common with other vernacular literatures which have developed in the western world, has retained the influence of its classical patrimony. Perhaps the most striking example of man's relationship to all nature occurs in Dostoevskii's *Crime and Punishment*. Raskolnikov, the central character of the novel, has committed the crime of murder and has thus lost within himself that Platonic orderliness which should reflect the harmony of nature in general. Sonia bids Raskolnikov to "bow down and kiss the earth" as a sign of repentance for his crime against nature, of which the earth is the primary symbol (Dostoevskii, 1967:433). A moral lapse, then, is not merely a civil crime or a religious sin, but an offence against the harmony of nature. When one person harms another, nature as a whole is harmed; it can follow, therefore, that man cannot harm any aspect of nature, especially the earth, without harming himself in the long run.

In addition to this wide tradition and its numerous variations, pre-revolutionary Russian literature saw the rise of an anti-urban literature with a special antipathy towards the imperial capital of St. Petersburg. Gogol's short story, "The Overcoat", Dostoevskii's early work, The Poor Folk, and Tolstoy's masterpieces, War and Peace and Anna Karenina, are works which clearly demonstrate their authors' bias against the capital (Gogol, 1943; Dostoevskii, 1966; Tolstoy, 1967, 1979). Boris Pil'niak's The Naked Year is an early Soviet rendition of the same theme. For Pil'niak (1928), Petersburg is a fungus which should be purged from the basically agrarian Russian land.

With the tardy advent of the Industrial Revolution to Russia, an anti-industrial fiction also sprung into existence. Kuprin's novel, Moloch, and Chekhov's short story, "A Doctor's Visit," are examples of a genre which portrayed the seamier sides of industrial life and the negative effects of factory life upon both the owners and workers, as well as upon the countryside as pollution began to take its toll (Kuprin, 1949; Chekhov, 1979).

In common with all vernacular literatures of the western tradition, Russian writing underwent a period of romanticism—a reaction to the restrictions of the neo-classicist movement which had preceded it. Romanticism was a rather broad revolt against classicism in the arts, rationalism in philosophy, and materialism. It is usually connected with political events which enhanced the rights of individuals at the expense of rights of the state; while classicism saw man as governed, romanticism saw man as governing. In literature the romantic hero refused to conform and opted for revolt rather than acceptance, a heroic defiance of the world in the name of a better ideal.

Romanticism also changed—or attempted to change—human perceptions of nature. Those under the influence of classicism tended to view nature as something to be conquered, something to be organized, something completely separate from human beings. It was common for these people to advocate formal gardens, usually squared parcels of well-manicured grass, flowers, and trees. Europe is full of this type of garden which flourished during the neo-classical period.

The romantics, however, held a completely different view of nature. For them, nature is a mirror reflecting human attitudes. The individual communes with undeveloped nature to nuture his conscience and to refresh his strength for the trials of life. Rather than formal gardens, romanticism prefers nature as a primitive wilderness, just as it adopted Rousseau's idea that man is a noble savage. Neither man nor nature needs to be governed by external forces.

Dostoevskii's Crime and Punishment has already been cited as a novel which contains the idea that man and nature are related; Dostoevskii's other novels, especially Brothers Karamazov also propose that view (Dostoevskii, 1957). In the latter novel Dostoevskii presents the view that all human beings are images of God and, therefore, are innately worthy of respect. If all people believe this, writes the author, then the dignity of each person will keep men from abusing each other. In the same novel, Dostoevskii goes much further and states that the earth is also the creation of God and therefore reflects in some way the glory of God. From the religious point of view, Dostoevskii then comes to the same conclusion which the Greeks and romantics had espoused earlier: there is a unity in the world, and man cannot harm nature without causing eventual harm to himself.

Leo Tolstoy's novel, Anna Karenina, presents another variation on the same theme. All of Tolstoy's major works contain this theme, but Anna Karenina presents it most forcefully. Any individual human being is only a small part of a large universe, and happiness depends upon the ability of the individual to discern and blend in with the processes of nature. The closer one is to the land, the happier that person will be. Agriculture, therefore, is to be preferred to industry, the country is superior to the city, and manual labor on the land is more wholesome than intellectual labor. One should study the processes of this earth, not attempt to subjugate and control them. According to Tolstoy, the further one strays from this vision of life, the more unnatural and unhappy life becomes. In Anna Karenina, for example, the heroine commits suicide because she remains dependent upon high society and is unable to appreciate the independent agrarian life which Levin, Tolstoy's hero in the novel, has come to prize through a process of soul-searching.

THE SOVIET WRITERS

Writers of the Soviet period have inherited a rich tradition which included the common Western concept of respect for the earth, a definite ill-feeling for urban life as opposed to the wholesomeness of rural, agrarian life, and uneasiness towards the effects of industry and technological progress. The fact of this tradition goes a long way to explain the silence of established writers during the First Five Year Plan, a silence usually attributed merely to their inability to write upon command. Stalin repaid many of these writers for their lack of cooperation by arresting them during the purges of the late 1930s.

The Five Year Plan was an intensive effort—a crash program—of industrialization and collectivization of agriculture. The purpose of the Plan was to change an agrarian nation into an industrialized country in the shortest amount of time possible. Agriculture was taken out of private hands and the peasants were organized into collective farms. The Plan was inaugurated with much ballyhoo in 1928 and concluded one year ahead of schedule in 1932, although by no means a complete success. Industrialization was slowed down by "wreckers"—in fact, mere incompetence in many cases—and collectivization was intensely resisted by the peasants. The Soviet government reacted with trials, executions, and military expeditions against the rebellious peasants.

The great majority of established Soviet writers, i.e., those whose talent had been acknowledged by the public and whose works were sought after, as opposed to Party hacks who churned out drivel upon command, confronted this phenomenon of crash industrialization with their background of being formed in the Western tradition and by preceding Russian literature; they were unable to paint a favorable portrait of the Five Year Plan in literature when requested to do so. Yuri Olesha, whose novel Envy and other works made him one of the most respected and popular writers of the 1920s, stated that industrialization was not his theme and refused to write upon the subject (Struve, 1950:247). Isaak Babel, whose short stories of life in Odessa and the Russo-Polish War of 1920-21 are considered classics of Soviet Russian literature, announced that he had discovered a new genre--the genre of silence (Hayward and Labedz, 1963:66).

One established writer who agreed to write upon the subject of industrialization after much persuasion was Boris Pil'niak, credited by many critics to be the best writer of the 1920s and now considered a non-person in the Soviet Union. Pil'niak's novel, The Volga Flows to the Caspian Sea, written at the request of Party authorities, wound up being a not-so-subtle condemnation of industrialization and its negative effects upon nature (Pil'niak, 1970). The problem here is the difficulty, if not the impossibility, of artistically justifying a phenomenon which runs counter to a traditionally accepted value--respect for nature and its processes. Industrialization, especially an intensified program of industrialization, means not only the advent of technological progress and its subsequent material comforts, but it also means doing battle with nature, a battle with its own subsequent effects: the tampering with natural processes and the potential ruin of the environment. Another destructive effect of industrialization, of course, is the stultifying and monotonous labor of the worker who must contribute long hours of work.

The physical ugliness of the locale--the belching smoke of the factory, the crowded tenements, shacks, or even barracks in the Soviet Union--and of the workers themselves--must have left a negative impression upon writers who were accustomed to cultivate beauty and refinement.

The Volga Flows to the Caspian Sea exemplifies the negative opinion which most Soviet writers had of the First Five Year Plan. The author opposes the grandiose designs of the Plan not only because they represent unwanted progress or are ugly, but also because he believes that they destroy the harmony of man's relationship with nature. In the novel the offence against nature is put most sharply by the fact that the engineers cause the river to flow backwards, an unnatural achievement which the author cites continually to symbolize the perverse aspect of the entire project and industrialization in general. In addition, the personal lives of the engineers are ruined as moral chaos sets in, and as the engineers themselves begin to regret the passing of the old way of life.

Pil'niak uses the entanglement of the engineers' marital affairs to reflect the unnatural quality of their project. As various husbands and wives fall in and out of love with each other and continually change housekeeping arrangements, the engineers are supposed to accept the situation in accord with the principles in vogue at that time in the Soviet Union. These principles, derived from the philosophy of N. G. Chernyshevskii, dictated calm rational acceptance of new romantic or sexual attachments and condemned an emotional refusal to recognize the change of affection as bourgeois selfishness.

Pil'niak, however, portrays the situation in a different light. In describing the unhappiness of the engineers who attempt to order their lives in accordance with the new morality, he suggests that it would have been preferable for them to have fought for the preservation of their families rather than meekly accept the situation. Pil'niak considers the latter alternative unreal because it denies normal human instinct. Throughout the novel there exists a connection between the personal relationships of the engineers and their occupation of conquering nature; their life, according to the author, is faulty on both counts because it is unnatural.

Pil'niak seems to be stating that material progress cannot be bought at the expense of nature and if the attempt to do so is made, nature will eventually exact a stern punishment, just as unhappiness is the result of an acceptance of an unnatural morality. The particular Five Year Plan project portrayed in The Volga Flows to the Caspian Sea—a gigantic dam—results in the inundation of a local town, the loss of valuable farm land in a time of famine, and the bewilderment of the local population as its age-old agrarian lifestyle is destroyed and the beauty of the countryside is transformed into industrial ugliness. Even the head engineer, Comrade Poletika, a respected member of the Party, begins to realize that the benefits of technology are tempered with destructive side-effects. As if to reward the engineer for coming to his senses, Pil'niak restores to him his wife and domestic happiness. Subtlety was not Pil'niak's strong point.

Pil'niak's final point is one which is more readily accepted now, but which was not in great favor in the Soviet Union at that time. He concludes from the close relationship of man to nature that people will eventually be poisoned if they continue to live in an increasingly decaying environment.

To summarize the First Five Year Plan in literature: established Soviet writers were unable to portray the events of the Plan in a favorable light, and one can logically conclude that one reason was the respect for nature and the earth which is imbedded in the intellectual tradition of Western civilization. This tradition clashed with the methods and goals of the First Five Year Plan and writers were unable to bridge the gap.

The 1932-1953 period is a bleak one in the history of the Soviet Union. Stalinism was to be found in all aspects of Soviet life and literature was no exception. By 1932 the Party had firm control of the publishing houses and literary journals and was in a position to dictate the content of literature. Dissent concerning industrialization, or even a depiction of its negative effects, does not appear in Soviet literature again until the 1950s, following the death of Stalin. Instead, Soviet writers praised industrialization lavishly and portrayed people who were interested in the preservation of the environment or against rapid industrialization as relics of the feudal past, saboteurs, lackeys of international capitalism, or, in the case of Party members, right deviationists.

During the 1950s, social problems again surfaced in Soviet literature, but they were always soluble; a happy ending was still mandatory. Industrialization was not to be disparaged because it helped the Soviet Union defeat the Germans in World War II. Technological progress was necessary for the Soviet Union to outdo America and take its rightful place among the great powers.

Only in the 1970s did Soviet literature begin to reflect real doubt about the negative aspects of technology and once again lament the passed beauty of unspoiled nature. This new development is associated with a group known as the village writers, a sort of catch-all term for authors who are interested in the natural quality of small village life and complain about the encroachments of industry upon the countryside and its consequent disruption of the environment. These writers, especially Vladimir Soloukhin, tackle the problems of pollution head on and complain about the destruction of nature (cf. Brown, 1978). They also ask the question, but very carefully, of course: is it all worth it? The fact that they ask the question, and the way in which the question is phrased, suggest that the answer is not affirmative.

The village writers also--once again very gingerly--deal with the fundamental problem in Soviet industrial life, the problem of the Plan. Michael Kupilik's essay in this volume goes into this factor in more detail. Briefly the problem is this: each factory manager is expected to deliver a quota each month, and his professional career depends upon his ability to fulfill the quota at the appointed time. Pollution controls-- usually costly, slowing or stopping production while they are installed and perhaps even after they are installed—are not the concern of the manager. His livelihood depends upon his ability to meet short-term goals, even if the result is a long-term mess. This situation is the norm in the Soviet economy and even a mild attack upon this system requires a certain amount of courage.

There is a very interesting political aspect to this development. The Soviet press, including artistic literature, is carefully controlled and when a note of dissent or criticism does appear in the Soviet Union, it usually signifies some support among Party authorities or, at least, among a small group within the Party elite. At this moment, however, the village writers are under severe attack by orthodox Soviet literary critics for trying to turn back the clock and for not having the correct view towards industrial progress. This literary debate then implies a concealed conflict within Party circles over the impacts of industrialization. The outcome of this debate remains to be seen, but the injection of the phrase "lack of class consciousness," a powerful epithet in official Soviet usage, may indicate that the village writers will be on the losing side.

Alexander Solzhenitsyn's novels also reflect the common tradition by carrying on the Tolstoyan legacy. In First Circle, for example, the educated and the powerful--engineers, physicists, famous authors, and politicians--lead unhappy and shallow lives, while the janitor at the scientific institute, a peasant who is temporarily away from the land, is comparatively well-adjusted (Solzhenitsyn, 1976). He is concerned only with his family and his land, and operates from humane impulses rather than from consciously formulated principles.

Solzhenitsyn uses the janitor as a teacher as the peasant instructs the educated in the art of living a happy and full life. The reader finds that Solzhenitsyn's solution to unhappiness is remarkably similar to Tolstoy's: stay close to the land, distrust material progress, especially attempts to improve upon the processes of nature, and follow instinct rather than theory. Readers may disagree with some of the points raised by both Tolstoy and Solzhenitsyn, but they are representative of a longstanding tradition in Western culture which posits a close relationship between man and the rest of nature.

So what can one say about Socialist growth and nature from a Soviet literary perspective? First, when Party controls are strict, as they were under Stalin and intermittently are under Brezhnev, environmental concerns are not dealt with by Soviet authors; when controls are loose, the common Western tradition and the traditions of pre-Stalinist Russian literature resurface and the negative effects of technological progress make their way into literature with disapproving comments by Soviet authors. Secondly, those writers who are attempting to alert their readers to the dangers of environmental degradation point to a problem which seems to occur in the United States as well as in the Soviet Union. The common tradition of respect for the earth and the need to stay close to the land, concepts which are canonized in literature, do not seem to have much meaning for the great majority of people. In a sense, this tradition is elitist; most peasants in the Soviet Union, unlike their fictionalized counterparts in literature, like industrialization and do not seem too interested in the perils of environmental degradation. In fact, they leave the land at the first opportunity and migrate to industrial sites in order to find more lucrative employment and to enjoy the bright lights of city life. Perhaps the blame for this phenomenon rests with the collective farm structure and its undeniable shortcomings; the fact remains, however, that for the sake of better-paying jobs, Soviet peasants desert their land for the factory.

This fact, however, does not deny the validity or timeliness of recalling the tradition through literature. As people throughout the world become more conscious of the problems facing an industrialized earth, they may discover for themselves the same traditions which philosophers and authors have transmitted for centuries.

FOOTNOTES

1. <u>Samizdat</u> literature refers to works which are passed around
illegally in the Soviet Union. This type of literature consists of
material which is not publishable in the Soviet Union for political
reasons. It is reproduced and disseminated by readers who type a new
copy of the works being read and then pass on both copies to other
readers, who in turn repeat the process until multiple copies are in
circulation. For more information concerning <u>samizdat</u> literature,
cf. Brown, 1978.

BIBLIOGRAPHY

Brown, Deming. _Soviet Russian Literature Since Stalin_. Cambridge: Cambridge University Press, 1978.

Chekhov, Anton. _Anton Chekhov's Short Stories_. New York: Norton, 1979.

Curry, W.C. _Shakespeare's Philosophical Patterns_. Baton Rouge: Louisiana State University Press, 1937.

Donne, John. _John Donne's Poetry_. New York: Norton, 1966.

Dostoevskii, Fedor. _Crime and Punishment_. Baltimore: Penguin, 1967.

_____. _The Brothers Karamozov_. New York: New American Library, 1957.

_____. "The Poor Folk" in _Three Short Novels_. New York: Bantam, 1966.

Gogol, Nikolai. "The Overcoat," in _A Treasury of Russian Literature_. New York: Vanguard Press, 1943.

Goldman, Marshall. _The Spoils of Progress_. Cambridge: MIT Press, 1972.

Guthrie, W. K. C. _A History of Greek Philosophy_. Cambridge: Cambridge University Press, 1962.

Hayward, Max and Labedz, Leopold (eds.). _Literature and Revolution in Soviet Russia_. London: Oxford University Press, 1963.

Highet, Gilbert. _The Classical Tradition_. New York and London: Oxford University Press, 1949.

Kuprin, Alexander. _Molock_. Moskva: Gos-izd, 1949.

Pilniak, Boris. _The Naked Year_. New York: Payson and Clarke, 1928.

_____. _The Volga Flows to the Caspian Sea_. New York: AMS Printing, 1970.

Plato. "Timaeus" in Benjamin Jowett (tran.) _The Dialogues of Plato_. Chicago: William Benton, 1952.

Solzhenitsyn, Alexander. _The First Circle_. New York: Bantam, 1976.

Struve, Gleb. _Soviet Russian Literature_. Norman: Oklahoma University Press, 1950.

Teilhard de Chardin, Pierre. _Le Milieu Divin_. London: Fontana, 1962.

_____. _The Future of Man_. New York: Harper and Row, 1964.

Tolstoy, Leo. _Anna Karenina_. New York: Penguin, 1979.

_____. _War and Peace_. Baltimore: Penguin, 1967.

Wheelwright, Philip. _The Presocratics_. New York: The Odyssey Press, 1966.

Part IV

Asia

13
Environmental Problems of the Green Revolution with a Focus on Punjab, India

Darshan S. Kang

INTRODUCTION

During the 1960s, agricultural science produced the great development popularly known as the "Green Revolution." While scientists, scholars, and cynics from the developed nations have described this achievement both as a "miracle" and a "hoax" (Paddock, 1970:897; Wade, December 20, 1974:1093), Third World countries have welcomed this revolution as a great blessing which has saved millions of people from starving to death. In some countries, the increase in per acre yield of grain and the resultant growth in annual food production has simply been phenomenal. Between 1967 and 1969, a period of two crops, the annual wheat harvest in Pakistan increased by about 60%. In Sri Lanka the rice crop increased by 35% between 1969 and 1971. The record harvest of 1966-67 turned the Philippines from a net importer of rice to a net exporter. In Asia, as a whole, the area under high yielding varieties of crops increased from only 200 acres in 1965 to 34 million acres in 1969 (Stover, 1976:39). Similarly, within the seven years from 1965 to 1972, India increased its wheat production from 11 million to 16 million tons—a record increase in food grain production unmatched by any other country in history (Brown and Eckholm, 1974:137).

In 1967, William and Paul Paddock expounded the "thesis of triage" to assign priorities for delivery of United States food aid to Third World countries which were expected to face serious famines by the year 1975 (Paddock, 1967:205-209). According to this thesis, they divided the hungry nations into three categories.

In category I were nations in which the trend in population growth had already surpassed agricultural potential. These nations were considered the "can't be saved" group and to send them food was considered a waste. Category II consisted of nations which had the necessary resources to buy food. These were called "walking wounded" and required no food aid in order to survive. Nations with a manageable degree of imbalance between food and population made up category III. They were included in a "can be saved" group, provided some time was bought for them with outside food aid.

The triage thesis was widely accepted and frequently quoted during the sixties and even early seventies, and famine was thought to hang like a sword of Damocles over the Third World. However, with the advent of the green revolution the threat of famine receded progressively, at least for the time being. As a result of reaping the harvest of the revolution many Third World countries moved up the triage scale. For example, the revolution has temporarily pushed India from Category I to II.[1] Other than the achievement of political independence, nothing is thought to have had a greater positive impact on the country during the twentieth century.

To most Third World citizens, the green revolution appears to be the final solution for their chronic famine problem, but for more detached analysts it is a bag of mixed blessings. In addition to immense benefits, the green revolution has also brought about some serious environmental problems. These problems, if not tackled expeditiously, may bring the entire process of the green revolution to a grinding halt. Harris even warns that the green revolution will trigger natural and cultural disasters of a size unprecedented in human history (Harris, 1972:28).

THE NATURE OF THE GREEN REVOLUTION

In order to understand the nature of such associated problems and to find solutions for them, we have first to understand the genesis of the green revolution. Traditionally, agricultural production is considered to be a function of land, labor, capital, and technology. Within the overall limits of these variables, agronomists try to maximize crop yields by intensifying the applications of irrigation, manures, chemical fertilizers, insecticides, pesticides, and weedicides to the traditional varieties of grains. These traditional varieties, characterized by tall and thin straw, typically convert the heavy doses of fertilizers into overall growth of the plant rather than increasing the grain yield. Commonly, the excessive growth of the plant causes the stalk to break, lodging the grain on the ground, which results in heavy crop losses. In these circumstances the biological capacity for increasing grain production does not exist or is extremely limited (Brown and Eckholm, 1974:134). The optimum fertilizer doses for traditional varieties are limited to approximately 40 kg. per acre. Thus, a technological barrier to increasing per acre yields exists when using traditional grain varieties.

But during the early sixties, Dr. Norman Borlaug, an American plant breeder, achieved a major break through this barrier by developing dwarf wheat varieties. This breakthrough was considered a great achievement in biological engineering which actually started the process of the green revolution. Indeed, Dr. Borlaug was awarded the 1970 Nobel Peace Prize for this work. The dwarf varieties also came to be known as "new seeds," "miracle seeds," "high yielding varieties" (HYV's), or "wonder wheats".

The important feature of these new varieties is not that they are particularly productive in themselves but that they can absorb three to four times higher doses of fertilizer than the traditional varieties and convert it into grain, provided proportionately heavy and frequent irrigation applications are also available (Hopkins, et. al., 1979:281-282). Other characteristics of these new varieties include:

1. heavy and early tillering,
2. dense plant population,
3. lack of sensitivity to day length,
4. early maturity (120-150 days as compared with 150-180 days for traditional varieties)
5. high susceptibility to insect and pest attacks.

Agricultural experts recommend frequent applications of insecticides and pesticides to ensure a successful harvest. Thus, the green revolution is not simply a product of miracle seeds, but also of exceptionally heavy use of other agricultural inputs--fertilizers, irrigation, insecticides, and pesticides. Figure 1 depicts the

Figure 1

YIELDS OF TRADITIONAL AND HYV GRAINS

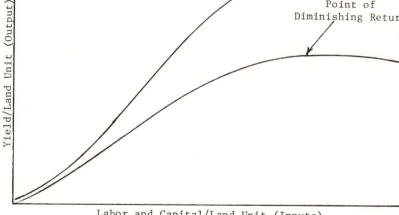

Source: adapted from Hoy (1980)

relationship between yield per land unit and the amounts of cooperating resources applied to the land for both traditional and miracle seeds. The latter are superior not only in raising yields for a given level of inputs, but in permitting more inputs to be applied before diminishing returns set in. The residuals from heavy use of these inputs, however, are responsible for causing several serious environmental problems. These problems will now be examined in a case study of the state of Punjab, in particular, and Third World countries, in general.

THE PUNJAB

The Punjab, India[2] is a classic example of diffusion of the green revolution and associated environmental problems (Poleman and Freebairn, 1973:127; Byres, 1972:104-108). It is a small state the size of West Virginia located in the northwestern part of India (Figure 2). Latitudinally, the Punjab coincides with Texas. The physiography[3] of the state is rather simple (Figure 3). With the exception of the northern foothills, it is essentially a flat alluvial plain with an average slope of less than 0.1%. The total relief is of the order of 2,000 ft. Climatically, it lies in the tropical desert, steppe and sub-humid zones. Eighty percent of its precipitation is received during the three monsoonal months of mid-June to mid-September, and the remaining twenty percent during the three winter months, mid-December to mid-March. A year-round growing season is available under irrigated conditions. Three major perennial rivers traverse the state. The whole state is made up of several good aquifers, which are pregnant with ground water. Traditionally, Punjab has been a leader in agricultural production and is popularly known as the California of India.[4] Indeed it currently supplies about 25 percent of India's total wheat requirement although the state occupies only 1.5 percent of the country's geographical area (Randhawa, 1977:656).

When high yielding varieties of wheat from Mexico were introduced into the Punjab during 1965-66, the resulting yield was an incredible 6.9 tons per hectare, and the annual food grains production of the state increased from 3 million to more than 7 million tons within the next six years (Figure 4). During 1969-70, 59 percent of the estimated acreage planted under new high yielding grain varieties in the non-communist nations was in India; and about half of that was in the Punjab (Ehrlich and Ehrlich, 1972:120). Thus the green revolution was on and so were the related environmental problems.

LAND-USE IMBALANCE

The first casualty of the green revolution in the Punjab has occurred on marginal lands. These lands, appropriate for grazing or forest use only, are being progressively broken for cultivation. This has already resulted in 84% of the geographical area of the Punjab being under cultivation today, whereas a comparable figure for the United States comes to 17%; for a wheat growing state such as Montana 13%, and for India as a whole to 42%. Only 4% of the Punjab is now under forest, and not a single acre of this contains a climax type vegetation (Figure 5). According to Spate, sound land management practices demand that 33% of the state's area should be left under natural vegetation (Spate and Learmonth, 1972:73). The Punjab obviously falls far short of this target.

The result of this pressure is an acute shortage of timber and firewood. For example, the bodies of dead Brahmins,[5] which earlier were cremated with sandalwood (Santalum album) or the wood of the pipal (Ficus religiousa) tree, now are burned with ordinary firewood. This has forced other castes to use cow-dung cakes instead of firewood for cremation. At the same time, Pakistan is experiencing severe timber shortages due to the shift in land-use. The price of domestic lumber has risen from rupees 15 a cubic foot in 1967 to rupees 80 in 1976 (Eckholm, 1979:27).

Similarly, the concept of wilderness has become foreign to the people of Punjab, in particular, and those of India in general. In order to experience wilderness one has to visit the downtown areas of the cities or the conventions of the political parties.

ENERGY SHORTAGE

Not only has the green revolution reduced the amount of wood available for fuel, by taking land from under the forest, but it also entails agricultural practices which are highly energy intensive. The increased demands for irrigation, fertilizers and pesticides which are the principal ingredients of the green revolution further accentuate the existing shortages of energy resources like petroleum, coal, and hydro-power. The irony is that the countries which earlier spent their foreign exchange to import food, are now spending the same on foreign oil and fertilizers to keep the revolution going. India, for example, is importing crude oil from the Soviet Union in trade for rice.

One important impact of energy shortages is that cow-dung, which should be applied to fields to maintain their fertility and proper soil structure, is burned as an energy source. It has been estimated by the World Bank analysts that in Nepal the amount of additional dung that will be burned in the year 2000 will reduce grain production by about one million tons. Each ton of cow-dung means a loss of about 50 kilograms of potential grain output (Eckholm, 1979:29).

Despite the fact that India and many other Third World countries import billions of dollars worth of oil annually, their per capita consumption levels are not high by world standards and shortages remain acute. The per capita consumption of energy in the U.S.A. is 370 times that of Bangladesh, and 57 times that of India (Barney, 1980, Vol. II:239). Currently many people in South Asia do not have sufficient energy resources available to cook their food and there are frequent complaints about black marketing in fuel and fertilizers in the press. In India, electrical energy is rationed and available to domestic, agricultural and industrial users for only a few hours a day. The responsibility for shortages does not lie only with excessive consumption, but also with repeated increases in petroleum prices by OPEC producers.

196

FIGURE 2

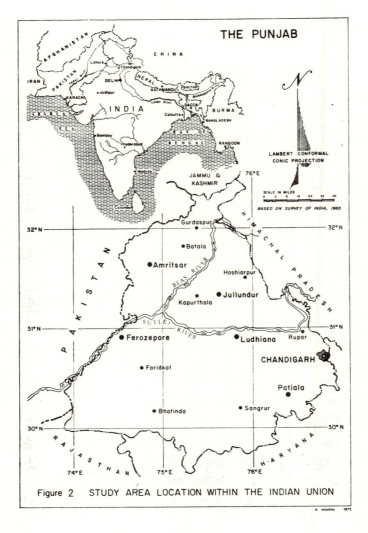

Figure 2   STUDY AREA LOCATION WITHIN THE INDIAN UNION

Source: Kang (1975)

FIGURE 3

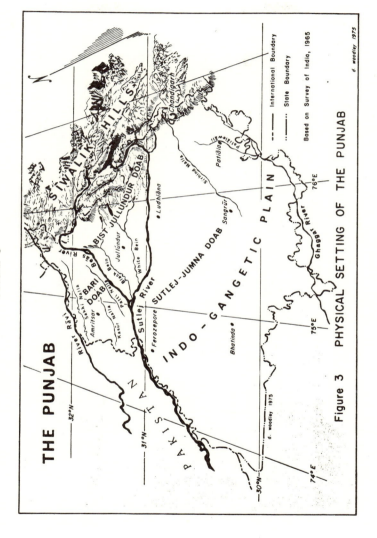

Figure 3   PHYSICAL SETTING OF THE PUNJAB

Source: Kang (1975)

198

FIGURE 4

PRODUCTION OF FOODGRAINS
(PUNJAB STATE)

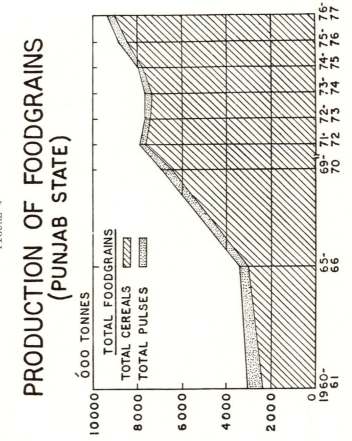

Source: Statistical Abstract of Punjab (1977)

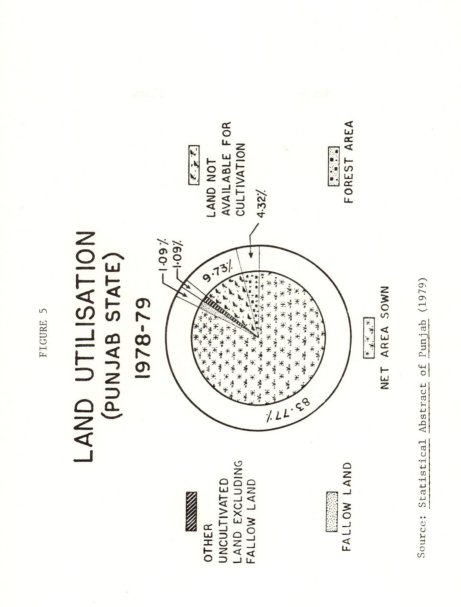

FIGURE 5

LAND UTILISATION (PUNJAB STATE) 1978-79

Source: Statistical Abstract of Punjab (1979)

DETERIORATION IN HYDRO-ENVIRONMENT

Deterioration in the hydro-environment is another problem facing the Punjab as a result of the green revolution. High yielding varieties (HYV's) cannot be grown successfully under dry farming conditions and in the absence of irrigation yield far less than the traditional varieties (Brown, 1970:22). Thus, whereas local wheat varieties require about 12 inches of irrigation in the Punjab, the HYV's require at least 36 inches (Uppal, 1961:16). To meet this intensive irrigation demand, billions of cubic feet of water are being transferred from one basin to another annually. In parts of Punjab, where ground water is plentiful, hundreds of thousands of tube wells with pumps have been installed replacing traditional open wells (Figure 6), and the area under irrigation is increasing very rapidly (Figure 7). These interventions in the natural hydrologic cycle have disastrous effects on the natural environment.

A very large portion of the water diverted from rivers for irrigation percolates downward and raises the water table. The rising water table brings up salts with it. Eventually, both water and salt rise sufficiently close to the surface to prevent the growth of plants. Technically, these problems are known as salt and water-logging, but some experts describe them as a cancer of the soil, because eventually soil deteriorates to such an extent that no crops will grow and the land will have to be abandoned (Brown, 1972:51). According to Calder, in the Indus Valley in Pakistan the population grows at the rate of 10 more mouths to be fed every 5 minutes. In that same 5 minutes in that same place, an acre of land is being lost through water-logging and salinity (Paddock, 1970:901). Salt and water-logging are also advancing rapidly in the river valleys of the Ganges, Helmand, Tigris, Euphratus, and Nile where intensive irrigation is carried out to grow HYV's (Barney, 1980, Vol. II:279). Several million acres have already been lost to salt and water-logging in Punjab, India and Punjab, Pakistan.

On the other hand, indiscriminate sinking of tube wells is causing a decline in the water table in other parts of the region due to "overcrowding". Dahlberg is of the opinion that an "assured" supply of irrigation water may be there for only a few more years (Dahlberg, 1979: 119). Large scale dessication of the regions of the world now supporting the green revolution is thus a real possibility.

The increased use of fertilizers and pesticides is causing extensive pollution of water resources. Eutrophication of village ponds, large scale nitrate contamination of the drinking water supply, and water-related diseases are all on the increase (Barney, 1980, Vol. II:342-43).

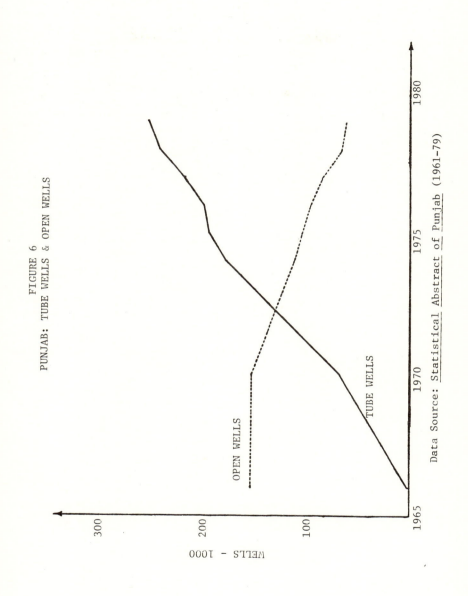

FIGURE 6
PUNJAB: TUBE WELLS & OPEN WELLS

WELLS - 1000

Data Source: Statistical Abstract of Punjab (1961-79)

202

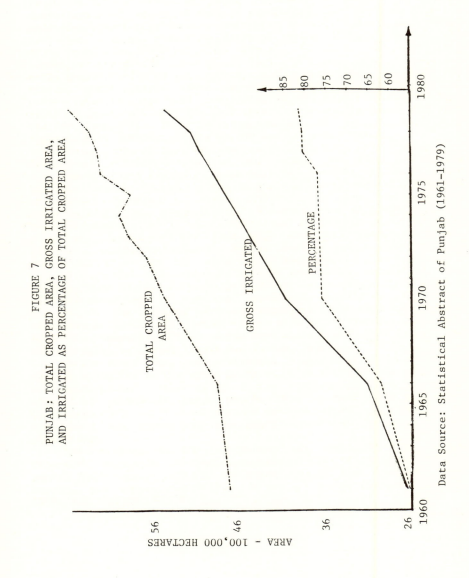

FIGURE 7

PUNJAB: TOTAL CROPPED AREA, GROSS IRRIGATED AREA,
AND IRRIGATED AS PERCENTAGE OF TOTAL CROPPED AREA

Data Source: Statistical Abstract of Punjab (1961-1979)

SOIL EROSION

The next victim of the green revolution is the soil itself.   On the plains, salt and water-logging are taking vast areas out of production.   In the foothills, where marginal lands have been transferred from forest to agricultural use, serious soil erosion problems are developing. The Prime Minister of India, Mrs. Gandhi, has recently pointed out that indiscriminate cutting of trees at the foothills of the mountains and in the plains has brought about climatic imbalances leading to floods, air pollution and drought (India News, July 6, 1981:8). Natural waterways are being choked with sand and silt, and the life of reservoirs is being reduced. Thus it is now estimated that Bhakra Dam reservoir in India, whose original design was based on a 150 year life expectancy, will now be silted up in 75 years. In Pakistan the new Tarbela Dam will be rendered useless in 50 years due to heavy silt load from its catchment. Because of severe erosion, caused by deforestation, the Ambuklao Dam in the Philippines has an expected economic life of just 32 years. Studies of 27 major reservoirs in India reveal them to be silting up at three times the expected rate, largely because of the deforestation linked to opening up of land for agriculture (Eckholm, 1979:31-32). During a visit to the Himalayas in 1979, the author observed large tracts of sloping land being converted from forestry to agricultural land use, making them more vulnerable to water erosion. Thus, the green revolution is indirectly contributing towards the exhaustion of natural resources—soil and water—which are the very basis of its existence.

DIMINISHING PLANT BREEDING STOCK

One of the most serious problems confronting the green revolution is that of genetic erosion. Global 2000 (Barney, 1980, Vol. II:288) reports that plant diseases are constantly evolving ways to overcome plant resistances, requiring plant breeders to develop new resistant strains. The tens of thousands of genotypes of the major crop species are the raw materials from which plant breeders work, but stocks of genetic raw materials are being reduced as natural habitats and traditional seed diversity are lost. In Turkey thousands of local wheat varieties have become extinct (Chedd, 1970:172). Increased reliance on a narrowing gene pool and more extensive monoculture of food staples creates the risk of sudden unanticipated widespread losses from disease in world food production.[6]

According to Randhawa, some of the HYV's like Kalyan-Sona have already become susceptible to brown rust (Randhawa, 1974:70). In 1971, Tungro virus carried by the rice leaf-hopper severely reduced yields of IR8 rice in the Philippines and completely prevented its being grown in Bangladesh. Another impressive new variety of rice[7]— IR24—is also susceptible to several diseases and pests (Allen, 1974:320). In Indonesia 5% of the 1975 rice crop was destroyed by a previously unknown pest which spread through HYV fields (Stover, 1976:41). Pakistan suffered a serious setback in food production during the crop year 1978-79 due to a sudden pest attack, and there is a local joke in Pakistan that the new miracle wheat has given rise to a new miracle locust (Wilkies, 1972:33).

CHANGING CROP PATTERNS

As a direct consequence of the green revolution's introduction in the Punjab, a very rapid change in the spatial patterns of land-use is taking place. Local varieties of crops are being grown in newly opened areas which were formerly forests or marginal lands. Traditional agricultural lands are now kept constantly under soil depleting crops like wheat and rice, rather than being rotated with soil building leguminous crops like pulses,[8] because the former yield greater immediate profits. This process implies a downward spiralling of agricultural land use--from legume to wheat to rice to wasteland. To illustrate, in Punjab, the area under wheat has nearly doubled and the area under rice has gone up by five times since the start of the green revolution (Figure 8). During the same period, the area under pulses (legumes) has been reduced by one-half (Figure 9). A paddy culture is being established which plays havoc with the soil structure and the quality of water on which human health depends. Dysentery and diarrhea caused deaths have increased more than five times since 1971 (Statistical Abstract of Punjab, 1979: 484). The time honored soil building agricultural practice of "green manuring"[9] is now buried in history.

SOCIO-ECONOMIC PROBLEMS

On the socio-economic side, there are serious problems of storage, marketing, and distribution of the fruits of the green revolution. In India, marketing networks and storage facilities are not adequate to cope with the boom in grain production. The consequences can be seen in the "mountains" of food grain stored in railroad stations, schools, and other open air places. Waste of food grains under these conditions is common in most Third World countries, and it has been estimated, for example, that about 15% of the food produced in India does not reach the consumer because of losses in storage and the need for seed.[10] Although food is now available in the market in plenty, many poor families simply do not have the money to buy it.

Due to the increased cost of agricultural inputs required for growing high yielding varieties, large landlords who can finance such costs reap the major benefits of the green revolution. From studies conducted at the International Rice Research Institute, it is estimated that whereas the total cash costs of production for the average Filipino rice farmer using traditional methods and varieties is about $20 per hectare, the cost rises to $220 when the new, high yielding varieties are grown (Wharton, 1969:470). Small landholders and landless peasants usually are not in a position to derive benefits from the green revolution due to lack of credit facilities to meet such costs. At the same time, because of the increased use of agricultural machinery, employment opportunities for rural landless labor are considerably reduced (Cant, 1974:30). Rozlucki has observed that with the exception of the Punjab, the actual income level of agricultural laborers in India did not rise as a result of the green revolution (Rozlucki, 1977:121). The rural rich are getting richer, while the poor in the rural population find it very difficult to maintain their economic status quo. Poleman and Freebairn notice a marked tendency for the rural poor to move to the already over-crowded cities, thus adding to their complex environmental problems (Poleman and Freebairn, 1973:86-86).

Cases of direct class-conflict are on the increase (Harris, 1972:30). In Tanjore, one of India's model IADP[11] districts, forty-two persons were burned to death in December, 1978, when two groups were fighting over the best way to gain a share of the benefits from the new varieties used by the landlords (Brown and Finsterbusch, 1972:142). The Ehrlich's record that resentment toward owners of large landholdings by the landless in India led to massive land grabs in 1970. Hundreds of thousands of landless farmers seized an estimated 32,000 acres of land in a single week (Ehrlich and Ehrlich, 1972:121-122). Naxalites[12] have begun "executing" rich landlords and other perceived class enemies. Thus, the green revolution is working both as a stabilizing and de-stabilizing factor for the economic, social, and political systems of the country. Even on the food front, although total food production in India has increased by more than 100 percent, per capita availability of food has only increased by 43 percent (Figure 10). It is still only 191 kgs. per year, as compared to 708 kgs. in the United States.

OTHER ECOLOGICAL PROBLEMS

Many other ecological problems have surfaced. For example, residuals from heavy applications of fertilizers, pesticides, and weedicides are accumulating rapidly. According to Punjab Government reports, the use of chemical fertilizers has increased 15 times since the inception of the green revolution (Figure 11), and the consumption of insecticides and pesticides increased eight-fold over a period of only three years--1966 to 1969 (Randhawa, 1974:95). The tragedy of the situation is that almost all the pesticides being used are of persistent varieties such as DDT. The local population is not yet fully aware of the consequences of the introduction of these poisons into the ecosystem. There was quite an uproar in the Indian Parliament only when the nation realized that "Garuda", the holiest of the holy birds in South Asia, was already extinct. The incidence of cancer, which was almost unknown in rural areas about two decades ago, has increased very rapidly, as have deaths from diseases like malaria, typhoid, and dysentery.

206

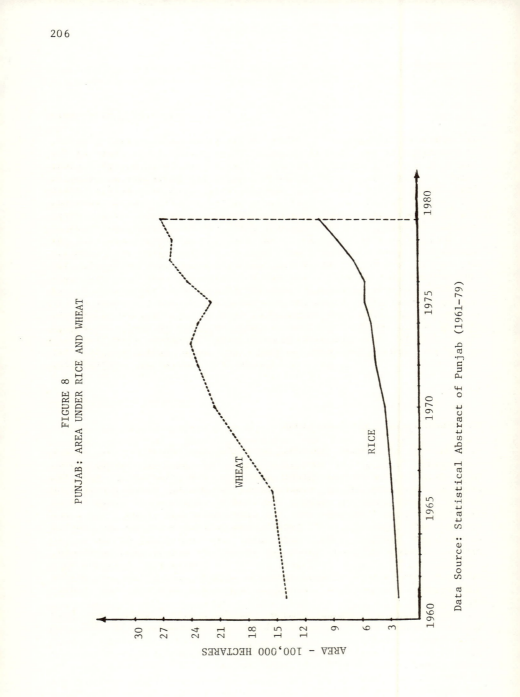

FIGURE 8

PUNJAB: AREA UNDER RICE AND WHEAT

Data Source: Statistical Abstract of Punjab (1961–79)

FIGURE 9

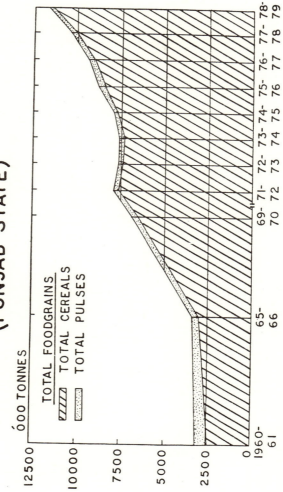

PRODUCTION OF FOODGRAINS
(PUNJAB STATE)

Source: Statistical Abstract of Punjab (1979)

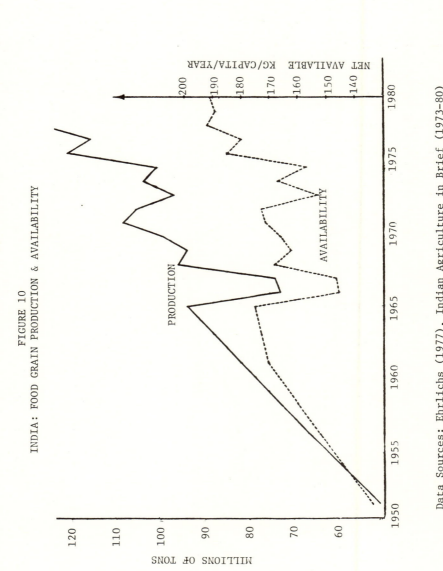

FIGURE 10

INDIA: FOOD GRAIN PRODUCTION & AVAILABILITY

Data Sources: Ehrlichs (1977), Indian Agriculture in Brief (1973-80)

209

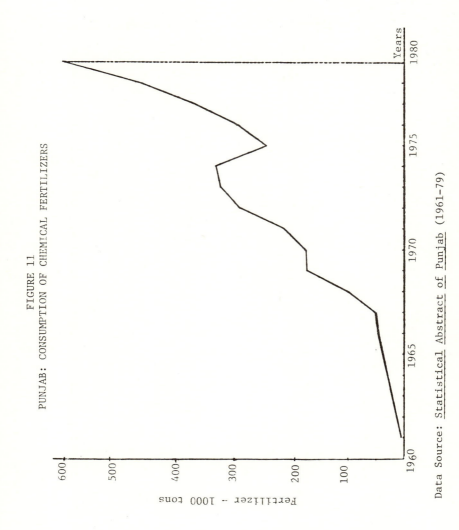

FIGURE 11

PUNJAB: CONSUMPTION OF CHEMICAL FERTILIZERS

Fertilizer — 1000 tons

Years

Data Source: Statistical Abstract of Punjab (1961-79)

210

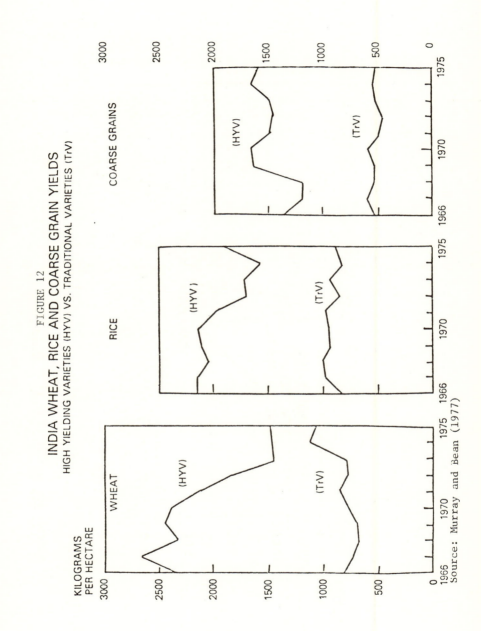

FIGURE 12
INDIA WHEAT, RICE AND COARSE GRAIN YIELDS
HIGH YIELDING VARIETIES (HYV) VS. TRADITIONAL VARIETIES (TrV)

Source: Murray and Bean (1977)

CONCLUSION

In the West, an environmentalist's fight is against waste, excessive corporate profits, and faulty exploitation of natural resources. In the Third World, it turns out to be a fight against the very existence of human life. Pure Western environmentalism is a luxury which Third World nations can ill afford. It is very hard to agree with Marvin Harris' statement that the green revolution is a hoax, and it is impossible to deny that the green revolution has saved some Third World countries from immediate starvation. On the other hand, it is equally hard to endorse the complacency of Third World countries which embrace the green revolution as a perennial success. To a great extent, it is a self-destructive system. The fertilizers, pesticides, and intensive irrigation practices which made the green revolution a sudden success will ultimately lead to its demise if the related environmental problems are not attended to immediately. The yields of HYV's have already started declining (Figure 12). Local specialists should join in developing a well-balanced and well-coordinated approach which could ensure resource utilization on a sustained basis. It will take much capital, considerable time, and persistent efforts to make the green revolution an ongoing success. Finally, the socio-economic salvation of the Third World does not lie only in the green revolution, but also in reversing population growth rates. It is true the green revolution has bought the people of the Third World some time for action. If they fail to act now the consequences, not only for them but for the world as a whole, can better be imagined than described.

FOOTNOTES

1. In fact, so far as the food situation is concerned, India has gone through a full cycle—from a very heavy importer to self-sufficiency, to an exporter, and back to an importing stage, after the introduction of HYV's. (India News, 12(27), July 17, 1981, p.1; Ehrlich, et al., 1977:337).

2. This statement is equally valid in the case of the Punjab, Pakistan.

3. For a detailed discussion of the physiography and hydrology of the Punjab see Uppal and Kang (1955).

4. For further information about the role of Punjab in Indian agriculture see Sorkin (1971).

5. A Brahmin belongs to the highest class in the hierarchy of the Indian caste system. Other major castes are Kashtriya, Vaisha, and Shudra, stated according to the descending order of their status.

6. According to Stover, this is what happened in the Great Irish Potato Famine of the 1830s and 40s (Stover, 1976:41).

7. IR8 and IR24 are high yielding rice varieties which were developed at the International Rice Research Institute in the Philippines.

8. Pulses are leguminous crops like peas and beans (Phaselous mungo), which are the principal source of protein in South Asia.

9. Green manuring involves growing of leguminous crops and plowing them back into the same field in order to maintain, if not improve, soil structure and fertility.

10. The seed rate for HYV's is three to four times higher than the local varieties. The high seed rate is essential to obtain larger plant population per unit area.

11. IADP stands for Intensive Agricultural Development Project. These projects are implemented in selected districts in India by providing special agricultural advisory services and inputs such as fertilizers, irrigation, improved seeds, insecticides, pesticides, weedicides, credit, and marketing facilities.

12. Naxalites are members of that faction of the Indian Communist Party, which follows Mao's principles. The name comes from the Naxalbari area in the West Bengal state, the site of communist uprisings in 1967.

BIBLIOGRAPHY

Allen, Robert. "New Strategy for the Green Revolution." New Scientist LXIII (August, 1974):320-321.

Barney, Gerald O. Study Director. The Global 2000 Report to the President I and II. Washington, D.C.: U.S. Government Printing Office, 1980.

Brown, Lester R. Seeds of Change: The Green Revolution and Development in the 1970s. New York: Praeger, 1970.

Brown, Lester R. and Eckholm, Erik P. By Bread Alone. New York: Praeger, 1974.

Brown, Lester R. and Finsterbusch, Gail W. Man and His Environment: Food. New York: Harper and Row, 1972.

Byres, T. J. "The Dialectic of India's Green Revolution." South Asia Review V (January, 1972):99-116.

Cant, R. G. "The Green Revolution: Implications and Examples from the Philippines." New Zealand Journal of Geography No. 56 (April, 1974):25-31.

Chedd, Graham. "Hidden Perils of the Green Revolution." New Scientist XLVIII, 724 (Oct. 22, 1970):171-173.

Dahlberg, Kenneth A. Beyond the Green Revolution. New York: Plenum Press, 1979.

Eckholm, Erik. Planting for the Future: Forestry for Human Needs. Worldwatch Paper 26. Washington, D.C.: Worldwatch Institute, February, 1979.

Ehrlich, Paul R. and Ehrlich, Anne H. Population Resources Environment: Issues in Human Ecology. San Francisco: W. H. Freeman and Company, 1972.

Ehrlich, Paul R. The Population Bomb. New York: Ballantine Books, 1969.

Ehrlich, Paul R., Ehrlich, Anne H., and Holdren, John P. Ecoscience: Population, Resources, Environment. San Francisco: W. H. Freeman, 1977.

Frankel, F. R. India's Green Revolution: Economic Gains and Political Costs. Princeton, N.J.: Princeton University Press, 1972.

Frankel, Sir Otto. "Genetic Changes in the Green Revolution." Ceres II, 5 (Sept./Oct. 1969):35-37.

Harris, Marvin. "How Green the Revolution." Natural History (June/July, 1972):28-30.

Havens, A. Eugene and Flinn, W. Green Revolution Technology: Structural Aspects of Its Adoption and Consequences. Geneva: United Nations Research Institute for Social Development, 1975.

Hewitt de Alcantara, Cynthia. "The Green Revolution as History." Development and Change V, 2 (1973-74):25-26.

Hopkins, Raymond F., Puchala, Donald J. and Talbot, Ross B. Food, Politics, and Agricultural Development: Case Studies in the Public Policy of Rural Modernization. Boulder, Colorado: Westview, 1979.

Hoy, Don R. (ed.). Essentials of Geography and Development. New York: Macmillan, 1980.

India, Government of. Ministry of Food and Agriculture. Indian Agriculture in Brief. 11th ed. Delhi: Manager of Publications, 1971.

Kang, Darshan S. Derivation of Hydro-based Crop Regions in Punjab (India). Unpublished Ph.D. dissertation, University of Nebraska, Lincoln, 1975.

Ladejinsky, Wolf. "Ironies of India's Green Revolution." Foreign Affairs XLVIII, 4 (July, 1970):758-788.

Mencher, Joan. "Conflicts and Contradictions in the Green Revolution: The Case of Tamil Nadu." Economic and Political Weekly IX, 6, 7, 8 (Feb., 1974): 315.

Millikan, Max F. and Hapgood, David. No Easy Harvest: The Dilemma of Agriculture in Underdeveloped Countries. Boston: Little, Brown and Co., 1967.

Murray, Francis S. and Bean, Louis H. World Food: A Three-Dimensional View of Production, Demand, and Nutrition. Washington, D.C.: Center for Strategic and International Studies, Georgetown, University, 1977.

Paddock, William C. "How Green is the Green Revolution?" Bioscience XX, 16 (1970):897-902.

Paddock, William and Paul. Famine - 1975! America's Decision: Who Will Survive? Boston: Little, Brown and Company, 1967.

Poleman, Thomas T. and Freebairn, Donald K. Food, Population, and Employment; the Impact of the Green Revolution. New York: Praeger, 1973.

Punjab, Government of. Economic and Statistical Organization. Statistical Abstracts of Punjab, 1968-1979. 11 volumes. Chandigarh, India: Economic Adviser to the Government, Punjab, 1969-80.

Randhawa, M. S. Green Revolution. New York: Wiley, 1974.

_____. "Green Revolution in Punjab." Agricultural History LI, 4 (Oct. 1977):656-661.

Rosenthal, Jerry E. "And What About the Green Revolution." Agenda III, 2 (March, 1980):5-7.

Rozlucki, Wieslaw. "The Green Revolution and the Development of Traditional Agriculture: A Case Study of India." Geographia Polonica 35 (1977):111-126.

San, Sudhir. Reaping the Green Revolution. Maryknoll, New York: Orbis, 1975.

Sharma, Hari P. "The Green Revolution in India: Prelude to a Red One?" In Imperialism and Revolution in South Asia. Kathlene G. Aberle and Hari P. Sharma (eds.). New York: Monthly Review Press, 1973.

Sorkin, Alan L. "In Punjab: The Green Revolution." Growth and Change II, 3 (July, 1971):36-41.

Spate, O. H. K. and Learmonth, A. T. A. India and Pakistan: Land, People and Economy London: Methuen, 1972.

Stover, Sue. "The Green Revolution: A Lesson in Ecology." The Kansas Geographer, No. 11 (Spring, 1976):39-52.

Sukhatme, P. V. "Human Protein Needs and the Relative Role of Energy and Protein in Meeting Them." In The Man/Food Equation, F. Steele and A. Bourne (eds.). New York: Academic Press, 1975, 53-76.

Uppal, H. L. Crop Patterns for the Bhakra Canal Area. New Delhi, India: Indian Council of Agricultural Research, 1961.

Uppal. H. L. and Kang, Darshan S. "Hydrology of Punjab with Special Reference to Ground Water." Proceedings of Symposium on Ground Water. New Delhi: Central Board of Geophysics, 1955.

Wade, Nicholas. "Green Revolution (I): A Just Technology Often Unjust in Use." Science CLXXXVI (December 20, 1974):1093-1096.

_____. "Green Revolution (II): Problems of Adapting a Western Technology." Science CLXXXVI (December 27, 1974):1186-1187.

Wharton, Clifton R. "The Green Revolution: Cornucopia or Pandora's Box." Foreign Affairs XLVII (1969):464-476.

Wilkes, H. Garrison and Wilkes, Susan. "The Green Revolution." Environment XIV, 8 (October, 1972):32-38.

14

Resource Scarcity and Population Growth: International Planning and Environmental Imperatives

Dennis J. O'Donnell

INTRODUCTION

Throughout the world, human activity affects the environment through diverse patterns of resource use. A good measure of world resource use—world output of goods and services—has increased approximately 4 percent per year since 1950 while population has increased approximately 2 percent per year. As a result, the growth of resource use, with its consequent environmental impact, has been roughly equally attributable to two factors: increasing population and increasing per capita consumption. (Brown, 1974:28). Projecting these past trends suggests that worldwide resource use will double in approximately 17 years.

This output growth has two properties. First of all, it has not been converted into an adequate standard of living for the world's peoples. Even with massive redistribution, total world output would not be enough to provide a decent material existence for the 4.3 billion people in the world. Secondly, it has proved to be environmentally damaging. Scientific and social literature suggests that we cannot indefinitely sustain world civilization at current rates of growth in resource consumption. Additionally, many scientists doubt that we can sustain even our current, let alone a higher, level of resource use without irreversible damage to our biosphere. We face the specter of a world unable to feed its millions, yet unable to tolerate the environmental impact of its inadequate efforts to do so. This possibility must be treated as a serious threat to our existence. The exact outcome of this dilemma is speculative. Yet the fear exists that we are not well enough organized as a world community to adapt our population and resource use patterns to a level consistent with a decent human existence and a sound environment.

In this paper it is argued that most of the detrimental environmental effects of human activity result from externalities, that is, situations in which the benefits and costs of decisions are not received or borne by the decision maker. A commonplace example is a

factory polluting the air. In the absence of regulations, the
factory's use of the air as a dumping ground is probably the cheapest
way of getting rid of wastes. The costs, in the form of health
effects, diminished visibility, and so forth, are borne by the public
at large. The factory owner is more than compensated for the
diminished quality of his own personal environment by the greater
profit realized.

The problem, of course, is not confined to factories. The world
is full of millions of decision centers embedded in a multitude of
economic, social and cultural settings. Individuals, communes,
governments, international organizations, and planning agencies are
all examples. Like the factory owner, they all share the incentive
to avoid paying the full costs of their decisions when it is possible
to do so. Whether it is the Soviet central planner allowing
pollution to destroy Turkish fishing in the Black Sea, the Indian
farmer having another unplanned child he cannot feed or educate, a
U.S. public power authority raising a smoke stack to disperse
emissions, thus meeting a local environmental quality standard, or a
cold, hungry Peruvian cutting wood to heat his house and cook his
family's food, all are transferring costs through the environment to
others by their decisions. They are all creating negative
externalities. In addition, decisions taken by each unit separately
may eliminate benefits available to others and society in general.
The farmers who destroys an apple orchard to provide a storage area
for vehicles may also have destroyed the possibility of beekeeping in
the area. The family that fails to immunize its children may raise
the risk to others of infection. These cases illustrate lost
benefits as externalities.

As a general rule, we observe that regardless of political-eco-
nomic organization, level of development or size of the decisions
making unit, cost transfers occur between decision making units in
our current world. In general, costs are transferred through the
environment where possible.

It is the thesis of this paper that externalities, and ultimately the current threat to the environment derive from the way we have
organized our decisions regarding resource use and population.
Systems of individual, collective, and international decision-making
make the generation of externalities possible. Similarly, changing
the level of resource use without reorganizing decision making will
fail to provide long run stability in our relationship to the
environment.

HIERARCHY AND ENVIRONMENTAL DECISION MAKING

Both aspects of environmental quality discussed in this paper —
population and resource use, involve decisions made at different
levels of aggregation. At one extreme, decisions are occasionally
made on an almost global basis through international organizations
involving most of the world's states. At the other extreme are
decisions taken by individuals. And in between lie regional,
national, state, local and family levels of decisions making.

To a substantial extent, this system of decision making evolved to meet the need for economic growth and political stability. But however useful it may be for that purpose, it makes the generation of externalities inevitable. This is because it permits decision makers to take actions with effects beyond their jurisdictions. In any particular environmental subsystem - airshed, watershed, ecosystem, and so forth - multiple decision making units are permitted to take actions inevitably affecting the whole subsystem.

The only way to eliminate externalities is to "internalize" them. This requires that the environmental costs of resource-use decisions be borne by the unit making them. This in turn implies that the jurisdiction of the decision making unit must coincide with the environmental subsystem affected by the decision. If the authority to pollute the air, for example, resides at the level of the airshed, it will be impossible to pass the pollution to another party. If pollution is permitted, and if the deciding authority is responsive to the interests of its constituency, it will be because the benefits of additional population or resource use are believed to outweigh the costs in diminished air quality. It is impossible for the benefits to be "ours" and the costs "theirs".

To reorganize decision making authority in line with this principle is, of course, a formidable challenge. Individual freedom, government authority, and national sovreignty would all have to be limited in important ways and new levels of authority created. For nations, however, this process is not unknown. In the European Common Market, for example, nations have found that their economic survival has required economic integration, loss of autonomy, and free movement of very diverse peoples throughout Europe.

If we create international authorities to exercise control over environmental systems which cross national boundaries, we destroy a "common property" right to an environmental resource. Consider, for example, the oceans. Though they are unowned, they are used freely by most nations. This free use makes them the common property of all, and subjects them to overuse and degradation. By placing such resources under international management, we remove from individual nations the the right to use them as common property. We invest that right instead with the managing authority, which both controls the resource and represents the interests of all parties that will be harmed by its degradation. Thus "internalizing" costs destroys valuable common property rights. This is another source of conflict in reorganizing decision making.

In many respects, the current hierarchy of decision making resembles an endangered biological system. Synecology is the study of relations between organisms within their environment (Hawley, 1973:27). In the synecology of an environmental unit, the associative relations between the organisms it contains will form an equilibrium both vertically and horizontally. The vertical or hierarchical structure must fit the overall survival imperatives of the environment. A biological system that failed to control component parts' external effects on the hierarchy of subsystems would perish. Our hierarchical decision making system operates with respect to the environment like such an ill-fated biological system. A nation that industrializes for its betterment and destroys its water resources is like an uncontrolled muscle that breaks a supporting bone; the individual that denudes a hillside of wood is like a parasitic cell drawing nutrients from the tissue it composes.

In the following section we examine two examples of the environmentally dysfunctional character of the way we make decisions regarding population and resource use. They display the problem as it occurs at very different levels of economic development and resource use and under different demographic pressures.

The first case is that of the Himalayan watershed, which is among the economically least developed areas of the world and is subject to burgeoning population pressure. The second case is the airshed of the North American industrial midlands and Northeastern coast, which is shared by Canada and the United States. This area exemplifies the highest level of economic development and population pressure due to urbanization.

THE FAILURE OF DECISION MAKING

The Ganges Watershed

The watershed of the Himalayan mountains drained by the Ganges is controlled by India, Nepal, Tibet, Bangladesh and Bhutan, five of the poorest over-populated nations on the earth. The watershed contains an environment deteriorating at an astounding rate through deforestation, erosion, flooding and water pollution (Eckholm, 1975:764-66). Nepal illustrates the problem of hierarchical decision making failing environmentally and leading to devastating international consequences down river. To quote Eckholm:

> Nepal has an exotic facade of romance and beauty...
> Population growth in the context of a traditional agrarian
> technology is forcing farmers onto ever steeper slopes,
> slopes unfit for sustained farming even with the
> astonishingly elaborate terracing practiced there.
> Meanwhile, villagers must roam further and further from
> their homes to gather fodder and firewood... Groundholding
> trees are disappearing fast among the geologically young,
> jagged foothills of the Himalayas... landslides that
> destroy lives, homes, and crops occur more and more
> frequently throughout the Nepalese hills... Topsoil
> washing down into India and Bangladesh is now Nepal's most
> precious export... The incidence of flooding by swollen
> rivers coming down from the mountains is increasing... the
> bed level of many rivers is rising from 6 inches to 1 foot
> every year....causing river courses to meander about, often
> destroying prime farmland (Eckholm, 1975:764-65).

The final resting place of much of the silt is the Bay of Bengal where in 1974 an Earth Resources Technology Satellite observed a new 40,000 square mile island being formed out of Himalayan silt (Sterling, 1976:14).

The process of population growth and environmental destruction initiates with families having additional children. Increasing the family size is a rational decision given labor needs and cultural and

social patterns and families have no incentive to deal with the
environmental consequences. But the watershed cannot support the
cumulative effects. The various decision making units below the
national level are unable to cope with population and resource use
externalities.

At the national level, Nepalese environmental decision making is
largely concerned with internal matters. Though some international
interaction on watershed management exists, the environmental
resource is controlled by none and deteriorated by all. As a river
system, the Ganges has the general property of one way causation and
little feedback (i.e., decisions down river do not affect the
upstream status). Inter-regional economic models do exist with
environmental effects built in (Coupe, 1977:21-31), but policy
application requires that the region be defined environmentally and
be a decision making unit. In the situation confronted by the five
nations in the Ganges watershed, national sovereignty issues and the
ability to externalize costs dominate the forces of regional
watershed cooperative management.

Theoretical economics suggests that a system of compensations
between the nations could develop to reduce the generation and impact
of externalities (Coase, 1971:509-512). Thus India could pay Nepal
not to cause flooding or Nepal could compensate India for the damage
done. These compensations could be "efficient" in the sense of
producing a net gain in social welfare. India would pay Nepal only
if the benefits it received outweighed the cost of flood control.
Nepal would compensate India only if to do so were less costly than
flood control.

Yet such an approach never resolves the issue of who pays whom.
There may be obvious technological considerations - it might, for
example, be easier to stop floods than to compensate their victims -
but the issue is likely to be debated on other grounds. A nation
which is forced to protect its environment and welfare by paying off
a neighbor not only unilaterally incurs the costs of environmental
cleanup, it also relinquishes rights to a common property resource
and an important measure of national sovereignty. These will be the
predominant considerations in any discussion of compensations (Dales,
1972:314-316).

The survival of the people in the Ganges watershed is linked to
the management of the watershed more than to the geopolitcal
organization of India or Nepal. The watershed will sustain life if
population control, migration policy, agricultural practices,
land-forest and animal management are intricately linked as an
ecosystem. This result is beyond Nepal's control and only a partial
concern of India. Currently the hierarchy of decision making in the
Ganges watershed is unevenly developed. While nations and family
units are well organized politically and culturally, regional,
community and sub-national decision making units are poorly organized
and lack legitimate legal or administrative authority over resource
use or population. Eckholm's description speaks clearly to the
environmental results of this situation.

Awareness of the problem is growing. To quote Nirmal Bista, "A
long term perspective on the stability of this fragile ecosystem
demands that the entire Himalayan region be considered as a unit from
an ecological point of view" (Bista, 1981:315). The current focus is

on regional energy use issues between India and Nepal, but broader
questions of watershed management and population control are under
discussion.

The Eastern U.S.-Canadian Airshed

Acid deposition is creating a rapidly deteriorating airshed in
the highly urbanized and industrial eastern part of North America.
World-wide, rain and snow now are from five to thirty times more
acidic than the unpolluted ice and snow deposited in glaciers prior
to the industrial revolution and recovered for analysis today
(Likens, 1979:43-4). In general, this increase in acidity is
attributable to the development of industrial urban society with the
accompanying heavy burning of fossil fuels and smelting of sulfide
ores.

The eastern North American airshed contains a population in
Canada and the U.S. of over 100 million people whose per capita
energy consumption is 61 times the level in India (Brown, 1974:32).
Energy use in this region is doubling every 17 years and mineral
consumption is moving at roughly the same rate (Brown, 1974:31,33).
Economic growth and modernization has increased the use of energy.
The area also has massive urban population concentrations. The
eastern North American airshed includes the second largest
conurbanized area in the world in the New York metropolitan area and
4 others with urban populations exceeding 5 million in 1980 (U.S.
Bureau of the Census, 1979). The process of industrialization-urban-
ization tends to concentrate sources of acid rain pollutants and
attempts to cope with the problem locally tend to spread pollution
across the airshed.

The concentration of sources in urban areas results from the
development of industrial complexes with large labor pools and
massive transportation networks. This leads progressively to
localized pollution problems. The response to local pollution has
typically been the establishment of local emission standards. The
polluters' response in turn has been to disperse emissions with
higher smoke stacks. As Likens states, "the trend toward building
taller stacks has turned the local problems (acid rain) into regional
ones. In 1955 only two stacks in the U.S. were higher than about
180 meters; now essentially all stacks are taller than that ... by
1975 at at least 15 stacks taller than 300 meters had been built in
the world" (Likens, et al., 1979:44). The potential of superstacks
is best seen by looking at the Sudbury, Ontario copper-nickel smelter
with its 400 plus meter stack. One percent of total annual world
sulfur emissions come from this smelter complex and during the past
decade sulfur emissions have equalled the amount emitted by all the
world's volcanoes (Likens, 1979:44-5).

Control of such a phenomenon as acid rain is essential to the
preservation of water quality, animal habitat, and fresh water
ecosystems that clearly cross multiple national boundaries. Local
emission standards have contributed to regional problems and have
generated incentives to pass on negative externalities to the
environment. We see in this case a highly developed urban-industrial
society with a hierarchical decision making system structurally

unrelated to the airshed as an environmental unit. The complexity of defining an airshed may be greater than for a watershed, but the general principle of management remains. The airshed as an environmental unit must integrate decisions controlling all sources and effects of acid rain. World weather patterns connect the airsheds and coordination at the global level among airshed management authorities is essential to complete the hierarchy.

The airshed must integrate decision making across national boundaries, semi-autonomous state and provincial boundaries, local and city jurisdictions. Unless the airshed's environmental needs control industrial activity and local population concentration and growth decisions, the problem will not be resolved.[1]

CONCLUSION

The eventual specification of decision making hierarchies and relevant environmental units is not unlike the evolution of a viable species in the natural world. Unless it is adaptable to environmental change, the species will not long endure. Recognition of such decision making problems as externalities, uneven hierarchical organization, national sovereignty conflicts and issues of individual versus collective freedom must lead to analysis and solutions. These problems have received some tangential attention in population control literature (see Berelson, 1979) and environmentally at such conferences as the 1977 World Water Conference in Mar del Plata, Argentina, and in the research of organizations such as the Energy Systems Program of the International Institute for Applied Systems Analysis. It is useful to note that coordination between the analyses of population and the environment is weak. Economic-demographic models as yet contain few if any environmental interactions (McNicoll, 1976). Major approaches to the analysis of world environmental carrying capacity are very weak in integration of population variables and processes (Robinson, 1973).

The international consequences of population and resource use on the environment have now become dangerous. Survival requires adaptation, and adaptation may require massive alteration in the nature and existence of decision making units, based on knowledge and the imperatives for integrated control. Economic and political systems are transient adaptive mechanisms. Our needs for a sustaining environment endure forever.

FOOTNOTES

    1. After many years of bickering over issues of responsibility arising from the fact that the United States, despite higher emission standards, caused more trans border pollution than Canada, with lower standards, a 1980 binational Commission on Transboundary Air Pollution has been established. A similar step has been taken in Europe under the U.N. Economic Commission for Europe.

BIBLIOGRAPHY

Balassa, Bela. The Theory of Economic Integration. Homewood,
    Illinois: Richard D. Irwin, 1961.
Berelson, Bernard, and Haveman, Robert. "On the Efficient Allocation
    of Resources for Fertility Reduction." International Family
    Planning Perspectives 5, 4 (December, 1979):133-152.
Bista, Nirmal K. (ed.). Development of the Himalayan Resources for
    Regional Cooperation and National Development. Kathmandu,
    Nepal: CEDA, June, 1981.
Boulding, Kenneth E. The Organizational Revolution. New York:
    Harper and Brothers, 1953.
Brown, Lester. In the Human Interest. New York: W. W. Norton &
    Co., 1974.
Center for Economic Development and Administration (CEDA). Migration
    in Nepal: A Study of Far Western Development Region.
    Kathmandu, Nepal: CEDA, Tribianuvan University, 1977.
Coase, Ronald. "The Problem of Social Cost." In Readings in
    Microeconomics, W. Breit and H. Hochman (eds.). New York:
    Holt, Rinehart and Winston, Inc., 1971.
Coupe, B. E. M. G. Regional Economic Structure and Environmental
    Pollution. Leiden, Netherlands: Martinus Nijhoff, 1977.
Dales, J. H. "The Property Interface." In Economics of the
    Environment, Robert Dorfman (ed.). New York: W. W. Norton &
    Co., 1972.
Eckholm, Erick. "The Deterioration of Mountain Environments."
    Science 189 (September 5, 1975):764-770.
Hawley, Amos H. "Human Ecology." In Population, Environment and
    Social Organization, Michael Micklin (ed.). Hinsdale, Illinois:
    The Dryden Press, 1973.
Likens, Gene E., et al. "Acid Rain." Scientific American, 241, 4
    (October, 1979):43-51.
McIntyre, Robert, and Thornton, James R. "Environmental Divergence:
    Air Pollution in the USSR." Journal of Environmental Economics
    and Management 1 (1974):109-120.
McNicoll, Geoffrey. "On Aggregative Economic Models and Population
    Policy." Papers of the East-West Population Institute 18
    (October 1971).
Olson, Mancur. The Logic of Collective Action: Public Goods and the
    Theory of Groups. Cambridge: Harvard University Press, 1965.

Robinson, Warren. "Review Symposium, The Limits to Growth: A Report for the Club of Rome's Project on the Predicament of Mankind. D. Meadows, et al." Demography 10, 2 (May 1973):289-295.

Simon, Herbert. "The Architecture of Complexity." The Science of the Artificial. Cambridge: The MIT Press, 1969.

Sterling, C. "Nepal." Atlantic (October, 1976):14-25.

U. S. Bureau of the Census. Statistical Abstract of the United States: 1979. Washington, D. C.: U. S. Government Printing Office, 1979.

Part V

Africa

15
Human Ecology, Desertification, Nationalism, and Population Growth in the Sahara

Fred W. Reed

INTRODUCTION

Except in those aspects with which we have frequent contact, we humans tend to perceive our world as relatively unchanging. Some changes take place at such a slow rate that we tend not to notice them unless we do careful measurements. Other changes go unnoticed because they occur in parts of the world with which we have little contact. An example is the change occuring in the Sahara desert. Only in the past eight to ten years, because of magazine and newspaper accounts focused on drought and starvation in the Sahel, have we become aware of the growth of the Sahara. But various estimates suggest that for some time the Sahara has been and continues growing southward at a rate of nearly 40 kilometers per year. Because of its size, slow rate of change and distance from us, however, most of us think of the Sahara as fixed in size with its growth only occurring during the past decade or so.

The Sahara desert has, at least during the past forty centuries, grown substantially. Plant and animal species have had their locales greatly altered or have become extinct. Humans, it would seem, have had substantial influence on the expansion of the desert. Small bands of humans, in their seasonal movements, have altered vegetation through burning, overgrazing, and hunting. In the last eighty years, governments have greatly accelerated "desertization" through their interference in the routine activities of humans who have traditionally inhabited the desert.

This paper has two general purposes. First, I would like to offer a description of the growth of the Sahara desert during the past six to eight thousand years. Second, I would like to relate briefly several theories concerning causes of this growth. These will concentrate especially on the role of nomads in the region.

GROWTH OF THE SAHARA

Current Size

Because of its great size, talking about the Sahara coherently is difficult for those of us whose frame of spatial reference is the United States. The present area of the Sahara desert according to Cloudsley-Thompson (1977) is 3.5 million square miles. Only four countries in the world are larger; the Soviet Union (8.6 million square miles), Canada (3.8 million square miles), and China and the United States (both at approximately 3.7 million square miles). Put another way, if all of the United States excluding California and Alabama were a desert, it would equal the area of the Sahara. Other deserts do not come close to the Sahara in size. The Australian desert, at 1.3 million square miles, has about one third the area of the Sahara, with the Arabian next largest.

Today, the Sahara borders the Mediterranean on the North of Africa, often touching the coast line and usually lying only a few miles from the coasts of Egypt, Libya, Tunisia, Algeria, Morocco, the Spanish Sahara, Mauritania, and Senegal. On the south, and east as well, the Sahara contributes a good deal to the geography of Ghana, Togo, Dahomey, Nigeria, Cameroon, the Central African Republic, Sudan, Ethiopia, Somalia, Kenya, and Tanzania. The Sahara divides the continent. Travelers speak of North Africa and Sub-Saharan Africa.

The Sahara is of Recent Origin

Because of its enormous area, it is easy to imagine the Sahara as having existed always at its present size. But comparatively recent investigations in pre-history indicate that the present size of the Sahara is of relatively recent origin. Not too long ago, the Sahara was a place full of life and vegetation.

Nor has the desert always been a dominant feature of Africa. Seven thousand years ago the site of Khartoum, the present capital of Sudan which is now well inside the Sahara, was receiving about 700 mm. (about 28 inches) of rainfall a year (Cloudsley-Thompson, 1977:40). This amount, which is easily twice that which falls across the mountains of Western Montana, is certainly not indicative of desert. At about the same time (ca. 7000 B.C.) the hippopotomus and other swamp animals ranged as far north as 400 miles north of the site of the present city of Timbuktu, which is in the center of Mali on the Niger River (Cloudsley-Thompson, 1977:47). At the end of Upper Pleistocene or about 8 thousand years ago, the central Sahara was covered by Mediterranean vegetation with forests of pine, cedar, and oak. The Sahara south of the Tropic of Cancer was full of lakes and active rivers. Most of these lakes and rivers and the vegetation remained until approximately three thousand years before the present.

Most recently, in 500 B.C. Hanno saw elephants on the Atlantic shores of Morocco in areas which are now desert. Other travelers of that era reported the presence of lions (which, incidentally, were common in Algeria until the arrival of the French). Cheetahs were common in the eastern part of what is now desert and were tamed and trained to course game. Antelopes, mouflon, ostriches and other kinds of game were common throughout the area which is now the Sahara. At present the desert contains the fossils of elephant, giraffe, rhinoceros, and hippopotomus (Cloudsley-Thompson, 1978: 417). Even as recently as 1820, the countryside of northern Sudan was heavily wooded, with game and lions reported to be abundant within 190 km. of Khartoum. Now wood used for fuel in Khartoum must be brought from as far away as 300 km. to the south (Cloudsley-Thompson, 1978:417).

Reasonable evidence exists to suggest that five to seven thousand years ago, much of the central Sahara was a rather humid area. The currently existing wind and rainfall patterns on the south were about 100 km. north of their present position. Rainfall was sufficient not only to maintain plant and animal life, but lakes and rivers as well (Cloudsley-Thompson, 1978:417). Such levels of rainfall have recurred periodically. As recently as the period between 1941 to 1951, the 100 mm. isohyet[1] moved 650 kms. to the north. This most recent movement of the 100 mm. isohyet appears to indicate a wet cycle which lasted until about 1965 (Brokensha, Horowitz, and Scudder, 1977:11).

That the desert's growth is recent is illustrated by the fact that within living memory parklike country in Somalia and the horn of Africa have been reduced to badly eroded wastes without plant cover. Only a few stumps show where junipers formerly thrived. Where lions were plentiful and the plains were reported to support abundant hartebeest, oryx, and gazelle, one now finds scorched and parched earth (Cloudsley-Thompson, 1977:42-43). In many places the earth has no top soil or plant life to protect it from wind and rains. Rains which fall in this desert simply rush through the wadis and provide little support for plant or animal life. The ability of the land to recover from physical impact has been so reduced that in the deserts of Libya, Tunisia, and Algeria, one can still clearly see the tracks of the Allied and German tanks which passed through in 1941-1943.

An idea of the extent of the desert can be had by noting that over one half of the country of Mauritania and three quarters of Niger are desert. In Kenya, which most of us associate with good rains and an abundance of wild game, only 18 % of the land is thought arable (AID, 1975:19).

CAUSES OF THE GROWTH OF THE SAHARA[2]

Climate, Fire, Agriculture, and Population

Let us ask what would account for the expansion of the Sahara.

It seems likely that despite the variations in the area's climate described above, desertization is not an exclusively climatic process and that man has contributed substantially to it. Indeed, Le Houerou contends that the expansion of the Sahara is not at all likely to have come about because of climatic changes in North Africa. The evidence available at present does not suggest that there have been any significant climatic changes in the area for the past two thousand years, and certainly no major changes during the past one hundred. Yet within the past one hundred years desertiza-

tion has substantially advanced. Indeed, the years since 1930 have
seen the greatest spread of the desert (Le Houerou, 1978:365). What,
then, are the human activities which have led to desertization?

Cloudsley-Thompson (1977) argues that the spread of the Sahara
could be largely due to man's development of fire and its subsequent
use in agriculture. Noting that much savanna occurs in places where
the average rainfall is 60 inches per year or more (a condition in
which one would be likely to find rainforest), he argues that the use
of fire permitted Africans to practice shifting agriculture in areas
which were previously rainforests. Burning permitted the agricultural use of the forest and developed the savannas which we now see
occupied by wild game and domestic herds. Areas near the 100-300 mm.
isohyet were most susceptible to conversion through burning and were
subsequently turned into desert through overgrazing. He also points
out that human caused burning differs substantially from naturally
occurring burning in its consequences. Humans often burn grazing
areas and trees at times during the year when rain is unlikely.
Natural lightning fires occur during periods of rain. Moreover, the
burnings which are started by farmers and nomads alike tend to weaken
as well as disfigure trees and other large vegetation. Clearly, fire
has been available for the past 50,000 years and the desert has not
been growing for any time near that long, but it is important to note
that until about 7,000 or 8,000 years ago societies on the southern
edge of the desert were primarily mesolithic. Their subsequent use
of fire may correspond with the fairly recent growth of the Sahara.

Farming in marginal areas is also cited as a major cause of
expansion of the Sahara. Le Houerou (1978) argues that in areas of
100-200 mm. (4 to 8 inches) of rainfall, crops are usually very poor
and farmers may get one crop out of each five to 10 cultivations.
Even in good years, the soil is left exposed to the wind for long
periods of time. The consequence of this exposure is apparent in
Tunisia where the sirocco removes approximately ten tons of topsoil
per month. In conditions where there is only a thin layer of
topsoil, such a loss cannot continue for long without extreme
desertization taking place.

Government farming programs offer greater hazards to the fragile
environments which border the Sahara than have traditional farmers,
who have usually been able only to scratch the surface of the earth
to plant their seeds. Their ability to affect markedly the tilth and
moisture content of the soil is extremely limited. Modern farming
methods, though, have brought machines to the task in these marginal
areas. Tractors permit deep cultivation and the consequent losses of
moisture and top soil. Modern agriculture, moreover, tends to be
monocultural, that is a single crop is grown in an area. Since pest
damage potentially affects the entire crop, monoculture offers
extreme long-term risks to the farmers who practice it. In the short
run, however, monoculture promises the possibility of participation
in dominant cash economies with great payoffs.

Population pressures have amplified the effects of agricultural
practices to accelerate the expansion of the Sahara. In many of the
arid areas of Africa, population pressures are often well beyond the
local carrying capacity of the land. Therefore, individuals migrate
to get jobs. In some areas 60% to 80% of the potential labor force
migrates to other parts of the country or to Europe. Money sent

home, in some instances, exceeds all other local income. In Tunisia in 1973, for example, the largest single source of foreign exchange was money sent from Europe by Tunisian migrants. Some of this money is used to buy tractors and other equipment to expand agriculture into areas previously thought too marginal for that use. According to Floret and Hadjej (1978), of the roughly 9 million hectares of good grazing land held by Tunisia at the beginning of the 1970s, 2.7 million hectares had been diverted to farming. They report that this added farming effort is prosecuted with the use of tractors and other motorized farming equipment.

Another cause of the growth of the desert is wood removal. The removal of trees may not directly affect climate, but it is clear that the presence of trees hinders the run-off of rain and provides feed for browsing animals, e.g. goats, camels, and giraffes. Throughout the area surrounding the Sahara trees have been and continue to be removed. Acacia scrub has long since been removed from the area around Khartoum, and charcoal for cooking fires must now be brought from great distances at high cost (Cloudsley-Thompson, 1978:418). Indeed, in some places in Africa, the purchase of cooking fuel has come to constitute the major single expense for families. Along the east coast of Africa there is frequently a thick cover of smoke coming from the fires used to make charcoal. Much of the charcoal is exported to Kuwait, Saudi Arabia, and the Gulf States where barbecuing is now fashionable. The consequence is continued desertization.

Nomadism and Desertization

The Nomadic Pattern. In assessing the role of nomads in the expansion of the Sahara, it is essential first to understand the human and physical ecology of the region.

The Sahara offers the outside observer an interesting view of mutually dependent human interaction. Subject to a variety of local variations, the network of relations around the border of the Sahara is nearly everywhere the same. The parties to the relation are two. First, there is a set of nomadic herders who spend a substantial portion of their year herding their cattle, sheep, and goats in the desert. These herders move great distances. For example, in Nigeria the nomadic herders range from as far south as the coastline itself to beyond the northern border of the country. At the same time, the herder shares a mutually dependent relationship with the sedentary farmer. Sedentary farmers, who inhabit the countryside surrounding the desert proper, look forward to the visits of the nomads during the dry season and after the harvest of crops. The nomads can be counted on to bring their sheep, goats, and cattle to graze off the stubble from the farmers' fields and to provide needed manure in exchange (Swift, 1977:450).

In addition to providing the farmer with manure, the nomad has historically provided and still provides a variety of services. Often farmers give nomads cattle to graze for them while on their seasonal rounds. In exchange the nomad gets the benefit of free milk and dairy products while moving about and returns the cattle to the farmer during the next season along with any calves, lambs, or kids that might have been born. This sort of trade tends, on one hand, to cement the relationship between the farmer and the nomad, ensuring the nomad's return to provide manure during the next year, and on the other hand reduces the concentrations of cattle in areas of limited grazing. Often the nomad gives sedentary farmers gifts of cattle or other livestock. During the early 1970s it was seen that Tuareg from out of the desert would return to those farmers to whom they had given livestock to collect on the goodwill which they had built up through the years (Swift, 1977:460).

In the rigorous environment of the desert nomadism offers advantages and survival techniques which no other way of can. First, since none of the desert routinely receives as much as 100 mm. of rainfall a year, the moisture available would not permit sedentary agriculture. By moving about, the nomad manages to develop what turns out to be an excellent (if difficult) living from the desert. The mobile nomad is able to take advantage of grazing at the peak of the growing season when grasses are best for digestion and nutrition of his stock. Grasses during this period are about 70% digestible while for dry grasses this figure falls to approximately 30% (Swift, 1977:460). Indeed, it is possible to argue cogently that if the nomads were not moving about making use of seasonal grazing, a substantial amount of pasture would simply go to waste.

Mobility also permits the maintenance of larger herds. In the areas where nomadism is usually found, rainfall is not only low but also highly variable. Local rainfall can vary by as much as 50% a year and may at times drop to zero. Clearly, localized immobile animal production would have to vary in the same manner. Since such variability in herd size is not possible, pastures would likely be undergrazed during good years so that herds might not be too numerous during the bad years. By moving about, sometimes over great distances, the nomad can "smooth out" the variability in rain to which he is subject.

Traditional nomadism in the area of the Sahara desert thus takes maximum advantage of a variable food supply. Nomadism is part of a web of interactions by which sedentary farmers and the nomad both profit. The farmer receives manure when he needs it. He is able to own a herd of animals without the burden of supplying labor or having the animals near when it is inconvenient. The farmer gets meat from time to time and also, with good fortune, will have an animal to sell for needed cash. The nomad's profits are also clear. He is supplied with animals to be used for dairy products throughout the year. During the time of the year when the desert gets hottest, he can move to the area where his farmer clients (patrons?) live and have a place to stay, eat, and get reorganized for the next round of movements.

Nomadic activity and the spread of the Sahara. Despite the intricate and longstanding pattern described here, nomadic activity has also been offered as a cause for the expansion of the desert. Cloudsley-Thompson (1978) argues that the nomads of the desert pose peculiar dangers to the fragile environment of arid areas. Because nomads often use a variety of livestock, their animals are not only able to take maximum advantage from an area but they are also able to completely overgraze it. Indeed, the sheep, cattle, and goats herded by desert nomads do not compete with each other for grazing. Rather, each species concentrates on its own peculiar grazing niche.

Although the grazing of nomadic herds can contribute to desertization, the fact that the nomadic pattern is ancient suggests its role in this regard was, until recently, minimal. Using the archeological evidence that herders were moving their animals throughout the desert region during the fifth and sixth millenia before the present, it can be strongly argued that the grazing and migration patterns which were in use and well established prior to the colonization of Africa contained considerable wisdom and proven survival value. The intrustion of "outsider moderns," however, appears to have altered the nomadic pattern to the detriment of the environment and nomadic society itself. This intrusion dates back to the colonial period and has continued under the influence of independence and nationalism.

Early efforts of colonial governments had major effects on the growth of the Sahara. In Niger, for example, the French colonists expanded security in the wild lands where the indigenous population had feared to graze their stock. With entire new areas of the country then available for grazing, the Fulani, a sub-Saharan group of herders, expanded their impact throughout what has now become desert both within and beyond the country's borders. The French also capitalized on a major problem for nomads in an arid area: the scarcity of water. Nomads seemed to be searching constantly for water for themselves and their animals. The French thus decided to drill boreholes to make water more accessible. They did not realize that there was already an existing intricate system of water sharing. Previously, the person who dug a well was able to decide who would use the water. These distributional limits on the water supply controlled the number of nomads and herds in an area. No such norm governed the use of government wells. Also, the water now seemed abundant. Nomads tended to stay near the boreholes with the consequence that areas of ten to fifteen km. around each borehole were overgrazed, bringing additional desert (Swift, 1977:474-475).

Independence came to most of the Saharan African countries towards the end of the 1950s or the beginning of the 1960s and further transformed the pattern of nomadic life.

One of the first tasks of any polity is to restrict its own population and the populations of its neighbors within their respective national boundaries. Clearly, nomadism in recorded history has not routinely restricted itself to national boundaries. In most instances, nomads have moved in response to environmental (food, grass, water) exigencies with little regard to the political divisions legislated by distant powers. Indeed, some of the nomad groups are known to have moved nearly one half of the distance across Africa in their annual cycle. Now, following independence, nomads were obliged to remain within externally imposed boundaries. In some instances there were clashes with governmental troops. In other instances the nomad simply moved further into the desert. In any event, pastoral mobility seems to have been sharply reduced with a consequent increase in the pressure on local grazing (Swift, 1977:474-475).

The new governments around the Sahara tended not to be so responsive to the nomads as they were to more sedentary citizens. Some of the reasons for this are readily apparent. Nomads, who felt little identification with the new nations, were not parts of the

more important political coalitions which took over governments
following independence. Nomads, because of their frequent travel
tended to be less educated than their more sedentary fellows.
Moreover, governments have little skill in offering services to
nomadic groups and rather prefer that the nomads stay in one place to
receive services. For example Somalia, which prides itself on the
nomad origins of its people, responded to recent droughts (with
United Nations assistance) by setting up programs oriented towards
settling the nomadic groups. Indeed, in roughly twelve years of
development work in the Saharan area of Africa, I have yet to see a
government devise a program for nomadic peoples which was compatible
with their continuing a nomadic life. What have they tried and what
have been the consequences?

One activity oriented towards settling nomads has been to drill
new boreholes to supply water for herds and to provide limited
irrigation. These projects have become somewhat successful adminis-
tratively, i.e. they have caused nomads to become semi-sedentary.
But as in the colonial experience, they have caused concentrations of
livestock to be formed in areas where heavy grazing cannot be
supported.

It was noted previously that traditionally the man or group that
dug a well would determine who would use the water. Through
centuries of customary usage, local norms concerning water use had
developed. The wells drilled by governments and the U.N. created
problems because there were no rules associated with the usage of the
newly available water. Feuds and fights resulted, and in a number of
instances, nomads asked governments to close the boreholes and went
back to digging shallower wells (Swift, 1977).

In the north of Africa, where petroleum has permitted more
extravagant projects, results of government intervention have been
more problematic. Some Libyan irrigation schemes have succeeded in
obtaining 14 cuttings of alfalfa a year. With such success,
sedentary farming is attractive. It must be remembered though that
sub-Saharan water is a fossil resource. At Al-Kufra oasis, with
50,000 hectares being irrigated by sprinklers, the water table is
sinking at the rate of 35 meters in 40 years. Date palms on the
border of the Sahara in Tunisia are succeeding in reducing the water
table 5 cm. per year. It would appear that some of the old ways may
be best - if not in the short run, then in the long run.

The role of population growth. One might also ask whether
population growth of nomads has caused an expansion of the desert?
Recent evidence suggests that it has not.

At the time when the French "pacified" areas of Niger, Chad, the
Central African Republic, and other Saharan countries, the Fulani
cluster of tribes and to a lesser extent, the Tuareg did expand
across the desert clear to Ethiopia on the eastern side of Africa.
More recently, however, research evidence points to self-imposed
population control. The Borora, a Fulani nomad group in Niger
exhibits a net population growth rate of 1.1% per year compared to
their sedentary neighbors' rate of 2.3%. Similarly, the nomadic
Tuareg exhibit a population growth of 1.1% a year while sedentary
Buzu have a growth rate of 2.4% (Brokensha et al, 1977).

SUMMARY

In this paper, I have tried to describe some of the changes taking place with respect to the growth of the Sahara desert. Even without precise measurement, it seems clear that the Sahara has grown substantially during the past century and that no single cause can account for the desert's growth. Observable changes in the weather pattern could only be partially responsible. Use for grazing of land with only marginal ability to recover certainly had an effect. The addition of new technologies which allowed increased density of animal and human populations on the borders of the desert contributed to the change. New technologies such as tractors and drilled wells permitted a more intensive use of land.

This paper attempted to offer a point of view, a hypothesis perhaps, that appears unrepresented in the literature. I have suggested that the Saharan region may have been capable of sustaining traditional nomadic land use with its exchange with the sedentary farmers. A number of national and international changes have drastically altered the intensity and extensity of nomadism. The increased world market in beef has resulted in greater efforts to maintain larger herds. Governmental attempts to restrict nomadism within national borders and tube wells for watering have localized and intensified land use. These national and international actions, I propose, contribute to the already complex web of factors causing the growth of the Sahara.

FOOTNOTES

1. The 100 mm.isohyet is a term used to describe the line along which there is a mean rainfall of 100 mm.(approximately 4 inches per year). The significance of the isohyet is that 100 mm. of rainfall seems to be the minimum necessary for sedentary habitation. While some animals and crops may require more moisture, 4 inches of rainfall on the average will permit farmers to count on getting crops with enough frequency to maintain their families. Also grazing is likely to be sufficient for a few animals.

2. Desertification is a term commonly used to describe the growth of unuseable land such as I have just described. I would like to use another term for the process: desertization. The use of the term desertization has been suggested by Le Houerou because desertification is a word frequently used to denote the general degradation of vegetation and soil conditions in arid, semi-arid, and humid zones. Le Houerou defines desertization as "the extension of desert landforms and landscapes to areas where they did not occur in the past". Thus it is distinguished from the general process of desertification which would include, for example, the regression of tropical forests into savanna.

238

BIBLIOGRAPHY

Brokensha, David W., Horowitz, Michael M., and Scudder, Thayer. The Anthropology of Rural Development in the Sahel. Binghampton, New York: Institute for Development Anthropology, Inc. July 1977.

Cloudsley-Thompson, J. L. Man and the Biology of Arid Zones. Baltimore: University Park Press, 1977.

_____. "Human Activities and Desert Expansion." The Geographical Journal 144, Part 3 (November 1978):416-424.

Ekwensi, C. Burning Grass: A Story of the Fulani of Northern Nigeria. London: Heinemann, 1962.

Floret, Christian and Hadjej, Mohamed S. "An Attempt to Combat Desertification in Tunisia." Ambio 6,6(1977):366-368.

Hawley, Amos H. Human Ecology: A Theory of Community Structure. New York: The Ronald Press, 1950.

Johnson, Douglas and O'Keefe, Phil. Overview of Physical and Socio-Economic Environments, Impact Situation in North Africa. Clark University. Overview Paper 4. February 1978.

Le Houerou, Henri Noel. "Man and Desertization in the Mediterranean Region." Ambio 6,6(1977):363-365.

Rand McNally. World Atlas. Imperial Edition. Chicago: Rand McNally and Co.:1970.

Swift, Jeremy. "Sahelian Pastoralists: Underdevelopment, Desertification, and Famine." Annual Review of Anthropology 6(1977):457-78.

16
China and Tanzania: Economic Development and Environmental Problems

Robert E. Eagle

> If present trends continue, the world in 2000 will be more crowded, more polluted, less stable ecologically, and more vulnerable to disruption than the world we live in now. Serious stresses involving population, resources, and environment are clearly visible ahead. Despite greater material output, the world's people will be poorer in many ways than they are today (Barney, 1980:1).

The above conclusion was the result of the most massive study of world environmental problems ever attempted by the United States Government. Commissioned by President Jimmy Carter, the study was an attempt to project what the world would be like if the U.S. and other nations continued to pursue their current policies. The report suggests that the nations of the world will have to take decisive action to alter the current trends (Barney, 1980:1-5).

As one looks at the issues that have held the attention of the political leaders of the world in the past decade, there is evidence of some concern for environmental problems. But these concerns have not been of as high priority as several other problem areas. For less developed countries, problems of economic development are generally of far greater salience than are environmental problems (Soroos, 1981). Basic human needs for food, safe water, shelter, education, health care, and employment opportunities are the items highest on the agendas of the world's poorer countries.

Economic development and environmental problems are not always thought of together. But if one stops to consider the nature and causes of environmental problems, it is clear that many, if not most, of the serious environmental problems in both developed and less developed countries are consequences of the activities we associate with economic development.

Often when world environmental problems are discussed, they are linked to the western, industrial, energy-intensive model of development. Sometimes in this context, suggestions are made for alternative models of development, especially for countries which have not yet developed so-called modern, industrial economies. For example, Dennis Pirages suggests rather than follow the industrial model, less developed countries should seek a different path to development: one with considerable emphasis on agriculture and which would use small-scale or "appropriate" technology that would be simpler, decentralized, and labor intensive (Pirages,1978:268-270).

A number of writers have treated alternative models of development and "appropriate" technology, particularly from a theoretical point of view. This paper examines the experiences of two countries--China and Tanzania--in which leaders have developed indigenous alternative models of development and have tried for a considerable period to use them to achieve development in their own countries.

The models of development created by Mao Zedong in China and Julius Nyerere in Tanzania have generated a great deal of interest around the world, particularly the Third World. Both models place emphasis on rural development, equality, self sufficiency, and frugality. Both leaders have opted for socialist economies within a one-party state. There are, of course, some important differences between the approaches that the two nations have taken and these differences will be brought out as the development of the two countries is described below.

The features of these development models mentioned above, particularly the elements of self sufficiency and frugality, have led a number of commentators to suggest that these two countries have devised paths to economic development that are much more compatible with the need to preserve the environment than have other development models, particularly those stressing industrialization, energy-intensive approaches to nearly everything, and urbanization.

CHINA

The most striking characteristic of China today is its tremendous population. Approximately 1 billion people, almost a quarter of the entire earth's population, live in a land area roughly comparable to that of the United States. The amount of cultivable land is only about 10% to 13% of the total land area.

The topography of China varies greatly, from tropical lowlands along the coast to the highest mountain in the world, from arid deserts to fertile farm land that has been producing for centuries.

There was a time centuries ago when China had a very impressive cover of trees and an abundance of wildlife. This is no longer so and it has been the driving force of population, probably more than any other factor, which has changed the face of China to what it is today.

China has the oldest continuing civilization on earth. For much of their history, the Chinese have considered their nation to include the only really civilized people in the world. Outsiders were looked upon as barbarians. It was thus a considerable shock to the Chinese when, in the nineteenth century, upstart Europeans and Americans appeared with superior weapons and other technology and made a virtual colony out of the nation.

The subsequent period from the Opium War to the Boxer Rebellion was a very humiliating one for the Chinese. It was followed by revolution led by Sun Yatsen, then civil war, and then occupation by the Japanese.

When the Chinese Communists emerged victorious over the somewhat corrupt and ineffective government of Chiang Kai-shek, Mao Zedong moved effectively to unite China and to give it sufficient strength to be respected and taken seriously. These accomplishments were so welcome to the Chinese people that they retained a profound appreciation for what Mao had done throughout the remainder of his life, although some of this political zig-zags in later years were unsettling, to say the least (Fraser, 1980:109ff.).

Mao was an avid reader, thinker, and writer, and his ideas for the economic development of China evolved continuously under changing circumstances. In the years prior to 1949, Mao gained some experience managing the base areas under Communist control. Then, from 1949 until 1957, China was under Soviet tutelage. The Soviet model of development was used as a guide, and much of the emphasis was on developing heavy industry.

When the break came between the Soviet Union and China, with the Russians withdrawing their assistance, Mao began to experiment with different approaches to economic development in China. The Great Leap Forward launched in 1958 was an attempt to make dramatic changes in China's economy. Nevertheless, Mao still allocated the major share of capital resources to industry, while to increase output in agriculture, he relied on massive reorganization. The Great Leap Forward took the Chinese peasants through several stages of land reform and reorganization, the final result being the formation of farming communes averaging about 5,000 people each. Since 80% of the people in China live in the country, this reorganization had a very substantial impact on the way of life in China.

According to Alexander Eckstein,

> Mao saw in the Great Leap an opportunity to fully emanci-
> pate China from reliance on the Soviet Union, and more
> importantly, to break out of the vicious circle of
> backwardness through a discrete leap, through a supreme
> effort, through a once-for-all mobilization effort designed
> to tap all the energies and latent capacities of the
> Chinese people. The hope was that one vast supreme effort
> could push China significantly upward in terms of its stage
> of development and thus launch the country on a path of
> more or less automatic and self-sustaining growth (Eck-
> stein, 1977:58).

The Great Leap thus involved not only the concept of self-reliance but also a very powerful feeling of impatience. Some of the elements of the Great Leap strategy, such as labor-intensive approaches to agriculture and the development of decentralized, small-scale industry, probably had considerable merit and the fact that they did not work out well does not necessarily negate their validity. Rather, the problems with the Great Leap had more to do with unrealistic expectations trumpeted by the leadership, particularly Chairman Mao, and the ineffective implementation of plans to realize these expectations (Eckstein, 1977:59).

In 1962, at the National People's Congress, Chou En-Lai announced a major change in the economic priorities of the Chinese. For the first time since the Communists came to power in 1949, agriculture was to be in first place, followed by consumer-goods production with investment-goods industries taking last place. These priorities represented a sharp break from the past.

This break resulted from the serious food crisis and famine of 1960 to 1962, which had indicated clearly to the Chinese leaders that a change of policy toward agricultural development was needed. Under the new policy, agriculture would receive major infusions of chemical fertilizers and industrial inputs. Mao and his comrades had concluded that relying solely on organic fertilizers (both animal and human manure) and merely reorganizing the use of human labor would not bring about the desired increases in agricultural production (Eckstein, 1977:59-63). It should be remembered that during this period China's population, already the largest in the world, was continuing to grow rapidly, while the amount of land available for agriculture was actually decreasing. As a result of these trends, the need for increased productivity in agriculture was a very major problem for the Chinese leadership, perhaps the most important domestic problem they faced.

It is interesting to speculate on how economic development in China might have proceeded under the model of development that had evolved by 1962 if it had not been for the Cultural Revolution. The ideas developed earlier in the evolution of Mao's thinking on economics did not all disappear. Many of them were retained, though often with different relative priorities. The Maoist model of economic development at this point contained all the basic elements that were to catch the interest of many people around the world: self-sufficiency, and labor-intensive agriculture and industry. It also included such injections of modern technology as were feasible, egalitarianism through socialism, and a strong dose of ideology and politics in economic affairs.

Some writers who have discussed the various elements of Mao's economic development model have pointed out that there are some significant tensions, perhaps even contradictions, among the different elements in the model. One part of Mao's model that has been a source of considerable controversy has been the quest for economic equality among the people. No state in the modern world has achieved complete equality among its citizens. Perhaps China has come as close to this goal as any other nation. The income spread between the top fifth of China's population and the bottom fifth is only 4 to 1, compared to 8 to 1 for the United States (Ding Chen,1980).

It was in pursuit of such ideological goals as equality that Chairman Mao launched the Cultural Revolution in 1966. It would be hard to exaggerate the disruptive effect that this Cultural Revolution has had on the Chinese economy. The discontinuation of higher education for ten years alone has had and will continue to have a major effect on China's attempts to apply new types of technology which require trained personnel. The terrorizing of millions of state officials caused not just a temporary disruption in economic activity, but has made most state officials even today extremely cautious about rocking the boat. This is an ironic result

for a political movement led by Mao, who believed that the inventive-
ness and creativity of the people was an important component of
progress in China.

With the intervention of the political struggles surrounding the
Cultural Revolution and its aftermath, it is difficult to make any
clear assessment of the economic development model which evolved
during the years of Mao's leadership. Probably the most important
assessment of Mao's policies is being made by his successors. It is
interesting and significant that a number of important changes in
economic development policy have been made since the "practice"
faction of pragmatists led by Deng Xiaoping won the factional
struggle for power in 1978, two years after Mao's death. The new
leaders have opened the doors to the import of foreign technology and
have encouraged foreign trade in general, a significant modification
of the policy of self-sufficiency. They seem eager for rapid
progress in acquiring new and sophisticated technology.

In the short time they have been in power, China's new leaders
have learned that there are limits to what can be achieved in
modernizing China's economy. Just as Mao and his comrades were over
optimistic in some of their economic planning, so have Deng and his
compatriots had to go through a process of scaling down their
expectations in the light of hard realities. After a year or so of
purchasing foreign technology, for example, China's new leaders
discovered that they had accumulated a considerable, indeed sobering,
foreign debt. They still talk of achieving modernization by the year
2000. But they will not be able to move as quickly as they seemed to
suggest during their first year in control of the government in
China.

Regardless of the somewhat flexible norms of the Chinese
development model, it is clear that economic growth has had adverse
effects on the environment.

The major environmental problems in China are related to the
land, water, forests, and energy resources. But the major force
behind the pollution and depletion of these resources is the
unbelievably large population.

According to recent estimates, the number of people in China is
close to 1 billion. The population has increased by 400 million
since the Communists came to power in 1949, and in one sense, this
increase is a tribute to the good management of the communist
leaders. They have improved sanitation and health care and therefore
dramatically reduced the incidence and effects of many types of
diseases. As a result, the death rate has dropped and life
expectancy has risen to 60.7 years for males and 64.4 years for
females. These are very impressive figures when compared with those
of other Third World countries such as India, which has life
expectancies of 41.9 years and 40.6 years, for men and women,
respectively (World Almanac, 1981).

This huge and growing population has been as much a curse as a
blessing to the Chinese, however. As with increasing populations in
other developing countries, the growing number of people makes it
very difficult to improve the per capita output in the country. The
Communist leaders have therefore encouraged smaller families in a
number of ways. Contraceptive devices and abortions are available
without charge. Birth control materials are available without

charge.   Birth control materials are openly displayed in stores and
store windows. Delayed marriage is actively encouraged.

As he was on many subjects, Mao was somewhat ambivalent on the
subject of birth control. He apparently was reluctant to push hard
for population control because it would have appeared as an admission
that the socialist economy was not capable of providing for the
people of China (Maloney, 1981). His successors, however, have shown
no such reluctance. The official policy in China now is to strongly
encourage one-child families, through the use of both rewards and
punishments. Children from one child families will be given a number
of important privileges in Chinese society, ranging from education to
jobs and other items of great importance. On the other hand, couples
will be penalized if they have more than two children by not getting
any extra food allocation for the third child (Maloney, 1981).

There is more support for these policies among the urban people
of China than among rural families. This is not surprising, for
additional children have some definite economic value in the rural
economy that they do not have in the city.

China's birth control policies have shown some notable results
in the years since the leadership started encouraging smaller
families. After decades of steady growth, the group of Chinese of
ages 5 to 10 is not much larger than the next oldest group, and
exceeds the group of ages 1 to 5 substantially, by about 20 million
(Ding Chen, 1980).   This difference is larger than the entire
population of Tanzania. Even with such sharp reductions in family
size, however, it will be many years until the population stabilizes.

Perhaps the most important resource in overpopulated China today
is agricultural land on which to grow the food to feed one fourth of
the world's population. The total amount of agricultural land in
China is decreasing, due to soil erosion, salinization, and the
growth of urban areas. If land is cleared to make new agricultural
land available, the shortage of forest resources becomes more
pronounced. No more than 13% of China's total land area is suitable
for cultivation, and about half of this land is irrigated. Some of
the irrigation systems are two thousand years old.   The maintenance
of soil quality is threatened by pressures to produce more food.

It is truly remarkable that the land of China has remained as
productive has it has through the centuries it has been cultivated.
One of the reasons that the soil fertility has held up so well is the
traditional heavy reliance on organic fertilizers. Animal manure,
particularly from the peasants' privately-owned pigs, accounts for a
very substantial portion of agricultural fertilizers. Human waste,
or night soil, is also a major fertilizer.

In recent years, however, predominately nitrogenous chemical
fertilizers, produced in local factories, have come into increasing
use. Most experts agree that in order to increase the short term
yield on China's farm land, the use of more chemical fertilizer will
be necessary. However, there is a long run trade-off involved.   The
fertility of the soil will not hold up as well with chemical
fertilizer as it has with the organic ones.

In addition to the deterioration of land, large-scale and rapid
deforestation has taken place, and reforestation efforts, even though
significant, have been inadequate to reverse the trend (Barker,
1981:30-39).   Awareness of the tremendous decline in forest resour-

ces, which has been occurring since 1949, is relatively recent and results in part from the greater availability of data following the Cultural Revolution.

Much of the wood cutting is for commercial timber. But an even greater portion of wood use is for fuel. There is a considerable problem of timber poaching, which is difficult if not impossible to control.

In South China, some forest areas are being cleared to create more agricultural land. The areas in China with the greatest forest cover today are the mountainous and remote parts of the country, which are mostly in the west, but even in these regions there are growing pressures on forest resources.

In China's major cities such as Beijing and Shanghai, there are major air pollution problems. In 1974 the government enacted environmental legislation similar to Japan's, establishing standards for air and water pollution. But as yet there are many places in China that are not in compliance with the standards.

John Fraser, a Canadian journalist stationed in China, noted about a day in Beijing that it was

> one of the five or six times a year you could easily see the beautiful Western Hills from Chang An Avenue, a double reminder of the antique splendor of Peking's natural setting and the density of uncontrolled pollution which normally affronted the city's atmosphere (Fraser, 1980: 321).

Floods and droughts have long been problems in China. Now major projects control the Yangtze and Yellow Rivers along with many other waterways. In the past 30 years, 70,000 dams have been built and irrigated land has increased by hundreds of millions of acres (Ding Chen, 1980). Hydroelectric power production has risen sharply. But both these dams and water quality in the rivers are threatened by future developments.

China's two largest rivers, the Yangtze and the Yellow, are subject to extreme siltation. This is due to the soils found on the loess plateaus of the Shansi and Shensi Provinces which the rivers drain and which are extremely vulnerable to erosion. As a result, the Yellow and Yangtze carry, respectively, the highest and second highest siltation loads in the world. This major and continuing erosion is degrading lands which were formerly suitable for farming, while the downstream dams are threatened by siltation. The Chinese are trying a number of erosion control methods, including terracing and check dams, with only partial success (Robinson, 1981:125-127).

As more chemical fertilizers and pesticides are applied in China's fields, the runoff will create more serious water pollution problems in the adjacent rivers. On the other hand, the current policy of recycling most human waste for use as agricultural fertilizer has made it unnecessary to dispose of this material in the nation's rivers. If the use of night soil for fertilizer is ever discontinued, some alternative method of treatment and disposal would have to be worked out.

Pollutants from industrial plants cause considerable water pollution in China. Although pollution cleanup standards have been on the books since 1974, much remains to be done before these standards are reached by all industrial plants.

In keeping with the Chinese maxim "All Waste is Treasure," the happiest solution to a water pollution problem is one where a use is found for the polluting substances. Orville Schell describes some of the approaches being taken in Shanghai to alleviate water pollution. These include changing from toxic to non-toxic chemicals in industrial processes, multiple-use planning to regain valuable chemicals from waste, and various purification measures (Schell, 1977:102-108).

In order to keep its already large cities from becoming even larger, China has a strict policy of controlling where its people are allowed to live. Thus a limited number of people are allowed, at least legally, in the large cities. This policy has helped to keep these cities manageable and to stem the tide of migrants into cities which one finds in most other developing countries. Of course, a considerable price is paid by the individuals subjected to such regimentation. Many people in China consider the cities much more desirable than the rural areas, and there is a great deal of frustration on the part of people who would like to live in a city but are not permitted to do so.

Some visitors to China remark about the interesting examples of small-scale or "appropriate" technology in use there. Not all the attempts at small scale technology have worked out, but a great many have. One current development of interest is the widespread use of small bio-gas plants. With manure as a starting material, these units extract usable methane gas and produce solid residuals which can be used as fertilizer. 7 million of these plants are in use in China, and a total of 70 million are planned for 1985 (Barney, 1980:200).

Another environmental problem which the Chinese face is desertification. A substantial program of building shelter belts has been undertaken to slow down this process.

TANZANIA

Like China, Tanzania has received considerable attention and interest as a possible model for development for Third World countries.

Tanzania lies on the east coast of Africa, just south of Kenya. Its land area is 364,900 sq. mi. (945,087 km^2). The estimated 1981 population is 17,950,000. The population is growing at a rate of about 3% per year. 90% of the people live in rural areas, with only 10% in urban areas. The largest city is the capital, Dar es Salaam, with a population of 851,522 in 1979.

Tanzania is mainly an agricultural country and is only modestly endowed with natural resources. At present, it is one of the 25 least developed countries in the world and one of the 14 poorest countries in Africa (Ayoade, 1980).

Two of the major assets of Tanzania are its beautiful scenery and abundant wildlife. In the northern part of the country on the Serengeti Plain and in the Ngorongoro Crater one can see elephants, giraffes, leopards, lions, zebras, buffaloes, and many varieties of antelope. This area is the principal basis of Tanzania's tourist industry. Nearby is Mount Kilimanjaro, at 19,340 feet the highest mountain in Africa. Tanzania is bounded by impressive lakes, including Lake Victoria and Lake Tanganyika, and has an extensive shore on the Indian Ocean.

Julius Nyerere has been the President of Tanzania since the country gained independence in 1961, except for an unusual period in which he stepped down from office for several months to contemplate in a quieter atmosphere the problems of the country and what should be done about them.

Nyerere's model of development was not put together immediately after independence. Rather, it evolved over several years. The clearest statement of the model was in a speech now referred to as the Arusha Declaration, which President Nyerere delivered in 1967. The main elements of the Declaration strategy were socialism, self-reliance, emphasis on rural development and the use of labor rather than capital, development of cooperative farming villages (called ujamaa in Swahili), and rules preventing government or party leaders from enriching themselves from sources other than their salaries.

Indicative of the interest that Tanzania's road to development has generated is the following comment by Richard H. Blue and James H. Weaver:

> We are convinced that (President Julius) Nyerere is one of the most creative thinkers on the subject of the development in the world. We believe the effort to build an agrarian socialist society that is equity based, village and community oriented, participative and democratic, and which places a high value on human freedom is one of the most important experiments in the world today.
>
> The model has obvious importance in Africa. Nyerere is widely respected throughout the continent. In fact, he is probably the most widely respected man in Africa today. Even the Tanzanians' enemies seem secretly to hope that the Tanzanian model is successful—so as to demonstrate to the world that it is possible to develop a successful and "authentically African" model of development.
>
> But we think the model may have wider implications than for Africa alone. It may ultimately be important in an evolutionary sense, if mankind is to evolve some way to live together in a humanly satisfying and ecologically sound system (Blue and Weaver, 1977:1-2).

The heart of Nyerere's development plan was the establishment of ujamaa, or cooperative villages. Over the course of several years, nearly all the rural people of Tanzania were resettled in villages in locations chosen by the government. Many of the people were not eager to leave the familiar lands on which they were living. In some cases, force was used in the relocation and there are stories of people being loaded into military trucks at gunpoint and driven to their new homes.

Nyerere's hope was that sizable communal plots would be the basis of prosperity in these cooperative villages. But in most cases, the communal plot system has not worked well, largely because the economic incentive structure did not encourage villagers to work the communal plots (Ergas, 1980).

The villages have served highly useful purposes, though, even if they have not lived up to President Nyerere's expectations regarding communal farming. One of the objectives of the new government after independence was to provide basic services such as health care, education, and water supply. These services can be delivered much more easily in sizable communities than they can to people scattered throughout the country as the population was prior to the establishment of the ujamaa villages. Since then notable progress has been made in these three areas.[1]

In the process of coping with worldwide inflation, a war started by Idi Amin of Uganda, and Tanzania's relative lack of natural resources, especially energy resources, President Nyerere and the other leaders of Tanzania have had to depart somewhat from the objectives set forth in the Arusha Declaration. Most dramatically, Tanzania has not been able to be self-sufficient economically and has, in fact, become one of the largest recipients of foreign aid per capita in the world. When President Nyerere sat with other world leaders at the Economic Summit meeting in Cancun, Mexico, in October of 1981, he did not speak as a stern proponent of self-sufficiency for all nations. Rather, he lectured the wealthy nations on the need for them to do more to help the poorer countries. He no doubt sympathized with Prime Minister Indira Ghandi of India who said, "It's hard to pull yourself up by your bootstraps if you don't have any boots."

The development of tourism also seems to threaten the principles of the Arusha Declaration. It was difficult for the nation's leaders to decide to promote tourism and to build the luxury facilities that would appeal to world travelers. This would mean, they knew, that some of the Tanzanian people to whom they had been preaching the virtues of frugality and a modest life-style would be working in hotels, restaurants, and transportation terminals where they would come into contact with wealthy, extravagant tourists whose life-style was anything but modest. Even so, economic necessity prevailed, and the country has done as much as it can to try to attract tourists and the hard currency they leave behind.

As in the case of China, Tanzania's development has not left the environment unscathed. Tanzania's most important environmental problems are related to the land, particularly to agriculture and forestry. Soil erosion and decline of soil fertility are evident in some areas, particularly in the most heavily populated farming areas where pressures on the land are the most intense. These problems grew considerably worse when the government's policy of villigization concentrated Tanzania's people into large villages. The locations chosen for these new villages were not all the best from an ecological point of view. Often they were chosen because they were close to a road. Some were simply not able to support all the people who were moved to live on them.

Overgrazing by livestock has resulted in serious depletion of the range in parts of Tanzania. This problem is particularly acute on semi-arid lands. In some such areas, only semi-desert is left even though, under less stress from overgrazing, the rainfall of 750 mm. per year should support woodland growth of considerable density (de Vos, 1975:73).

As throughout the Third World, Tanzania is also experiencing deforestation. The government has set aside a generous amount of land in forest reserves in addition to the national parks. But it has not been possible to patrol all these reserves adequately, and some cutting therefore continues.

As results of overgrazing and deforestation, some man-made sub-deserts are found in Tanzania, as well as in Kenya, Botswana, and Lesotho. To deal with this problem as well as to protect soil more generally, shelterbelts are being planted in Tanzania, as they are in China (de Vos, 1975:133).

One environmental problem unique to Africa is the tsetse fly. Found only in tropical Africa, it probably creates the continent's worst insect problem. There are large areas of land unused by man because of tsetse infestation.

The tsetse fly carries the animal parasites that cause African sleeping sickness, which infects humans, and also a deadly disease called nagana, which infects cattle and horses. Nagana is sufficiently pervasive that it has been estimated that if the tsetse fly could be completely eliminated, cattle production in Africa would double. A good deal of land in southern Tanzania is tsetse infested, and operations are under way to clear the land of this infestation to make more land available for agriculture and livestock production (de Vos, 1975:148-151). While the stakes in eliminating the tsetse fly are large, a controversy has nevertheless developed over the need to eliminate wildlife and clear vegetation in the process. For some the environmental costs of eradification are unacceptably high.

In Tanzania, relatively little fertilizer, either organic or chemical, is used. The same is true of "mixed farming", a method where cattle are allowed to graze over the fields at certain times of the year, leaving organic fertilizer in their wake. This practice could be effectively used in Tanzania in many more areas than it is now (de Vos, 1975:176).

In Tanzania at present the pressure of the people on the land is not as great as in countries such as Kenya and China, where the amount of arable land per person is half of that of Tanzania (The World Almanac, 1981).

CONCLUSION

There are a number of similarities between China and Tanzania in terms of economic development and environmental problems. Both countries have for lengthy periods been under the leadership of a charismatic and politically dominant figure who has tried to guide the economic and political development of the country along original paths of the leader's own creative derivation. The models of development did not come into being immediately after their rise to political leadership. Rather, they evolved over several years as a result of reflective thinking coupled with experience in leading the nation.

At one stage in their evolution, the development models of China and Tanzania included the concepts of self-sufficiency as nations, minimum urbanization through agricultural development and small-scale decentralized industry, equality, and socialist economic organization under the tutelage of a one-party political system.

Since these models were developed and implemented in national economic planning, leaders in both countries have made significant changes in the prescriptions they contain.

They have turned away from the idea of total self reliance toward greater acceptance of outside aid, imported technology, outside investments by private enterprise, and foreign trade in general. China, with its large size and vast resources, is much closer to being self-sufficient than is Tanzania.

They have put more emphasis on industry while trying to do as much as possible with agricultural development. They have become more pragmatic in their approaches to economic problems.

The socialist economic approach appears to be well entrenched in China. But modifications in the system are being considered and tried on an experimental basis. These encourage more productivity and efficiency through incentive and reward systems that depart from earlier approaches which emphasized equality regardless of performance.

For several years, on the other hand, there has been some criticism inside and outside Tanzania of its socialist economic system. As long as Julius Nyerere remains president, it is unlikely that drastic changes will be made. Rather, more gradual and limited changes seem likely.

In seeking to achieve equality, both China and Tanzania have faced the problem of government bureaucrats becoming an elite class. Both governments have tried through education, exhortation, and other means to develop in government employees a political and social outlook in harmony with the goal of egalitarianism. But in both countries this has proved to be very difficult. It was largely because of this problem that Mao, in desperation, launched the Cultural Revolution in 1966. This exercise, however, appears to have created more problems than it solved. It seems unlikely that Nyerere would follow a similar course.

The leaders of China and Tanzania have been concerned with the values not only of bureaucrats but indeed of whole societies. They have attempted to inculcate in their people a new set of values, including less emphasis on material consumption. The rest of the world has been watching these experiments at changing values with considerable interest. From what evidence is presently available, it appears that these attempts have been much less successful than their promoters had hoped.

China and Tanzania have faced some similar environmental problems. In both countries there are examples of land used in ways that are inappropriate both agriculturally and environmentally.

The major environmental problems of both countries concern land and forest resources. Of these, soil erosion and declining soil fertility are the most critical. Desertification and deforestation have led to significant reforestation projects, but remain as unsolved problems.

Tanzania has done a magnificent job of preserving wildlife in a system of national parks. Its national forest reserves have been some help in maintaining natural forest resources. In China, the press of its large population has eliminated most of the large animal species that roamed the land in earlier times.

What relationships, if any, can be discerned between economic development in these two countries and their environmental problems? Despite their relatively low levels of economic development, both countries have significant environmental problems, most of them resulting from man's economic activities. The unusually large siltation in China's Yangtze and Yellow Rivers, for example, is aggravated by land use practices on the fragile loess highlands where most of the soil erosion occurs.

On the other hand, because of their low level of economic development, the environmental problems in these countries are generally less severe than similar problems in countries with technologically more advanced economies.

Matters of economic development are generally accorded a higher priority in these two countries than environmental problems. It seems safe to say that the leaders of China and Tanzania will be judged more on the performance of the economies under their direction than on their success in alleviating environmental problems. The Chinese leaders aspire to create a powerful, modern, socialist nation by the year 2000. Given their impressive resource base, including abundant energy resources such as coal and oil, they have a real chance of reaching their goal. In Tanzania, President Nyerere has been looking toward large industrial projects to improve his nation's economy. But the paucity of natural resources in Tanzania, including virtually no major energy resources, will make economic progress slow and difficult. It will be interesting to see how much effort China and Tanzania make to prevent further deterioration of the environment as they pursue their goal of economic development.

FOOTNOTES

1. Julius K. Nyerere, The Arusha Declaration: Ten Years After. Dar es Salaam, 1977. This is a thorough and remarkably candid assessment of both the accomplishments and the shortcomings of the Tanzanian model of development in its first 10 years.

252

BIBLIOGRAPHY

Adelson, Charles E. "Western Tourism and African Socialism." Africa Report. (September-October, 1976):43-47.

Ayoade, J. A. A. "Teaching African Politics: Problems and Prospects." Teaching Political Science, 7 (July 1980):389-406.

Barker, Randolph and Rose, Beth (eds.). Cornell University Workshop on Agricultural and Rural Development in China Today: Implications for the 1980s. Ithaca, N.Y.: Cornell University, 1981.

Barney, Gerald O. The Global 2000 Report to the President of the U.S. Volume I. The Summary Report. New York: Pergamon Press, 1980.

Blue, Richard N. and Weaver, James H. A Critical Assessment of the Tanzanian Model of Development. Development Studies Program, Occasional Paper No. 1, Agency for International Development, Washington, D.C., 1977.

Chen, Ding. "The Economic Development of China." Scientific American 243 (September 1980):152-165.

de Vos, Antoon. Africa, The Devastated Continent? The Hague: Dr. W. Junk b.v. Publishers, 1975.

Eckstein, Alexander. China's Economic Revolution. Cambridge: Cambridge University Press, 1977.

Ergas, Zaki. "Why Did the Ujamaa Village Policy Fail? -- Towards a Global Analysis." The Journal of Modern African Studies 18 (1980):387-410.

Fraser, John. The Chinese: Portrait of a People. New York: Summit Books, 1980.

Maloney, Joan M. "Recent Developments in China's Population Planning: Notes and Comments." Pacific Affairs 54 (Spring 1981): 100-115.

Nyerere, Julius K. The Arusha Declaration: Ten Years After. Dar es Salaam, 1977.

Pirages, Dennis. Global Ecopolitics. North Scituate, Mass.: Duxbury Press, 1978.

Robinson, A. R. "Erosion and Sediment Control in China's Yellow River Basin." Journal of Soil & Water Conservation 36 (May-June 1981): 125-127.

Schell, Orville. In the People's Republic. New York: Vintage Books, 1977.

Soroos, Marvin S. "Trends in the Perception of Ecological Problems in the United Nations General Debates." Human Ecology 9 (1981):23-45.

The World Almanac. New York: Newspaper Enterprise Association, Inc., 1981.

17
African Approaches to Environmental Stress: A Focus on Ethiopia and Nigeria

Peter Koehn

> Let them come and see men and women and children who knew
> how to live, whose joy of life had not yet been killed by
> those who claimed to teach other nations how to live.
>
> Chinua Achebe[1]

The African continent is currently experiencing serious national and transnational environmental problems, including air and water pollution, erosion, drought, reduction of genetic diversity, inadequate waste disposal, the dumping of toxic wastes by foreign companies, and desertification (Ware, 1975; Caldwell, 1975; Lateef, 1980:180-93; Gupte, 1980:1; Africa (London), No. 108, August 1980:10-16, 75-6; U.S.,C.E.Q. and Department of State, 1980:33-4, 99, 144; Robinson, 1979:1; New York Times, August 31, 1980, p. 13; Wells, 1977:19-25; U.N.E.P., 1980:4; 1977:8-12; IUCNNR, 1980). The principal concern of this chapter is with forces that directly and indirectly threaten one of Africa's most valuable and valued physical resources: the land.

It would be difficult to overstate the importance of land to Africans. In 1979, cultivators and pastoralists who depend on the land for their livelihood comprised over 75 percent of the economically active population in approximately three-fourths of the countries located in Sub-Saharan Africa (U.S. Department of State, 1979:1-10). Furthermore, in most parts of Africa, land serves other vitally important social, cultural, and political functions. For some, it provides the basis for individual and corporate identity. Some Africans value their land as a sacred trust and link between past, present, and future generations. In certain places, one's social status is defined in terms of land use rights (see Hoben, 1973:7-10; Famoriyo, 1979:13, 20) and, almost everywhere on the continent, control over land constitutes an important source of wealth and political power (see Markovitz, 1977:280-2; Eckholm, 1979:6; Girma Negash, 1981:36-7).

In most of Africa, land is a fragile as well as a precious resource. On the continent's limited arable lands,[2] soils tend to be shallow in depth, devoid of humus, and easily leached of nutrients and minerals (Bohannan and Curtin, 1971:24-5; Norman, Pryor, and Gibbs, 1979:9-10). This fragile resource is being subjected to increasing stress from a number of natural and social sources, including unfavorable and erratic climatic conditions, forest destruction, wind and water erosion, population pressures, ecologically destructive agricultural and livestock practices, weapons destruction, and unregulated urban expansion (U.S., C.E.Q. and Department of State, 1980:33, 144, 224).

Today, 17 of the 26 countries in the world threatened by mass starvation are found on the African continent. Across Africa, food production increases averaging 1.3 percent per annum over the past decade have failed to keep pace with the estimated annual population growth rate of nearly 3 percent. If these trends continue unabated, Africa's farmers will only produce an estimated 80 percent of the continent's food requirements by 1985 (Jaynes, 1980: 1, 14; Bisrat Aklilu, 1980:387-8; Pirages, 1978:89-90). Yet, most African countries are finding it increasingly difficult to afford escalating food imports. In the face of dire World Food Council predictions that the 1980s will be a decade of perpetual food crises in Sub-Saharan Africa (see Africa, No. 108, August 1980:10), aricultural production pressures on arable and marginal lands will continue to mount in scope and urgency. The primary objective of this chapter is to analyze the environmental and socio-economic consequences of the principal responses to such pressures that have been adopted to date in the two most populous countries in Africa: Ethiopia and Nigeria.

ETHIOPIA

Although Ethiopia is one of the 25 poorest countries in the world, it is endowed with a large land mass, fertile soils, and great diversity in terrain, elevation, and climate (Assefa Kuru, 1978:213; Cohen and Weintraub, 1975:1). In spite of these advantages, food production increased at a less rapid rate than population in the latter years of Haile Selassie's rule, and more than 200,000 peasants perished in the wake of the drought and famine which afflicted Ethiopia between 1970 and 1974 (Cohen, Goldsmith, and Mellor, 1976:8; Shepherd, 1975:37-39). In 1980, the Ethiopian government reported that roughly one-sixth of the country's 30 million inhabitants risked starvation in the face of another drought affecting much of East Africa (Africa (London), No. 108:13, 16; Jaynes, 1980:1).

While Ethiopia has been beset by chronic food production shortfalls over the past decade, the country's political system and its agricultural sector have experienced considerable transformation during this period. These changes necessitate that the agrarian conditions and approaches that prevailed during Emperor Haile Selassie's imperial regime be clearly distinguished and analyzed separately from those that have been introduced since the 1974 military coup.

Land and Agriculture Under Emperor Haile Selassie

Insecurity of tenure constituted a central feature of the pre coup agricultural system, with important implications for land use. In the ten southern provinces, where 60 percent of Ethiopia's rural population lived, the majority of farmers labored under the virtual absence of legal or political protection from arbitrary and sudden eviction. These tenant farmers also found it nearly impossible to obtain compensation for any improvements they made on or to the land. When they increased the value of the land by planting trees, digging ditches, etc. or raised the yield of their harvest, the landlord usually responded by increasing their rent (which amounted to 75 percent of the harvest in some areas). Under such onerous and insecure conditions, southern peasants had no incentive and showed little inclination to increase food production, adopt agricultural innovations, conserve trees and water resources, control erosion, or invest in improved soil fertility (Cohen and Weintraub, 1975:17, 34-55; Stahl, 1974:90; Holmberg, 1976:2-3; Eckholm, 1979:31; Dunning, 1970:298-99). In much of the northern part of Ethiopia, farmers worked fragmented and scattered landholdings under corporate tenure systems.[3] By the late 1960s, northern peasants found it increasingly difficult to maintain a subsistence level of food production in the face of soil erosion and infertility, relatively high population densities, and shrinking plot size brought about by deforestation,[4] rapid population growth, and the nature of prevailing land tenure systems. Corporate tenure systems also prevented northern farmers from obtaining commercial or government credits since, under the imperial legal order, land could not be mortgaged in the absence of an individual title (Markakis and Nega Ayele, 1978:59-60; Disney, 1976:42; Dunning, 1970:296-7).

In Ethiopia, about 85 percent of the labor force depends upon agriculture for a livelihood. The vast majority are subsistence farmers who cultivate extremely small plots using simple, locally available inputs (Disney, 1976:39; Tesfai Tecle, 1975b:1-3).[5] The non-monetary sector accounted for an estimated 75 percent of total agricultural output, more than 90 percent of Ethiopia's food production, and about 45 percent of the country's Gross Domestic Product in the pre-coup period (IBRD, 1973:I,3; Liebenthal, 1976:2). Nevertheless, the imperial government demonstrated little interest in this sector. Under the Third Five Year Plan (1968-73), it devoted only 1 percent of total expenditures to the improvement of peasant agriculture (Cohen and Weintraub, 1975:5, 8). Ellis (1978:9) adds that "intermediate technology was lacking and little effort was being made to develop any."[6]

Ethiopia's Third Plan emphasized the rapid development of large-scale commercial farms producing crops for export. To stimulate capital-intensive agriculture, the imperial government exempted tractors and other heavy equipment, farm fuel (through 1973), pesticides, and fertilizer[7] from import duties, while it taxed imported hand tools such as sickles and spades (Cohen, 1975:348; Blaug, 1974:130). To satisfy western multinational corporations and their agents, Haile Selassie offered foreign firms making agrarian investments of $200,000 or more a three to five year income tax holiday (Dunning, 1970:285; Cohen and Weintraub, 1975:8; Brietzke,

1975:48-9). Many of the large commercial plantations encouraged by Haile Selassie's legal order used fertile lands for the production of luxury crops or inedible commodities destined for export abroad (see Bondestam, 1975:539, 546; Lofchie, 1975:554; Koehn, 1979:52-4, 64n; Stahl, 1974:71-5; Markakis and Nega Ayele, 1978:56; Assefa Kuru, 1978:218; Reimer, 1975:129).

The consequences of the imperial government's agricultural strategy are starkly illustrated by reference to commercial development of the Awash river basin, which began in the early 1960s. By 1970, 60 percent of the land brought under cultivation in the Awash valley had been devoted to cotton production, while sugar plantations claimed another 22 percent of the cultivated area. The discharge of effluents into the Awash river by industries involved in the processing of cash crops and the indiscriminate use of insecticides on commercial farms adversely affected the health of pastoralists and animals in the valley (Bondestam, 1975:430; Flood, 1976:66; also see U.S., C.E.Q. and Department of State, 1980:35). To make way for these profitable plantations, moreover, the government had forcibly evicted Afar pastoralists from their traditional low-land pastures.[9] Eviction from the flood plains of the Awash valley led to overgrazing on the less fertile lands to which the Afar had to move, malnourished herds, and greater dependence upon adequate rainfall for survival. Perhaps one-fourth of the Afar people living in the lower Awash valley perished when drought hit the area in the early 1970s (Bondestam, 1974:423-31; Mohammoda Gaas, 1974:2, 5).

Haile Selassie's government began to devote some attention to the cultivation of food crops for domestic consumption in the latter years of imperial rule. As in the agricultural export sector, official policies favored mechanized farming schemes in the production of food for local markets. Foreign assistance in the form of grants, loans, and advisers provided by various donors (see Lele, 1975:202-3; Stahl, 1974:94-5, 75; Stryker, 1979:353) supported agricultural development projects in Chilalo (sponsored by Swedish aid agencies), Ada (financed by U.S. A.I.D. loans and grants) Wollamo (conceived and principally funded through World Bank loans), and Shashemene and Negele (assisted by U.N.F.A.O. fertilizer credits). In the absence of land reform, a small group of wealthy and middle-income agricultural entrepreneurs became the principal beneficiaries of project inputs in each area. Absentee landlords and other large-scale and "progressive" farmers secured favored access to credit, fertilizers, and extension services, introduced high-yield crop varieties and mechanized farming, and profited from commercial grain production. Mechanized agricultural production threatened the long-term carrying capacity of the soil and diminished the importance of traditional tenant and small owner- occupied farming arrangements. Thus, the rate of eviction of tenant families by landlords increased dramatically in the project areas (Stahl, 1974;75-7, 103-5, 126-67; Cohen, 1975:348-9; 1980b:114-5; Ellis, 1972:118, 126, 138; 1978:8-9; Liebenthal, 1976:5; Gilkes, 1975:126-9; Tesfai Tecle, 1975a:92-4, 100-3; 1975b:30).[10]

At the time of the famine which afflicted Ethiopia in the early 1970s, then, the following patterns prevailed in rural land use and agricultural practices: (1) rapidly expanding adoption by small numbers of large-scale farmers of mechanized agriculture and green revolution inputs subsidized and promoted by foreign donors and imperial government policies and land allocation practices; (2) diminished food production for domestic consumption and rising exports of certain cash crops; (3) tenant insecurity, exploitation, and eviction; (4) increasing marginalization and vulnerability of peasant farmers and pastoralists; and (5) widespread, unattended soil erosion and deforestation.[11] As a result of these developments, previous disparities in resource distribution and income-generating opportunities within the agricultural production sector had become far more pronounced. In addition to having an adverse impact on project environments,[12] the wholesale importation and implementation of green revolution strategies and inputs required the substitution of scarce national resources (capital, foreign exchange, management, heavy machinery, fuel) for Ethiopia's abundant ones (farm labor, oxen, traditional skills and knowledge, locally made tools). The limited attempts made to introduce improved small-scale agricultural implements proved unsuccessful. For instance, the Ministry of Agriculture's Extension and Project Implementation Department (EPID) did not manage to sell a single one of the 5,000 improved ox-drawn implements it planned to make available to small holders in 1973 and 1974. During this same period, however, EPID sold 10,000 tons of fertilizer and 123 tons of "improved" seeds (Gill, 1975:110; Green, 1974:97).[13]

Post-coup Developments

In September 1974, the Derg, a committee of military men, overthrew Emperor Haile Selassie, terminated imperial rule, and assumed political power (see Koehn, 1975:7-21). The Derg quickly introduced a series of radical policy measures aimed, among other objectives, at transforming the economics of agricultural production and the traditional power structure of rural society. The Derg's program focused principally on land tenure arrangements. Specifically, the military government nationalized without compensation all land (from the largest to the smallest holdings), abolished tenancy and all tenant obligations, and guaranteed use rights for pastoralists over land they customarily grazed their herds on. Its 1975 Land Reform Proclamation, furthermore, granted former tenants and hired laborers possessory rights to farm the land they had previously tilled—up to a ceiling of 10 hectares per family—and full rights of possession over the fruits of their labor. The Proclamation prohibited the employment of hired labor by individuals and the sale, exchange, mortgage, or lease of land holdings. In addition, the Derg nationalized agri-businesses controlled by foreign interests and all other large-scale mechanized farms, including the extensive holdings of the royal family. The military government turned some of these enterprises into state farms, while it redistributed the land area of others among landless peasants according to collective farming principles.[14]

Another crucial aspect of the Derg's rural policy involved the formation of a network of local peasant associations, with their own elected leadership.[15] Each association encompassed an area of at least 800 hectares. The Derg delegated a number of major responsibilities to peasant associations, including distributing available land

in the area; adjudicating disputes over land among members;
conserving soil, water, and local forests; building schools,
clinics, and feeder roads; and organizing marketing cooperatives and
defense squads.

The Impact of Derg Reforms

In analyzing the short-and long-term impact of the Derg's
reforms, it is fruitful to consider peasant agriculture independently
from state farms, as each involves a fundamentally different approach
to land use.

Peasant Agriculture. For much of the Ethiopian peasantry,
conditions improved considerably in the first years following the
military coup. In particular, the abolition of onerous land rents
and other obligations to landlords placed former tenants in control
of the fruits of their labor. This action removed a pivotal
constraint (Cohen, 1980b:132-4, 137; Eckholm, 1979:21, 24, 31-4) on
increased food production and resource conservation by small-scale
cultivators. Many peasant families responded to these radical
changes in their legal/political environment by consuming a larger
portion of their increased harvest, thereby reducing undernourishment
among the rural populace (Gilkes, 1976:664; Holmberg, 1976:12;
Stahl, 1977:70; Tesfai Tecle, 1975b:71). From a long-term
perspective, the most fundamental changes brought about by the Derg
have been the elimination of the rural elite's power base through
sweeping land reform measures, and the empowerment of the peasantry
through the formation of local peasant associations.[16] According to
official figures, approximately 25,000 associations with a combined
membership of nearly 7 million peasants had been established by late
1977 (cited in Ottaway, 1977:79, 89).

Nevertheless, the new government often failed to provide peasant
associations with the resources needed to perform the crucial local
activities they had been assigned (Koehn, 1979:62-3; Cohen,
Goldsmith, and Mellor, 1976:28; Stahl, 1977:80-1; Cohen, 1980b:137)
and it continued to neglect urgently needed environmental
preservation measures and the development and adoption of improved
agricultural implements adapted to diverse local conditions (Bisrat
Aklilu, 1980:388-91, 399).[17] For instance, in one of the few field
studies of peasant associations conducted in the post-coup period,
Michael Stahl (1977:74-6, 80-1) discovered that peasants in western
Wollega had realized the importance of checking the advancing gullies
that deprived them of scarce farm land, and had shown great interest
in planting trees on denuded hills and slopes. Both afforestation
and gully checking are primarily labor-intensive activities which the
new peasant associations are particularly well suited to tackle
through collective action. Unfortunately, however, the military
government failed to provide associations with the basic inputs
(seedlings and technical advice) required for the successful
execution of such undertakings. Like the imperial regime it had
overthrown, the Derg subsidized and promoted the application of
inorganic fertilizers (with the aid of a $15 million World Bank loan)
and generally failed to facilitate the adoption of small-scale,
conservation-based innovations (Tesfai Tecle, 1975b:80-1; Stahl,

1977:82).[18]

Moreover, the Derg's initial efforts to promote peasant empowerment and small-scale agriculture underwent a major reversal in 1977. After seizing power following a shoot-out at a meeting of the ruling military council which eliminated his chief rivals, Major Mengistu Haile Mariam proceeded to impose new central government controls over peasant associations, and diverted their attention from rural development activities to maintaining law and order and raising funds and materials for use by the Ethiopian military in its struggle to crush "anti-revolutionary and anti-unity" forces in rebellious parts of the country--including Tigre, Eritrea, and the Ogaden (Cohen and Koehn, 1980:283-7; Markakis and Nega Ayele, 1978:189-91).

State Farms and Mechanized Agricultural Schemes. The second major aspect of the Derg's agricultural strategy has been the creation of state farms. State farms have continued to employ the same capital and energy-intensive techniques utilized by the former capitalist owners of the land. In one of its first acts after assuming power, the Derg mobilized all available tractors and, with the help of reallocated credits from previously unutilized World Bank funds, ploughed the land on many state farms (Liebenthal, 1976:6; Ottaway, 1975:49).[19] In spite of this effort, coupled with heavy fertilizer applications, total state farm production reportedly decreased by 50 percent in the first post-reform harvest.[20]

Major Mengistu has placed increasing emphasis on resettlement schemes and state farms, mechanized agriculture, improved seeds, and other green revolution inputs over the past four years (Africa Research Bulletin, Economic, Financial, and Technical Series, Vol. 15, No. 11, Dec. 31, 1978, p. 4927; Harbeson, 1980:7; "Mengistu Tries Planting Politics at Ground Level," The Guardian, Nov. 2, 1980; "6,000,000 Dispossessed," 1981:17-18; D. Ottaway, 1980). In these vital respects, Major Mengistu's approach to agricultural production and rural land use closely resembles that promoted by the imperial government prior to the military coup d'etat, except that this time Ethiopia is primarily relying upon Soviet, Eastern European, and Cuban advice, technicians, and equipment rather than western capitalist involvement.

Summary Assessment

There is considerable controversy over the impact of the Derg's policies on national food harvests. Firm food production figures have never been available in Ethiopia. African crop censuses are notoriously unreliable (see Cohen, 1980a:689, fn 2, 3). Official figures have been over-estimated for propaganda purposes, and underestimated as the result of increased on-farm consumption, hoarding, peasant suspicion of government authorities (Stahl, 1977:12), or state efforts to secure international assistance. It is remarkable, nonetheless, that all available macro-level statistics on post-coup food production patterns in Ethiopia are uniform in direction if not in detail. A variety of Ethiopian government/international agency sources (cited in Holmberg, 1976:11; Gilkes, 1976:664; Cohen, 1980a:688-9; Ottaways, 1978:201n) all show national food production in 1975-76 surpassing the previous year's harvest by 10-20 percent. Ethiopia's total food grain harvest declined slightly in 1976-77, but remained substantially above the 1974-75 level, according to Ministry of Agriculture/FAO (cited in Cohen, 1980a:689) and U.S. Department of Agriculture (1980:5) statistics.

Although the precise figures are debatable, the available evidence demonstrates that Ethiopia did not experience the "substantial decline in production" that many hold will invariably occur immediately following the implementation of a radical land reform program (see Cohen, 1980a:686; Cohen and Weintraub, 1975:87). This conclusion holds even though embittered former landlords organized armed bands that harassed peasant cultivators, and farming activity in Eritrea had been disrupted by warfare (Ottaways, 1978:72-3, 77). The surprising performance of the agricultural sector in Ethiopia during the first two post-reform harvests has been attributed to political changes and increased peasant production (Koehn, 1979:61-3), to the extension of food crop cultivation to new lands (Stahl, 1977:48), and to favorable rainfall (Cohen, Goldsmith, and Mellor, 1976:20-1; Cohen, 1980a:688, 690; Ottaways, 1978:76). The "good weather" thesis, however, is not borne out (at least for the 1975-76 harvest) by studies of local rainfall patterns. Much of the Ethiopian countryside continued to experience drought or below normal rainfall during the long rainy season of 1975 (Ethiopia, CFNIS, 1975; Ethiopia, RRC, 1975; Shepherd, 1975:79; also see Ottaways, 1978:77). Moreover, available estimates of later harvests lend further weight to the argument that political factors have exerted a major impact on national food production in Ethiopia. According to Ministry of Agriculture/FAO statistics, total food grain production declined so precipitously in the 1977-78 harvest that it fell below output for 1974-75 for the first time since the land reforms (cited in Cohen, 1980a:689; also see U.S., Department of Agriculture, 1980:5). This sharp decline in food production, which does not appear to have been reversed in 1978-79 (see Cohen, 1980a:690), coincides with Major Mengistu Haile Mariam's rise to power within the Derg, with his move to divert peasant associations into militaristic activities, and with the regime's renewed emphasis on capital and energy-intensive agricultural schemes (primarily state farms).

The Mengistu regime also shares responsibility for another type of environmental destruction that is currently afflicting the Horn of Africa: _weapons_ destruction.[21] In southeastern Ethiopia, people already stricken by the 1980 drought have been bombed off their land by the Ethiopian air force, and have seen their camel herds destroyed by machine-gun fire. An estimated four million Ethiopians are currently living as refugees outside the country's borders. Half of this number are concentrated in refugee camps in the drought and poverty stricken nation of Somalia, where they have demolished the surrounding countryside foraging for food and firewood (Jaynes, 1980:1: U.S., Department of State, 1980:1; _Africa_ (London), No. 108, Aug. 1980: 13, 16; "6,000,000 Dispossessed," 1981:5-84; Girardet, 1981).

NIGERIA

Nigeria is the most populous country in Sub-Saharan Africa and one of the ten most populous in the world. Its current population is estimated at 90-100 million persons, with more than half living in the 10 northern states. The country's 357,000 square miles, roughly twice the size of California, encompass several ecological zones, from sudanic savanna in the far north to tropical rain forests along the coast (see the map in Awa,1980:5-7;also Norman, Pryor, and Gibbs, 1979:9-13).[22] Over the last decade, Nigeria has become a major oil-exporting country.[23] Nevertheless, roughly 70 percent of the country's labor force are principally engaged in agricultural activities, and Nigeria's per capita GDP has only reached about $500 (U.S., Department of State, 1979:6-7; I.B.R.D., 1974:5, 30; Nigeria, "National Report," 1975:2-3; Norman, et. al., 1979:1; Matlon, 1979:8; Davies, 1981:70).

Nigeria is currently experiencing most of the environmental pressures mentioned at the beginning of this chapter, including soil erosion, loss of natural vegetation, deforestation, desertification, urban water pollution, unregulated chemical and industrial contamination, and even oil spills (Nigeria, NCAZA, 1978; New Nigerian, April 2, 1980, p. 15; June 6, 1980; August 11, 1980, p. 1; van Apeldoorn, 1978; Goddard, 1974:262-3; Nigeria, "National Report," 1975:4-5, 10-11).[24] Soil erosion and deforestation are particularly serious problems in the northern states. In 1978, the National Committee on Arid Zone Afforestation declared a zone of about 125,000 square kilometers to be "easily prone to desertification". This land area spreads across the five northern most states (Borno, Kano, Sokoto, Bauchi, and Kaduna) and carries about one-fourth of Nigeria's population (see Map 1). After touring the affected area, committee members reported grossly inadequate public afforestation efforts and deficient management practices, but directed most of their criticism at traditional agricultural practices--particularly shifting cultivation and indiscriminate bush burning.[25] According to the Committee's report:

> Because of the extent of [shifting] cultivation over the years the natural grazing areas of the Arid Zone have dwindled to a point where over-grazing of the natural range and grazing reserves is...a serious problem. Shortage of grass especially in the dry season results in herders cutting down trees and tree branches to provide supplementary feed to their animals.
>
> Annual bush fires are common.... These fires are most often started deliberately by cattle rearers hoping to encourage an early flush of green grass, or by hunters to expose game.... Such fires restrict the growth of the tree species which are able to survive. They also reduce the rate of regeneration by destroying seeds, seedlings and young trees (Nigeria, NCAZA, 1978:III 3-8, II 4-9, 12-14).[26]

262

MAP 1
NIGERIA: STATE BOUNDARIES

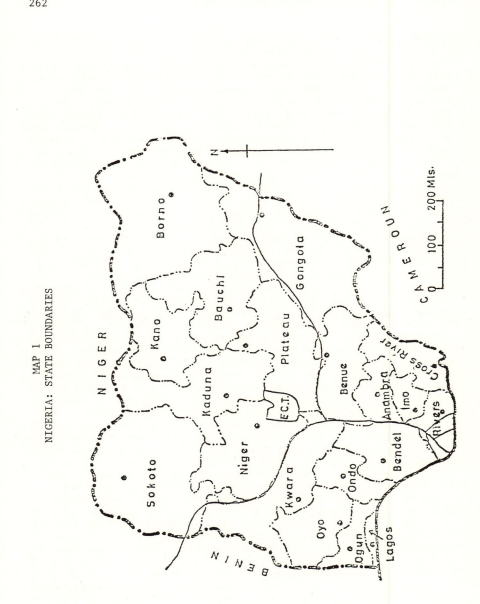

There are strong indications, however, that the increasing importation and introduction of "modern" methods of large-scale, commercial crop production poses a more serious threat to Nigeria's natural resources and to the welfare of peasants and pastoralists than traditional, subsistence-oriented agricultural practices. After reviewing national trends with respect to agricultural products and policies, we will examine in detail the mounting stress which federal government-promoted irrigation schemes and World Bank-sponsored agricultural development projects are placing on Nigeria's land and people, particularly in the northern states.

Food Production

Over the past decade, food production in Nigeria has grown at an average annual rate of less than 2 percent, while population has increased more than 3 percent per annum (see Awa, 1980:2; Cowell, 1981b:3; Matlon, 1979:8; Forrest, 1977:77; "Nigeria's Fourth," 1981:567; U.S.D.A., 1980:5). Nigeria has experienced dramatic decreases in agricultural commodity exports[27] and increases in food imports since 1973, the year in which the country began to reap huge revenues from the sale of its oil on the world market. By 1976, Nigeria's exports consisted almost entirely of crude oil (Freund, 1979:96-7; Forrest, 1977:77-8). Today, the extraction and sale of petroleum resources accounts for nearly 50 percent of Nigeria's GDP and supplies more than 80 percent of total federal government revenues. Agriculture's contribution to GDP has decreased consistently from 61 percent shortly after independence (1962/63), to 50 percent in 1970/71, and to less than 20 percent at present (Famoriyo, 1979:1-2; Matlon, 1979:8; I.B.R.D., 1974:126; Nwosu, 1977a:36n; Joseph, 1978:230-2; Shagari, 1980:2469).

At present, Nigeria must import millions of metric tons of food (particularly rice, wheat, maize, and meat) in order to satisfy domestic needs. The country's food import bill has risen rapidly as a result. In 1980, Nigeria spent $2.3 billion on food imports, an eight-fold increase over its 1975 expenses (de Onis, 1981:9; Hecht, 1981; Cowell, 1981b:3; Freund, 1979:97; Forrest, 1977:78-9; New Nigerian, August 5, 1980).[28] Projections based on Club of Rome data forecast an $11 billion annual deficit in Nigeria's food trade by the year 2001 if malnutrition is to be eliminated by the end of the century (cited in Shaw, 1980:561; also see Omole, 1979:4-7). Moreover, food imports currently are claiming a larger proportion of Nigeria's petroleum revenues which are declining due to falling world prices and production cutbacks.

Confronted with an increasingly expensive agricultural trade deficit, escalating food prices in politically influential urban centers, and the prospect of growing dependence on certain western countries for required food supplies (Shaw, 1980:562; Forrest, 1977:78-9; Wallace, 1979a:2; Oculi, 1979:63-4), the Federal Military Government (FMG) began to take domestic food production problems more seriously in the mid-1970s (Garba, 1979:II; Forrest, 1977:77). Nigeria's Third National Development Plan (1975-80) referred to agricultural development as the country's highest priority (Williams, 1976b:136; Matlon, 1979:9; Wallace, 1978/79:

55). Nevertheless, the crop production sector received less than 10 percent of annual state and federal government budget allocations under the Murtala/Obasanjo regime (Anise, 1980:19; Forrest, 1977:77; Wallace, 1979a:7-8; Hecht, 1981).[29] The technocratic approaches to agricultural development initiated and promoted by the FMG during this period also essentially ignored both the small-scale peasant farmers who produce the lion's share of Nigeria's food crops and the environmental dangers inherent in a strategy guided by the overarching principle that "big is beautiful." Large-scale irrigation schemes and rural development projects, commercial farms operated by parastatal organizations, fertilizer, and credit constituted the primary ingredients in the FMG's agricultural policy for the Third Plan period (Forrest, cited in Wallace, 1979a:9; Forrest, 1977:80; Williams, 1976b:136-7; Oculi, 1979:70-1; NES, 1980:5).

The FMG launched five specific types of projects in the mid-1970s aimed at increasing food and/or cash crop production: (1) river basin development schemes (irrigated farming); (2) integrated rural development projects (designed and assisted by the World Bank); (3) the National Accelerated Food Production (NAFP) Programme (provision of a coordinated package of inputs); (4) the Operation Feed the Nation (OFN) campaign (distribution of highly subsidized chemical fertilizer supplies for application on staple food crops);[30] and (5) agricultural credit schemes (operated primarily through the Nigerian Agricultural and Cooperative Bank set up in 1973). These projects reflect several common, linked features. They are based on the assumption that the wide adoption of western technology offers the key to increased agricultural production. They rely extensively on imported machinery, expertise, chemical fertilizers, pesticides, and "improved" seeds. They endeavor to involve producers more deeply in commercial farming. And they tend to be capital and bureaucratic (management) intensive in nature (Wallace, 1978/79:66; 1979a:3, 5, 8, 20-5; 1979b:7; Joseph, 1978:231; Matlon, 1979:10n; Forrest, 1977: 79-80; Nwosu, 1977b:141-2).[31] In terms of socio-economic results, these agricultural programs have failed to generate significant increases in food or cash crop production, and have left Nigeria even more heavily dependent upon imports and foreign interests than prior to their implementation. Furthermore, they have undermined the ability of the vast majority of the country's rural populace to remain agriculturally productive and self-sufficient, both directly in terms of their impact on land and socio-economic relations and indirectly through neglect of peasant cultivators and pastoralists and the diversion of desperately needed resources into the hands of a small group of relatively wealthy farmers, private businessmen, and civil servants (see Wallace, 1978/79:61, 71; 1979a:4-5, 31; 1979b:7; 1980a:75; Forrest, 1977:80; Oculi, 1979: 69-70, 73; Palmer-Jones, 1980:2, 10-11; D'Silva and Raza, 1980:14-16).

Of the five types of agricultural programs instituted by the FMG, the irrigation schemes and the World Bank-designed and assisted development projects have received far greater emphasis and absorbed much higher levels of government expenditures (Forrest, cited in Wallace, 1979a:9). In view of the scope and significance officially attached to these projects, particularly in the savanna region in the north of Nigeria, it is important to explore their social and

environmental impacts in some detail. The next sections of this
chapter, therefore, take a critical look at a major river basin
irrigation scheme and a model integrated agricultural development
project that are located in two of the northern states.[32]

The Bakalori Irrigation Project

Massive irrigation projects absorbed the largest proportion of
federal government spending on agriculture under the military. The
FMG established seven River Basin Development Authorities in the
northern states. Each Authority is charged with undertaking an
expensive irrigation scheme aimed at increasing domestic food and
cash crop production by making water available for agricultural
purposes. Through irrigation and double cropping, the official
expectation is that small farmers will grow and market more and
different crops, and improve their economic standing in the process
(Wallace 1978/79:60; 1979a:9-10; 1980b:1-2; Garba, 1979:II;
Oculi, 1979:71). Evidence gathered through independent research
efforts indicates, however, that the overall impact of these projects
to date has diverged considerably from this expectation. Moreover,
the Authorities failed to devote attention and resources to mitiga-
ting the adverse consequences inflicted on the project environment by
these undertakings. These findings are illustrated in this chapter
by reference to one of the schemes, the Bakalori project at Talata
Mafera in Sokoto State.[33]

The Bakalori project was designed in Rome by an Italian
consulting firm and initiated in the early 1970s by the Sokoto Rima
River Basin Development Authority without prior consultation with the
people living in the affected area or thorough study of local farming
systems, customs, and social and economic relations (Wallace, 1980c:
4, 44; 1978/79:63-4).[34] By 1977, the Bakalori dam had been built and
a large area had been flooded.

The first burden of the project fell upon the people of Maradun.
Although some 15,000 inhabitants of this area had lost their homes,
their town, and their farmlands to the dam site, the government had
not yet begun to construct its promised "improved" housing in 1977.
Furthermore, no new farmlands had been made available to those whose
land had been expropriated for the project. Indeed, the farmers
affected by construction of the Bakalori dam still had not been
allocated their promised new farmlands three years later. A new town
had been constructed for former residents of Maradun by 1980. Tina
Wallace (1980b:2-3) graphically describes New Maradun in the following terms:

> Not far from the walls of the sophisticated elaborate
> engineering of the Bakalori dam, expensively constructed
> out of imported materials according to Italian designs, is
> a new town, New Maradun. The town is signalled by rows and
> rows of corrugated roofs in straight lines. Underneath the
> roofs, square mud houses stand in serried ranks under the
> glare of the sun. No trees shade the houses, no bushes
> grace the area.... Every third house stands empty, some
> have lost their roofs already, the walls are crumbling....

> [T]here is only one central watering place, a dirty pool
> fed by a pump on the river. Those who live on the
> outskirts of this straggling settlement must walk three kms
> to reach this pond.

In addition to not receiving new farm plots, the people displaced to
make way for the Bakalori dam and project headquarters had not been
paid the compensation they are legally entitled to for the loss of
their economic (i.e., fruit or nut bearing) trees, and for crops that
could not be cultivated over three wet seasons from 1977 to 1980
(Wallace, 1980b:7, 14n; 1980c:8-9, 36).[35]

The Sokoto Rima River Basin Development Authority is currently
preparing 2,100 hectares of sprinkler-irrigated land for residents of
New Maradun at a place named Fankarawa, nearly ten kilometers away
from the new settlement. According to Wallace (1980b:4; 1980c:10):

> Fankarawa is a barren wasteland where no one has ever
> farmed even though there is a history of land pressure in
> this densely populated area. The land is rocky, the
> contractors use dynamite to blast the rocks to lay the
> pipes. Where there is soil, it is thick clay, difficult to
> drain. The farmers say they cannot farm there, the
> consultants are unsure whether it is a viable agricultural
> area. The sprinkler project will remunerate the Italian
> contractors, but may not provide the people of New Maradun
> with a means of livelihood.

Elsewhere on the Bakalori project, contractors leveled about
3,500 hectares of land for a surface irrigation scheme, using
laser-beam technology and bulldozers. In this area, fertile topsoil
has disappeared and virtually all trees have been destroyed.[36] The
affected zone currently resembles a desert, and the project lies
within the region of Nigeria designated as most highly prone to
desertification (Nigeria, NCAZA, 1978:III-3). No new trees have been
planted for shade or as windbreaks. When allowed to return to their
now sandy, infertile lands that had been denuded of vegetative cover,
farmers in the surface irrigation area still had not been compensated
for the loss of three wet season crops, expropriation by the
Authority of twenty-five percent of their land as a contribution for
road and canal construction, and destruction of their economic and
firewood trees and the grazing land that had supported their
livestock. The combined impact of these unmitigated alterations in
environmental conditions and neglect of the economic consequences
associated with project intervention in the surface irrigation area
has forced many small landholders into debt; some have been
compelled to rent or sell their land on the scheme for little money
to large-scale farmers from the locality or to wealthy outsiders
engaged in absentee farming (Wallace, 1980b:6-7, 11; 1980c:20, 37).

The third type of land adversely affected by the construction of
the Bakalori dam is the rich _fadama_ along the banks of the Sokoto
river. The river no longer overflows its banks downstream of the new
dam. As a result, dry season farming has ceased altogether on an
estimated 20,000 hectares or more of highly productive _fadama_ land
where it had only occasionally been disrupted by serious floods in

the past. No compensation or programmatic attention has been paid to
the villagers affected, many of whom already have been deprived of a
crucial source of food and income (Wallace, 1980b:7-8;   1980c: 17,
37).[37]

An overall performance assessment of the Bakalori project
reveals the extent to which the costs associated with large-scale
irrigation schemes in the northern states of Nigeria outweigh the
limited benefits they have provided.   At great environmental and
social cost, at the sacrifice of 20,000 hectares of productive fadama
land in the dry season, and at a financial outlay to date of roughly
$.3 billion (Wallace, 1980b:8; New Nigerian, Feb. 28, 1980, p.1),
the Sokoto Rima River Basin Development Authority had managed to
place a total of 1,000 hectares of land under irrigated cultivation
by the 1979/80 season.[38] However, local farmers had become so
disaffected with various aspects of the Bakalori scheme that they
erected road blocks aimed at disrupting work on the project in late
1979. In February 1980, more than 5,000 angry farmers effectively
blocked all access to the dam. This action resulted in a complete
stoppage in the flow of irrigation water and the destruction of
nearly all the crops which project staff had planted on the 1,000
hectare area (Wallace, 1980c:1; New Nigerian, Feb. 28, March 5, 10,
April 30, May 5, 14, 1980).[39]

The adverse social and environmental impacts observed on the
Bakalori project are directly related to the technocratic approach to
agricultural development in the north of Nigeria that has been
promoted by the River Basin Development Authorities. The other
schemes have shown similar tendencies to abuse natural resources,
particularly land.[40] Only a minute proportion of the small farmer
population has been served by these large-scale irrigation projects,
while heavily subsidized yields have consistently been lower than
projected. The main beneficiaries of the schemes have been large and
absentee farmers, foreign contractors, and project staff (Palmer-Jones, 1980:2, 7, 10-11;   Wallace, 1979a:10-18, 31;   1978/79:
67-72;   1980b:8).   Undeterred by the performance record compiled by
existing projects, the FMG set in motion additional programs aimed at
creating 274,000 hectares of irrigated land over the next decade at
an estimated cost of $4 billion, or $14,400 per hectare (cited in
Wallace, 1979a:10;   also see Palmer-Jones, 1980:1, 4; I.B.R.D.,
1974:79).[41]

The Funtua Agricultural Development Project

The integrated rural development project constitutes the second
type of major agricultural undertaking launched by the FMG in several
northern states. Each of the seven projects initiated by 1979 in
Nigeria has been planned, managed, and evaluated by staff employed or
trained by the World Bank. They follow a common design that has been
popular with the Bank since 1973 (Wallace, 1980a:62, 77n; D'Silva
and Raza, 1980:1).[42] Bank loans provide 33-51 percent of the funds
used to finance project activities. Project loans must be repaid in
foreign exchange over a twenty year period at annual interest rates
of between seven and eight percent. In each contract negotiated with
the World Bank, Nigeria is required to expend 40 percent of the loan

abroad—on salaries and emoluments for expatriate staff, tractors, other vehicles and equipment, fertilizers, pesticides, etc. (Wallace, 1980a:62-3; Olinger, 1979:105-6).[43]

The FMG commissioned the first two integrated agricultural development projects in 1975. One of these, the Funtua Agricultural Development Project (FADP), is located on some of the best agricultural land in Kaduna State. FADP encompasses an area of 7,590 square kilometers (about 10 percent of the state's land area). Expenditure on the project amounted to about 70 million dollars over the period 1975-80, with 51 percent of the funds derived from the World Bank loan, 43 percent from state government funds, and the rest supplied by the federal government. The stated objectives of the Funtua project are to increase agricultural productivity and small farmers' incomes. The FADP design is devoted to bringing about change in the traditional farming system through top-down, technocratic intervention. It concentrates on the coordinated provision and application of technology packages in order to achieve targeted increases in crop production. The principal components in the package are high-yield seeds which require irrigated cultivation and intensified applications of inorganic fertilizers, herbicides, pesticides and expert advice. Tractor hire units have also been established. The main crops for which packages are provided at Funtua are sorghum (guinea corn), maize, groundnuts, and cotton (D'Silva and Raza, 1980:1-3; Wallace, 1979a:18; 1980a:64-5; Forrest, 1977:80).

World Bank officials and FADP staff operate on the assumption that the implementation of a technocratic approach to agricultural production that is based on the adoption of "improved" inputs and modern farming techniques is a necessary and sufficient condition for increasing domestic food supplies and improving living conditions for the rural masses. The project has completely ignored other crucial local issues, including the unequal distribution of land, wealth, and power, rural health conditions, the needs and practices of pastoralist groups, the role of women, the place of non-farm economic activities, exploitative marketing arrangements, prevailing political arrangements and bureaucratic orientations, rural industrial development, and environmental stress (Wallace, 1980a:64, 66, 76; Oculi, 1979:71; Matlon, 1979:104). It is not surprising, therefore, to discover that FADP's approach to agricultural development has produced results that depart dramatically from its official objectives. Dr. Brian D'Silva, one of the few independent researchers to conduct a carefully designed study of FADP's impact on agricultural production during the first three years following its inception, reports that in spite of the massive infusion of resources (including an impressive extension worker to farmer ratio that "has not been achieved even in most developed countries", low interest loans for tractor purchases, and government price supports), project yields have consistently been disappointing for the maize, improved sorghum, groundnut, and cotton crops (D'Silva and Raza, 1980:4-6, 9-11, 13, 16-8).[44] Moreover, key inputs provided by this expensive project (particularly fertilizer, credit, and extension visits) have been disproportionately concentrated on large-scale and progressive farmers, while the bulk of the farmers in the area, who are classified as small-scale and traditional, have been neglected

(D'Silva and Raza, 1980:7-8, 11, 14-6, 18; Wallace, 1980b:10-11; 1980a:69,75; 1979a:18-20).[45]

The Funtua project has also placed increasing pressures on the land, although its adverse environmental consequences are less visibly striking in the short term than those inflicted by the large-scale irrigation schemes. In this regard, it is important to note that FADP is situated in an area where farmers traditionally practice complementary mixed cropping of cereals and legumes, rely heavily on manure to maintain soil fertility, and apply inorganic fertilizers only to priority crops (D'Silva and Raza, 1980:12; Wallace, 1980b:9; Norman, et. al., 1979:29, 56-9, 76, 112; Matlon, 1979:86). However, all of the technology packages introduced on the Bank-assisted scheme promote monocropping.[46] The high-yield sole crop varieties emphasized by FADP require applications of chemical fertilizers in quantities that threaten to produce serious soil acidification problems in the area (D'Silva and Raza, 1980:12, 17; Wallace, 1980b:9; Abalu and D'Silva, 1979).[47] Moreover, the new varieties are less resistant to local weeds than traditional ones, a situation likely to encourage farmers to use potentially harmful chemical herbicides that have previously been unknown in the area (D'Silva and Raza, 1980:17).[48]

Agricultural Policy Following the Return to Civilian Rule

Elsewhere in this volume, Darshan Kang documents the environmental casualties associated with the green revolution in Punjab, India. Nigeria's military rulers and external creditors chose to ignore the serious implications of such evidence for the nation's own natural resources. They embarked on essentially the same mid-1960s green revolution strategies that had already been shown to result in adverse social and economic as well as environmental consequences (see Stryker, 1979:329-31; Abubakar, 1980:51-7; Dahlberg, 1979:49, 67, 90; Stahl, 1974:129, 135-8).[49] And, when the familiar warning signs of acute and unattended stress on the land began to surface on the massive irrigation schemes and integrated agricultural development projects launched in the northern states,[50] officials showed no concern and made no effort to modify prevailing policies and approaches or to mitigate their impact.

The civilian political party leaders who replaced Nigeria's military rulers in October, 1979 (see Koehn, 1981) have pressed for the introduction of "modern" technological inputs on an even wider scale in the agricultural sector.[51] Shortly after President Shehu Shagari assumed office, he set out to make Nigeria self-sufficient in food and cash crops by 1985 (New Nigerian, May 22, 1980, p.1).[52] In January 1980, the Shagari administration commissioned a team of Nigerian and World Bank experts "to examine in depth the food situation in Nigeria and to identify broad programmes and strategies that will lead to an early achievement of self-sufficiency" (Gusau, 1981:74). Nine months later, President Shagari announced that Nigeria would realize this objective through a multi-billion naira "Green Revolution Programme."[53] In support of this program, the President proposed to allocate 13 percent of the federal government's capital expenditures in the 1981 financial year on agriculture and water resources.[54]

The central components in the Green Revolution Programme set forth by President Shagari with assistance from the World Bank advisers have now been incorporated into Nigeria's 82 billion naira Fourth National Development Plan (1981-85). Not surprisingly, the program concentrates on expansion of integrated agricultural development projects and large-scale irrigation schemes. According to the Federal Minister of Agriculture, the new government was so "impressed by the success of the integrated agricultural development projects...started on a pilot basis in Funtua, Gombe and Gusau..."[55] that it decided "to establish similar projects in all [19] states of the Federation by 1983" (Gusau, 1981:74-5).[56] More than 2.3 billion naira (4.1 billion dollars) has been reserved for expenditures on these projects over the Fourth Plan period. The Plan calls for the federal and state governments to contribute approximately 65 percent of this sum in direct budgetary allocations.[57] The Shagari administration plans to cover the remaining 800 million naira in project costs through IBRD loans ("Nigeria's Fourth," 1981:567; Gusau, 1981:75).[58] The new government also intends to multiply the amount of land to be placed under Bakalori-like irrigation schemes to be run by eleven River Basin Authorities. In 1980, the federal government instructed each of the eleven Authorities "to carry out feasibility studies on irrigable areas within their locality and co-opt them in their programme" (New Nigerian, May 22, 1980, p.1).[59]

The Fourth National Development Plan also emphasizes the creation of large-scale mechanized agricultural enterprises. Through joint ventures with state governments and private "technical partners both within and outside the country", the National Grains Production Company plans to establish a 4,000 hectare mechanized grain farm in each of the 19 states by 1985.[60] With the aid of International Finance Corporation loans and expanded national agricultural credit schemes, the Shagari administration is promoting similar joint state/private commercial ventures into large-scale estates devoted to the cultivation of cash crops such as oil palm, cotton, rubber, and cocoa through chemical-intensive farming techniques (New Nigerian, May 22, 1980, p.1; August 5, 1980; December 9, 1980, p.1; Gusau, 1981:76, 79; Shagari, 1980:2472; "Nigeria's Fourth," 1981:565, 567; Africa Research Bulletin, EFT Series, Vol. 17, No. 9, Oct. 31, 1980, p. 5687).[61] The federal government continues to provide tractors to cooperative societies and farmer associations "at 50% subsidy", to allow duty-free importation of farm machinery, and to offer direct financial assistance to state governments for land-clearing projects (Gusau, 1981:76; "Nigeria's Fourth," 1981:567). These policies and programs have been deliberately fashioned to foster rapid and extensive mechanization of the agricultural sector, a central ingredient in the administration's overall green revolution strategy. In a statement reflecting the key underlying assumptions that shaped the Fourth National Development Plan, Nigeria's top agricultural official openly asserts that "human labour as a source of energy on the farm has become not only scarce and expensive but unattractive. Human labour must therefore be replaced systematically through the introduction of farm machinery" (Gusau, 1981:76; Davies, 1981:69).[62] The present government's predilection for technological solutions in the food production arena has even led it to "attach high priority to the development of mechanised fishing..." (Gusau, 1981:77).

The expanded provision of subsidized fertilizer supplies also constitutes a central component in the new government's Green Revolution Programme.[63] In 1980, the Shagari administration dramatically increased the importation and subsidized supply of inorganic fertilizers, with scant regard for the environmental consequences of this action (Gusau, 1981:76).[64] The Fourth Plan calls for further purchases of 3.13 million metric tons of fertilizers at a cost of nearly 850 million naira (U.S. $1.5 billion) to the federal and state governments between 1981 and 1985 ("Nigeria's Fourth," 1981:567-8).

In virtually every facet of its Green Revolution Programme, the Shagari administration has opened new doors for foreign involvement and profit making. The government's emphasis in agricultural planning and budgeting on large-scale privately run enterprises has been deliberately designed "to attract foreign private investment...." Moreover, "agricultural production and processing have been transferred from Schedule II to III of the Nigerian Enterprises Promotion Act which means that foreigners can now own up to 60 percent of the equity in an agricultural enterprise" ("Nigeria's Fourth," 1981:565; emphasis in original).[65] The greatly increased capital outlays on modern technological inputs called for by the Fourth Development Plan guarantees that Nigeria will provide an expanding market for fertilizers, agricultural machinery, insecticides, herbicides, and improved seeds manufactured abroad and continue to be a major employer of expatriate technical assistance.

Western agri-business concerns are eager to capitalize on Nigeria's belated interest in the green revolution. Concomitantly, successive U.S. administrations, bent on reducing a multi-billion dollar balance of trade deficit recorded in recent years due to American fondness for Nigerian crude oil,[66] have actively promoted U.S. corporate interests in capturing a large share of Nigeria's growing market for imported agricultural commodities and inputs. In July 1980, former Vice President Walter Mondale traveled to Nigeria to undertake negotiations related to these subjects. His meetings with top Nigerian government officials (including Vice President Alex Ekwueme) and subsequent discussions held between Presidents Carter and Shagari in Washington in October led to the signing of bilateral agreements aimed at increasing U.S. public and private sector involvement in Nigeria's Green Revolution Programme. The memoranda of understanding signed by the two vice presidents in July specifically call for increased scientific, technical, and research exchanges, and cooperative governmental efforts to expand agricultural trade and encourage and facilitate participation by U.S. private business firms in joint farming ventures in Nigeria (Hecht, 1981; West Africa, No. 3323, April 6, 1981, p. 763).[67] As a direct outgrowth of these agreements, a Joint Agricultural Consultative Committee (JACC) has been set up to promote and monitor U.S. agri-business ventures in Nigeria. The JACC, which is headed by former U.S. agriculture secretary Orville Freeman,[68] consists of corporate executives from 26 large U.S. companies and Nigerian representatives drawn from the private and public sectors.[69]

The composition of the JACC leaves little doubt that the U.S. government and business communities intend to use their favored status with the Nigerian government to push high-technology agricultural inputs and investments. This approach is particularly appealing to the Reagan administration, which views deeper involvement by the U.S. private sector in the "development" process in general and in international agri-business activities in particular as one of the most important ingredients in a low budget foreign aid policy that will simultaneously save African economies from disaster and benefit American business interests (Crocker, 1981a:3; Hartwell, 1981).[70] The export of U.S. agricultural technology occupies center stage in this policy approach. This emphasis is consistent with the personal beliefs of President Reagan, which are clearly articulated in a revealing passage taken from his "heartwarming personal correspondence as Governor of California" (von Damm, 1976:97):

> The greatest technological revolution in world history hasn't really been in space or any of the other exotic industries, but in American farming. We produce more food for more people with less labor and fewer workers in the field of agriculture than any other nation on earth....
>   Foreign aid over these past decades should have concentrated less on food distribution abroad and more on the export of American farming know-how. I still think that is a good idea in the present world situation.... [emphasis added].[71]

To the delight of U.S. corporations represented on the JACC, Nigeria's present political leadership has indicated that it also is impressed with the potential applications of U.S. technological inputs in the agricultural sector.[72] In fact, President Shagari has publicly hailed the Joint Agricultural Consultative Committee as a body that "will take care of the large-scale farming projects" proposed as part of his Green Revolution Programme (New Nigerian, October 10, 1980, p.1). And, Nigeria's Minister of Agriculture emphasized prospects for greater U.S. involvement in supplying Nigeria with farm machinery, pesticides, and improved seeds at a meeting with American members of the JACC (Hecht, 1981).[73]

These trends are particularly disturbing in the case of Nigeria, which, unlike most African countries, possesses sufficient funds from current oil revenues to protect its land, embark on conservation-based rural development, build on local inputs and proven traditional, diverse, labor-intensive food production techniques, and meet the basic needs of the small-scale farmers who produce more than 90 percent of the country's food crops.[74] Instead, the Nigerian government has opted to recycle a large share of its petrodollars among foreign agri-business corporations, contractors, and consultants that specialize in intensive technology operations which push increasing numbers of small-scale, traditional cultivators and herders on to marginal farm lands.[75] The Shagari administration also continues to mortgage Nigeria's oil production assets to obtain World Bank loans for overseas purchases of green revolution inputs that accelerate domestic environmental destruction, enhance the economic standing of a privileged group of large-scale and "progressive" farmers, and fail to generate substantially increased local production of staple food crops.[76]

CONCLUSIONS

In Ethiopia and Nigeria, as well as elsewhere in Sub-Saharan Africa, the agricultural production methods placing the greatest stress on the environment and posing the most serious threat to the long-term carrying capacity of the land are not African in inspiration or design, and often not even in their financing and execution.[77] Given the historical record of disregard for and abuse of farm land and small farmers amassed by both the U.S. and the U.S.S.R.,[78] it is not surprising to discover that the energy- and capital-intensive projects which "experts" in both countries have conceived and promoted for export to Africa and elsewhere in the Third World emphasize exploitative rather than conservationist approaches to agricultural development.

The destructive internal and international environmental consequences associated with the growing wholesale transfer of modern agricultural technology as a substitute for traditional, ecologically adapted and environmentally sensitive practices have been overlooked and/or underestimated by most students of international relations and environmental studies (see, for instance, Zartman, 1979:80-1). As long as powerful institutions within the United States and the Soviet Union continue to entice countries possessing rich agrarian potential (such as Ethiopia's) and vast mineral resources (such as Nigeria's) to follow their large-scale, fossil fuel and chemical-based crop production paths (see Dahlberg, 1979:109-11, 114, 120, 129, 163, 221) and Third World elites persist in uncritically adopting these models,[79] there is little ground on which to dispute the pessimistic global food supply forecasts generated by those who are closely monitoring soil and climatic conditions (Pirages, 1978:95-102, 188; U.S., C.E.Q. and Department of State, 1980:32-41, 109-10, 225-6; Munn, 1977:78-85; Crittenden, 1980).

An alternative path is available, however, that would enable Sub-Saharan Africa to sustain increased food production and would involve a more equitable distribution of resources (see Dahlberg, 1979:90, 172, 176-92, 212-27; Pirages, 1978:268-9). This path requires greater self-reliance and enhanced local, mass control over and cooperation in agricultural planning, research, investments, and project execution.[80] It hinges on the advancement of small-scale, ecologically informed, and conservation-based responses to local rural development needs and environmental stresses that build on the traditional practices and insights of peasant farmers and pastoralists,[81] and are supported by popular local leaders. Above all, countries like Ethiopia and Nigeria need to develop African approaches to food production and to avoid western ones.

FOOTNOTES

1. Chinua Achebe, No Longer at Ease (1960:45).

2. According to U.N.F.A.O. estimates, only 16% of Africa's land mass offers soils with no serious limitations for agriculture (cited in IUCNNR, 1980).

3. See Stahl (1974:81) for the location of corporate landholding areas. On northern land tenure systems, see Hoben (1973); Bauer (1975:240-41); Gilkes (1975:113-14); Cohen and Weintraub (1975: 31-4). An advantage of the northern rist system is that fragmentation and the division of land use rights into scattered plots of different fertility may encourage crop diversification and can serve as a hedge against total crop failure (Brietzke, 1976:642). Hoben (1973:51) also found that high status household heads in Gojjam attempted to obtain fields in more than one altitude zone in order to diversify their crops. Nevertheless, malnutrition is endemic in the north and Tigre province in particular has been stricken by famine on a recurrent basis (Bahru Zawde, 1976:53).

4. See U.S., C.E.Q. and Department of State (1980:144); Shepherd (1975:70-1).

5. In 1971, the application of nigrogenous fertilizer in Ethiopia "averaged around 0.25 kg per hectare of farm land (excluding permanent pasture). The corresponding figure for the United States was 40 kg/ha..." (Gill, 1975:109n).

6. For a detailed, critical analysis of the limited efforts undertaken to develop improved small-scale agricultural implements, see Gill (1975:111-12). The adoption of western technology "in toto" constituted the officially prescribed solution to Ethiopia's low agricultural productivity during this period (Gill, 1975: 109).

7. To encourage expanded fertilizer application on small as well as large-scale farms, the government also held down its domestic market price by funding a subsidy of $4-6 per quintal from 1971 to 1974 (Bisrat Aklilu, 1980:398, 390-1; Stahl, 1974:153).

8. A handful of foreign-dominated enterprises controlled and managed more than half of these cultivated lands (Bondestam, 1974:431-8). The World Bank helped to finance irrigated farms in the Awash valley (Liebenthal, 1976:4).

9. The imperial government granted land use rights over these rangelands to large-scale enterprises at nominal rents (Gill, 1975:109). For details regarding the adverse consequences for peasant farmers and pastoralists of imperial government land grant practices and the expansion of mechanized agriculture on to grazing lands, see Stahl (1974:64-8, 104,127).

10. Cohen (1975:349) reports that "one study in the northern part of Chilalo, where the [CADU] project has operated the longest, estimates that as of 1971, 20-25 percent of the pre-CADU tenant population had been evicted." Gill (1975:109-10) calculates that the introduction of a single, standard type tractor of 50-65 horsepower "would create perhaps three or four new jobs but would displace between 40 and 120 traditional cultivators."

11. On the severe soil erosion and deforestation problems afflicting Ethiopia and the government's failure to embark on urgently needed conservation projects, see Assefa Kuru (1978:215-20). Tesfai Tecle (1975a:97) notes, however, that the Wollamo project had completed "about 130 kms. of contour terraces, protecting some 700 hectares from water erosion..." by 1972.

12. For instance, Assefa Kuru (1978:218) maintains that mechanized farming has caused serious denudation of arid zones in Ethiopia, while the mass migrations of families and cattle brought about by the displacement of tenant farmers and pastoralists from agricultural development project and commercial plantation areas has resulted in "an increased rate of shifting cultivation."

13. In the Chilalo project area, the adoption of inexpensive, ox-drawn devices also lagged far behind the introduction of chemical fertilizers (Gill, 1975:110-11).

14. For further details regarding the Derg's radical land measures, see Koehn (1979:57-8); Cohen and Koehn (1977:3-62).

15. Proclamation 31 of 1975 initially barred former landlords and former owners of 10 hectares of land or more from membership in peasant associations.

16. Delegates elected by the members of local associations participate in a series of higher-level (district, regional, etc.) bodies that possess specific powers and responsibilities. The system culminates in the nation-wide All-Ethiopian Farmers Association, which is linked to the central government. For details, see Cohen and Koehn (1980:280-6); Ottaway (1977:83-4).

17. Gill (1975:115-6) contends that "the need for appropriate intermediate farm technology has become more urgent than ever" in light of provisions in the Land Reform Proclamation of 1975 that prohibit most farmers from hiring agricultural labor and the opportunities available through peasant associations for acquiring such implements and encouraging their use by members on a shared basis.

18. Holmberg (1976:11) reports that the purchase and application of fertilizer increased dramatically among small-scale agricultural producers under the new regime. Heavy applications of nitrate fertilizers accelerate the decomposition of soil organic matter, thereby reducing the soil's capacity to retain moisture (U.S., C.E.Q. and Department of State, 1980:33, 106), and can produce other threats

to health and the environment (U.N.E.P., 1978:9).

19.   Ethiopia received 3 percent of all IDA credit funds allocated
between 1961 and 1978 (Stryker, 1979:333). According to Liebenthal
(1976:1), "the Bank Group committed credits of U.S. $107.5 million
for five projects, a record level of lending" to Ethiopia, from July
1974 to June 1976. He adds that Ethiopia received the World Bank's
first loan to any African country in 1950. By 1976, "Bank group
disbursements accounted for over one-third of total disbursements of
medium and long-term debt to Ethiopia."

20.   See Ottaways (1978:77, 201n).   They report, however, that
production on state farms in the Rift valley and Chilalo district
"was very good." On the positive side, in the first years following
the coup, the Derg converted major plantations and large commercial
farms from export commodity production to the cultivation of cereals
and other food crops for domestic consumption (Holmberg, 1976:11).

21.   Merryman (1979:13) shows how armed conflict between the Kenyan
army and Somali nationalist forces in the mid 1960s increased Somali
pastoralists vulnerability to drought. For a thorough analysis of
the effects of various weapons systems on arid and tropical
ecosystems, see Robinson (1979:35-68).

22.   On soil fertility in the different regions, see Mabogunje
(1965:13-4);   Norman, et al. (1979:9-10). For general regional
patterns of agricultural production and consumption, see I.B.R.D.
(1974:127); Omole (1979:2).

23.   The largest single share (40 percent) of Nigeria's high-
quality, low-sulfur crude exports is shipped to the United States.
In recent years, Nigerian supplies have provided between 13 and 17
percent of total U.S. oil imports (Martin, 1980:1; Africa Research
Bulletin, EFT Series, Vol. 17, No. 7, August 31, 1980, p.5612).

24.   The January 1980 Texaco oil blow-out in Rivers State
reportedly affected about 1,200 square kilometers of land inhabited
by an estimated 230,000 people (New Nigerian, August 11, 1980, p.1).
      President Shagari's 1981 budget proposal calls for the
allocation of 1 percent of all revenues accruing to the federation
account to "continuing ecological problems;   soil erosion, desert
encroachment, flood control among others" (West Africa, No. 3307, 8
December 1980, pp. 2469, 2477; New Nigerian, September 2, 1980,
p.1).   In June 1980, the Federal Minister of Housing and Environment
announced that the government would mandate that environmental impact
assessments be undertaken before it would approve the execution of
major projects called for in the Fourth National Development Plan
(New Nigerian, June 6, 1980).

25.   The Committee also attributed the rapid depletion of
vegetation and deterioration of the general environment occurring
within the zone to the high concentration of livestock in the area
coupled with poor range management, environmentally destructive road
and building construction projects, and uncontrolled cutting of trees

for use as firewood and charcoal in rural and urban areas (NCAZA, 1978:II 9-10, 12, 16-17). The author is grateful to Dr. Ango Abdullahi, Committee Chairman and Vice Chancellor of Ahmadu Bello University, for making this report available.

26. Further south, the newly elected Governor of Niger State expressed public concern in June 1980 over the alarming rate at which forests are being recklessly destroyed in that state. At the same time, some state governments have moved to withdraw the reservation status attached to certain forests (New Nigerian, June 9, 1980, p.13; Nov. 22, 1980, p.1). At the national level, Nigeria banned the export of all wood-based products in 1976. However, wood still provides 90 percent of the energy used for cooking in this oil(and natural gas)-rich country. L. I. Umeh, forest management expert in the Federal Department of Forestry, recently predicted that Nigeria will run out of wood in 1995 if current practices remain unaltered (New Nigerian, November 18, 19, 22, p.1; also see Gusau, 1981:78; New Nigerian, July 3, 1979, p.II; May 22, 1980, p.3). After reviewing similar projections, the World Bank mission studying long-term options for Nigerian development (I.B.R.D., 1974:129) nevertheless concluded that Nigeria could substantially increase forestry output and exports to Western Europe "by using existing forests more intensively, [and] establishing plantations of quick-growing trees...."
On the adverse effects of deforestation and agricultural burning on the earth's atmosphere (i.e., the accumulating concentration of carbon dioxide), see U.S., C.E.Q. and Department of State (1980:59n, 83).

27. Especially groundnuts, cocoa, and palm oil (Hecht, 1981; I.B.R.D., 1974:127; Gusau, 1981:75). Between 1960 and 1967, palm produce supplied an average of 22 percent of Nigeria's export earnings. By 1979, the country had become a net importer of thousands of metric tons of palm oil (Africa Research Bulletin, Economic, Financial, and Technical Series, Vol. 17, No. 9, October 31, 1980, p.5687).

28. Nigeria's food production deficit for 1979/80 is officially estimated at "2.6 million tonnes of grain equivalents, and [it is] estimated that at the present rate of increase in food production, the deficit will increase to 5.3 million tonnes of grain equivalents by 1985" (Gusau, 1981:74).

29. Several critical analysts view the FMG's sudden interest in and modest expenditures on increased food production as mainly directed toward "checking urban inflation and keeping wage costs low" (Forrest, 1977:77-8; also see Wallace, 1978/79:56-7; 1979a:5-7; Shenton and Freund, 1979:14-19; Shenton and Watts, 1979:57-60).

30. The FMG sold fertilizer at 25% of cost through 1979 (D'Silva and Raza, 1980:12).
In 1977, the government added mechanized land clearing as one of the priority activities of the OFN program. Oculi (1979:70-1,68) notes that "the Federal Government in 1977/78 alone 'disbursed...

about 100 million Naira for clearing 15,000 hectares of land for the use of both large and small scale farmers.' This constituted government subsidization at the rate of over 600 Naira for clearing each hectare and the likelihood is that most of the land cleared went to officials and local leaders." More recently, "Operation Feed the Nation" has promoted poultry farming, partly through the heavily subsidized importation of corn (see New Nigerian, July 16, 1979, p.9).

31. Most of the programs and inputs emphasized by the FMG are consistent with advice tendered in the late 1960s by a team of U.S. agricultural development "experts" (Eicher and Johnson, 1970:386-9). However, the U.S. agricultural economists advocated that the Nigerian government concentrate on adopting policies aimed at the "immediate expansion of export and import substitution crops...." Specifically, "primary attention should be given to cocoa, oil palm, groundnuts, and cotton..." (Eicher and Johnson, 1970:385-6). Oculi (1979:64) shows how, again based on the advice of foreign experts, Nigeria's agricultural policy promoted the production and export of cash crops in the form of raw materials during the early 1960s. He attributes the country's declining ability to produce enough food for domestic needs, the impoverishment of the bulk of its farmers, and increasing malnutrition to the "neo-colonial and anti-food policy" pursued during this period. Also see Forrest (1977:77).

32. On the limited impact of NAFPP (initiated in 1974) and OFN (launched in 1976) on food production and the tendency of both programs to benefit a privileged elite group of farmers, see Wallace (1979a:21-6); Forrest (1977:80); Joseph (1978:232); Awa (1980:9-14); Freund (1979:97); Nwosu (1977b:142-3); Matlon (1979:102). On the failure of agricultural loan schemes to benefit sizeable numbers of poor farmers, see Wallace (1979a:27-30); Awa (1979:9-11); NES (1980:5); Williams (1976b:137); Oculi (1979:70-1); New Nigerian, August 5, 1980; Nwosu (1977a:37-8).

33. For a detailed study of the impact of the Kano River Irrigation Project, see Wallace (1979b). Also see "Resettlement Drama," West Africa, No. 3323 (6 April 1981), pp.745-6; Wallace (1979a:10-18; 1978/79:66-72; 1980b:3-7); Palmer-Jones (1980).

34. This situation arises frequently in Africa, reflecting in part the absence of legally mandated social and environmental impact statements. Stevens (1978:3) calls for the involvement of social scientists at the inception of development projects; i.e., prior to the award of contracts. Also see Dahlberg (1979:129).

Through 1980, the Nigerian government continued to rely on advice from visiting foreign experts in attempting to deal with problems on the Bakalori project (Wallace, 1980c:5; also see Wallace, 1979b:7). On the drawbacks inherent in this approach, which typically treats local farmers as obstacles to development and external technicians as its catalyst, see Williams (1976b:136); Dahlberg (1979:49, 174); Wallace (1978/79:61-3; 1979a:10-11, 31); Bisrat Aklilu (1980:399).

35. In addition, they "have not even received all the compensation they were eventually promised for their housing" (Wallace, 1980c:9). Disputes over the payment of compensation have characterized major resettlement exercises in Nigeria in recent years (see New Nigerian, August 18, 26, 1980, pp. 1, 9; Stevens, 1978:2; Wallace, 1979a: 16-17; Aliyu and Koehn, 1980:2,9; Aliyu, Koehn, et al, 1979:127-40; New Nigerian, March 10, 1979, p.1).

36. In one 338 hectare area alone, contractors cut down "over 1,000 economic trees, plus many smaller, non-economic ones" (Wallace, 1980b:6).

37. Damming of the Sokoto river has also deprived some downstream villages of their water supply and fishermen of their livelihood (Wallace, 1980c:17,36-7). In the long run, "downstream from extensive irrigation projects the water may become too saline for further use, unless expensive desalinization measures are undertaken" (U.S., C.E.Q. and Department of State, 1980:35, 101; also see Le Houerou and Lundholm, 1976:220-1; Ambroggi, 1980:104-6).
   In addition, Fulani cattle herders traditionally cross the project area with huge herds each dry season. Project officials have now decided that Fulani herders must no longer traverse the irrigation scheme, "but no alternative arrangements or plans have been made to accommodate their very real needs" (Wallace, 1980c:17, 45). For a report on the negative impact of new irrigation projects in the Senegal river valley on traditional Fulani herding patterns and the environment, see Dash (1981).

38. SRRBDA staff planted most of the 1000 hectares (out of the 3,500 hectares constructed) placed under cultivation in 1979/80 as disaffected local farmers refused to engage in irrigated farming. When complete, the Bakalori project is projected to irrigate 24-26,000 hectares of land, at an estimated cost in excess of $.8 billion (Wallace, 1980b:7-8, 11; 1980c:1; also see Forrest, 1977: 79).

39. As many as 200 protesting farmers may have lost their lives when police stormed the roadblocks on April 26 although official estimates placed the death toll at 25. The Authority made certain concessions regarding compensation for those displaced by the dam and for farmers who had lost crops or trees, and work on the project recommenced in May 1980 (New Nigerian, April 17, 23, 29, May 5, 14, June 19, July 1, 1980).

40. On the damage to land resources brought about by large-scale irrigation projects elsewhere in the world, see U.S., C.E.Q. and Department of State (1980:33, 101).

41. In addition, by 1979 the FMG had placed six massive hydro-electric power generation schemes under contract or study that would require flooding more than 24,000 square kilometers of land (Iliasu, 1980:5ff). Three days prior to handing over power to their civilian successors, the FMG authorized execution of the largest of these projects, a $4 billion scheme at the confluence of the Niger

and Benue Rivers near Lokoja in Kwara State that would have displaced 270,000 people and flooded some 800 villages and towns. In the face of protests from the local populace and politicians, the Shagari administration cancelled the Lokoja dam project less than one year later (New Nigerian, September 29, 1979; June 4, 1980, p.1).

42. The main ingredients in the World Bank's integrated package approach are agricultural inputs (fertilizers, pesticides, new seed varieties, and farm machinery), extension and credit facilities, marketing assistance, and infrastructural development (including the construction of dams and rural feeder roads). See Nigeria, FADP (1977); Wallace (1980a:65-6); Stryker (1979:330-1); I.B.R.D. (1974:31). The I.B.R.D.-assisted projects in Nigeria bear a striking resemblance to the package projects initiated in Ethiopia in 1971 with support from the World Bank's soft-loan affiliate, the International Development Association (IDA). See Lele (1975:8, 14, 203); Stahl (1974:94-5, 106-7).

43. On the advantages accruing to western industrial economies from World Bank development assistance loans and credit conditions, see Lappe, Collins, and Kinley (1980:90-2); Stryker (1979:329-30, 332); Oculi (1979:65-6); Olinger (1979:105). The Bank's lending to Nigeria has closely paralleled the overall shift noted by Stryker (1979:326-29, 334) from a nearly exclusive concentration on financing physical infrastructure to a more diversified strategy under which agricultural sector projects (including cash crop schemes) currently receive about one-third of all loans (see Olinger, 1979:103-6; Freund, 1979:100).

44. It is interesting to observe that of the four crops promoted by FADP, only sorghum can be categorized as a staple food source in Nigeria. The high-yield maize introduced on the project is primarily grown for animal feed (Wallace, 1980b:8, 11; D'Silva and Raza, 1980:2-4, 10, 12; Shenton and Watts, 1979:61). Moreover, some farmers believe that improved sorghum ("short Kaura") yields less food value (defined as the amount of pounded grain available) than the traditional variety (D'Silva and Raza, 1980:9). On the marketing and drought risks and loss of self-sufficiency experienced by peasants adopting the high-yield single crop varieties pushed by the project, see Wallace (1979a:20; 1980b:9, 11-12, 1980a:72).

45. FADP's Chief Project Evaluation Officer explicitly stated in 1978 that project staff " prefer the trickle down approach from farmer to farmer, accepting that some will thereby benefit later than others. As a consequence of this preference, we concentrate on our notorious 'progressive farmers'" (cited in D'Silva and Raza, 1980:13). Those monitoring trends in the project area also have observed growing absentee farming by businessmen and civil servants, increasing land transfers (sale and rent of land to wealthy individuals), rising income disparities, and the creation of an expanding landless class of agricultural laborers required to work at low wages (Oculi, 1979:67-8, 71; D'Silva and Raza, 1980:18; Wallace, 1980b:10-13; Shenton and Watts, 1979:61). For an incisive analysis of the security and incentives for investment in land

improvements provided by customary tenure arrangements, and the negative impact of current tendencies toward individual private tenure in villages near the project area, see Ega (1979:290-7). Also see Williams (1976b:147); Matlon (1979:72-3, 101); Payer (1980:43-4).

Furthermore, the concentration of scarce agricultural inputs on the project area has necessitated that the needs of farmers living elsewhere in Kaduna State be neglected (Wallace, 1980a:70, 73-4). All of these outcomes, including the progressive farmer bias, the failure of the "trickle down" approach to improve peasant living standards, and the financial and administrative impossibility of replicating the conditions introduced on integrated package projects on a wide scale, have been experienced on similar Bank-designed and sponsored agricultural development schemes elsewhere in the Third World—including Ethiopia nearly a decade earlier (Stahl, 1974:94, 116, 122-3, 126-9, 133-8, 152; Liebenthal, 1976:5; Lele, 1975:203-4; Payer, 1980:31-5, 38-44; Stryker, 1979:330-2; Lappe, Collins, and Kinley, 1980:72-4, 80, 88; Leonard, 1973:3, 5 ff; also see Norman, et al., 1979:89, 102, 107; Pirages, 1978:227; Thiesenhusen, 1978:167-72).

46. Monocropping, the heavy application of fertilizers, and the more intensive hand weeding required by the new crop varieties all have accentuated the existing scarcity of farm labor during the peak bottleneck period, a factor that may be contributing to the disappointing yields recorded on the Funtua project (D'Silva and Raza, 1980:17; Wallace, 1980b:9-10; Norman, et al, 1979:88-9, 102). On the labor spacing and more dependable nature of the inter-cropping farming techniques traditionally practiced in the north of Nigeria, see Norman, et al (1979:63, 76). For an analysis of the disruptive consequences for traditional labor patterns brought about by the introduction of inorganic fertilizers and improved seed varieties in Ethiopia, see Gill (1975:116).

47. Widespread expansion in inorganic fertilizer applications has been FADP's most dramatic impact on the farming system in the project area. While only 40 percent of the farm households in three Kano State villages sampled by Matlon (1979:22) applied chemical fertilizers in 1974/75, 77 percent of the taxpayers in five FADP project villages surveyed by Gana (1980:3) had already utilized this input by August 1975. Moreover, the quantity of subsidized fertilizers (predominantly superphosphate and calcium ammonium nitrate varieties) sold by the project's farm service centers increased from about 9,000 metric tons in 1976/77 to more than 18,000 metric tons in 1977/78 (cited in Gana, 1980:5; D'Silva and Raza, 1980:15; Nigeria, FADP, 1977). Norman, Pryor, and Gibbs (1979:88-9, 108, 75) express concern that the "increased use of biological-chemical technology" may lead to the long-term decline of soil fertility in the northern states, and call for research on "whether domestically kept livestock can provide sufficient manure to maintain soil fertility." See also U.S., C.E.Q. and Department of State (1980:33, 106). On the relationship between land deterioration, peasant marginalization, and the economic interests of multinational corporations, see Oculi (1979:69); Payer (1980:31-2).

48. From 1976-1978, FADP also sold over 55,000 litres of insecticides, more than 6,000 spraying machines, and 48 tractors (cited in D'Silva and Raza, 1980:15; Nigeria, FADP, 1977). By 1978, FADP only supplied "chemicals and sprayers as well as expensive items" on credit (New Nigerian, May 10, 1978). The introduction of highly mechanized, tractor-based agricultural techniques on lands where hand labor has constituted the only source of power for most cultivators further disturbs the delicate ecological balance of the area (see Norman, et al, 1979:32; Matlon, 1979:17, 22; and Famoriyo, 1979:110 on the other region of Nigeria). Also see Dahlberg (1979:82-3, 90, 111, 113, 150) and U.S., C.E.Q. and Department of State (1980:108-9) on the harmful effects of pesticides and the unsustainable nature of fossil fuel energy intensive agricultural systems over the long run.

49. Indeed, the World Bank has recently been criticized in Ghana for importing outmoded and inappropriate green revolution strategies from Nigeria on a project similar to FADP (cited in D'Silva and Raza, 1980:19).

50. See the statement made by the Emir of Zaria in his address to the Sixth International Conference on Water and Waste Engineering in Africa, reported in New Nigerian, April 2, 1980, p.15.

51. The campaign platforms adopted by each of the five political parties officially certified to contest the 1979 elections all promote this objective, as their published manifestos (New Nigerian, April 19, 1979, p.3; July 3, 1979, pp.I-II) demonstrate.

52. The Shagari administration subsequently delayed its target date for national self-sufficiency in cash crops to 1987 ("Nigeria's Fourth," 1981:567; Cowell, 1981b:3). With respect to food production, the Federal Minister of Agriculture, Ibrahim Gusau (1981:74,79), offered this more qualified assessment in November 1980: "In order to completely eliminate the food deficit by 1985 domestic production of crops will need to increase by about 6.6% annually between 1980 and 1985. For fisheries and livestock annual increase of about 11.3% will have to be achieved over the same period.... However, indications are that agricultural growth rates in excess of 4% per annum are extremely difficult to achieve and sustain over a 5 year period."

53. All of the approaches recommended in June 1980 by the National Committee on Green Revolution (which replaced the OFN Committee in February), including "large projects like the dams and irrigation schemes of the river basin development authorities, the procurememt and distribution of fertilizers..., mechanisation, land clearing, ... and integrated rural development" have been given a central place in the President's program (New Nigerian, June 23, 1980, p.4; Gusau, 1981:72-4,79; Africa Research Bulletin, EFT Series, Vol. 17, No. 1, February 29, 1980, p.5401).

54. The President's 1981 budget proposal for this sector amounted to 1.16 billion naira (U.S. $2.08 billion), second only to his

proposed allocation of 1.42 billion naira on industries (Shagari, 1980:2472). The new civilian governments allotted about 11 percent of their combined capital expenditures to agriculture in the 1980 fiscal year, compared with the 6-7 percent budgeted by the FMG for this sector between 1975 and 1979. According to the Minister of Agriculture, federal and state governments are expected to allocate "not less than 15%" of new capital expenditures, or more than 13 billion dollars, on agriculture over the course of the Fourth Plan period (Gusau, 1981:79; also see Cowell, 1981b:3).

55. The Federal Director of Rural Development, Omoefe Oyaide, evaluated these projects as "successful" on the grounds that (1) a huge number of farmers were involved, and (2) they resulted in increased production (West Africa, No.3323, April 6, 1981, p.770). However, the Federal Government officially placed the national crop production growth rate at an unimpressive 1 percent in 1981 ("Nigeria's Fourth," 1981:567). Moreover, as Lappe, et al. (1980: 88, 56) point out "the Bank likes to count beneficiaries by counting the number of people living in the area where a Bank project takes place. If two million people live in the area and half are said to be poor, then the Bank's public relations department simply assumes one million poor people will benefit." The Bank has used such counting methods to arrive at the conclusion that its projects in northern Nigeria are reaching "'more than a million people'" (cited in Wallace, 1980a:71), while independent analysts contend that the vast majority of farmers in the project areas have been unaffected and have not even experienced 'trickle down' benefits (Wallace, 1979a:20).

56. A twentieth ADP is planned for the new Federal Capital Territory at Abuja (West Africa, No. 3323, April 6, 1981, p.770). Ten integrated agricultural development projects modeled along the same lines as FADP were in operation by 1981. In addition, "an Accelerated Development Area Programme (ADA) is to be implemented for residual areas not yet encompassed by the ADPs. The programme would apply the core elements of the ADP approach such as improved extension, input distribution and rural feeder roads in a simplified package which could later be upgraded to full ADP status" ("Nigeria's Fourth," 1981:567). It is noteworthy that the Federal Government's proposed extension of the integrated agricultural development program to cover all of Kaduna State (where FADP is located) has not been carried out due to the resistance of the PRP Governor of the state. In November, 1980, Governor Balarabe Musa rejected both the idea of implementing the program state-wide (originally endorsed by the military government) and the terms of the 100 million naira I.B.R.D. loan agreement about to be signed for financing the project expansion. A release issued by the Governor's press secretary on November 18, 1980 explained that the Kaduna state executive differed with both the World Bank and the Federal Government on "'some major agricultural policy directions of the project and the control and remuneration of foreign staff.'" Regarding policy differences, "the release stated that expatriates... in control of the Funtua Project ...encouraged massive application of chemical fertilizer by the farmers 'as though this is all that modern farming methods mean.'"

The release maintained that although this approach is "certainly in the interest of big foreign corporations which derive huge...[profits] from the sale of chemical fertilizers," it is "not in the long term interest of farmers in the state, because massive application of chemical fertilizers would damage the soil and cause other serious ecological destructions likely to render the whole area into an acidic wasteland in the long run." Finally, the statement maintained that the Kaduna state executive preferred to encourage cultivation of the food staples grown in the area (New Nigerian, November 11, 19, 1980, 1980, pp. 1,11,17). In 1981, a majority of the members of the NPN-controlled house of assembly in Kaduna State voted to impeach Governor Balarabe Musa.

57. Planned federal government expenditures of 580 million naira on the ADP/ADA program represent more than an eleven-fold increase over allocations at this level during the Third Plan period (1975-80). See Gusau (1981:75).

58. The Minister of Agriculture cited the 800 million naira figure as the amount "which will be loaned to the rural development programme" over the Fourth Plan period following his meeting with Robert McNamara, then President of the World Bank, in October 1980 (Gusau, 1981:75; West Africa, No. 3323, April 6, 1981, p.770; also see New Nigerian, December 9, 1980, p.1; Africa Research Bulletin, EFT Series, Vol. 17, No. 5, June 30, 1980, p.5560).

59. In May 1980, the Minister of Agriculture announced that the federal government now plans "to put at least 270,000 hectares of land under irrigation through its river basin authorities by 1982" (New Nigerian, May 22, 1980, p.1).

60. Five such farms already had been incorporated by mid 1980 in Niger, Oyo, Kaduna, Kano, and Bauchi states (New Nigerian, August 15, 1980, p.1).

61. In many respects, Nigeria's Fourth National Development Plan (1981-85) resembles Ethiopia's Third (1968-73) Plan (see Stahl, 1974:74-5). The outcomes associated with the agricultural policies pursued by the imperial Ethiopian government during the Third Plan period have been analyzed above.

62. According to the authors of the Fourth Plan, "apart from increased output, agricultural mechanisation primarily is a means of reducing the tedium of farm operations and the unattractiveness of farming as an occupation. There will be a lot of mechanisation since it has obvious advantages including the possibility of large-scale clearing of land and its preparation for irrigation.... On a global scale it will have the long-term effect of releasing labour permanently to industry and services without a drop in agricultural production" ("Nigeria's Fourth," 1981:567, 566).

63. "Next to seeds, the use of fertilizer is the most important in ensuring high productivity", according to the Federal Minister of Agriculture (Gusau, 1981:76).

64. The Shagari administration quickly terminated state government involvement in the distribution of fertilizers. Pending the establishment of a new national fertilizer marketing board, the 11 river basin authorities have been directed to undertake this function (New Nigerian, August 18, 1980, p.19). The government reduced the rate at which it subsidizes fertilizer prices from 75% to 50% in 1979 (D'Silva and Raza, 1980:12).

65. General Obasanjo actually first proposed to effectuate this transfer in 1978 (cited in Wallace, 1979a:30). Decree No. 3 of 1977 had increased the indigenous equity participation requirement for Schedule II enterprises to 60% effective 31 December 1978 (Collins, 1977:145). In his incisive analysis of the impact of the FMG's indigenization decrees, Collins (1977:143, 131, 135, 137) concludes that "the overall picture which thus emerges...is one of a tightening nexus between government and foreign capital.... The state must now protect even more the interests of foreign capital in which the local bourgeoisie has a stake." Also see Joseph (1978:230), Oculi, (1979:70); Osoba (1979:69-71).
      Furthermore, Nigeria's Fourth Plan (1981:565) assures potential investors that the "fiscal incentives already provided by government for companies wishing to go into large-scale agricultural production, e.g., income tax relief for pioneer enterprises,... will be maintained and improved upon...." [emphasis added]. For a list of the incentives which General Obasanjo offered specifically "'for modern and large production farmers'" in 1978, see Wallace (1979a:30).

66. The United States recorded a balance of trade deficit with Nigeria in excess of 9 billion dollars in 1980, its highest with any country in the world. In 1980, farm commodities worth 348 million dollars comprised about one-third of the total value of U.S. exports to Nigeria and roughly 20 percent of Nigeria's total food import bill (Hecht, 1981; Cowell, 1981a; West Africa, No. 3323, April 6, 1981, p.763; Africa Research Bulletin, EFT Series, Vol. 17, No. 7, August 31, 1980, p.5612).

67. This agreement included the opening of Nigerian trade and investment centers in the U.S., and the installation of a new U.S. Department of Agriculture trade office in Lagos. The memorandum of understanding on agriculture also provided for the establishment of an inter-governmental working group to design and implement specific agricultural projects in Nigeria. The first project undertaken as a result of this agreement consisted of a soil survey of Nigeria conducted with the assistance of a team of U.S. Department of Agriculture experts sent to Nigeria by the Reagan administration. A second memorandum of understanding calls for cooperative projects in the energy area, including: environmental protection against pollution resulting from oil production; deep on-shore and off-shore oil exploration and production; extraction of Nigeria's coal resources; solar energy research; and exchange of information on hydro-electric power schemes (Africa Research Bulletin, EFT Series,Vol. 17, No. 7, August 31, 1980, pp.5611-12; West Africa, No. 3323, April 6, 1981, p.763).

68. At a public forum held at the University of Montana in 1975, Freeman (1975:7, 15) expressed his conviction that all of the major crises facing the world (nuclear destruction, famine, deterioration of the biosphere, inflation, unequal distribution of wealth) can be overcome through "production. And I would add, more production — much more production." He went on to state that "never in its history has mankind had the potential to produce as profusely as it can today. Science and technology have placed great power at man's disposal.... The potential to produce what people need and desire is almost unlimited." By the time of the 1975 meeting, Freeman had already become preoccupied with finding ways to recycle petrodollars, which he identified as the key to increased production. The paramount, immediate question according to Freeman is "will the billions of dollars that have been wrenched suddenly from the oil-consuming countries and deposited in the OPEC countries be recycled into productive use in time?"

69. The U.S. members of the Committee represent giant agri-business and financial concerns, including farm equipment manufacturers (FMC Corporation, Allis-Chalmers, Ford Motor Company); fertilizer, pesticide, and seed producers (Pfizer, Occidental Petroleum, Whittaker); food processing operations (Carnation, Pillsbury, Ralston Purina); and financial institutions (Chase Manhattan, First National Bank of Chicago). See Hecht (1981); Young (1981). President Shagari has described the U.S. members of the JACC as "top American experts on agriculture" (New Nigerian, October 10, 1980, p.1).

70. Earlier this year, U.S. Agriculture Secretary John Block promised support for the JACC (West Africa, No. 3323, April 6, 1981, p.763). More recently, Assistant Secretary for African Affairs Chester Crocker (1981b:2-3) specifically hailed the fledgling JACC as the administration's prime model "of the contributions and benefits of private sector involvement in Africa to which we are giving encouragement" and expressed the hope that this novel experience will provide the basis "for developing similar relationships with more African countries."

71. This perspective is not restricted to officials in the Reagan administration. Andrew Young, who made numerous diplomatic visits to Africa on behalf of the Carter administration, refers to Sokoto State as "the heartland of Nigeria's green revolution, the region that Nigerians hope will one day sprout Iowa corn, San Joaquin Valley fruits and vegetables, Georgia peanuts, Mississippi Delta cotton and—especially—Louisiana rice." Young foresees U.S. agri-businesses helping Nigeria accomplish rates of agricultural output similar to those experienced in the United States provided that "U.S. technology and Nigerian oil wealth" can be brought together. He maintains that "the land is ready and so is the government, but people and technology have yet to be put together to produce the desired results." He further advises American businessmen that "food production on a massive scale in a nation like Nigeria is profitable and in the U.S. national interest" and notes that "the market for American farm methods is enormous in this country." Young

particularly singles out "trucks, tractors, combines and processing machinery of all varieties" as "very much in demand" (Young, 1981; also see Shaw, 1980:561; Oculi, 1979:67). Young's mention of "San Joaquin Valley fruits and vegetables" is instructive. According to the Global 2000 Report, "about 400,000 acres (160,000 hectares) or irrigated farmland in the San Joaquin Valley currently are affected by high, brackish water tables that pose an increasingly serious threat to productivity" (U.S., C.E.Q. and Department of State, 1980:101).

In similar fashion, Tom Farer (1979:169-70), who views poverty in the Horn of Africa as "more a consequence of failures in production than of distribution," advocates that the U.S. continue to be involved in teaching Ethiopia how to "increase agricultural production."

72. Oculi (1979:67) points out that increasing Nigerian purchases of foreign-manufactured agricultural equipment must also be attributed in part to "the emergence of a new capitalist class of importers whose wealth depends on the continuation of the phenomenon and who seek to influence policy makers accordingly."

73. Thus far, major U.S. corporations have shown more interest in expanding exports of American technological inputs and food crops than in investments in Nigerian agricultural enterprises in spite of the Nigerian government's willingness to provide foreign agri-business concerns with tax holidays, tariff exemptions, and special credit facilities (see Hecht, 1981; Young, 1981; Osoba, 1979:68). The central place of expanding exports in U.S. business and government strategy is reflected in a recent report (de Onis, 1981:9) that a "technical assistance" agreement had been reached under which "American rice growing and milling companies will invest in new mills and farm projects...increasing Nigerian rice production, in exchange for guaranteed imports of 250,000 metric tons of American rice." In his December 1980 budget message, President Shagari (1980:2472) announced that "this Administration intends to further facilitate the importation of those food items ['like rice'] for which there is an identified gap between local production and demand. ...Henceforth, licenses will no longer be issued to individuals but direct to Government Agencies adjudged competent to import and sell...[such items] at controlled prices."

74. See Oculi (1979:70, 72); N.E.S. (1980:5); I.U.C.N. (1980); Langdon and Mytelka (1979:208-11); Williams (1976b:136); Norman, et al (1979:63, 75, 104); Famoriyo (1979:110); Shenton and Watts (1979:55); Okaiyeto (1980:20); "Nigeria's Fourth" (1981:567); Davies 1981:70).

75. Nigeria's Minister of Agriculture, Ibrahim Gusau, holds the view that "if you can afford to have [a] mechanized system ... [of agricultural production], it is all well and good" (Davies, 1981:69).

76. The World Bank's increasing involvement in Nigeria has not been confined to the agricultural sector. Over the past two years, major Bank loans also have been negotiated for electric power, urban

housing, and highway construction projects (Africa Research Bulletin, EFT Series, Vol. 17, No. 7, August 31, 1980, p.5628; New Nigerian, December 9, 1980, p.1).

The attraction of Nigeria's market and petrodollars to foreign investors is revealed in the fact that by 1978 the country had already become "the largest recipient of Bank finance in sub-Saharan Africa and the seventeenth largest of the total of 116 countries to which the Bank had lent money" (Olinger, 1979:105-6). For an analysis of the limited role played by the World Bank in promoting international environmental preservation (and monitoring environmental impacts) and the constraints under which it operates in this policy arena, see Le Prestre (1981:10-33).

77.   Certain indigenous practices also have placed added stress on the land in light of the growing population pressures experienced in some parts of Ethiopia and Nigeria (Bivins, 1980:8; Matlon, 1979:17, I.B.R.D., 1974:129; Gill, 1975:109). In general, however, traditional African agricultural implements and cultivation techniques have been adapted to local ecological conditions and are sensitive to the critical need to preserve fragile natural resources (Gill, 1975:116; Dahlberg, 1979:227; Stahl, 1977:18; Merryman, 1979:14; Franke and Chasin, 1980:237; Huntington, Ackroyd, and Deng, 1981:49-53). According to Shenton and Watts (1979:55), "agronomists working in northern Nigeria have come to realize that ancient, indigenous planting methods, intercropping and crop rotation patterns are well suited to the conditions of rainfall variability which predominate in Hausaland, as well as to the character of local soils." Also see Norman, et al (1979:63, 75, 104); Famoriyo (1979:110). For an analysis of the environmental and economic benefits of the traditional Ethiopian plough (ard), see Gill (1975:112-3).

Moreover, closer investigation often reveals that it is the introduction of "modern" agricultural schemes and techniques (including mechanization and eviction, large commercial farms) that has forced peasants and pastoralists to engage in ecologically destructive practices. See Assefa Kuru (1978:218); Stahl (1974:104, 127); Swift (1977:28); Walls, 1977:25; Dash (1981); U.S.,C.E.Q. and Department of State (1980:60n); Eckholm, (1979:28-9).

78.   See the Kupilik and Barrett and Kemmis contributions to this book; U.S., Presidential Commission on World Hunger (1980:12); U.S.,C.E.Q. and Department of State (1980:101-5); Dahlberg (1979: 146, 163); Crittenden (1980); Eckholm (1979:30).

79.   Bisrat Aklilu (1980:399) maintains that "the wholesale importation and implementation of agricultural innovations without careful experimentation and adaptation has become the norm among LDC's." During a visit to the U.S. aimed at promoting the transfer of western technology to Nigeria, General Obasanjo is reputed (Osoba, 1979:68) to have made a statement to the effect that "'America is the nearest thing in the world to man being in total control of his environment.'" Also see Wallace (1978/79:73).

80.   Ethiopia embarked on major steps in this direction immediately

following the overthrow of Emperor Haile Selassie in 1974. Under Major Mengistu Haile Mariam, however, the Derg began in 1977 to re-assert centralized control over peasant association activities and to divert their attention and scarce national resources into military and security operations.

In Nigeria, government officials, business and landed elites, and traditional authorities tend to dominate agricultural policy making and to control resource allocation decisions at the local (project) level (see Yahaya, 1979:20-4, 27-8; Shenton and Watts, 1979:61; Koehn, 1980:4-13, 24-38; Wallace, 1980a:67; 1980b:2-7, 11; 1979a:29-30; Williams, 1976a:45-6; Opio-Odongo, 1980:10-11; Hay, Koehn, and Koehn, 1980:18, 20, 23; Freund, 1979:93-4; Palmer-Jones, 1980:10-11). On the need for the creation of new institutional arrangements that involve popular local leaders and promote peasant participation in rural and community development, see Yahaya (1979:28-31); Oculi (1979:70); Matlon (1979:104); Stahl (1974:105, 166-7); Mortimore (1978:220-4); Dahlberg (1979:131); Lateef (1980:195); Wallace (1980a:76).

81. For specific suggestions along these lines that take into consideration the kinds of natural and social conditions found in rural Ethiopia and/or Nigeria, see Gill (1975:112-3); Famoriyo (1979:110); Norman, et al. (1979:104, 107, 113); Mortimore (1978:224-5); Merryman (1979:12); New Nigerian, April 23, 1979, p.5; Macpherson and Jackson (1975:103-18); Swift (1977:26-30); Lateef (1980:189-90, 198, 215-6); Scrimshaw and Taylor (1980:87-8); Bisrat Aklilu (1980:399).

BIBLIOGRAPHY

Abalu, George O. I.; and D'Silva, Brian. "Integrated Rural Development and the Environment:Some Lessons From an Integrated Rural Development Project in Northern Nigeria." Paper presented at the International Conference on the Environment, Arlon, Belgium, September, 1979.

Abubakar, Sanusi. "Notes on the Green Revolution as a Specific Experience in Rural Development." Nigerian Journal of Public Affairs, 9 (May,1980): 51-9.

Achebe, Chinua. No Longer at Ease. London: Heinemann, 1960.

Aliyu, A. Y.; Koehn, Peter H.; et al. First Report on the Establishment of a Unified System of Administration for the Federal Capital Territory (Abuja). Zaria: Department of Research , Management, and Consultancy, Ahmadu Bello University, 1979.

Aliyu, A. Y.; and Koehn, P. H. "Proposal for a Unified System of Administration for the New Federal Capital Territory of Nigeria." Nigerian Journal of Public Affairs, 9 (May, 1980):1-21.

Ambroggi, Robert P. "Water." Scientific American, 243 (September, 1980):101-16.

Anise, Ladun. "Desubsidization: An Alternative Approach to Governmental Cost Containment and Income Redistribution Policy in Nigeria." African Studies Review, 23 (September, 1980): 17-37.

Assefa Kuru. "The Environmental Impact of Agriculture in Ethiopia." Environmental Conservation, 5 (Autumn, 1978): 213-21.

Awa, Njoku E. "Food Production Problems of Small Farmers in Low-Technology Nations: Some Evidence From Nigeria." Cornell International Agriculture Mimeograph 79. Ithaca: Cornell University, June, 1980.

Bahru Zawde. "A Historical Outline of Famine in Ethiopia." In Drought and Famine in Ethiopia, Abdul Mejid Hussein (compiler). African Environment Special Report No. 2. London: International African Institute, 1976.

Bauer, Dan. "For Want of an Ox...: Land, Capital, and Social Stratification in Tigre." In Proceedings of the First United States Conference on Ethiopian Studies, 1973, Harold G. Marcus and Jon Hinnant (eds.). East Lansing, Michigan: African Studies Center, Michigan State University, 1975, 235-48.

Bisrat Aklilu. "The Diffusion of Fertilizer in Ethiopia: Pattern, Determinants, and Implications." Journal of Developing Areas, 14 (April, 1980): 387-99.

Bivins, Joseph T. "The 1960's and early 1970's in Mahuta (Funtua LGA): Processes of Indigenous Change." Paper presented at the Seminar on Change in Rural Hausaland, Bagauda Lake, February,

1980.

Blaug, Mark. "Employment and Unemployment in Ethiopia." International-
al Labour Review, 60 (August, 1974): 117-43.

Bohannan, Paul and Philip Curtin. Africa and Africans. Revised
edition. Garden City, N.Y.: Natural History Press, 1971.

Bondestam, Lars. "People and Capitalism in the North-Eastern
Lowlands of Ethiopia." Journal of Modern African Studies, 12, 3
(1974): 423-29.

_____. "Notes on Multinational Corporations in Ethiopia." African
Review, 5, 4 (1975): 535-49.

Brietzke, Paul. "Law and Rural Development in Ethiopia." African
Studies Review, 18 (September, 1975):45-62.

_____. "Land Reform in Revolutionary Ethiopia." Journal of Modern
African Studies, 14 (December 1976):637-60.

Caldwell, John D. The Sahelian Drought and Its Demographic
Implications. OLC Paper No. 8. Washington, D.C.: Overseas
Liaison Committee, American Council on Education, December,1975.

Cohen, John M. "Effects of Green Revolution Strategies on Tenants
and Small-scale Landowners in the Chilalo Region of Ethiopia."
Journal of Developing Areas, 9 (April, 1975):335-58.

_____. "Analyzing the Ethiopian Revolution: A Cautionary Tale."
Journal of Modern African Studies, 18 (December, 1980a):
685-91.

_____. "Green Revolution in Ethiopia: The Politics of Rural
Development in a Blocked and Inequitable Society." In Analyzing
Political Change in Africa: Applications of a New
Multidimensional Framework, James R. Scarritt (ed.). Boulder:
Westview Press, 1980b, 107-45.

Cohen, John M.; Goldsmith, Arthur A.; and Mellor, John W. Revolu-
tion and Land Reform in Ethiopia. Rural Development Occasional
Paper No. 6. Ithaca, N.Y.: Cornell University, Center for
International Studies, 1976.

Cohen, John M.; and Koehn, Peter. "Rural and Urban Land Reform in
Ethiopia." African Law Studies, 14, 1 (1977):3-62.

_____. Ethiopian Provincial and Municipal Government; Imperial
Patterns and Postrevolutionary Changes. East Lansing, Mich.:
African Studies Center, Michigan State University, 1980.

Cohen John M.; and Weintraub, Dov. Land and Peasants in Imperial
Ethiopia. Assen: Van Gorcum and Company, 1975.

Collins, Paul. "Public Policy and the Development of Indigenous
Capitalism: The Nigerian Experience." Journal of Commonwealth &
Comparative Politics. (July, 1977):127-50.

Cowell, Alan. "Nigerian Official, Warning U.S., Talks of Oil Curbs."
New York Times (July 27, 1981a).

_____. "Nigeria, Rich With Oil, is Dependent on U.S. and Other
Nations for Food." New York Times (August 15, 1981b):3.

Crittenden, Ann. "America's Topsoil Eroding Away at Alarming Rate."
New York Times (as cited in Missoulian, November 6, 1980).

Crocker, Chester A. "Strengthening U.S.- African Relations." Current
Policy No. 289. Washington, D.C.: U.S. Department of State,
Bureau of Public Affairs, June 20, 1981a.

_____. "U.S. Interests in Africa." Current Policy No. 330.
Washington, D.C.: U.S. Department of State, Bureau of Public
Affairs, October 5, 1981b.

Dahlberg, Kenneth A. Beyond the Green Revolution; The Ecology and
    Politics of Global Agricultural Development. N.Y.: Plenum
    Press, 1979.
Dash, Leon. "Sahelian Herders Rebuilding After Drought." Washington
    Post (September 1, 1981).
Davies, Fela. "Interview with the Minister of Agriculture on the
    Green Revolution in Nigeria." Africa Agriculture, (1981):
    67-71.
de Onis, Juan. "Rice Shortage in Nigeria Brings Charges of
    Corruption." New York Times (January 18, 1981):9.
Disney, Richard. "Some Measures of Rural Income Distribution in
    Ethiopia." Development and Change, 7 (January, 1976):35-44.
D'Silva, Brian; and Raza, M. Rafique. "The Funtua Agricultural
    Development Project: Its Impact on the Area's Farming System."
    Paper presented at the Seminar on Change in Rural Hausaland,
    Bagauda Lake, February, 1980.
Dunning, Harrison C. "Land Reform in Ethiopia: A Case Study in
    Non-Develpment." U.C.L.A. Law Review, 18 (December, 1970):
    271-307.
Eckholm, Erik. The Dispossessed of the Earth: Land Reform and
    Sustainable Development. Worldwatch Paper 30. Washington,
    D.C.: Worldwatch Institute, 1979.
Ega, L. Alegwu. "Security of Tenure in a Transitory Farming System:
    The Case of Zaria Villages in Nigeria." Agricultural
    Administration (1979): 287-98.
Eicher, Carl K.; and Johnson, Glenn L. "Policy for Nigerian
    Agricultural Development in the 1970's." In Growth and Develop-
    ment of the Nigerian Economy, Carl K. Eicher and Carl Liedholm
    (eds.). East Lansing, Mich.: Michigan State University Press,
    1970, 376-92.
Ellis, Gene. "Man or Machine, Beast or Burden: A Case Study of the
    Economics of Agricultural Mechanization in Ada District,
    Ethiopia." Unpublished Ph.D. dissertation, University of
    Tennessee, 1972.
_____. "Land Tenancy Reform in Ethiopia: A Retrospective
    Analysis." Paper presented at the Fifth International Conference
    on Ethiopian Studies, Chicago, 1978.
Ethiopia. Consolidated Food and Nutrition Information Service.
    "Current Situation in Drought-Affected Areas." CFNIS /33/75.
Ethiopia. Relief and Rehabilitation Commission. "August 1-20
    Rainfall Review." Unpublished report. Addis Ababa:RRC, 1975.
Famoriyo, Segun. Land Tenure and Agricultural Development in
    Nigeria. Ibadan: Nigerian Institute of Social and Economic
    Research, University of Ibadan, 1979.
Farer, Tom J. War Clouds on the Horn of Africa: The Widening Storm.
    Second, revised edition. New York: Carnegie Endowment for
    International Peace, 1979.
Flood, Glynn. "Nomadism and Its Future: The 'Afar'." In Drought and
    Famine in Ethiopia, Mejid Abdul Hussein (compiler). African
    Environment Special Report 2. London: International African
    Institute, 1976.
Forest, Thomas G. "The Economic Context of Operation Feed the
    Nation." Savanna, 6 (June, 1977):75-80.
Franke, Richard W. and Chasin, Barbara H. Seeds of Famine: Ecolo-

gical Destruction and the Development Dilemma in the West African Sahel. Montclair, N.J.: Allanheld/Universe, 1980.

Freeman, Orville L. "Interdependence: The Bottom Line (Global Crisis Spells Opportunity)." In Montana and the Rest of the World; Proceedings of the Third Public Affairs Forum held in Missoula, February 13-14, 1975. Bozeman: Cooperative Extension Service, Montana State University, 1975, 1-21.

Freund, William. "Oil Boom and Crisis in Contemporary Nigeria." Review of African Political Economy, 13 (May-Aug., 1979):91-100.

Gana, Jerry A. "Diffusion of Agricultural Innovations and Rural Development: A Case Study of Funtua and Malumfashi Areas." Paper presented at the Seminar on Change in Rural Hausaland, Bagauda Lake, February, 1980.

Garba, Joseph N. "The Military Regime and the Nigerian Society." New Nigerian (28 September 1979):I-III.

Gilkes, Patrick. The Dying Lion: Feudalism and Modernization in Ethiopia. New York: St. Martin's Press, 1975.

_____. "Ethiopia: More Decentralization as Land Reform Progresses." African Development 9, 7 (1976):663-5.

Gill, Gerard J. "Improving Traditional Ethiopian Farming Methods." Rural Africana 28 (Fall, 1975): 107-18.

Girardet, Edward. "Ethiopia, Somalia: Each Want Other to Concede First." Christian Science Monitor (March 17, 1981).

Girma Negash. "The Role of Symbolic Politics in the Power Contest Between Regime Leaders and the Leftist Opposition in the Ethiopian Revolution, 1974-1977." Paper presented at the Western Association of Africanists Meeting, Colorado Springs, March 6-7, 1981.

Green, David A. G. Ethiopia: An Economic Analysis of Technological Change in Four Agricultural Production Systems. East Lansing, Michigan: African Studies Center, Michigan State University, 1974.

Gupte, Pranay B. "Greedy Sahara Devours Land Along Its Borders." New York Times (September 15, 1980):14.

Gusau, Ibrahim. "The Green Revolution Policy of the Federal Government." Africa Agriculture, 1 (1981):72-9.

Harbeson, John W. "Revolutionary Participation in Ethiopia." Rural Development Participation Review, 2 (Fall, 1980):6-9.

Hartwell, Jay. "Capitalism Can Boost Economies of Africa, High U.S. Official Says." Honolulu Advertiser (August 29, 1981).

Hay, Richard; Koehn, Eftychia; and Koehn, Peter. "Attitudes of Local Government Administrators in the Northern States Toward Rural and Community Development." Paper presented at the National Seminar on the Role of Local Government in Social, Political and Economic Development held at the Institute of Administration, Ahmadu Bello University, 28-30 April 1980.

Hecht, Robert. "U.S. Looks for Increased Involvement in Nigeria's Agriculture." African Economic Digest (February 27, 1981).

Hoben, Allan. Land Tenure Among the Amhara of Ethiopia; The Dynamics of Cognatic Descent. Chicago: University of Chicago Press, 1973.

Holmberg, Johan. "Pricing Strategies for Agricultural Produce in a Changing Society: Rural/Urban Contradictions in Ethiopia." Paper presented at the 19th Annual Meeting of the African

Studies Association, Boston, 1976.

Huntington, Richard; Ackroyd, James; and Deng, Luka. "The Challenge for Rainfed Agriculture in Western and Southern Sudan: Lessons from Abyei." _Africa Today_, 28, 2 (1981):43-53.

Iliasu,Salihi. "Developing Nigeria's Water Resources (1) and (2)." _New Nigerian_ (July 4, 1980):5 ff; (July 5, 1980):5.

International Bank for Reconstruction and Development. _Nigeria: Options for Long-Term Development_. Report of a mission sent to Nigeria by the World Bank. Baltimore: The Johns Hopkins University Press, 1974.

_____. _Agricultural Sector Survey_, 3 vols. Washington, D.C.: IBRD, Agricultural Projects Department, Report No. PA-143a, 1973.

International Union for Conservation of Nature and Natural Resources. _World Conservation Strategy; Living Resource Conservation for Sustainable Development_. Nairobi: UNEP, 1980.

Jaynes, Gregory. "A Parched, Warring Africa Facing Famine." _New York Times_ (September 15, 1980):1 ff.

Joseph, Richard A. "Affluence and Underdevelopment: The Nigerian Experience." _Journal of Modern African Studies_ XVI (June 1978):221-39.

Koehn, Peter. "Ethiopian Politics: Military Intervention and Prospects for Further Change." _Africa Today_, 22 (April-June, 1975):7-21.

_____. "Ethiopia: Famine, Food Production, and Changes in the Legal Order." _African Studies Review_, 22 (April, 1979):51-71.

_____. "The Involvement of Local Governments in Nigeria's National Development Planning for the 1980s; A Comparative Analysis of Bauchi and Kaduna Capital Project Proposals." Paper presented at the Department of Research, Management, and Consultancy Seminar, Institute of Administration, Ahmadu Bello University, Zaria, 5 June 1980.

_____. "Return to Civilian Rule: The Nigerian Experience." Paper presented at the Annual Meeting of the Western Political Science Association held in Denver, 26-28 March 1981.

Langdon, Steven and Mytelka, Lynn K. "Africa in the Changing World Economy." In _Africa in the 1980s; A Continent in Crisis_. New York: McGraw-Hill Book Company, 1979, 123-211.

Lappe, Frances M.; Collins, Joseph; and Kinley, David. _Aid As Obstacle_. San Francisco: Institute for Food and Development Policy, 1980.

Lateef, Noel V. _Crisis in the Sahel: A Case Study in Development Cooperation_. Boulder, Colorado: Westview Press, 1980.

Le Houerou, H. N.; and Lundholm, B. "Complementary Activities for the Improvement of the Economy and the Environment in Marginal Drylands." In _Can Desert Encroachment Be Stopped? A Study With Emphasis on Africa_. Ecological Bulletins No. 24. Stockholm: Swedish Natural Science Research Council, 1976.

Lele, Uma. _The Design of Rural Development; Lessons From Africa_. Baltimore: Johns Hopkins University Press, 1975.

Leonard, David K. "Why Do Kenya's Agricultural Extension Services Favor the Rich Farmers?" Paper presented at the Sixteenth Annual Meeting of the African Studies Association, Syracuse, N.Y., 1973.

Le Prestre, Philippe G. "The Role of the World Bank Group in the
    Formation of International Environmental Policy." Paper
    presented at the Annual Meeting of the International Studies
    Association, Philadelphia, March 18-21, 1981.
Liebenthal, Robert. "Certain Development Issues in Ethiopia and
    Their Relationship to Rural/Urban Balance: A Perspective Based
    on World Bank Experience." Paper presented at the 19th Annual
    Meeting of the African Studies Association, Boston, 3-6
    November, 1976.
Lofchie, Michael F. "Political and Economic Origins of African
    Hunger." Journal of Modern African Studies, 13 (Dec.,
    1975):551-67.
Mabogunje, Akin L. "Land,People and Tradition in Nigeria." In The
    Politics and Administration of Nigerian Government, L. Frank-
    lin Blitz (ed.). New York: Frederick A. Praeger, 1965, 11-36.
Macpherson, George; and Jackson, Dudley. "Village Technology for
    Rural Development: Agricultural Innovation in Tanzania."
    International Labor Review (Feb.,1975):97-118.
Markakis, John; and Nega Ayele. Class and Revolution in Ethiopia.
    Nottingham: Spokesman,1978.
Markovitz, Irving L. Power and Class in Africa. Englewood Cliffs,
    N.J.: Prentice-Hall, Inc.,1977.
Martin, Douglas. "Nigeria also Raising Its Oil Price." New York
    Times (Dec. 31, 1980):1.
Matlon, Peter J. Income Distribution Among Farmers in Northern
    Nigeria: Empirical Results and Policy Implications. African
    Rural Economy Paper No. 18. East Lansing, Mich.: Department
    of Agricultural Economics, Michigan State University, 1979.
Merryman, James. "Ecological Stress and Adaptive Response: A Study
    of Drought Induced Nomad Settlement in Northern Kenya." The
    Pan-Africanist, 8 (July, 1979):6-16.
Mohammoda Gaas. "The Afar or the Danakil Plight." Ethiopian Herald
    (April 17,1974):2.
Mortimore, Michael. "Grain Reserves at the Village Level in
    Drought-Prone Areas of Nigeria." In The Aftermath of the 1972-74
    Drought in Nigeria: Proceedings of a Conference Held at
    Bagauda, April, 1977, G. Jan van Apeldoorn (ed.). Zaria:
    Federal Department of Water Resources and Centre for Social and
    Economic Research, Ahmadu Bello University, 1978.
Munn, R. E. "The Greenhouse Effect." Mazingira, 2 (1977):78-85.
Nigeria. Funtua Agricultural Development Project. The Funtua
    Agricultural Development Project. Funtua:FADP, 1977.
Nigeria. National Committee on Arid Zone Afforestation. Report of
    the National Committee on Arid Zone Afforestation to the Federal
    Military Government of Nigeria. Lagos: NCAZA, 1978.
Nigeria. "National Report." Interim version presented at the United
    Nations Conference on Human Settlements, Vancouver, 31 May- 11
    June, 1976. Nairobi: U.N., Habitat, June, 1975. A/CONF .70/NR
    /54.
Nigerian Economic Society. "Economic Policy of the Military Regime;
    Summary of Proceedings of the NES Annual Conference held in Kano
    from April 30 to May 3, 1980." New Nigerian (May 29, 1980):5ff.

"Nigeria's Fourth National Development Plan." West Africa, 3320 (16 March 1981):558-69.

Norman, David W.; Pryor, David H.; and Gibbs, Christopher J. N. Technical Change and the Small Farmer in Hausaland, Northern Nigeria. African Rural Economy Paper No. 21. East Lansing, Mich.: Department of Agricultural Economics, Michigan State University, 1979.

Nwosu, Humphrey N. "Nigeria's Third National Development Plan, 1975-80: Major Problems to Implementation," Africa Today, 24 (Oct.-Dec., 1977a):23-38.

_____. Political Authority and the Nigerian Civil Service. Enugu:Fourth Dimension Publishers, 1977b.

Oculi, Okello. "Dependent Food Policy in Nigeria, 1975-1979." Review of African Political Economy, 15/16 (May-Dec.,1979):63-74.

Okaiyeto, Peter O. "Classification of Farmers in Nigeria." New Nigerian (March 10,1980):20.

Olinger, John P. "The World Bank and Nigeria." Review of African Political Economy, 13 (May-Aug., 1979):101-7.

Omole, T. A. "Nutrition and Food Objectives in National Development and Planning." Paper presented at the Think Tank/ University of Ibadan Conference on Food and Nutrition Policy for Nigeria in the 1980's, Ibadan, May, 1979.

Opio-Odongo, Joe M. A. "The Inertia of Rural Development in Hausa-land: An Explication of a Structural Incongruence Hypothesis." Paper presented at the Seminar on Change in Rural Hausaland, Bagauda Lake, February, 1980.

Osoba, Segun. "The Deepening Crisis of the Nigerian National Bourgeoisie." Review of African Political Economy, 13 (May-Aug., 1979):63-77.

Ottaway, David B. "Ethiopia Tests Collectives." Washington Post (Dec.5, 1980).

Ottaway, Marina. "Land Reform and Peasant Associations: A Prelimi-nary Analysis." Rural Africana, 28 (Fall, 1975):39-54.

_____. "Land Reform in Ethiopia 1974-1977." African Studies Review, 20 (Dec., 1977):79-90.

Ottaway, Marina and David. Ethiopia: Empire in Revolution. New York: Africana Publishing Company, 1978.

Palmer-Jones, R. W. "Why Irrigate in the North of Nigeria?" Paper prepared for the Seminar on Change in Rural Hausaland, Bagauda Lake, February, 1980.

Payer, Cheryl. "The World Bank and the Small Farmer." Monthly Review, 32 (Nov., 1980):30-46.

Pirages, Dennis. The New Context for International Relations: Global Ecopolitics. North Scituate, Mass.: Duxbury Press, 1978.

Reimer, Richard. "Ethiopian Agricultural Exports: A Brief Survey." Rural Africana, 28 (Fall, 1975):119-37.

Robinson, J. P. The Effects of Weapons on Ecosystems. UNEP Studies 1. Oxford: Pergamon Press, 1979.

Scrimshaw, Nevin S.; and Taylor, Lance. "Food." Scientific Ameri-can, 243 (Sept., 1980):78-88.

Shagari, Shehu. "Budget of Cautious Optimism." West Africa, 3307 (Dec. 8, 1980):2469-76.

Shaw, Timothy M.;   and Fasehun, Orobola.   "Nigeria in the World
    System: Alternative Approaches, Explanations, and Projections."
    Journal _of_ _Modern_ _African_ _Studies_, 18 (Dec., 1980):551-73.
Shenton, Bob; and Freund, Bill.   "The Incorporation of Northern
    Nigeria into the World Capitalist Economy." _Review_ _of_ _African_
    Political _Economy_, 13 (May-Aug., 1979):8-20.
Shenton, Bob; and Watts, Mike. "Capitalism and Hunger in Northern
    Nigeria." _Review_ _of_ _African_ _Political_ _Economy_, 15/16 (May-Dec.,
    1979):53-62.
Shepherd, Jack. _The_ _Politics_ _of_ _Starvation_. New York: Carnegie En-
    dowment for International Peace, 1975.
"6,000,000 Dispossessed in the Horn of Africa." Special Issue.   _Horn_
    _of_ _Africa_, 4, 1 (1981):5-84.
Stahl, Michael. _Ethiopia:_ _Political_ _Contradictions_ _in_ _Agricultural_
    Development. Stockholm: Raben and Sjogren, 1974.
_____. _New_ _Seeds_ _in_ _Old_ _Soil:_ _A_ _Study_ _of_ _the_ _Land_ _Reform_ _Process_
    _in_ _Western_ _Wollega,_ _Ethiopia,_ _1975-76_. Research Report No. 40.
    Uppsala: Scandinavian Institute of African Studies, 1977.
Stevens, Phillips, Jr.   "Social Science Involvement in African
    Development Planning." _African_ _Studies_ _Review_, 21 (Dec.,
    1978):1-6.
Stryker, Richard E. "The World Bank and Agricultural Development:
    Food Production and Rural Poverty." _World_ _Development_, 7 (March,
    1979):325-36.
Swift, Jeremy. "In Defence of Nomads." _Mazingira_, 2 (1979):26-30.
Tesfai Tecle. "An Approach to Rural Development: A Case Study of
    the Ethiopian Package Projects." _Rural_ _Africana_, 28 (Fall,
    1975a):87-105.
_____. _The_ _Evolution_ _of_ _Alternative_ _Rural_ _Development_ _Strategies_
    _in_ _Ethiopia_. African Rural Employment Paper No. 12.   East
    Lansing, Mich.: Department of Agricultural Economics, Michigan
    State University, 1975b.
Thiesenhusen, William C. "Reaching the Rural Poor and the Poorest:
    A Goal Unmet." University of Wisconsin _Land_ _Tenure_ _Center_
    Reprint, 136 (1978).
United Nations Environment Programme. _The_ _State_ _of_ _the_ _Environment;_
    Selected _Topics_ _1977_. Nairobi: UNEP, 1977.
_____. _The_ _State_ _of_ _the_ _Environment_ _1978_. Nairobi:UNEP, 1978.
_____. "Women, Environment, and Development." Environmental Brief
    No. 5/80. Nairobi:UNEP, 1980.
United States, Council on Environmental Quality and Department of
    State.   _The_ _Global_ _2000_ _Report_ _to_ _the_ _President_ _of_ _the_ _U.S._
    Volume I. New York:Pergamon Press, 1980.
United States, Departrment of Agriculture, "World Agricultural
    Situation," WAS-24. Washington, D.C.: Department, December,
    1980.
United States, Department of State.   "Basic Data on Sub-Saharan
    Africa." Special Report No. 61. Washington, D.C.: Department,
    Bureau of Public Affairs, December, 1979.
_____. "Somali Relief: US Policy." _Gist_ (August, 1980).
    Washington, D.C.: Department, Bureau of Public Affairs.
United States, Presidential Commission on World Hunger.   _Overcoming_
    World _Hunger:_ _The_ _Challenge_ _Ahead_. An abridged version of the
    Report of the Presidential Commission on World Hunger.

Washington, D.C.: U.S. Government Printing Office, June, 1980.

van Apeldoom, G. Jan, editor. The Aftermath of the 1972-74 Drought in Nigeria; Proceedings of a Conference Held at Bagauda in April, 1977. Zaria: Federal Department of Water Resources and Centre for Social and Economic Research, Ahmadu Bello University, 1978.

Von Damm, Helene. Sincerely, Ronald Reagan. Ottawa, Ill.: Green Hill Publishers, Inc., 1976.

Wallace, Tina. "Planning for Agricultural Development: A Considera- tion of Some of the Theoretical and Practical Issues Involved." Nigerian Journal of Public Affairs, 8 (1978-79):54-78.

_____. "Agriculture for What? Problems and Strategies of Nigeria's Food Policy in the Third Development Plan." Paper presented at the Department of Research, Management, and Consultancy Seminar, Ahmadu Bello University, Zaria,1979a.

_____. Rural Development Through Irrigation: Studies in a Town on the Kano River Project. C.S.E.R. Research Report No. 3. Zaria: Center for Social & Economic Research, Ahmadu Bello University, 1979b.

_____. "Agricultural Bonanza? Some Crucial Issues Raised by the World Bank Agricultural Development Projects in Nigeria." Nigerian Journal of Public Affairs, 9 (May, 1980a):61-78.

_____. "Agricultural Projects and Land." Paper presened at the Seminar on Change in Rural Hausaland, Bagauda Lake, February 29-30, 1980b.

_____. "Report on Some of the Social and Economic Issues and Problems Raised on the Bakalori Irrigation Project." Unpublished paper. Zaria: Department of Research and Consultancy, Ahmadu Bello University, March, 1980c.

Walls, James. "Man's Desert: The Mismanaged Earth." Mazingira, 2 (1977):19-25.

Ware, Helen. "The Sahelian Drought: Some Thoughts on the Future." Ouagadougu: U.N. Sahelian Office, March 1975. ST/SSO/33

Williams, Gavin. Nigeria; Economy and Society. London: Rex Collings, 1976a.

_____. "Taking the Part of Peasants: Rural Development in Nigeria and Tanzania." In The Political Economy of Contemporary Africa, Peter C. W. Gutkind and Immanuel Wallerstein (eds.). Beverly Hills, Calif.: Sage Publications, 1976b, 131-54.

Yahaya, A. D. "Local Government as an Agent of Rural Development: An Evaluation." Nigerian Journal of Political Science, 1 (June, 1979):20-31.

Young, Andrew. "Gone Fishing in Argungue." Washington Post (March 9, 1981).

Zartman, I. William. "Social and Political Trends in Africa in the 1980's." In Africa in the 1980s; A Continent in Crisis. New York: McGraw-HillBook Company, 1979, 69-119.